OHIO'S KINGMAKER

Ohio's Kingmaker

Mark Hanna, Man & Myth

William T. Horner

OHIO UNIVERSITY PRESS ✦ ATHENS

Daverpont

Ohio University Press, Athens, Ohio 45701
www.ohioswallow.com
© 2010 by Ohio University Press

To obtain permission to quote, reprint, or otherwise reproduce or distribute
material from Ohio University Press publications, please contact our rights and
permissions department at (740) 593-1154 or (740) 593-4536 (fax).

Printed in the United States of America
Ohio University Press books are printed on acid-free paper ⊗ ™

17 16 15 14 13 12 11 10   5 4 3 2 1

Library of Congress Cataloging-in-Publication Data
Horner, William T., 1968–
  Ohio's kingmaker : Mark Hanna, man and myth / William T. Horner.
    p. cm.
  Includes bibliographical references and index.
  ISBN 978-0-8214-1893-2 (cloth : alk. paper) — ISBN 978-0-8214-1894-9 (pbk. :
alk. paper)
  1. Hanna, Marcus Alonzo, 1837–1904. 2. Politicians—United States—Biography.
3. McKinley, William, 1843–1901—Friends and associates. 4. Legislators—United
States—Biography. 5. United States. Congress. Senate—Biography. 6. United
States—Politics and government—1865–1900. I. Title.
  E664.H24H66 2010
  328.73'092—dc22
  [B]
                              2009048947

For my family, Heather, Tricia, and Ellie,
   the amazing people who make my life so happy.

For my parents, Bob and Judy Horner,
   without whom none of this would be possible.

For Mary Lou Carver,
   who has given me as much love as my own mother.

For Ron Carver,
   a great man who would have enjoyed this book.

Contents

CONTENTS

Illustrations

Acknowledgments

I owe many people thanks. First and foremost, thanks go to my wife, Dr. Heather Carver, who encouraged and advised me through the process of writing this book and everything else. Without her love and support, life would be far less worthwhile. Second, I thank my parents, my in-laws, and my extended family for their unceasing support over the years. Third, I would like to thank my colleagues in the Department of Political Science at the University of Missouri. Thanks especially to departmental chair John Petrocik for his continuing support. Fourth, my thanks go to Ting Yan, whose work as a research assistant at the early stages of this project helped to give it shape. Fifth, I thank Karl Rove for granting me interviews about various aspects of this project. Finally, I thank the editors at the Ohio University Press and the outside reviewers who made this book much better than it would have been otherwise. Of course, any errors, flaws, or poor writing that remain herein are entirely my fault.

INTRODUCTION

Mark Hanna in
the Twenty-first Century

n 1999 and 2000, many people in the press drew paral-
lels between the 1896 presidential campaign of William
McKinley and that of George W. Bush. According to
reporters who covered the campaign, this was largely
due to Bush's chief political strategist, Karl Rove, who
spoke often of McKinley, even going so far as to fax entire copies of
The Presidency of William McKinley, the University of Texas historian
Lewis Gould's book, to reporters.[1] Rove was an oft-covered figure in
Texas politics for two decades before he worked to help make then-
Governor Bush a frontrunner for the Republican presidential nomination. By distributing McKinley materials, he was making the point
that he saw important parallels between the political environments at
the end of the nineteenth century and the end of the twentieth century.
These comparisons led reporters to recall a figure largely forgotten in
modern American politics, Marcus Alonzo Hanna, friend and advisor to
William McKinley. The trouble, however, is that in recalling Hanna,
journalists relied on the worst, most inaccurate information about him.

Why does it matter if the reputation of a figure who died a hundred
years ago is besmirched by the reporters of today? In part, because
of the way this false impression of Hanna is used. As time passes,
scholars may agree with today's journalists and find that there were
many valid reasons to criticize the actions and power of Karl Rove.
There may well be ways he handled winning elections of which both

Democrats and fair-minded Republicans would disapprove. Building a case against Rove with a false interpretation of the historical record, however, does nothing but cause well-informed readers to question the veracity of everything else that was reported about him.

One of the most dangerous aspects of modern political journalism is its reckless disregard for history and, at the same time, its impact on history. Journalists print and broadcast what they believe to be true at the moment. They either do not know what occurred in the past or often seem as if they do not care. At the same time, what reporters write or broadcast today becomes part of the historical record and will be archived; a future historian in fifty or a hundred years may consider what they produced to be reliable information, but it is not. Journalism is, at best, a rough draft of history. Unfortunately, however, what reporters produce affects history because when people read or watch the news, they respond to it.

The United States went through an economic transition around the end of the nineteenth century as rapid industrialization began to shift the economy away from agriculture. The country was poised not just at the beginning of a new century but the beginning of a new way of life. William McKinley and his advisor and campaign strategist Mark Hanna sensed this change. They wanted the country to acknowledge it and wanted to help facilitate the shift. More than one hundred years later, Rove saw the United States not only on the verge of another new century but also in the midst of yet another major economic transition, from one based on manufacturing to one based on service. During the campaign in 1999 and 2000, Rove spoke often with reporters both about this parallel and the campaign's plans to duplicate something else from the 1896 election. Just as the economic transition at the end of the nineteenth century was accompanied by a long period of hegemony for the Republican Party, Rove argued that the economic transition at the end of the twentieth century boded well for a new period of Republican hegemony in the twenty-first.

Many reporters took the analogy between the two elections further than Rove wanted them to, however, and soon stories began to appear that offered not just comparisons of the McKinley era and a possible Bush era but also of Mark Hanna and Karl Rove. Many of the comparisons were less than flattering, as reporters asserted that McKinley was a president who was controlled by a political master, Mark Hanna,

FIGURE I.I. Nominis umbra (the shadow of a nominee). Cartoon by Homer Davenport, *New York Journal*, September 19, 1896, 3

and further suggested that Bush was under the control of the Hanna-reincarnated Karl Rove. The problem with these comparisons is that they were usually made with careless disregard for historical facts.

Stories that suggested Karl Rove was Mark Hanna, version 2.0, or that Mark Hanna was Karl Rove's role model began to proliferate. These comparisons continued with some regularity throughout Rove's association with the Bush administration, and other comparisons were made as well. From 1999 through Rove's resignation from the White House staff in 2007, more than three hundred media reports mentioned the names of both Rove and the fictional puppetmaster Svengali, from George du Maurier's novel, *Trilby;* several dozen mentioned both Rove and Earl of Warwick, the fifteenth-century kingmaker involved in the reigns of both Henry VI and Edward IV; and more than 150 articles and at least five books mentioned both Karl Rove and Mark Hanna, often referring to Hanna as "William McKinley's Karl Rove."[2] Are comparisons between Hanna and Rove well founded? The answer, in a word, is no.

The published books and unpublished research about Mark Hanna paint the picture of a complicated man who was, at times, cutthroat in business and politics but who was, at his core, a good and decent man who believed the things he did were for the betterment of the country. To be sure, Hanna was, in part, driven by personal ambition—he wanted to be a president-maker, as is evidenced by the fact that William McKinley was not the first candidate he backed—but he was also driven by an understanding that the times were changing, that the economy of the country was no longer primarily agricultural, and that it would never be so again.

Hanna's perceived political agenda was objectionable both to many when he lived and many in the twenty-first century, spurring coverage that focused not only on alleged parallels between him and Rove but between McKinley's presidency and that of George W. Bush. For instance, columnist Linda McQuaig wrote in the *Toronto Star,* "If the Bush presidency resembles anything, it's that of William McKinley, who occupied the White House in the late 1890s at the height of the era of unchecked corporate power. Bush strategist Karl Rove has been likened to the McKinley strategist (Mark Hanna), who believed government should be run by, and for, big business."[3] To McQuaig, George Bush was William McKinley, Karl Rove was Mark Hanna, and the interests of business controlled all four men, to the detriment of society. However, it is important to consider the intent, as well as the consequences, of the policies a person advocates when trying to assess his legacy. Hanna is rarely given that consideration in modern reporting.

It is also important to understand that Hanna was not a one-man band. His role was overestimated and demonized by his critics at the end of the nineteenth century, and it continued to be overestimated and demonized by many who referenced him in the late twentieth and early twenty-first centuries as an example of where things started to "go wrong" in American politics. In many ways, the coverage of Hanna was unchanged a century after his death. Despite the fact that several highly respected scholars have argued that Hanna's legacy was much different from the biography that was written about him by the partisan press of his age—a press that was led by William Randolph Hearst's reporters—it is the Hearstian legacy of Hanna's Svengali image that persists.

In 1896, misinformation about Hanna in the press was to be expected for two reasons. First, Hanna lived in an era of blatantly partisan journalism, and consumers knew which outlets were which. People read the publications that aligned with their own political points of view, and those points of view were reinforced by what they read. There were newspapers that lauded Hanna and newspapers that reviled him in accordance with the political predisposition of their editors and publishers. In comparison, the modern press is largely nonpartisan and objective in its coverage of politics, the alarmist claims of watchdog groups notwithstanding.

One hundred years ago, journalism was a very different, very partisan business, and for many journalists who wrote for publications sympathetic to the Democrats, facts about Hanna took a back seat to painting a picture of an evil man who promoted Republicanism at any cost. On the other hand, there were publications that favored the Republicans that wrote scathingly about William Jennings Bryan and much more positively about Hanna. However, the positive image was not nearly as compelling and, as a consequence, the impression of Hanna that survives today is almost universally negative.

The portrait of Hanna that has stood the test of time is of a man who was grossly obese; a cutthroat attack dog for the "Trusts"; a cigar-smoking man clad in a suit covered with dollar signs who stood side by side with a titanic figure representing the trusts and a tiny, childlike William McKinley. He will forever be known as "Dollar Mark," thanks to Homer Davenport and the many other political cartoonists who drew him as a malevolent presence. Positive impressions of Hanna in the Republican media stood no chance against the powerful prose and darkly humorous cartoons produced by the incendiary journalists who worked for Democratic newspapers. The most

XXXV

FIGURE I.2. As they go to the polls. Cartoon by Homer Davenport, reprinted in *The Dollar or the Man? The Issue of To Day,* ed. Homer Davenport and Horace L. Traubel (Boston: Small, Maynard, 1900), 35

influential of these were owned by William Randolph Hearst, whose publications were the driving force behind the negative impression of Marcus Alonzo Hanna that survives today.

Hearst had two main motives behind the misleading coverage of Hanna. First, Hearst was one of the few Democratic publishers who openly supported William Jennings Bryan, so the coverage in his newspapers was a political choice. Second, however, was a strong profit motive. Hearst sold many newspapers on the East Coast because very few other newspapers in the East, including traditionally Democratic newspapers, supported Bryan. Today, in the era of giant media conglomerates, the ideological motive is missing from much of American journalism, but the profit motive is as strong as ever and continues to have a profound influence on the accuracy and quality of reporting.

If this were the only factor that influenced the coverage of Hanna, we might expect that the evolution of journalistic standards from 1896 to the present day might have had an effect on the tone, substance, and accuracy of reporting about Mark Hanna a century after his death. However, the second reason misinformation about Hanna in the press of his day was to be expected is that journalists rarely let facts get in the way of a good story. Newspapers offered compelling dramas on a serialized basis, giving readers details guaranteed to keep them coming back; faithful stories are almost never as compelling as embellished versions of the truth. Painting Hanna as a robber baron set on stealing America's working class blind certainly made for a much more compelling story than did presenting him as a dedicated politician.

Unlike the shift away from partisan journalism that took place in America during the early part of the twentieth century, there has been no shift in modern journalism away from the importance of presenting compelling storylines to attract an audience and of making a profit. The price of the profit motive is frequently paid through bad journalism. Concern about the financial imperative extends beyond the consumers of media coverage to journalists themselves. In the Pew Research Center's annual analysis of the state of the news media in America, the Project for Excellence in Journalism found in 2008 that more than two-thirds of all journalists (Internet, national, and local) feel that "increased bottom-line pressure is seriously hurting the quality of news coverage, rather than just changing the way news organizations operate."[4] Whether poor coverage is the result of cuts in newsroom budgets, as many journalists complain; time pressures; the pursuit of a compelling story at the expense of reality; or all of the above, journalism is often inaccurate and misleading.

Inaccurate journalism, whatever its cause, is a serious problem in American society because the public depends on accurate reporting if it is to be well informed about politics. As Mitchell Charnley, a respected professor of journalism, writes in his textbook *Reporting,*

What accuracy means literally is that every element in a news story, every name and date and age and address, every definitive word or expression or sentence, is a precise and unequivocal statement of a verifiable certainty. Not only that: it means also correctness of general impression, correct perspective achieved by the way the details are put together and by the emphases they are given. If the meaning and the imperative need for accuracy are easy to understand, the quality itself is not easy to attain.[5]

Charnley points out the hard task of juggling the many details reporters have to handle in their work, but the news media, if they are to be the watchdogs of democracy, have an obligation to be especially vigilant, no matter the difficulty. Unfortunately, both the public and scholars, including Charnley, find that the news media are frequently in error. A majority of the public certainly seems to have doubts about the accuracy of the news media in the United States. In the Pew Research Center for the People & the Press's annual survey of attitudes about the news media, it was consistently found that more than 50 percent of people surveyed felt that news-media stories were often inaccurate.[6] The fact that the public has such little faith in the watchdogs for democracy is, in and of itself, discouraging. Even more discouraging is that studies of accuracy in journalism have consistently revealed equally disappointing findings. The first such study was conducted in 1936 by Mitchell Charnley, who found that roughly half of all stories published in three Minneapolis daily newspapers contained errors.[7]

In a 2002 study, journalism researcher Scott Maier found that things remain largely unchanged in the twenty-first century. Using methods similar to Charnley's, who asked the subjects of stories to comment on the accuracy of the reporting about them, Maier found an average of 1.5 errors in stories in the *Raleigh News & Observer* during the period he analyzed.[8] Maier argues that this finding is discouraging in part because the *Columbia Journalism Review* rated the Raleigh newspaper as one of the best in the country—if one of America's best newspapers has so much trouble with accuracy, it implies there may be far greater problems at other newspapers. Maier writes, "It has been suggested that errors in newspapers are not as widespread as the public perceives. But with more than half of locally produced stories containing one or more errors, as news sources found in this study, the public's claim to finding errors regularly in their daily newspapers seems hardly far-fetched."[9]

Maier expanded the scope of his research in a 2005 study that examined fourteen newspapers of different sizes from across the country and found largely the same thing he found in his Charlotte study. Maier writes, "This study's central finding is sobering: More than 60% of local news and news feature stories in a cross-section of American daily newspapers were found in error by news sources, an inaccuracy rate among the highest in nearly seventy years of research, and empirical evidence corroborating the public's impression that mistakes pervade the press."[10] Worse than making errors, perhaps, is the fact that there is often little effort made to correct them. In 2007, Maier examined more than one thousand errors of fact published in ten newspapers from across the country and found that when newspapers do make errors, they almost never make the effort to correct them: "98 percent of the 1,220 factual newspapers errors examined went uncorrected. The correction rate was uniformly low for each of the 10 newspapers studied, with none correcting even 5 percent of the mistakes identified by news sources."[11]

Accuracy is of dubious quality not only in newspapers but also in television journalism, which, according to the 2008 state-of-the-news-media report, a majority of Americans cites as its primary source of news. The same study finds that people trust television journalism more than print journalism.[12] Unfortunately, that trust may be misplaced. In a 2001 study by Newslab, in which researchers interviewed television news managers from across the country, researchers found "that errors are common in both large and small markets, occurring at least once or twice a week. In just over a quarter of newsrooms surveyed, managers said errors get on the air every day."[13] In another study's examination of accuracy of local broadcast news, the researchers surveyed the subjects of news stories broadcast on five Cleveland television stations and found that "one person in three said that important information was left out of a story; one person in five complained that his or her interview was taken out of context, and nearly one in five thought the coverage of a particular event was overblown and sensationalized."[14]

A later study, conducted in 2004 by Newslab and Kent State researchers Gary Hanson and Stan Wearden found that 35 percent of news stories contained errors.[15] In addition to measuring the accuracy of these television stations, Newslab's researchers Deborah Potter and Amy Mitchell also asked television journalists about practices and policies for both preventing and correcting errors. They found that there is often a disturbing lack of precaution in preventing errors from being made in the first place. They also found that there is "a substantial gap between the importance journalists place on reviewing information before air and the frequency with which this actually happens in their newsrooms" and that caution about preventing errors from reaching the air was high with only certain kinds of stories, like investigative pieces and stories run during sweeps periods when there was the greatest chance the stations could get into legal trouble.[16]

In a separate analysis, researchers also found that many stations have little in the way of formal policies for correcting errors when they are broadcast. The report found that "two-thirds of the journalists responding to the survey said that on-air corrections are made at their stations, at least some of the time. The trouble is that many of them could discern no formal process for determining when and how to issue a correction" and that "fully one out of five respondents said they work at a station where there either is no corrections policy, or where errors are treated as an internal matter to be handled in a post-mortem meeting or a discrepancy report."[17] The relative lack of concern about accuracy and policies to correct errors when they are made is disturbing for those who depend on television news for information.

The unfortunate reality is that there is nothing new about inaccuracy in the modern age of so-called objective journalism. When Adolph Ochs purchased the *New York Times* in 1896, he bought a Republican-leaning newspaper with a small circulation. As such, it fit right in with all newspapers of the day by serving particular political interests. As the twentieth century arrived, Ochs and his editors began to move the *New York Times* toward a new kind of reporting that was objective and unbiased. The model proved economically successful, and the newspaper's circulation began to increase quickly. The *New York Times'* model of objective journalism was soon adopted by other newspapers whose publishers saw the economic opportunity that kind of coverage afforded. The economic success of objective journalism spurred the creation of schools of journalism, first at the University of Missouri and then at institutions like Columbia University and Northwestern University. These schools helped to establish professional standards of objective reporting, and people began to accept the notion that the news media are the so-called watchdogs for democracy.

However, inaccurate reporting does great damage to the possibility that the news media can play the role of watchdogs for democracy. For instance, Gary Hanson and Stan Wearden write that errors in television journalism result in "significant loss of credibility at three key levels—the story, the journalists, and the news organization itself."[18] In print journalism, the consequences of inaccuracy are equally profound, according to Scott Maier: "When the public distrusts what they read and see on the news, the media not only lose customers but, research suggests, community and democracy wither as the public becomes increasingly disengaged."[19] Craig Silverman, a Canadian journalist who recently wrote a book about inaccuracy in the press and who documents media errors on the Web site Regret the Error writes,

> Media errors exert an untold—and, of course, unchecked—amount of power in our world. . . . When the press makes mistakes, especially egregious ones, it gives ammunition to those who would curtail its power through increased regulation or legislation that could potentially restrict press freedom and have a corollary effect on freedom of speech. . . . When the seemingly powerful media cannot exercise its freedom, average citizens naturally suffer the impact.[20]

The vast majority of the public depends on the news media for information about politics.

When the news media get the facts wrong, they create problems for the members of the public who are interested in learning about current events. Much research documents the fact that there are many people with little or no knowledge about politics.[21] It is important to point out that the lack of knowledge is not necessarily due primarily to inaccuracy by the news media but to a complete lack of interest in news and politics for some citizens. Researcher Markus Prior found compelling evidence to support the notion that, since people now have the ability to watch whatever they want thanks to the proliferation of media outlets on cable, satellite, and the Internet, many choose anything but news or current-affairs programming.

Prior suggests this new reality is a powerful explanation of the continued existence of the knowledge gap that exists between the people in this country who are well informed about politics and the rest who are not. A large number of people who do not know much about politics do not have that knowledge because they are not interested in seeking it out. In the new media universe, where hundreds of channels are available, such people do not have to watch any news or coverage of politics if they do not wish to. When there were only a handful of channels in each market, each of which broadcast news at basically the same time, people were not able to avoid news if they were going to have the television on. Now, there is always a rerun of *Friends* on somewhere, and viewers can easily choose not to watch the news.[22] Overall, news consumption has declined precipitously over the last decade-plus. As the Pew Research Center for the People and the Press reported, use of all news media declined from 1994 to 2006. In that period, use of television news dropped from 72 percent to 57 percent; use of the newspaper dropped from 49 percent to 40 percent; use of radio news dropped from 47 percent to 36 percent; and even use of the Internet for news, which the center started measuring only in 2004, dropped from 24 percent to 23 percent in two years.[23]

Despite the fact that some people are directly to blame for their own lack of knowledge about politics because of deliberate avoidance, those who do seek information about public affairs are often ill served by the media outlets they turn to. To remain profitably competitive in the constantly evolving television market, news coverage has changed, becoming softer and less newsworthy, hoping to attract people who are not interested in news. A study of local television news by the Lear Center, a cooperative venture between scholars at the University of Southern California and the University of Wisconsin, found that the largest part of an average thirty-minute local news broadcast was devoted to commercials. The largest portion of the small, roughly twenty-two-minute news hole that remained was given over to sports and weather, which averaged close to 6.5 minutes per newscast, more than one-fourth of the time available. Serious news of all sorts, including elections and politics, received considerably less attention.[24] Meanwhile, the nightly news programs aired by the big-three broadcast networks have become something resembling miniversions of the news magazines that have proliferated on each of the networks, rather than actual newscasts. A small number of hard-news stories occupy the first few minutes of a typical broadcast, while the rest of the news hole is given over to news magazine-style reports. In fact, these reports are often short teases for longer versions of the stories that will air later in the evening on *Dateline NBC* or *20/20*. Cable news networks like CNN, MSNBC, Fox News, and even CNN's *Headline News* offer far less coverage of hard news than they once did and primarily offer talk shows, often with ideologically charged hosts, throughout their broadcast schedules.

When the lack of interest in public affairs that many people feel is combined with the fact that many other people's knowledge of politics is negatively affected by both indifference to actual news coverage by media outlets and by the frequent errors those same media outlets make and only infrequently correct, much of the public is left with little idea of what is going on in American politics. The mischaracterization of Karl Rove as the second coming of Mark Hanna is one graphic example of the poor quality of information about politics that is frequently reported in the news media. This book addresses oft-repeated errors about Mark Hanna not just to correct the misperceptions that many people have but also to demonstrate how once an error becomes part of the news media's common knowledge, it is repeated over and over and affects the coverage of politics in the news media a century later.

The contemporary political media make their greatest mistakes when they speak authoritatively about current events without putting them into context or, conversely, when they try to put current events in context by inappropriately comparing them to past events. The first problem is exemplified by a cover story in the October 21, 2007, edition of *Time*. The article, "The Incredibly Shrinking Court," presented the thesis that the Supreme Court has gradually become irrelevant as an institution of government. The reporter, David Von Drehle, wrote, "This trend—a steady shrinking of the judicial role in public policy and a handing over of issues to the states . . . points to an obvious question about the highest court in the land. How much does the Supreme Court matter anymore?" He adds,

> The irony is that the Court's ideology is playing a dwindling role in the lives of Americans. The familiar hot-button controversies—abortion, affirmative action, the death penalty, police powers and so on—have been around so long, sifted and resifted so many times, that they now arrive at the court

in highly specific cases affecting few, if any, real people. . . . What was once salient is now mostly symbolic.[25]

Von Drehle examines *Brown v. Board of Education* (1954) and comments that while that case affected millions, the Court's recent desegregation cases affect only a few hundred people.

The problem with Von Drehle's analysis is that it lacks historical context and is, therefore, very misleading to readers who might not have any knowledge of the Supreme Court beyond what they read in his story. The Court has always waxed and waned in importance in the history of the United States, as is true of the other two branches of government. Even if one accepts Von Drehle's contention that the Court's importance waned in 2007, which is an arguable contention, it does not mean the Court will be irrelevant for the rest of time. Journalists' jobs are to report what is happening today, but when they fail to put current events into context, it is impossible for the consumers of the news media to know what is really happening.

While Von Drehle erred by ignoring history, the news media's coverage of one of America's most historically controversial figures, Senator Mark Hanna, illustrates the second problem—misusing history to make misinformed points about politics today. Studying coverage of Hanna in the media of his day becomes more than a mere historical curiosity when it is considered as an example of how the failure to understand the past makes it difficult to report intelligently about the present. Inaccurate coverage of Hanna in the waning days of the nineteenth century became the basis of comments and coverage by pundits and journalists in the waning days of the twentieth century.

What reporters wrote about Hanna during his own time had an impact on the general public, politicians, and even some academics who wrote the history of the Gilded Age, despite the fact that they knew they were writing about an era in which the media were openly and unabashedly partisan. That partisan coverage continued to have an impact a century later. One high-profile and misinformed example of the lasting weight of the words reporters wrote about Hanna between 1896 and his death was the attention devoted to him in 1996 by Senator Bill Bradley in his autobiography *Time Present, Time Past*. What Bradley wrote about Hanna was informed by inaccurate reports about the Ohioan, and what Bradley wrote was later quoted by journalists who reported Bradley's complaints about the excesses of campaign finance when he ran for the presidency in 2000. Fiction, when it is repeated often enough, seems to become fact.

In his book, Bradley offers first praise, then condemnation of Hanna. Bradley refers to an interview he gave during his high-school years in Missouri in which he noted Hanna as one of his heroes, along with Billy Graham and St. Louis Hawks' basketball player Bob Pettit. He wrote, "I knew about Hanna because I had written a paper on the 1896 presidential election. A few years ago, my high-school history teacher reminded me that its theme had been 'Money is power.'"[26]

Bradley assigned blame to Hanna for the sharp escalation in campaign spending in American elections, writing, "Modern political fundraising began in William McKinley's campaign for president in 1896. It was an innovation of Marcus Alonzo Hanna, a successful Cleveland entrepreneur who made his money in the coal-and-iron business."[27] He elaborated further: "After Hanna was rejected for service in the Cleveland Civil Service Reform Association, he opted for the world of politics. He was a Scotch-Irish man of action, a politician who scoffed at the bookish and preferred the company of men with money."[28] According to Bradley, Hanna's decision to turn to politics was motivated by the anger of rejection, but it is hard to know how Bradley arrived at this conclusion. There was no specific mention of the Cleveland Civil Service Reform Association in either of the published biographies of Hanna, which both chronicled his early involvement in local politics: *Marcus Alonzo Hanna* by Herbert Croly and *Hanna* by Thomas Beer.

Herbert Croly wrote about Hanna's early involvement in politics and suggested that Hanna tried to organize fellow businessmen to get involved in politics and challenge the power of local political bosses:

> In this connection, it should be remembered that the first phase of the municipal reform movement all over the country took just this form of an attempt to renew the interest of business men in local politics. . . . As a business man and an active politician he was fighting the fact that business and politics were being specialized and divided. He was seeking to escape from the awkward alternative of being obliged either to fight the political mercenaries or to conciliate them.[29]

Both Croly and Thomas Beer emphasize Hanna's independence from established political authorities, including his support of a Democratic mayoral candidate, Charles Otis, because Hanna and other business-men felt the Republican nominee was unacceptable.

Thomas Beer addresses Hanna's entry into politics, but his inter-pretation is very different from Bradley's. To Beer, Hanna's behavior was motivated by a pragmatic analysis of reality:

> It was not until 1880 that Mr. Hanna shrugged and con-sented, and perhaps the experience of hearing himself called a rich busybody at a meeting of reformers was the conclusion of his first political mood. He knew, by that time, that machinery ruled in politics and that the machin-ery was companionably to be oiled by money. This image itself appeared in cartoons in the time of Grant. All was ap-propriate. Factories vomited cheap furniture and cheaper machines on the country, and the vital machinery of cities cast up cheap men into place. Behind this apparatus was a point of reality: one might quietly rule in politics without being a politician. One might be an engineer.[30]

In Beer's view, Hanna adapted to failure by changing his tactics, whereas Bradley portrayed Hanna's actions as little more than a temper tantrum.

Bradley also incorrectly characterized Hanna as the creator of the modern system of campaign finance when, in describing his own ef-forts to help Patty Murray, then a candidate for the U.S. Senate from Washington state, he wrote,

> I said that of all the things someone could give, time and money were the two most important. . . . As I spoke, I couldn't imagine Woodrow Wilson saying what I was saying. For LBJ, the gathering would have been too insignificant. Harry Truman would have frowned at the direct solicita-tion, and Mark Hanna, the man who started us down this crazy fund-raising path—well, Mark Hanna was popping a chocolate into his mouth and smiling.[31]

This assertion was incorrect in several ways. First, as is demonstrated later, Hanna's methods were not innovative—they had been used by his predecessors. He might have used them more effectively than they were used in the past, but even that conclusion is open for debate. Second, Bradley also ignored the major changes in electoral politics throughout the twentieth century as the country moved away from a system of rule by the parties to one of popular democracy via primaries. This change made campaigning much more difficult and much more expensive, especially as the costly medium of television became dominant. Hanna raised a great deal of money for McKinley, but even in current dollars, it was not excessive in comparison to the money spent in contemporary presidential elections. In 2004 and 2008, over a billion dollars was spent. In 2008, Barack Obama alone raised more than three hundred million dollars.

Bradley's mischaracterization of Hanna, however, is not confined to finances. He also incorrectly describes Hanna as the "Republican Boss" of Ohio, when he was not even the "Republican Boss" of Cleveland. Bradley suggests incorrectly that McKinley stayed home in the famous "Front Porch Campaign" at Hanna's behest, when the historical record suggests something much different. McKinley was not the first candidate to run a front-porch campaign, nor was it Hanna's decision for him to do so.

Bradley implied that while Hanna admired McKinley, the president owed not only his political success but his financial liquidity to Hanna. McKinley experienced a brush with bankruptcy on the cusp of his presidential campaign in 1896, but it was addressed immediately by a group of his close friends, which did not include Hanna in the beginning. Hanna only became aware of the crisis after a plan to respond to it was already in place. Bradley also asserts that Hanna, a Republican, was the first politico who "explicitly legitimized protecting the rich," and, as such, Republicans have "never had much trouble raising money." However, McKinley's direct predecessor, the Democrat Grover Cleveland, was well supported by business, and business only reluctantly came to McKinley's aid in 1896 out of fear of what would happen if Bryan was elected.

Finally, Bradley reported incorrectly that Hanna did all he could to disrupt the presidency of Teddy Roosevelt, considering him an "impulsive idealist."[32] It is true that Hanna was not happy to have Roosevelt get the vice-presidential nomination in 1900, but the two men accomplished a great deal together after McKinley's assassination, and Roosevelt went to visit Hanna on his deathbed. Hanna was never a serious threat to Roosevelt's presidency.

Perhaps the strangest thing about Bradley's assessment of Hanna is that while he is critical of the Ohioan, he also laments that he did not have a comparable figure in his own political stable. Bradley notes, "As I made my way in politics I never forgot the story of McKinley. For a time, I searched for my own Mark Hanna, who could meld organization and money into an unbeatable political machine. Then again, I knew there was another standard."[33] The other standard Bradley touted was Woodrow Wilson, whom he described as "naïve" about political money. Bradley wrote admiringly of Wilson as a man of ideas, suggesting that money is not everything in politics and that ideas matter. Ideas are certainly important in politics, but when citing Wilson as an example of the triumph of ideas over money, it should be remembered how he actually won the presidency in 1912. It was not so much the power of his ideas as the fact that Theodore Roosevelt ran a very strong third-party campaign that split the Republican vote and ensured the defeat of the incumbent Republican with the money, William Howard Taft.

When Bradley summarizes how he saw himself and his role in the political world in 1996, he includes another shot at Hanna: "Political leaders need to redefine our circumstances. For Mark Hanna, politics was a matter of weighing the economic interests of business, labor, and farmers and giving business the advantage."[34] What he wrote was not incorrect so much in substance as it was in motive. It is not wrong to argue that Hanna favored business interests, but he did so out of a genuine belief that what was good for the business community was good for society as a whole. Hanna believed America and its economy were in transition, and he believed that what benefited industry also helped labor. To Hanna, what was good for business and labor was good for the country. To attack him as selfish is not a fair characterization of his record or his views.

Later, after the publication of his book, Bradley turned his criticism of Hanna into a criticism of Karl Rove in the campaign of 2000, when he sought the Democratic presidential nomination. In a speech during the campaign, Bradley addressed the parallels that many, thanks in part to Rove's own efforts, drew between the campaigns of 1896 and 2000. He said that McKinley "sat on his porch in Ohio, carefully spinning sound bites that positioned him as a 'new Republican' while Hanna promised the financiers and titans of that era that their interests would be protected in the McKinley White House."[35] Once again, what Bradley said was not so much wrong in fact as it was in tone and innuendo. Hanna promised business leaders their interests would be safer if McKinley were president, but it did not mean he was offering the titans of business free access to the office. It was not his access to give, and, as president, McKinley was very careful to keep outsiders in check. Rather, Hanna was addressing real concerns in the business community about the proposals of William Jennings Bryan, the Democratic nominee. In making this statement, Bradley again played on the popular perception that Hanna ushered in a new era in which the party was captured by moneyed interests. Before the Republicans were captured by moneyed interests, however, the Democrats of Grover Cleveland were captured by moneyed interests. The popular perception is not always right, and the popular perception of Hanna is a case in point.

Bradley's 1996 book was part of his groundwork for his presidential campaign in 2000. What he wrote had an impact, especially on reporters, who pulled quotes from his book without analyzing them. What he wrote was taken as fact when, in reality, Bradley was careless with the facts. He relied primarily on inaccuracies that were reported by politically motivated reporters a century earlier; as a consequence, he made fundamental errors in what he wrote, and his errors were accepted as fact by journalists who reported his comments when he was running for the 2000 Democratic presidential nomination.

Karl Rove was frequently referred to in the press as a modern-day Hanna doppelganger who controlled George W. Bush. Painting Karl Rove as a sinister puppeteer set on controlling everything that happened in the White House, if not the entire government, was just as compelling from 1999 to 2007 as similar coverage of Mark Hanna was from 1895 to 1904. Unfortunately, the public is ill served by this reporting because the comparison is woefully inaccurate, and the portrait that most modern journalists paint of Hanna as Svengali or Warwick is simply wrong. It is impossible to assess presidents and presidencies while the president is still in office or has recently left office, so the extent of Karl Rove's influence in the White House has yet to be understood fully. Although careful analysis may show that Rove had an unprecedented level of power, journalists are inaccurate when they compare him to Hanna.

While is not unusual for journalists, columnists, and pundits to get things wrong, particularly when they cover complicated issues, policy arenas with which they are unfamiliar, or anything that requires some knowledge of history, there are few personas in American politics that have been as widely—and wildly—analyzed as Mark Hanna and Karl Rove. Beginning in 1999, many in the media and in politics freely made the comparison between the two men. Many also insisted, inaccurately, that Rove invited the comparison by telling people that Hanna was his political idol.

There were two predominant themes in the coverage of Karl Rove during the Bush years: Rove as the "Architect" (Warwick) and Rove as Svengali. In coverage of Rove as the Architect, a nickname bestowed on him by President Bush that both men may well now regret, reporters often used language that was praiseful, noting his achievements as a campaign strategist; but they also always speculated, often with suspicion, about his motives. In their coverage of Rove as Svengali, the news media focused on his role as an advisor to the president in a way that was often accusatory and alarmist in nature.

Frequently, the memory of Mark Hanna was invoked in both kinds of reporting, almost always in a negative context. At best, the modern portrayal of Hanna in the news media is unbalanced. At worst, it is entirely untrue. Considering that the image of Hanna that survives today poorly represents the real man, it raises questions about the coverage of Karl Rove that depicts him as a second coming of Hanna. If reporters blithely rely on an inaccurate view of Hanna, how much does that inaccurate view contribute to a similarly inaccurate view of Rove? This is not to suggest that modern reporters were politically biased in their coverage but, rather, that they were guilty of something far worse: careless disregard of the facts.

There have thus far been a limited number of "insider" accounts of the Bush administration and Karl Rove's role in it. Until the spring 2008, the best-known accounts were books by reporter Ron Suskind, who collaborated with the former treasury secretary Paul O'Neill in a critique of George W. Bush's economic policies; and by a former government terrorism expert, Richard Clarke, who provided a critical analysis of the Bush administration's war on terror.[36] Each book included criticisms of Karl Rove's role in various aspects of the Bush administration. Until May 2008, the single most critical analysis of Rove's influence came from John DiIulio, Bush's first director of the White House Office of Faith Based and Community Initiatives, after

DiIulio left the administration. He alleged that policy decisions were largely made by Rove and that they were always made with politics as the most important consideration. DiIulio subsequently recanted his critique after his comments were published in an article by Ron Suskind in *Esquire.*[37]

In May 2008, a book by former Bush press secretary Scott McClellan was published.[38] In it, McClellan is scathing in his criticism of the Bush administration's public-relations efforts. His book, an instant best seller, is also noteworthy because McClellan is easily the closest to the Bush inner circle to write critically about the forty-third president and the people who surrounded him, including—prominently—Karl Rove. It is also open to easy criticism—not surprisingly, most of this criticism came from those who were on the inside of what McClellan calls "the bubble"—because McClellan was a willing participant and major player for a long time in the very efforts about which he writes so critically.

Despite these high-profile, insider accounts, however, most people who worked in the Bush White House remain extraordinarily close-mouthed, and what has been reported about Rove in the press to date is based less on known facts than on rumor, conjecture, and informed speculation. It may be true that Rove's influence as an advisor or a behind-the-scenes power broker was unprecedented while he worked in the West Wing. However, analyses of presidential administrations take years to flesh out with careful scholarship, and only time will reveal Rove's actual influence.

What is definitely true, however, is that Mark Hanna does not make an apt comparison to Karl Rove, largely because the image of Hanna that has been portrayed in modern accounts of him is wrong. Comparisons between Hanna and Rove fall apart under even the most superficial scrutiny because their official positions were not the same. Hanna was elected to the Senate, while Rove served as an aide to the president, with an office in the West Wing. The two jobs cannot be easily compared, if only for the vastly different access to the president that a Senate office and a West Wing office afford.

Perhaps more importantly, if the comparisons made by reporters between Hanna and Rove were inappropriate, their errors were compounded when they extended the comparison to the presidents Hanna and Rove served, William McKinley and George W. Bush. So too were modern comparisons of the elections of 1896 and 2000. Inaccurate reporting has consequences, one of the most important of which is an ill-informed public. In turn, an ill-informed public can make incompetent choices.

Mark Hanna was an important figure in American political history; for that reason alone, he deserves to be understood better. Not only does understanding him better help correct Hanna's legacy, it also helps us to understand better the time in which we live. This book is not an examination of the role played by Karl Rove in the Bush administration but, rather, a study of the real role played by Mark Hanna in American politics as the country emerged from the shadows of isolation and became a world power at the turn of the twentieth century. However, by better understanding Hanna's true legacy, it may give pause to all who jump to easy—and often inaccurate—conclusions about politics in the present day.

Unfortunately, the news media that cover politics in the United States frequently operate on the basis of knee-jerk, spur-of-the-moment analyses of events. Rarely are history and the need to make careful analyses of complicated situations considered by reporters. Instead, reporters are pressured to make snap judgments with little concern for the consequences. The problem with this for the American people is that, because the media are our main sources of information about politics, we often end up with distorted views of reality. Our media-constructed perceptions of political characters like Mark Hanna and Karl Rove are examples of this problem. In the abstract, perhaps, it does not matter that people remember Mark Hanna. However, when Hanna's name is invoked, incorrectly, as an example of how what was wrong with politics a century ago is even more wrong with politics today, then the public is led astray and led away from what is really important, which is to understand what is really going on in the government and politics when they go to the voting booths to cast their ballots.

CHAPTER ONE

Mark Hanna—A Man Very Much Misunderstood

ark Hanna was not a born politician. It was not until after he had worked to build a variety of family businesses that he turned his attention fully to politics. Saying more than that about Hanna, supporting any statements that go deeper than that brief remark is difficult. For a man who was the focus of so much attention by the press of his day, there is remarkably little surviving evidence to prove that Hanna was a real person. Neither Hanna nor President William McKinley left much in the way of written records, which makes it difficult to understand Hanna's legacy fully.

There are only two published biographies of Mark Hanna, and only the one by Herbert Croly was written by an author with access to his papers and his contemporaries. Much of the Croly book is based on interviews, currently archived at the Library of Congress, that were conducted by James B. Morrow, a reporter and editor for the *Cleveland Leader.* Croly's 1912 book, *Marcus Alonzo Hanna: His Life and His Work,* gives readers an impression of Hanna as a man and politician that is much more favorable than much of what was printed in the popular press of his day.

It is unfortunate that a man who was the center of so much attention when he lived has received so little scholarly attention since his passing, but the lack of historical documents and records about Hanna is undoubtedly part of the reason for that. Croly was effectively handpicked by the Ohioan's family to write about their patriarch, but Croly's words of praise for the man deserve more credit than one might ordinarily give such a biography because the author's political views differed significantly from Hanna's.

Were Croly a hack of questionable character and skill, we would be left without any reasonable account of Hanna's life, and we might be left to wonder skeptically about the positive tone of the biography. Fortunately, given the book's importance as the only work about Hanna that approaches something like scholarly inquiry, this is not the case.

Croly's book was part of a series on political leaders published between 1882 and 1916 called the *American Statesmen Series*, edited by John Torrey Morse Jr. The series featured many well-known and highly respected authors—and politicians—including Carl Schurz, Henry Adams, Henry Cabot Lodge, E. M. Shepard, and Theodore Roosevelt. As Arthur M. Schlesinger Jr., the editor of the reissue of the series in the 1980s, writes, "The authors were mostly from outside the academy, and they wrote with the confidence of men of affairs. Their books are generally crisp, intelligent, spirited and readable" and deserve attention today "on their merits as well as for the vigorous expression they give to an influential view of the American past."[1] Fortunately for the otherwise scant historical record about Hanna, Croly fit in well with the crowd Schlesinger describes, and his personal reputation lends credence to his biography of Hanna.

While Croly was an influential and well-respected writer of his day, today he is best remembered as a founder and first editor of the *New Republic* and for his book *The Promise of an American Life,* which was a progressive treatise about ways to improve America. This work suggests two things about Croly: that he was a highly principled man and that his principles were not necessarily those of Mark Hanna. In *The Promise of an American Life*, Croly wrote of many ideas that Hanna would have disdained. Under his stewardship, the *New Republic* became a champion of progressive ideas. The historian James Ford Rhodes, who won the Pulitzer Prize in 1916 for his series of books *The History of the United States since the Compromise of 1850*, addressed the choice of Croly as Hanna's biographer in his 1922 book about the McKinley administration:

> Popular knowledge of a man of action who left few letters,
> did not keep a diary nor write a book depends largely upon

his biographer and, in this respect, Hanna was exceptionally happy. His son selected Herbert Croly, who made the work a labor of love and has presented the real Mark Hanna with remarkable perspicacity and skill. Some of Hanna's friends, on hearing of the selection, may have shuddered at the thought of an author with socialistic proclivities undertaking the biography of a strong individualist; yet the accomplished editor of the American Statesmen series had chosen Carl Schurz, an avowed tariff reformer, to write the life of Henry Clay and the wisdom of this selection had been fully demonstrated. Even so was the choice of Herbert Croly to write the life of Mark Hanna. One may learn from that book what manner of man was Hanna when he determined to bend all his energies to the nomination of McKinley in 1896.[2]

To Rhodes, Croly was a man of personal integrity whose generally positive look at the life of Mark Hanna was lent extra credibility thanks to Croly's apparent ideological differences with his subject.

As is the case with so much of Hanna's story, however, some additional explanation is necessary. Rhodes was Mark Hanna's brother-in-law; Hanna's wife, C. Augusta Rhodes Hanna, was James Rhodes's sister. The familial connection, however, is mitigated by the fact that the two men stood on opposite sides of the political fence. Rhodes, like his father, Daniel P. Rhodes, was a staunchly conservative Democrat and a cousin of Stephen A. Douglas, Abraham Lincoln's great political rival.

Regardless of Croly's credentials as Hanna's biographer, his work remains the most authoritative source of information about Hanna's life. The job was difficult, as there was precious little record for Croly to rely upon, fewer than ten years after Hanna's death. As Croly wrote in the introduction, "No political leader of similar prominence in modern times has left such a slim public record of his characteristic achievements."[3] The few paper records left behind by Hanna were made available to Croly for the book, and then most were destroyed by Hanna's family when the book was finished.[4]

Much of the record of Hanna's relationship with William McKinley, both personal and political, thus went completely undocumented. As

Croly writes, "Only about a score of letters and some four telegrams written by Mr. McKinley to Mr. Hanna have been preserved; and the great majority of these are trivial in character. It is, consequently impossible to find any significant indications in their correspondence of the increasing intimacy between the two men."[5] McKinley was reluctant to commit anything to paper, and many historians have suggested that when he did put his thoughts on paper, he was writing with his biographers in mind. One contemporary of McKinley, Charles Willis Thompson, a longtime editor of the *New York Times,* noted that McKinley's careful control of his image even extended to photographs. Thompson wrote, "He would never consent to be photographed in a negligent pose, and always took the most meticulous care about every detail of his appearance and his posture."[6]

Historian Margaret Leech, a McKinley biographer, suggested that a major reason for the lack of written communication between Hanna and McKinley was that both men relied on personal go-betweens and the new technology of the day, the telephone, rather than committing anything of importance to paper.[7] Regardless of the reasons for the lack of written documents to aid in compiling a biography of Hanna, the consequence of that absence was the same—there was very little left to suggest that Hanna ever existed outside the pages of the newspapers. Hanna spoke with some frequency to reporters, even to those from the paper that treated him the most harshly, Hearst's *New York Journal.* While many of his comments were printed in newspapers, his public comments do not necessarily shed much light on the real workings of his relationship with McKinley or about himself and his family.

The press, particularly Hearst's newspapers, often reported on Hanna's private life and the lives of his children. His son Dan, who went through a scandalous divorce, and his daughter Ruth, who was a Washington debutante during Hanna's years in the Senate, received frequent attention in the press, but this reporting took place without Hanna's cooperation. He believed firmly in a sharp separation between his public self and his private life. Writer Joe Mitchell Chapple reported that, during an interview, Hanna told an anecdote about his childhood that would have cast him in a favorable public light. However, Hanna asked that the story never be made public while he was still alive "because these things are apt to be misunderstood, and I prefer to have the people appreciate me for my public work and nothing else."[8] Hanna was not always comfortable in the public spotlight, but he did not shun it. The longer he was in politics, the more comfortable he became, and he seemed thoroughly to enjoy taking the stage during his Senate reelection campaigns in 1898 and 1904 and during McKinley's reelection campaign in 1900. Still, it was always important to him to keep a wall between his personal and public lives.

Hanna and His Politics

Hanna was, and still is, understood by many as a man intent on accruing personal power and making financial gains. People who see him in that light argue that he took those pursuits to their logical extreme in his quest of the White House for William McKinley. Hanna no doubt enjoyed the power and prestige he commanded late in his life, but it is wrong to assume that his involvement in politics, or with the Republican Party, was motivated by a desire to benefit himself directly.

In large part, his personal circumstances dictated that Hanna was intently focused on becoming a businessman, not a politician, for much of his life. This does not mean his family was apolitical. His father Leonard was a Whig and an outspoken proponent of the temperance movement. He once ran unsuccessfully for Congress as a Whig from the family's hometown of New Lisbon, Ohio. Still, though, politics was not the family business. Because of his father's ill health, Mark Hanna devoted his youthful energies to the family grocery business. With his brothers, he took over the family business, which merged several times with other companies and eventually combined with the Rhodes family's considerable business empire when Mark married Augusta Rhodes. Hanna eventually emerged as the head of that enterprise, and under his guidance, it expanded and diversified. Eventually, the family's holdings included a wide array of interests, including a theater in Cleveland, a street-car company, mining interests, a shipping company, a ship-building company, and many other concerns.[9]

While he was not always a politician, as a businessman Hanna believed that it was appropriate for, even incumbent upon, the government to do everything it could to help business. Many critics of Hanna interpret this belief to mean that his later involvement in politics was inspired entirely by a desire to help his bottom line by getting the cronies of big business into elective office. This accusation may well have been the case in the most basic sense in that he wanted people in office who shared his belief that government should help business because it was good for the country, but it is inaccurate to assert that he was motivated solely by a desire to line his own pockets. Hanna held the firm belief that the future of the country depended on a symbiotic relationship between business and government.[10] As Croly wrote, Hanna "made no sharp distinction between private and public interest."[11] To Hanna, one did not exist without the other.

Croly explained how this attitude influenced Hanna's decision to get involved actively in elective politics:

> To understand Mark Hanna's point of departure in politics we must bear in mind (1) that he was an industrial pioneer, and instinctively took to politics as well as business; (2) that in politics as in business he wanted to accomplish results; (3) that politics meant to him active party service; (4) that successful party service meant the acceptance of prevailing political methods and abuses; and (5) finally that he was bound by the instinctive consistency of his nature to represent in politics, not merely his other dominant interest, but the essential harmony between the interests of business and those of the whole community.[12]

From Croly's perspective, Hanna was an advocate of corporate-friendly policymaking, but it was not unprincipled or driven by personal greed. As a businessman, what was good for business in general was also good for Hanna personally, but Croly believed that improving his own bottom line was not Hanna's primary motivation. Rather, he was driven by his conviction that a healthy country necessitated a healthy economy and that a healthy economy required cooperative government policies. Hanna's philosophy continues to dominate much of American public policymaking today and is favored by both Republican and Democratic politicians. Despite the rhetoric of political campaigns, both parties do much to facilitate American business. Hanna's ideological goal of advancing harmonious relations between government and business was not the only reason for his interest in politics, however.

It sells Hanna short to argue that business was his only public-policy concern. If Hanna cared only about business, he could have done well to throw his support behind Grover Cleveland, a Democrat who was a strong supporter of business interests; or to ally himself with men like Jay Gould, a titan who supported Democrats; or even to go along with his own father-in-law, who was a big business Democrat. But Hanna was a steadfast Republican long before the party came to be known as the party of business.

In addition to his interest in fostering the relationship between government and business, Hanna was also motivated to get involved in politics by a strong sense of patriotism for his home state of Ohio. He began actively to promote Ohio as an important player in national politics even before politics became his full-time pursuit. Every presidential candidate whom Hanna devoted his organizational and financial resources to was an Ohioan, beginning with his efforts on behalf of James Garfield in 1880.

Most historians assume that Hanna and McKinley first met in the 1870s, but it was not until the end of the 1880s that they became close political partners. As historian Clarence Stern wrote,

> In the pursuit of his long cherished ambition to place in the presidential chair an Ohioan friendly to the interests of business, Marcus Alonzo Hanna had at the Republican national convention of 1888 concluded that McKinley was the man for that office. This decision to cast McKinley in the role hitherto disappointingly filled by John Sherman reflected Hanna's capacity for so adjusting his approach to a desired goal as to improve the chances of success.[13]

From Stern's perspective, Ohio patriotism was a major influence on Hanna, and there is ample evidence to support this assertion.

Hanna—A Republican, but Why?

Early in his biography, Herbert Croly addresses Hanna's basic political philosophy, which Croly felt was informed by a desire to do what was best for the country. This objective, Hanna clearly felt, was best served by the Republican Party. Croly wrote,

> He went into business partly as a bread-winner and partly because it took business to keep him busy. He went into politics as a citizen. The motive, in so far as it was conscious, was undoubtedly patriotic. That he should wish to serve his

country as well as himself and his family was rooted in his make-up. If he proposed to serve his country, a man of his disposition and training could do so only by active work in party politics. Patriotism meant to him Republicanism. Good government meant chiefly Republican government. Hence the extreme necessity of getting good Republicans elected, and the absolute identity in his mind and in the minds of most of his generation between public and party service.[14]

The link between patriotism and the Republican Party to which Croly referred happened early for Hanna. Hanna and his family were on the Union side in the Civil War. Since the leader of the Union, Abraham Lincoln, was a Republican, Hanna became a Republican at an early age. He was a Republican first and foremost because, in his mind and in the minds of many, the Republicans kept the Union together. Hanna's own service in the military during the Civil War was brief, but he did serve, contrary to reports on the pages of Democratic publications during the buildup to the Spanish-American War. In those partisan newspapers, he was frequently accused of sending a replacement for himself to avoid service in the military—a practice that was quite common among well-heeled northern families—because he was afraid to fight. He did, in fact, send a replacement, but the circumstances of the decision speak to something other than cowardice. At the outbreak of the Civil War, Hanna's father had just died, leaving him the only one in the family with enough experience to run the business. Hanna and his younger brother, Howard Melville Hanna, decided together that Howard should join the military while Mark stayed home to manage the family's finances. However, late in the war, Hanna was apparently unable to resist the call of duty and joined the 150th Regiment of the Ohio Volunteer Infantry as a lieutenant, where he was on active duty for just one hundred days. Sensitive about the criticism of his scant military record, he generally avoided the topic.

Hanna spoke publicly about his military service once, in an address to the Grand Army of the Republic, an influential organization of Union veterans of the Civil War, of which he was a member. He spoke to the group on September 12, 1901, while the world waited to see if William McKinley would recover from the gunshots that eventually killed him. Croly recounted the speech in his book, quoting Hanna:

This is my first visit to a camp-fire. As you all know, I have been one of you but a short while. To the question why I did not exercise my right to be enrolled, I will say that I never supposed I was entitled to stand with the men who were veterans of four years' terrible war. I am but a four months' man. In 1861 I might have enlisted, but circumstances prevented me. My father was on a sick bed. I did the best I could. I sent a substitute. Four years later I had the honor to be drafted. We did have a brush with General Early, but that was all. For that reason I did not think I was entitled to become one of your comrades.[15]

Clearly, Hanna was uncomfortable about his war record. In reality, his military service was more extensive than several presidents who did not serve, ranging from early presidents like John Adams, John Quincy Adams, and Martin Van Buren to McKinley's predecessor Grover Cleveland to a range of presidents from William Howard Taft through Franklin Roosevelt to one of our most recent presidents, Bill Clinton. Hanna certainly did not deserve the criticism that was heaped upon him more than thirty years after the fact by the partisan journalists who made careers out of criticizing him. Chief among his antagonists was William Randolph Hearst, who also never served in the military, a self-financed promotional tour in Cuba during the Spanish-American War notwithstanding.

Today's Republican Party is considered to be the party of big business, but when Hanna came of age, there were strongly probusiness factions of the Democratic Party. When Hanna married into the Rhodes family of Cleveland in 1864, he found his in-laws to be staunchly conservative Democrats who felt that the Democratic Party was the party to protect business interests. Before his marriage to C. Augusta Rhodes, her father, Daniel P. Rhodes, tried mightily to prevent her wedding a young Republican. The elder Rhodes was scandalized by the marriage of his daughter to the young Republican, and it took many years to wear the roughest edges off the relationship between Rhodes and his son-in-law. When they were first married, Hanna's wife reported that her father said to Hanna, "It is all over now, Mark, but a month ago I would liked to have seen you at the bottom of Lake Erie."[16]

After the wedding took place, Rhodes took years to warm up to his son-in-law and worked hard to try to make Hanna dependent on the

Rhodes family's benevolence. Hanna and his father-in-law shared many similar ideas about business and public policy, but their allegiance to different parties was a serious obstacle at the beginning of their relationship.

As a leader of the Republican Party at the end of the nineteenth century, Hanna became a driving force, along with men like Charles Dawes, in getting the party to depend less on the shirt-waving campaigns of the post–Civil War years. As Croly writes, "Probably no man in the country contributed more liberally, considering his means, to the war-chest of his party than did Mr. Hanna."[17] The presidential candidates he supported most energetically, Senator John Sherman and William McKinley, felt similarly to Hanna on the business issues he wanted the Republican Party to adopt.

Hanna and his colleagues turned the Republicans into a much more business-friendly party, but it was not an easy challenge. Many titans of big business at the end of the nineteenth century, such as the banking Rothschild family, were strong supporters of Democratic candidates. Grover Cleveland, the president who bookended Benjamin Harrison's four years in office, was a progold, probusiness Democrat who refused to endorse William Jennings Bryan in 1896 or 1900. Probusiness Democrats broke away from the Democratic Party in significant numbers during the campaign of 1896, appalled by Bryan's economic ideas; formed the National Democratic Party; and nominated their own presidential candidate, John M. Palmer. While Hearst's newspapers, including the *New York Journal,* and Democratic newspapers in the West supported Bryan, most Democratic newspaper publishers from the East, like Joseph Pulitzer, chose not to support Bryan.

Hanna's Early Days in Politics—Lessons Learned and a Path Chosen

Mark Hanna was steeped in politics from an early age. His father, though sickly through much of Mark Hanna's youth, was an activist who instilled in his son an interest in politics, though politics did not come to dominate Hanna's attention until late in life. For most of his adulthood, Hanna was a businessman with an interest in a number of industries, including groceries, theater, railroads, oil, mining coal and iron, shipping, and ship building.

Hanna's earliest serious involvement in politics centered on an effort to organize fellow businessmen to get involved in politics and challenge the power of local political bosses for the good of the business community.

Mark Hanna's active involvement in politics began in 1869 with his election to the school board in Cleveland.[18] In the 1870s, he got more involved in partisan politics, and, even at that early stage of his career, he demonstrated maverick tendencies that stayed with him throughout his career.

As historian James Rhodes explained, Hanna helped to break up the existing Republican machine that controlled Cleveland politics because he did not think the way it operated was good for the city. As part of that effort, he worked to elect a probusiness Democrat, Charles Otis, as mayor in 1873, and he rallied his fellow businessmen to oppose the Republican nominee, John Huntington, because he felt the Democrat was more qualified than anyone the Republicans had to offer.[19] Croly assessed this early action by Hanna as a search for a new kind of politics:

> In this connection, it should be remembered that the first phase of the municipal reform movement all over the country took just this form of an attempt to renew the interest of business men in local politics. . . . As a business man and an active politician, [Hanna] was fighting the fact that business and politics were being specialized and divided. He was seeking to escape from the awkward alternative of being obliged either to fight the political mercenaries or to conciliate them.[20]

Both Croly and another biographer, Thomas Beer, emphasized Hanna's independence from established political authorities.

Despite his activism in local politics, Hanna never became what could be described as a machine politician on the local level, like Boss Tweed in New York or Tom Pendergast in Kansas City. Politics did not come naturally to him, and he became adept in politics only after considerable trial and error.[21] Herbert Croly observes that Hanna's early political career was hampered by his lack of experience and connections, writing, "His peculiar success in business had been due largely to the formation of a group of loyal and permanent human relationships. His subsequent success in politics was to be due largely to the creation of similar ties; and the time had not yet come when the really helpful and permanent ties could be formed."[22] Even when he formed those ties, Hanna never became a boss in the traditional sense. In addition to not being a local boss, Hanna was never the boss of the Ohio state Republican Party that many newspaper columnists, like Alfred Henry Lewis, who wrote for William Randolph Hearst's newspapers, often accused him of being. During Hanna's life, control of Ohio politics was split between northern and southern Ohio, with southern Ohio controlled by Joseph Foraker, and Hanna frequently found his desires thwarted.

Hanna quickly came to believe, after being defeated in attempts to win local Cleveland offices, that real power lay not in holding office but in being an engineer who orchestrated political events. To biographer Thomas Beer, Hanna's early political behavior was motivated by a pragmatic analysis of reality:

> It was not until 1880 that Mr. Hanna shrugged and consented, and perhaps the experience of hearing himself called a rich busybody at a meeting of reformers was the conclusion of his first political mood. He knew, by that time, that machinery ruled in politics and that the machinery was companionably to be oiled by money. This image itself appeared in cartoons in the time of Grant. All was appropriate. Factories vomited cheap furniture and cheaper machines on the country, and the vital machinery of cities cast up cheap men into place. Behind this apparatus was a point of reality: one might quietly rule in politics without being a politician. One might be an engineer.[23]

While Hanna understood this was the path he wanted to take, it took considerable trial and error before he succeeded. Even when he was successful, he found that success did not necessarily result in the kind of power he might have desired. Hanna helped elect Joseph Foraker governor of Ohio in 1885, but his relationship with Foraker soon deteriorated, and the state party split into factions, causing Hanna's influence in Ohio to slip. Even when his closest ally, William McKinley, was elected governor in 1891, Hanna was frustrated in the pursuit of some of his goals.

While Hanna tried, with varying levels of success, to be influential in his home state, he clearly wanted to have an impact on the national level, and much of his political activities in Ohio were done with an eye toward winning a bigger prize. When Hanna supported William McKinley's gubernatorial campaigns, for instance, one of his a primary objectives was to help McKinley keep his name before the public in preparation for the 1896 presidential campaign. In an era before the direct election of U.S. senators by the public, Hanna got involved in state-legislative races because he hoped to ensure the election of state legislators who were sympathetic to his preferred U.S. Senate candidates, like John Sherman (or, later, Hanna, himself).

Hanna began his involvement in national politics as a supporter of two fellow Ohioans, Congressman James Garfield and Senator John Sherman. This work led him, eventually, to yet another fellow Ohioan, William McKinley, but Hanna's single-minded devotion to McKinley and his political career was far from lifelong, as is often asserted.

Much is made of Hanna's love for and devotion to McKinley, and the two grew to be very close; but the truth is that Hanna developed a taste for the rough-and-tumble world of presidential politics during the 1880 campaign of James Garfield, long before he became friendly with McKinley. Hanna subsequently campaigned for John Sherman in 1884 and 1888, dedicating significant effort to getting Sherman the Republican presidential nomination. After that nomination went to Benjamin Harrison in 1888, Hanna gave up on getting Sherman elected president and began to look for another candidate, who turned out to be McKinley.[24] Once he began to work on McKinley's behalf, he was completely dedicated to the major's success, but Hanna's relationship with Sherman belies the enduring myth that his political energies were always focused on getting McKinley elected president.

CHAPTER TWO

1880—Hanna Buys Trouble
with the Press and Helps Elect Garfield

nderstanding Mark Hanna as a real person is hampered by his image in the media. Hanna's enduring image in popular culture is overwhelmingly negative, thanks largely to coverage of him on the pages of the newspapers of William Randolph Hearst. However, Hearst's writers and cartoonists did not invent the negative image of Hanna that still exists today. His problems with the media began before he became a nationally known politician in the 1890s, and those problems came courtesy of a fellow Republican.

By 1880, Hanna was well known as a prominent businessman in Cleveland. He owned many businesses. Among these was the *Cleveland Herald*, a Republican newspaper that was published from 1819 to 1885, when its assets were divided between the *Cleveland Plain Dealer* and the *Cleveland Leader*.[1] Hanna's purchase of the *Herald* coincided with his first real involvement in presidential politics, as he jockeyed for a chance to represent Cleveland's Republicans at the national convention and, later, raised money for the party's nominee, James Garfield, in innovative ways.

Though the newspaper was never more than a minor part of Hanna's empire financially, it had a significant and lasting effect on his public image. Hanna owned the *Herald* from 1880 to 1885, and as long as he owned it, he was confronted by a furious rival, Edwin Cowles, the publisher of the other Republican paper in town, the *Cleveland*

Leader. For Cowles, the publishing of a Republican newspaper was a lifelong passion, and Hanna's challenge outraged him. During the time the owned the *Herald,* therefore, Hanna was the recipient of furious press criticism from his Republican rival. This was Hanna's first extended experience with negative coverage in the press, and, if he considered it at all, it was no doubt vexing to him that the bad press that haunted him through the last quarter century of his life began with a Republican newspaper.

Hanna bought the *Herald* from a former Republican member of Congress, Richard Parsons. His main competition, the *Leader,* was first published in 1844 under the name of *Ohio American* and was renamed the *Leader* in 1854. It was founded, and edited for several decades, by Edwin Cowles, who was eighteen years old at the time he started the paper.[2] As an owner, Cowles was an innovator. Under his ownership, the *Leader* was the first newspaper in Cleveland to have a printing press, called a perfecting press, which allowed for printing on both sides of the paper at once. The machine also folded the newspapers after they were printed.[3] As editor, Cowles was an advocate of abolition and, like Hanna, was a major supporter of the Republican Party in its nascent days.[4] Following the Civil War, he remained committed to keeping the Republican Party's reform ideal alive, supporting the Reconstruction of the former Confederate states, as well as other causes, like temperance.

Journalist Charles E. Kennedy, who was the city editor of the *Herald* when Hanna owned it, wrote that Cowles was "one of the most able and fearless of the early abolitionists."[5] Kennedy also asserted, "Unlike many other newspaper owners Cowles was not to be shifted from a course by the expediency of the moment. He was unafraid. His newspaper was unfettered. His one great mastering and moving impulse was the 'Grand Old Party,' loyalty to which was at times bad medicine for his newspaper property, but a loyalty grounded in absolute confidence and belief."[6] He was, according to Cleveland historian and journalist James Wallen, "of the Dana and Greeley type—an editor of personality and power."[7]

Cowles also had an intolerant side. In the post–Civil War years, he was an outspoken opponent of the Catholic Church. He was the head of the Order of the American Union, an anti-Catholic organization that preceded the formation of the American Protective Association, a group that caused the McKinley campaign some heartburn in 1896. Kennedy explained, "No one who was close to Edwin Cowles ever doubted the sincerity of the man in his attacks upon the Catholic church. To his intense and somewhat single track mind its rapid growth in the United States and its alleged domination of the Democratic party seemed a frightful menace, possibly entailing ultimate return to the days of the Inquisition, the removal of the Vatican to these shores, and a swallowing of the state by the church in one large future gulp!"[8] Kennedy added that Cowles's obsession with the Catholic Church was ultimately the undoing of his newspaper. He wrote, "[Cowles's] other conspicuous mistake, an unmerciful war upon a particular kind of religion, no doubt had something to do with the ultimate decline of his newspaper, for it was persisted in long after our people were awakening to a better understanding and toleration of religious views. His was a narrower age."[9] That downfall, however, came long after his rivalry with Hanna. It was this strongly opinionated man, intolerant of those who differed with him, who Hanna ran up against when he bought the financially failing *Herald* and tried to breathe new life into it.

As Kennedy related, the history of the *Herald* and the *Leader* was marked by bitter rivalry that predated Hanna's entry in the newspaper business. Under Cowles's leadership, the *Leader* pushed the *Herald* from first to second place in terms of circulation long before Hanna bought the *Herald*. When Hanna bought the paper, he outraged Cowles by pulling a William Randolph Hearst–like heist of the *Leader*'s editorial and writing staff, hiring away many *Leader* employees.[10] As was reported in the *New York Times,*

> A sensation has been caused in newspaper circles here by the sale of the Hon. R.C. Parsons's stock in the Cleveland *Herald* to a syndicate of wealthy citizens, headed by Mark Hanna, owner of the Opera-house. A march has been stolen on the *Leader* by the engagement of all of its staff except two by the new management of the *Herald,* the arrangement to go into effect at once. The *Leader* is in a predicament, as its very bone and sinew have been taken. John C. Keiffer, formerly of the Philadelphia *Press,* is to be editor and general manager of the *Herald,* and he will be assisted by J. H. Kennedy, for eight years one of the editors of the *Leader.*[11]

For Cowles, whose ownership of the *Leader* was part of an ideological mission, the aggressive move was unforgivable.

J. B. Morrow, who after Hanna's death in 1904 collected the many personal statements that were a key part of Herbert Croly's raw material for Hanna's biography, was a reporter for the *Herald* when Hanna staged his raid on the *Leader*. Sensing an opportunity, Morrow left the *Herald* and was promptly hired by Cowles at the *Leader*. Morrow wrote, "The first move the new management of the *Herald* made was to hire nearly every good man on the *Leader*. The argument was that inasmuch as the *Leader* was prosperous the men employed on it must have contributed to its success; therefore, it was good business policy to get those men."[12] Cowles was so angered by this move that he made making Hanna's life miserable a top priority for as long as Hanna owned the paper. Morrow summed up Cowles's anger in this way: "The methods of Mr. Hanna's opposition to the *Leader* aroused the fighting spirit of Edwin Cowles and for several years the *Leader* made Mr. Hanna a target for attacks and ridicule. Although he gave the *Herald* but little of his personal attention he was regarded as its chief owner and manager, and the *Leader* made him conspicuous by its abuse of him throughout his ownership of that property."[13] Cowles was a powerful enemy of Hanna because he had a ready-made platform, published daily, from which to attack him.

As Hanna became more prominent in Cleveland, he collected enemies, and Cowles was happy to capitalize on that fact. As Croly observed, "His fights with the petty 'bosses,' and his aggressive methods and ways had raised in his path a number of aggrieved men, who, like Mr. Cowles, were eager to oppose any candidate or measure which he advocated, and who were already describing him as a 'boss' unscrupulously grasping after money and party."[14] Cowles used his newspaper to paint a very negative portrait of Hanna as a corrupt party boss. This image, while largely untrue, stuck with Hanna throughout his career in politics, even after Hanna sold the *Herald* and Cowles stopped attacking him.[15] The fact that Cowles stopped his attacks on Hanna as soon he sold the *Herald* should have reduced the credibility of what was published in the *Leader* about Hanna when he owned the newspaper but, after five years of relentless attacks, the damage was done.

Despite Cowles's virulent treatment of Hanna, many defended his actions as the *Herald*'s owner. Herbert Croly portrayed Hanna's

actions as the publisher of the *Herald* as those of a man honestly trying to promote a political point of view. He wrote, "In assuming the
management of the *Herald,* Mark Hanna had no ulterior personal
purpose," and in buying the newspaper, Hanna gave himself "a costly
mirror in which his ardent Republicanism was reflected."[16] Croly's
view of Hanna's ownership of the *Herald* was also shared by some
journalists who worked in Cleveland in the 1880s.

Like J. B. Morrow, reporter Charles E. Kennedy was situated in the
middle of the battle between the two papers. He began his career in
journalism working for Cowles at the *Leader,* but he was one of the
journalists whom Hanna lured to the *Herald* with "a fifty per cent increase in salary."[17] He wrote that the *Herald* "was Republican in politics, but much more independent and fair in its dealings with party
questions than the *Leader,* which, under the direction of Cowles,
rated most Democrats as traitors and canonized even the least worthy
of the Republican leaders of that period."[18] Hanna was not pure as the
driven snow, and Kennedy acknowledged that during Hanna's ownership of the *Herald,* the *Leader,* "with some degree of truth, characterized
the freshly invigorated *Herald* as the organ of the Union Club, for it
was patent that the street railroads and other capitalized interests in
which Hanna was involved never got the worst of it in the *Herald* columns." Defending Hanna and the *Herald,* however, Kennedy added,
"throughout the entire Hanna regime labor in no other Cleveland
newspaper received fairer treatment."[19] This last statement is important because it provides a defense against one of the most common
critiques of Hanna: that as an industrialist, he was virulently antilabor
and antilabor union. In Hearst's cartoonist Homer Davenport's depic-
tions of Hanna, the grotesque figure of Hanna was frequently in close
proximity to, or standing on, a skull bearing the name of Labor.

Another journalist who agreed with Kennedy's positive assessment
of Hanna's stewardship of the *Herald* was one of his editors, J. H. A.
Bone, who wrote, "He did not attempt to make his unprofitable newspaper pay by using it to advance his other business interests. . . . Mr.
Hanna never meddled with the editorial department and rarely came
to the office. . . . He was a Republican, and the *Herald* was a Republican newspaper. Beyond that he had no personal political policy."[20]
Bone's comments were reiterated by James H. Kennedy, the older
brother of Charles E. Kennedy. James H. Kennedy was the managing

editor of the *Herald* while Hanna was its owner. James Kennedy commented on Hanna's managerial style, asserting that Hanna paid very little attention to the paper once he bought it:

> Of course he was a Republican and the *Herald* was a Republican newspaper and on all political questions the paper reflected his personal opinions, but he did not attempt to influence the paper in the least in local matters. He never gave us any instructions concerning the street railroads of Cleveland and he was at that time a very large owner and possibly the president of the West Side Street Railroad Company. He made no attempt to use the paper to promote his own interests, to punish his personal or business or political enemies or to reward his friends.[21]

For those who worked for Hanna, he was a fair boss and a fair publisher. These men remained loyal to him after his death, for it was important to them that no one thought he used his media outlet for personal gain.

It is natural to treat this characterization of Hanna with skepticism, but there is evidence that Hanna's purchase of the newspaper was more or less an impulse purchase. The demands of the rest of his business empire kept Hanna from being involved in the day-to-day management of the paper in the way that media tycoons like Pulitzer and Hearst or single-minded zealots like Edwin Cowles were. After he tried and failed to put the *Herald* in first place by raiding the staff of the *Leader*, Hanna moved on, selling the paper after just five years. It is not clear whether Hanna knew Cowles eased off him when he sold the *Herald*, but that is in fact what happened. When Hanna sold out, Cleveland no longer had a Republican newspaper taking almost daily shots at Mark Hanna.

J. B. Morrow felt Hanna had been treated unfairly by Cowles, despite Hanna's aggressive raid on the *Leader*'s staff:

> From the spring of 1880, therefore, until the *Herald* was finally broken up and sold, Mr. Hanna was the subject of the *Leader*'s attacks and its merriment. He was belittled in everything that he undertook and was pictured as being a dictator and a boss in politics. There was no foundation for either charge. Mr. Hanna was an active and progressive

man, but he gave no evidence of being dictatorial or of wishing to dominate local politics. He was a worker in his ward on the West Side on election day and he attended the conventions, but in no sense could it be said that he was ambitious personally. He was never a candidate for office and was devoting all of his time to his business.[22]

Morrow's memory of the turbulent conflict between Hanna and Cowles is significant because, while Morrow was a Republican, he never worked for Hanna. In fact, as has been pointed out, when Hanna bought the *Herald,* Morrow left the paper to work for the *Leader.*

The *Cleveland Herald* never made money during Hanna's ownership, and in 1885, Hanna the businessman divested himself of the newspaper. He sold part of the paper's assets to Edwin Cowles and part to man named Liberty E. Holden, who owned the *Cleveland Plain Dealer,* a Democratic newspaper. Coverage of the sale in the *New York Times* lamented the loss of the *Herald* and lauded Hanna's tenure as the newspaper's last owner: "The absorption of the *Herald* blots out the oldest Republican newspaper not only in Cleveland, but in Northern Ohio. . . . Mr. M. A. Hanna bought the paper at the ebb of its existence, and succeeded in making it an excellent paper and a formidable rival of the *Leader.*"[23]

In the sale, the physical remains of the *Herald* went to the *Plain Dealer,* and the subscription list went to Cowles and the *Leader.* What the *Leader* got in the deal was of great symbolic value to Cowles. As Kennedy wrote, "The *Leader* portion consisted in securing the scalp of a hated rival and the satisfaction of publishing for a few months the words 'and *Herald*' in small letters under its own title."[24] Croly wrote that the *Leader* "celebrated its victory in an editorial article, which described its defeated competitor as an able and a fair protagonist—a fact which no one could have suspected from a perusal of the *Leader's* pages a few weeks earlier."[25] With the exception of some celebratory flair on its masthead, however, the rest of the *Leader's* criticism of Hanna stopped as soon as he got out of the news business.

Selling the paper to Cowles was, according to Croly, a "judicious piece of backsliding" that "served at once to allay the enmity of Mr. Cowles. Thereafter Mr. Hanna was as amiably treated by the *Leader* as was any other good Republican."[26] Of course, while the sale eliminated one enemy for Hanna, it added to the strength of another. Liberty Holden and the *Plain Dealer* happily took up the mantle of the *Leader* as the city's leading critic of Hanna and remained critical of him throughout his life.

Since the physical entity that was the *Herald* became part of the *Plain Dealer,* Hanna's sale had the unintended consequence of strengthening a newspaper that portrayed him as a corrupt, big-business, party boss. The *Plain Dealer* was not the only anti-Hanna, Democratic newspaper in town. In addition to the *Plain Dealer,* another paper that attacked Hanna unmercifully was the *Cleveland Press.* J. B. Morrow wrote, "After Mr. Hanna sold the *Herald* he continued to figure more or less in the newspapers, although the *Leader* thereafter let him alone. He long had been a subject of ridicule by the *Leader* and then the *Press,* an afternoon newspaper, sensational and unscrupulous, took up the work of attacking Mr. Hanna where the Leader left off."[27] Morrow suggested that the *Press* used attacks on prominent citizens of Cleveland to draw attention and increase circulation and concluded, "My own theory is that the *Press* aroused more antagonism to Mr. Hanna than any other influence in Cleveland."[28] Morrow was clearly angered by the *Press*'s negative coverage of Hanna, writing, "Mr. Hanna was a shining mark for its attacks and for years was misrepresented in the columns of that newspaper. Prejudice, created first by the *Leader,* and then increased and kept alive by the *Press,* continued until near the close of Mr. Hanna's life."[29]

The irony is that Hanna's troubles with the press began with a Republican newspaper. Hanna's reputation as a ruthless, win-at-any-cost politico, first forged in a newspaper war with another Republican, continued to stay with him long after the war was over. His reputation was played up in the Democratic press in Cleveland, and, as Hanna became more prominent, it made the leap to the national press, most especially in the publications of William Randolph Hearst. As Croly observed,

> In the succeeding years he became more and more conspicuous is local business and politics, and the kind of attack which a Republican newspaper had begun was continued, although with less persistence, by Democrats. The *Plain-Dealer* referred to him, sometimes obscurely and sometimes overtly, as a "Boss" and as an aggressive and a greedy man. The *Press* . . .

took for a while a corresponding line of comment. He was pictured as overbearing, grasping, and as indifferent to the rights of others. An attempt was made to prejudice popular opinion against him by representing him as hostile to business prosperity of Cleveland. . . . Such misrepresentations continued for many years and contributed to establishing locally a distorted popular impression of Mr. Hanna long before he became a national political leader.[30]

Hanna's troubles with the press did not begin with Hearst and the *New York Journal*. The Hearst reporter who was most often charged with the task of attacking Hanna during the campaign of 1896, Alfred Henry Lewis, no doubt took cues from the Democratic press in Cleveland, which took their cues from the poison pen of Republican Edwin Cowles, though the abuse at the hands of Hearst rose to new levels.

Despite the virulence of Cowles's anger toward Hanna, the *Leader* was never in serious danger. Cowles vanquished the *Herald* as a rival long before Hanna had bought it and, despite Hanna's considerable skill as a businessman, the paper never succeeded. As Croly wrote, "The contest was bitter, because the rivalry between the two newspapers, as well as lively personal feelings, was involved. But the *Herald* and its owner were always being beaten by the *Leader* and its owner."[31] When Hanna sold the *Herald*, the *New York Times* had kind words to write about his time as a publisher, but, for Cowles, Hanna was simply an interloper, a nuisance to be aggressively dispatched.

The anger his purchase of the *Herald* engendered in Cowles was a lesson for Hanna in how much politics differed from business. For Hanna, business was business; in very few circumstances did he let anger or resentment get in the way of progress, either in business or politics. Others were not like him, however, and Edwin Cowles was not the only Cleveland businessman who was annoyed by Hanna's tactics, especially as he began to involve himself in politics. Despite his reputation as the man who helped make the Republican Party the party of business, Hanna was not appreciated by the money men of Cleveland because of his different, independent way of thinking. As James Ford Rhodes related, Hanna's independent streak "was inherent in himself and gained for him the dislike of the solid financial men of Cleveland, who had built up the city and were naturally the dominant figures in its financial circles."[32] Hanna shook up his own party, but that was not his only problem. Many of Cleveland's business leaders, like his own father-in-law, were Democrats. These factors, in addition to five years of negative coverage from a Republican newspaper, had a detrimental impact on Hanna's reputation in his hometown. As Croly wrote, "These personal enemies in his own bailiwick were a source of embarrassment to him throughout the whole of his political career. His political enemies were more than outweighed by his political friends, but the political friendships of these early years were, with one or two exceptions, not his permanent political friends. He had still to make a number of mistakes and failures before he knew what he could do in politics, and with whom he wanted to cooperate."[33] For Hanna, politics and business were intermingled, and he approached one in much the same way he approached the other.

One of his attorneys, Andrew Squire, reported, "Mr. Hanna's business characteristics were absolute accuracy, honesty and integrity. His early business associates were his late business associates. The men and firms with whom he did business twenty years ago were doing business with him at the time of his death."[34] This was true of Hanna's relationships in politics. He was comfortable with certain people, and they remained his allies throughout his unusual political career. His many allies point to this characteristic as a strength, but also as a weakness, suggesting that, to his detriment, Hanna was sometimes the last to notice a relationship had gone sour, such as happened during the campaign of 1888 when his relationship with Joseph Foraker collapsed. Before that happened, however, Hanna spent eight years learning about high-stakes politics and positioning himself to be a leader in the Republican Party.

Mark Hanna's first appearance in the "national" media came during the 1880 presidential campaign, when he received notice from newspapers such as the *New York Times* for his support of James Garfield's campaign. He played a prominent role in promoting Garfield's candidacy in the Cleveland area, and his efforts expanded to business communities of other cities across the country. Once Hanna got a taste for politics and a public role at this level, he stayed with it until his death in 1904. As James Rhodes wrote, "From that time on he never lost an opportunity to identify himself with any Republican movement. Although he had never read Cicero, he shared the Roman's belief that he must keep himself constantly before the public."[35]

During the 1880s, the Republican Party was a party in turmoil, both across the nation and in Cleveland. At the national level, the party was divided into factions: the Stalwarts; moderates, who were derisively referred to by the Stalwarts as the "Half-Breeds"; and the reformers. The Stalwarts, led nationally by New York senator Roscoe Conkling, opposed the more conciliatory stance that Rutherford B. Hayes took toward the South in the post-Reconstruction era that was ushered in by the scandal-tainted election of 1876. They supported protective tariffs and opposed any move to dismantle the patronage system. The so-called Half-Breeds, who stood between the Stalwarts and the advocates of many types of reform, favored Hayes's lenient treatment of the South and supported moderate civil-service reforms.

In the buildup to the 1880 Republican national convention, the *Cleveland Leader* supported James G. Blaine, a senator from Maine and former Speaker of the House who fell into the Half-Breed category. Hanna's *Herald,* meanwhile, endorsed John Sherman, who was leaving the Hayes administration, where he had served as secretary of the treasury. Like Blaine, Sherman was also more or less a Half-Breed candidate. The third potential candidate in the mix, backed by the Stalwarts, was U. S. Grant, the first Republican president to serve two full terms in office. He almost certainly would have been willing to serve a third consecutive term in 1876, but the Republican Party honored the tradition established by George Washington and more fully articulated by Thomas Jefferson of serving just two terms when it nominated Rutherford B. Hayes, another Civil War general, in his place.[36]

Grant, after traveling abroad for the better part of three years, returned to the United States a willing candidate of the so-called Stalwart branch of the fractured Republican Party. Grant was a man with great popular appeal despite the scandals of his presidency, so it seemed natural that he would make a good candidate for the Republicans. At the convention, support for Blaine and Grant divided most of the delegates. In the first several ballots, Blaine and Grant each received around three hundred votes, while Sherman repeatedly received around one hundred votes. Blaine was the most popular Republican of his day, but he was dogged by allegations of corruption as a congressman. These allegations had scuttled his presidential aspirations in 1876, and they continued to haunt him in 1880.

At the convention, Sherman's campaign was managed by Ohio congressman James A. Garfield, a former Civil War general who had just been elected to the U.S. Senate. Like Sherman, Garfield was a moderate, and he gave the speech placing Sherman's name in nomination at the convention. Sherman's presidential aspirations were always derailed by one event or another. In 1880, it was the eloquence of Garfield's speech that was largely responsible for ending Sherman's campaign. James H. Kennedy, who reported on the convention for the *Herald,* recollected that the delegates, especially the members of the Ohio delegation, responded with great enthusiasm to Garfield's speech for Sherman. Despite that enthusiasm, Kennedy reported, it was still a great surprise to everyone, especially the pro-Sherman Ohio delegation, when Garfield ended up with the Republican nomination.[37]

James Kennedy's brother, Charles, wrote of the Ohio delegation's excited response to Garfield's speech, as well as the surprise everyone felt when Garfield ended up as the nominee. Of the enthusiastic response to Garfield's speech, Charles Kennedy wrote, "Of course this was more an expression of local pride and loyalty than any attempt at prophesy, for it was generally thought that if the nomination came to Ohio at all it would go to Sherman, who had the support of the entire Ohio delegation. But fate and Garfield's great nominating speech decided that once again Sherman was to be thwarted in his Supreme ambition."[38] After more than thirty ballots were taken without arriving at a nominee, Garfield emerged as a candidate. As Garfield gained momentum and Sherman saw he stood no chance of winning, he released his votes to Garfield after the thirty-third ballot. On the thirty-sixth ballot, Garfield won the nomination.[39] Garfield received 399 votes to 306 for Grant and forty-two for Blaine. To appease the Stalwarts, the delegates gave Garfield a Stalwart vice-presidential nominee, Chester A. Arthur, who was a virtual unknown outside New York. Garfield's opponent in the campaign of 1880 was Winfield Hancock, yet another Civil War general.

During the general election campaign in 1880, Hanna gained national attention for the first time. Croly called the early 1880s Hanna's "experimental period," in which he slowly expanded both the scope and volume of his political activity. He had not yet, according to Croly, "come to realize what he wanted in politics or what were the ways and means of attaining success in this less familiar region."[40] Despite that, however, Hanna gained notice within Republican circles in Cleveland and beyond for his work on behalf of Garfield's campaign. As Croly wrote, Hanna was "intensely interested" in Garfield's campaign "because the candidate was not only from Ohio, but from the vicinity of Cleveland."[41] First, as a leader in the Cleveland business community, Hanna was widely credited with creating the Business Man's Republican Campaign Club. The club organized men of industry across the country to campaign on behalf of Garfield, raising money and holding events and parades to rally support.[42]

Following Hanna's death, Charles Leach spoke of Hanna's efforts in 1880: "He suggested, or if he didn't suggest it he helped to organize a business men's league which did effective work in the campaign."[43] In parenthetical comments included in the statement, J. B. Morrow wrote, "I think it to be a fact that a considerable sum of money was raised in Cleveland for General Garfield's personal use during the campaign. He was a poor man, worth, perhaps $25,000, and the Republicans of Cleveland thought he ought to be relieved of all anxiety concerning his individual expenses. He had to remain at his home in Mentor and to entertain a large number of public men who came to see him. To this fund, of course, Mr. Hanna must have been a generous contributor."[44] Senator Charles Dick, who was appointed to Hanna's seat in the U.S. Senate after Hanna's death and who was an integral part of McKinley's campaign operations in 1896 and 1900, argued that Hanna was critical to Garfield's success:

> It is my judgment that Mr. Hanna had as much to do with the election of Mr. Garfield as any single individual in the country. Garfield was being assaulted in the most vicious manner. . . . It was in that campaign that Mr. Hanna conceived and developed an organization known as the business men's league, an organization of business men of the country to work for Garfield's election. It started in Cleveland, went all over Ohio and spread from Ohio into all the States. It was that movement of business men, which in my judgment, was more effective than any other single influence in the campaign which resulted in Garfield's election.[45]

From Dick's perspective, 1880 marked Hanna's emergence as a critical player in Republican presidential politics.

Hanna probably did not deserve as much credit for Garfield's victory as Senator Dick wanted to give him, but at the same time, his actions in helping to set up the businessmen's club were clearly important for Garfield, who had a very tough campaign and won with only a very narrow plurality of the popular vote. Even the *Leader*, whose pages were so vehemently anti-Hanna, seemed to understand the importance of the club, for there were many positively toned articles published by the newspaper about the club.[46] It may have been an exaggeration to give Hanna sole credit for creating the concept of the Business Man's Club, but he was a founding member of the Cleveland club and was also a major source of money—both his own and money that he raised from others—for the Garfield campaign. The club was one of the earliest signs that the Republican Party was destined to become the party of business, and Hanna was a force in that transition.[47]

Hanna recruited support from the business community with the argument that what was good for the Republican Party was good for business and, further, what was good for business was good for the country. He was a trailblazer in connecting business interests with the Republican Party in an era when the Republicans were not the accepted party of business as it is today. Hanna, in fact, played a critical role in carving that niche for the party. As Malcolm Moos observed, Hanna was "bound by the instinctive consistency of his nature to represent in politics not merely his other dominant interest (business) but the essential harmony between the interests of business and those of the whole community."[48] As Hanna achieved personal success in business, he also came to believe that there were integral connections between business, government, and prosperity for the nation. It is not wrong to suggest that he acted politically with business interests in mind. On the other hand, to argue that Hanna fought for business interests out of some selfish instinct, as Hearst's writers and many other critics asserted, is dubious.

Beyond the creation of the club, Hanna was also credited by some with orchestrating an important event during the campaign. Because the Republican convention was contentious, thanks in large measure to the split between the Stalwarts and the rest of the party, it was critical for Garfield to have the best-known names in the party on his side. James G. Blaine did his part for Garfield, campaigning for him strongly and earning appointment as secretary of state in return.[49]

Getting Blaine's endorsement was comparatively easy since both men were moderates in the Republican Party. In the case of U. S. Grant, however, there was a great deal more uncertainty. Grant was a Stalwart, and it was unclear to what extent he would support Garfield, who was at best tolerated by the large faction of Stalwarts in the party who favored Grant. Getting the former president to support Garfield's candidacy was important from both a symbolic and practical perspective.

There are competing views about the extent to which Hanna was involved in bringing the men together. What is clearly true is that a large meeting of Republicans was scheduled in Warren, Ohio, to demonstrate to the public that there was no split in the Republican Party. Both Grant and Senator Roscoe Conkling, the country's leading Stalwart, traveled to Ohio to lend their support to Garfield's campaign. As the *New York Times* reported, Hanna was waiting in Cleveland to escort Grant and his party to the gathering. The paper further reported about the purpose of the gathering:

> The 35,000 who to-day assembled in mass convention here to hear and see Gen. Grant and Senator Conkling, and to give some marked expression to their Republicanism, have said to the Nation that all stories of Republican lukewarmness or apathy in the Nineteenth Ohio, or Gen. Garfield's, District are Democratic lies, put forth with a purpose and told without any foundation. More than that, the meeting has warmed the few doubting ones in this corner of the state, and will set them to work with new zeal.[50]

At the gathering in Warren, Grant spoke first, briefly, to introduce Conkling, who spoke for two hours. As was reported by the *New York Times,* in his opening remarks, Grant spoke of why he was a Republican. He and his supporters were Republicans who still waved the bloody shirt, but Grant also spoke of other reasons, including the party's support of business interests, to show that the Republican Party was superior:

> I am a Republican as the two great political parties are now divided, because the Republican Party is a national party seeking the greatest good for the greatest number of citizens. . . . But I am a Republican for many other reasons.

The Republican Party assures protection to life and property, the public credit, and the payment of debts of the Government, State, county, or municipality, so far as it can control. The Democratic Party does not promise this; if it does, it has broken its promises to the extent of hundreds of millions, as many Northern Democrats can testify to their sorrow. I am Republican as between the existing parties because it fosters the production of the field and farm and of manufactories, and it encourages the general education of the poor as well as the rich. The Democratic Party discourages all these when in absolute power.[51]

Grant worked to position the Republican Party in this speech as a party with something for everyone, Stalwart or not.

Garfield was not present in Warren for the large gathering. He chose, as was common in the day, to remain aloof from such campaign appearances. As McKinley would do later, Garfield ran a front-porch campaign from his house. This was in keeping with tradition, but it was also a reflection of Garfield's meager finances. Garfield's comparatively modest means motivated Hanna to work hard on his behalf in Cleveland, raising money from well-heeled Republicans. Following the meeting in Warren, the Grant-Conkling party, accompanied by Hanna, stopped in Mentor, Garfield's hometown.

The meeting in Mentor, however, was nothing like the speaking marathon that took place in Warren. There was a small parade from the train station to Garfield's house, followed by a brief public appearance in which Grant, Conkling, and other members of the party made short greetings to the crowd. After a quick meeting between the visitors and Garfield, Grant and Conkling left. Following the visit to Mentor, the party, including Hanna, returned to Cleveland. The following day, Grant traveled to Chicago, while Conkling stayed in Cleveland, spending the day with Hanna. Conkling gave an address at the Cleveland Armory, in which he spoke largely about the importance of protective tariffs. He closed his two-hour speech, a repeat of his effort in Warren the day before, with words of endorsement for Garfield and his running mate, Chester Arthur.[52]

According to Croly, Hanna was in charge of transportation for the Grant-Conkling party while in Ohio; thus, Hanna was responsible for arranging the visit with Garfield. According to Croly, during the journey, Hanna engineered an out-of-the-way stop in Mentor. Croly's source for this version of events came mainly from reporter James Kennedy's story in the *Herald*. The fact that the account came from a reporter in Hanna's employ suggests the possibility that Hanna's role was overstated. Kennedy's version, which was quoted directly by Croly, was as follows:

> Mr. Hanna called at the house and was shown into the dining room. "General," said he, addressing Grant, "it has been arranged that we return to Cleveland by way of Mentor, and if you propose to stop and see General Garfield, we shall have to start in a very short time." He made this announcement in public so as to bring the question straight to the attention of Grant. Conkling did not want to go to Mentor, and when he did not want to do anything he had a way of emphatically looking the part. His brow was like a thunder cloud. Grant saw the danger and did not dodge the issue. "We will go to Mentor," he said to Mr. Hanna, and Conkling sullenly acquiesced. According the train was stopped at General Garfield's town, and the distinguished Republicans paid their respects to the standard-bearer, whereby the country was given a still more striking proof of the willful harmony which prevailed in the Republican party.[53]

This is a compelling story that demonstrates Hanna's willingness to take charge early in the campaign. The trouble is, however, that there are good reasons to doubt its veracity.

First of all, the *New York Times'* coverage offered no details about Hanna's involvement in the planning of travel arrangements, only that he was part of the party that traveled with Grant and Conkling from Warren to Mentor. Historian Thomas Edward Felt argued that Kennedy and Croly created a myth when they gave so much credit to Hanna. Felt, relying on an entry in Garfield's personal diary, suggested that the timeline of events did not support the idea that Hanna deliberately arranged a meeting between Garfield and Grant. Garfield's diary implied that he knew, well in advance, of the meeting with Grant and that it was not a spur of the moment maneuver by Hanna, as Kennedy and Croly reported. Felt argued that it was

Grant's decision to visit Garfield and not Hanna's: "It was a good story, and not an incredible one at the time. But Hanna's debut as a manager of presidential futures had no such early or dramatic opening. He would learn the business, but slowly and thoroughly, not in a flash of atavistic genius."[54] However, Felt did not dispute the more general assertion in Kennedy's and Croly's accounts—that Hanna was important enough in the state's Republican organization, as early as 1880, to be responsible for arranging transportation for the Grant-Conkling party while they were in Ohio. It is not clear that it matters tremendously which version of Grant's trip to Mentor is correct. However, perception is a large part of reality, and if Hanna was perceived at the time as the organizer of the meeting, especially in his home city and state, then it certainly contributed to his credibility as a politico, early in his career. Whether Hanna instigated or simply facilitated the meeting between Grant, Conkling, and Garfield is less important for Hanna's reputation than the fact that he was part of making it happen and that he received credit at the time for his role. While there is some uncertainty as to the extent of Hanna's efforts for Garfield, his efforts were significant and, more importantly, did not go unnoticed.

It is also worth noting that Hanna's support for Garfield is evidence of his strong sense of Ohio patriotism because, ideologically, Garfield was not a man to whom Hanna would naturally have felt inclined. Hanna believed in playing by the rules of the game of politics, and the rules of the game at the time included patronage. Garfield was a moderate who believed in at least a measure of patronage reform. Given that they almost certainly had different views on this core fact of political life in the Gilded Age, Hanna's desire to promote a fellow Ohioan for Ohio's sake must have been strong, indeed.

Garfield won the election, but by such a narrow margin that it remains one of the closest races in history. He had only the barest of pluralities of the popular vote, beating his Democratic opponent, Winfield Scott Hancock, by fewer than ten thousand votes. In the Electoral College, Garfield's margin was more comfortable, with 214 votes to Hancock's 155. It is certainly possible that part of his success in the states with the most Electoral College votes, like Ohio with twenty-two votes, was due to the efforts of Hanna and his business colleagues. When Garfield was declared the winner, the *Herald* ran an editorial with a headline from Psalm 146, verse 8: "The Lord openeth the eyes of the blind! The Lord loveth the righteous!"[55] Hanna played no role in Garfield's administration, nor did he appear interested in doing so. Given the depth of his efforts on Garfield's part, he surely would have been entitled to ask for something. It is possible that he chose not to ask because he knew he and Garfield differed on the propriety of such requests. Or perhaps he chose not to ask because he was content with the fact that he helped elect an Ohioan to the White House. Regardless, the fact that he did not pursue a position in Garfield's administration should give pause to critics who argue he was motivated solely by a desire for personal power.

James Garfield was president for only four months before an assassin named Charles J. Guiteau killed him. Guiteau was a mentally ill office seeker who was motivated to murder by anger over Garfield's efforts to reform the patronage system. Garfield challenged Roscoe Conkling on the patronage-reform issue by appointing an old political enemy of Conkling's to be the collector of the Port of New York. This precipitated a crisis in the Senate as senators were torn between the tradition of senatorial courtesy, in which a senator was granted wide latitude in determining who would fill appointed political positions within his state, and a desire not to embarrass the newly elected president. In the end, Conkling resigned, and Garfield got his nominee. It was a symbolic victory for patronage reform, but, unfortunately for Garfield, patronage reform was his undoing. After he shot Garfield, Guiteau yelled, "I am a Stalwart and now Arthur is President!"[56] It took nearly three months for Garfield to succumb to his wounds, but when he died, Arthur became president. In deference to his fallen predecessor, Arthur retained many of the civil-service reforms initiated by Garfield, despite the fact that he was a Stalwart.

Hanna's service to Garfield concluded when he served as chairman of the Cleveland committee responsible for taking care of the Garfield funeral party when it arrived. Garfield's body lay in state in Cleveland's Public Square and was subsequently laid to rest in Lakeview Cemetery.[57] Lakeview Cemetery has been the final home for many prominent northern Ohioans, including Hanna.

Throughout the campaign season of 1880, Edwin Cowles attacked Hanna repeatedly in the pages of the *Cleveland Leader*. During the buildup to the Republican convention, the two men supported different presidential candidates, with Hanna supporting Sherman and Cowles supporting Blaine. Neither of their candidates emerged with the nomination, and both men supported Garfield in their newspapers. Cowles, however, engaged in a bitter campaign against Hanna's preferred congressional candidate, the incumbent Amos Townsend, who supported the growing ties between business and the Republican Party.

Townsend's opponent for the Republican nomination in 1880 was William Rose, a former mayor of Cleveland who supported the social agenda of the reform wing of the party. In the primary, the *Herald*'s support of Townsend was challenged by the *Leader*'s support of Rose.[58] Rose's candidacy was turned back at the Republican's district convention, in which Hanna and other allies of Townsend were in charge of the proceedings. While an independent candidate was nominated by some social reformers angry about Rose's defeat, the *Leader* announced that it would support Townsend in the general election. At the same time, however, as historian Fred Shoemaker observed, Cowles blamed Hanna for an independent Republican's running against Townsend and the Democratic nominee. To Cowles, Hanna's interference engineered the defeat of the proper candidate and brought dissension to the party.

Cowles wrote in the *Leader* that his paper would support Townsend because "the party is not to blame for the indiscreet conduct of . . . Mr. Hanna, and it should not be permitted to suffer for it."[59] Townsend won the election, but the bloodletting in the period before his nomination was significant. The split between Cleveland Republicans in 1880 was a recurring story throughout Hanna's career in politics. Indeed, his strongest, most vicious rivals throughout his political career often came not from the Democrats but from his hometown and from within his own party.

Cowles's anger toward Hanna boiled over yet again during Cleveland's mayoral election of 1883. The Republican nominee was George Gardner. Edwin Cowles, referring to Hanna as "Marcus Aurelius" in the *Leader*, accused him of getting Gardner the nomination purely for his own benefit and announced that his paper would not support the nominee.[60] The nickname Marcus Aurelius stuck with Hanna for the rest of his career, popping up frequently in articles and cartoons. It was clearly intended as an insult by Cowles, implying that Hanna was behaving like a dictatorial Roman emperor, and there were plenty of dictatorial emperors to choose from in Roman history. Just as obviously, Cowles chose Marcus Aurelius because he and Hanna shared the name Marcus. Cowles's clever wordplay demonstrated a lack of historical understanding, however, as Marcus Aurelius was a highly respected philosopher who was considered to be one of the Roman Empire's most enlightened leaders.

Cowles attacked Hanna regularly in his newspaper. Croly wrote, "The *Leader* charged Mr. Hanna with responsibility for the nomination, which was considered undesirable for no other reason, apparently, than the candidate's association with the owner of the *Herald;* and Mr. Gardner's election was consequently fought with bitterness, and finally with success, by Mr. Cowles."[61] Gardner lost the election and, as Fred Shoemaker wrote, the entire Republican slate was defeated by Democrats in Cleveland. By 1883, the anger Cowles felt toward Hanna finally became so great that he was not able to set it aside for the good of the party as he had in 1880.

CHAPTER THREE

The Sherman Years

hile Mark Hanna was a strong supporter of James Garfield and of Ohio Republicans in general, his participation in presidential politics attained new heights in 1884 and 1888 as he worked actively on behalf of Senator John Sherman, the Ohioan thought to have the greatest chance to become president in 1880 before Garfield took everyone by surprise.

Hanna was a strong and active supporter of the candidacy of John Sherman in 1884, but Sherman was not as enthusiastic a candidate as he had been in 1880, and there were several opponents among the Republicans. The strongest candidate was James G. Blaine, a perennial favorite but a man beset by concerns about his scandal-tainted past. Sherman was a significant player in 1884 if only because, as a favorite son of Ohio, he held the loyalty of its delegates. For Hanna, part of the drama of the 1884 campaign took place before the convention, when he sought election, for the first time, as a delegate to the national convention.

The Convention of 1884

There were to be two delegates from Hanna's Cleveland district, but there were three candidates in the race. Besides Hanna, the other two candidates were a young Republican named A. C. Hord and Hanna's sworn enemy, Edwin Cowles. As the *New York Times* reported, "The Hon. Edward Cowles, editor of the *Leader,* and a prominent Blaine man, will unquestionably be selected as one of the delegates to Chicago."[1] Hord was the son-in-law of a well-known Democrat, and many at the district meeting believed that he would provide a vote for Chester Arthur at the convention. The ultimate hope of those who supported Hord was to get Arthur nominated because nearly any Democrat would be able to beat the unpopular president in the general election.[2] As the *New York Times* reported, Hord was "compelled repeatedly to pledge himself before he could secure a great many of the votes," but despite doubts about his motives, Hord was elected first, receiving 181 votes to Cowles's seventy-three and Hanna's fifty-four.[3] This assured Hord of being a delegate and left the remaining spot to a direct competition between Cowles and Hanna. In a head-to-head contest, Cowles won by a margin of 198 to 107. Both he and Hord were instructed by the Twenty-first District to vote for Blaine. Winning the delegate's spot was obviously a sweet victory for the *Leader*'s editor. As Croly wrote, Cowles "needed no other motive for coveting the honor than a desire to prevent Mr. Hanna from winning it."[4]

Despite the loss in Cleveland, Hanna still had a chance at the state Republican convention where he was a candidate to be a delegate-at-large. Hanna was nominated by his Twenty-first District. His opponent was Dick Parsons, the former congressman from whom he had purchased the *Herald*. Hanna won the election, but any satisfaction he might have felt in victory was tempered by the suggestion that he had stolen it. Parsons was bitter about losing to Hanna, and many Ohio newspapers alleged that the at-large spot had been stolen from Parsons through nefarious backroom dealing.[5]

It was the kind of charge that would be repeated in various contexts throughout Hanna's career. The press thoroughly enjoyed accusing Hanna of wrongdoing, despite the fact that there was rarely any credible—or, at least, unchallenged—evidence to support such allegations. Like many accusations made against Hanna during his career, there was no significant proof of Parson's charges, and he remained an at-large delegate.

After winning the election, Hanna seemed likely to be a "Sherman man." Supporting Sherman fit in with Hanna's combined interests of Ohio patriotism and supporting Sherman's probusiness record, though Hanna did not officially commit himself to a particular candidate while he was at the state convention. His likely support of Sherman put him at odds with the two instructed delegates, Cowles and Hord. It was not surprising, of course, that Hanna found himself on the opposite side of the fence from Cowles.

There was considerable enthusiasm for Blaine at the Ohio convention, but Sherman, a favorite son, was not forgotten. The *New York Times* reported that an attempt to make it impossible for Ohio's delegates to vote for Sherman was defeated:

> A resolution was offered in the delegation meeting that all delegates to Chicago should be requested to vote for no man for President whose election would jeopardize Republican control of the United States Senate. This pointed at Sherman and was voted down. . . . J. O. Converse, the Chairman of the State Central Committee, is a very good specimen of a Sherman man under a coating of Blaineism. He is a delegate from the Nineteenth District, which is very strong for Blaine, and is under instructions for Blaine, yet he admits that the Sherman men are rather thick, and that he would not be called to very strict account if he should find it necessary to change from Blaine to Sherman. There are a great many other delegates who are in the same position.[6]

Hanna, expected to be a Sherman man, was not the only at-large delegate elected who was a supporter of the senator. General John Beatty, another Sherman man, was also selected as an at-large delegate.[7]

The Ohio state convention went very well for Sherman supporters, who managed to obtain several significant victories over the pro-Blaine forces. As the *New York Times* reported, "Although the Blaine men were in a clear majority and came under repeated instructions, the Sherman managers outgeneraled them, captured the organization of the convention, nominated Sherman men to the positions of Secretary of State and member of the Board of Public Works—which constituted two-thirds of the ticket—chose three of the four delegates at large, and came within close sight of getting the fourth."[8] Among the other at-large delegates chosen along with Hanna at the convention was a man who became another giant in Republican Party politics, in and out of Ohio: Joseph B. Foraker, a judge from Cincinnati.

Joseph Foraker was the Republican gubernatorial nominee in Ohio in 1883, before he and Hanna became friendly at the 1884 convention.

Foraker lost his first gubernatorial election, but he was renominated in 1885 and won. Hanna played a large part in his election. He served on Foraker's campaign committee and worked hard on Foraker's behalf in Cleveland, despite the fact that Hanna was becoming well known in Ohio politics 1885 and there was some talk of nominating him for governor. Hanna demurred, preferring to work behind the scenes. Croly wrote, "He was seeking political power by means of close association with popular leaders; and for the time being Mr. Foraker was the man of his choice."[9]

Though the relationship between Hanna and Foraker later soured, it began with promise. Hanna wrote to Foraker during the national convention, "Among the few pleasures I found at the convention was meeting and working with you. And I hope soon to have the pleasure of insuring the acquaintance under more peaceful and comfortable circumstances. I feel that the occasion was one which will be a great benefit to you in the future, for I hear nothing but praise for you on all sides, all of which I heartily endorse and will hope to be considered among your sincere friends."[10] In another letter, sent a few days later, Hanna wrote: "I assure you, my dear fellow, it will not be my fault if our acquaintance does not ripen, for I shall certainly go for you whenever you are within reach."[11] This is an interesting statement in hindsight, considering the way that the relationship between the two men fell apart four years later.

After they split in 1888, each man blamed the other for the breakdown in their relationship, but Foraker was clearly more bitter about it than Hanna. Foraker saw his break with Hanna as the reason that McKinley, and not he, benefited from Hanna's assistance in presidential politics, and it led him to years of sour comments and attempts to frustrate Hanna's objectives.[12] For a time following the 1884 convention, Hanna was as close to Foraker as he would later be to McKinley. When the relationship fell apart, it had profound consequences for the Republican Party in Ohio, dividing it into at least two, and sometimes more, factions. The split endured for the duration of the men's careers.

From 1884 until about the time of the Republican convention in 1888, however, Hanna and Foraker were strong allies. The strength of their relationship was noted by Ohio congressman Theodore Burton, a biographer of John Sherman, who wrote, "After the convention of 1884 Mr. Hanna became more prominently identified with state politics and grew to be a very warm partisan of Foraker."[13] Despite his coyness at the Ohio convention, Hanna was clearly on the record as a Sherman supporter by the time he got to the national convention in Chicago. As the delegates gathered, Hanna got the chance to become more familiar with the man to whom he is now forever linked, William McKinley. McKinley and Hanna shared an apartment while at the convention.

When they gathered in Chicago, the votes of the Ohio delegation remained split between Blaine and Sherman, the state's favorite son. As the *New York Times* reported,

> It is apparent that the political managers who came so near capturing the late Republican State Convention for Sherman as against Blaine, who was an acknowledged choice of the majority of the people, are still at work and have made a gain of some moment. . . . Judge Foraker, who seems to be the leader of the Sherman forces, was asked if there had been or was to be a conference among the Blaine and Sherman men for the purposes of agreeing on some compromise. He responded: "There has been no such meeting and there will be none.[14]

The split in the delegation continued for days as the convention proceeded. The Sherman forces hung together, despite their numerical disadvantage. Joseph Foraker made his mark on the national party with his speech placing Sherman's name in nomination.

For a while, the picture presented in media outlets like the *New York Times* was of a harmonious delegation. The pro-Sherman forces were depicted as happy to cast their votes for Blaine if the time came, and the Blaine delegates were similarly painted as happy to cast their votes for Sherman if, for some reason, Blaine's candidacy became untenable. Behind the scenes, however, there was considerably more tension and even the public pretense of harmony in the group fell apart on June 13, thanks to a bitter fight for the chairmanship of the Ohio State Committee, which was a barometer of the delegation's feelings about Sherman and Blaine. The *New York Times* reported, "The surface harmonious look and the general good feeling which prevailed up to midnight in the deliberations of the committee were dispelled after that hour."[15] The delegation remained divided between Blaine and

Sherman supporters, despite the fact that Sherman had almost no support outside Ohio.

In the end, Blaine easily won the party's nomination in Chicago. While Hanna supported Blaine after the convention by raising money for him in Ohio, he worked far less enthusiastically for him than he had for Garfield. Hanna was certainly disappointed that Sherman was not nominated. He supported Sherman for both geographic and ideological reasons. Sherman was an Ohioan, and Hanna clearly intended to support candidates from Ohio. After all, he had worked very hard for Garfield, despite the fact that Garfield's reform-minded views about patronage were far from a perfect match with Hanna's. He was more philosophically aligned with Sherman, so if Hanna supported Garfield, he obviously would support Sherman. Croly wrote of Hanna's feelings about Sherman, "That Ohio should possess a statesman eminently qualified for the presidency but denied as yet the opportunity of being a candidate was more than unfortunate; it was unjust. His national patriotism and his local pride were both aroused by the project of placing so eminent a man in so high an office. Thereafter the idea fermented in his mind."[16] For Hanna, Sherman was the right man for Ohio and for the nation.

Blaine lost the election to Grover Cleveland in 1884 in one of the most vitriolic races in presidential election history, as the supporters of each candidate did their best to drag the other candidate through the mud. Cleveland, a financially conservative Democrat, overcame negative press coverage of his prepresidential personal dalliances during the campaign. For Blaine, it was not an affair of the heart that got him in trouble but, rather, his apparent willingness to use his public position to increase his personal wealth and that of his friends. Cleveland was the governor of New York, and in the summer of 1884, a newspaper in Buffalo revealed that Cleveland had fathered an out-of-wedlock child with a widow named Maria Halpin.

Blaine, on the other hand, had been fighting charges for years that he used his position in the Congress to aid companies by supporting friendly policies. In return, the companies made sure Blaine and his allies benefited financially. As historians Martin and Dorothy Rosenberg noted, "The voters faced a hard choice: between a state governor who had dallied with a widow and refused to marry her when she became a mother, and a profiteering congressman who had urged laws to favor his partners and line his pockets. The choice . . . was between a private immoralist and a public immoralist."[17] Cleveland won the tight election, thanks largely to his narrowly won victory in the state of New York. This win was due, at least in part, not to anything Blaine did but to something he failed to do. At a rally in New York in the week before the election, a Protestant minister named Samuel D. Burchard gave a speech in which he said, "We are Republicans and don't propose to leave our party and identify ourselves with the party whose antecedents have been rum, Romanism and rebellion."[18] In his speech following this introduction by Burchard, Blaine failed to refute the minister's anti-Catholic sentiment. This was translated by the press as acceptance of the remark by Blaine, alienating New York's large Catholic population. How much did Blaine's failure to address Burchard's comment cost him? Given the extreme closeness of the vote in New York, it might have cost him thirty-six electoral votes, which was the difference in the election. Cleveland won New York by just over one thousand votes.[19] It is entirely plausible that at least that many people were angry enough about Blaine's seeming support for Burchard's anti-Catholic views to make them vote for Cleveland.

Like 1880, the election of 1884 was very close in terms of the popular vote. Cleveland won by fewer than one hundred thousand votes, and his margin of victory in the Electoral College, 219 to 182, was due entirely to his slim victory in New York.[20] In losing, Blaine fulfilled his own prophecy made in 1876 when he called himself the "Henry Clay of the Republican Party," suggesting that he, a great statesman, would never become president.

Political scientist Malcolm Moos summed up the election with an unattributed quote:

> "We are told that Mr. Blaine has been delinquent in office but blameless in private life, while Mr. Cleveland has been a model of official integrity but culpable in his personal relations. We should therefore elect Mr. Cleveland to the public office which he is so well qualified to fill and remand Mr. Blaine to the private station which he is admirably fitted to adorn."[21]

As is the case in every campaign, many factors combined to ensure Blaine's loss, but no matter what the exact equation was, the election signaled a changing of the guard in the Republican Party. Though Blaine was still a player in 1888, he was no longer the darling of the party. Seeing this, Mark Hanna was more motivated than ever to help Sherman win the office he felt the senator deserved.

The Convention of 1888

In a letter to Foraker shortly after Blaine's loss in 1884, Hanna wrote, "I feel sure now in looking back over the results of the campaign that John Sherman would have been the strongest candidate; and I believe that he will be the strongest man in 1888."[22] In retrospect, Hanna came to realize that he was confiding in a man whose faith in Sherman was no longer as high as his own. The proceedings at the Republican National Convention in 1888 at Chicago exposed cracks in the relationship between Hanna and Foraker. As J. B. Morrow observed: "There is no doubt in my mind that the break in the very friendly relations between Foraker and Hanna occurred in Chicago."[23]

Between 1884 and 1888, Hanna's ambition for Sherman grew significantly. By 1888, Hanna was determined to get the Republican nomination for Sherman. According to Croly, he was motivated not only by his belief that Sherman was the best man for the job but also by personal desire:

> The idea appealed to him because of its apparent practicability, because of its peculiar desirability, and because the work demanded for its realization was suited to his opportunities and abilities. At that time he had no ambition or hope of personal preferment. He was a business man with a collateral interest in politics. As a business man he could not afford the time for a slow and steady climb up the political ladder. Nevertheless he wanted to be associated with large political events and achievements. If he was going to interest himself in electing other men to office, why not the biggest man he knew and the highest office in the land?[24]

Whatever mix of reasons he had, Hanna was most definitely a Sherman man in 1888. Despite his support for Sherman in 1884, Hanna did not actually meet the senator until 1885. When they met, a positive relationship quickly developed between the two men, just as the bond between Hanna and Foraker had grown closer. Both Sherman and Foraker were impressed with Hanna's conduct at the convention in 1884, working to line up votes for Sherman. Although his efforts failed, many prominent Ohio Republicans learned for the first time that Hanna had a gift for political strategy.[25] By 1888, Hanna's troubles with Edwin Cowles were over, and he was easily appointed to the national convention as a delegate from Cleveland.

The Ohio at-large delegates were Foraker, McKinley, and two other well-known Ohio politicians, Congressmen Benjamin Butterworth and Charles Foster. Hanna was widely regarded as Sherman's manager at the convention. As J. B. Morrow reported, "It was acknowledged . . . that he was the leader of the Sherman forces in Ohio. He stated early in the spring of 1888 that he purposed to have a splendid organization for Mr. Sherman in Chicago, at the national convention, and that he purposed to have all the rooms that were necessary to make that organization effective 'if I have to buy a block,' as he expressed it."[26] However, Hanna's role as Sherman's manager in 1888 did not yet mean that he had emerged as a major figure in Republican Party politics at the national level. As Hanna biographer Thomas Beer relates, "Mr. Hanna was nobody in particular in the hotels of Chicago. . . . Mr. Hanna was now an actual millionaire . . . but he was not conspicuous; he was technically not in politics at all. He spent money on politicians. There was a difference, in 1888, which has since disappeared."[27]

Unlike 1884, Sherman was the nominal frontrunner at the time the delegates arrived in Chicago for the convention, but James G. Blaine continued to cast a shadow over the Republican Party. Despite Blaine's rather frequent pronouncements that he did not intend to be a candidate in 1888, he still had many supporters at the convention who awaited word from their leader. This introduced an element of great uncertainty at the convention. According to Morrow, "Mr. Hanna didn't believe Blaine's nomination was possible," but Hanna's personal opinions had very little influence on the many that supported Blaine.[28]

In the end, Hanna was right about Blaine, mostly because Blaine continued to refuse to allow his name to be considered, but his skills as a prognosticator were limited. As Morrow reported, "He did not foresee the nomination of Benjamin Harrison."[29] Hanna also failed to predict the events that led to Harrison's nomination. The 1888 convention had a profound effect on the rest of Hanna's political life, in large measure because it culminated in the breakup of his relationship with Joseph Foraker.

Foraker was no doubt thankful for the help he had received from Hanna in his gubernatorial campaigns, but, as McKinley would later do, Foraker was willing to use Hanna while holding him at arm's length when it was politically expedient to do so. Despite the important role Hanna played in his election in 1885, Foraker was not sufficiently grateful enough to thank Hanna by letting him control any significant state patronage in the Cleveland area. Later, when McKinley became governor, he gave Hanna more patronage authority than Foraker did, but as president, McKinley was often aloof from Hanna and gave at least as much power to other, less financially helpful friends. Not one to hold grudges, however, Hanna wholeheartedly supported Foraker in his reelection bid in 1887, increasing his financial commitment to the governor. For his part, Foraker continued to be willing to use Hanna's money while giving back as little as possible.

At the same time Hanna was playing an important role in Foraker's political fortunes, he was also becoming more involved in Republican politics in Cleveland. This became possible after he sold the *Herald,* which brought an end to the withering criticism Edwin Cowles published about him in the *Leader.* It did nothing to insulate him from the attacks of Democratic newspapers like the *Press* and the *Plain Dealer,* but their criticism was to be expected.[30]

As his stature continued to grow, Hanna wanted to be able to dispense important patronage jobs, especially in northern Ohio, a privilege he no doubt felt he had earned thanks to his efforts on Foraker's part. Unfortunately for Hanna, Foraker largely refused to grant Hanna the authority that by tradition he probably had earned. Foraker's refusal to grant Hanna the patronage power he wanted began with Foraker's election in 1885 and extended beyond his reelection in 1887.

One position Hanna very much wanted to be able to dole out was the lucrative job of oil inspector for the state of Ohio. When Foraker was elected, Hanna supported William M. Bayne for the job. Hanna felt Foraker should appoint Bayne in return for his service to Foraker's campaign. At the same time, William McKinley, then a congressman, also had a candidate for the job, Captain Louis Smithnight, whom he likewise pressured Foraker to appoint. Hanna backed away from his candidate and, according to Foraker, requested that McKinley's candidate be appointed. While Hanna was friendly with McKinley, the reason he backed down was to extricate Foraker from a sticky situation. In a letter, Hanna expressed both frustration with and loyalty to Foraker: "I had a call from Major McKinley and his oil inspector candidate. The Major is never behind-hand with his claims. I tell him he 'wants the earth,' and it looks as if I were getting about where I generally do in politics—'left' with no asset except my reputation of being a good fellow and always accommodating. However, I told McKinley I only cared for you in this matter."[31] This letter is instructive for two reasons. First, it clearly shows that in 1885 Hanna was working to further Foraker's career, not McKinley's. It also shows that while Hanna understood political reality, he was still not happy that his work on behalf of winning candidates, like Foraker, was not rewarded as he felt tradition demanded. Whatever prestige Hanna might have been able to claim from his close association with the governor was certainly diminished by his inability to influence important patronage assignments.

Two years later, when Foraker was reelected governor, Hanna again pressed for Bayne to get the job, while McKinley urged Foraker to keep his man, Captain Smithnight. Foraker largely dismissed both men and appointed an ally from Cincinnati, George Cox (later known as "Boss" Cox and a perpetual thorn in Hanna's side) to the position. While he made McKinley's man, Smithnight, a deputy inspector, Foraker once again ignored Hanna's candidate altogether.

After Hanna's death and nearly twenty years after the Ohio patronage incidents, Foraker gave a statement to J. B. Morrow in which he suggested the oil inspectorship was the reason his relationship with Hanna fractured. As Foraker told Morrow, "Mr. Hanna no longer wanted Smithnight retained in office and made a request that I appoint W. M. Bayne, of Cleveland. So the situation was this: McKinley had a candidate; Hanna had a candidate and I had a candidate. I appointed Cox and Cox made Bayne deputy oil inspector for Northern Ohio. This appointment was the occasion of the break in the friendship between Mr. Hanna and myself." Foraker further suggested that Hanna became McKinley's ally to spite him: "I have often thought since that my appointment of Cox made McKinley President. Mr. Hanna transferred his friendship from me to McKinley and I have believed was willing to show me what he could do for his friends when his friends were willing to carry out his requests."[32] Given the fact that Hanna later accepted many insults from McKinley on patronage questions, this seems unlikely. It is also a bit of doublespeak on Foraker's part because he clearly implied in the statement that Hanna was a president maker who could have made him president, but in his autobiography denigrated Hanna's abilities as a president maker, arguing that McKinley's election was a fait accompli, no matter who ran his campaign.

Foraker was a bitter man in his later years, presidential ambitions frustrated. It was ridiculous for him to argue that Hanna devoted the time and resources to McKinley because he desired revenge against him, but the fact that Hanna and McKinley escorted each other to greater heights than Foraker ever reached clearly bothered him. Despite Foraker's insistence that the oil inspectorship shattered his good relations with Hanna, Foraker's duplicitous behavior at the Republican convention in 1888 was, in fact, the primary cause of the rift.

J. B. Morrow noted in his parenthetical comments in Foraker's statement that he did not feel Foraker was straightforward in describing his relationship with Hanna:

> I am inclined to think that Senator Foraker's memory in respect to the cause of his disagreement with Mr. Hanna at the time he mentioned was not exactly as he states it to be. I was at the convention in 1888 and know Senator Foraker brought great scandal to the Ohio people who were there and to the delegates by his secret work with Mr. Blaine's friends. . . . Mr. Foraker was then at the height of his fame in Ohio and a great swarm of his partisans came on from Columbus and paraded the streets of Chicago with a band of music and banners and badges shouting for him for President. My understanding of events at that time was that Mr. Hanna became thoroughly angered at what he thought was Senator Foraker's bad faith.[33]

Morrow was not alone in expressing this view. Congressman Theodore Burton commented on this matter: "Foraker said that Mr. Hanna was offended because he would not appoint Colonel Smithnight oil inspector in Ohio. But those of us who have lived in Ohio understand that there was something more important than a mere state office that caused the break in the friendship between Foraker and Hanna. . . .

Those of us who understand local conditions in Ohio believe that Mr. Hanna was disgusted with Foraker's attitude previous to and during the Republican national convention of 1888."[34] Although Sherman was far from a shoo-in at the convention, Hanna felt the senator was harmed by Foraker's actions. Few matters were as important to Hanna as electing Ohioans to the White House, and he no doubt saw Foraker as no better than a traitor.

Perhaps Burton's strongest evidence against Foraker's claim that the patronage dispute killed his relationship with Hanna was his description of the outcome of a similar dispute he had with Hanna. In late 1890, the Cleveland Post Office had a postmaster vacancy. Since it was Burton's district, he supported a candidate for the position, even though he had just lost his reelection bid. Hanna supported a different candidate—the very same William M. Bayne whom he wanted Foraker to appoint as oil inspector in Ohio. McKinley, who, like Burton, had just been defeated for reelection to Congress, was asked by Postmaster General John Wanamaker who he thought should get the position. Burton related the event this way: "He understood the practices and ethics of politics and clearly told Wanamaker that I was entitled to the Cleveland appointment. He took a position against Mr. Hanna and my candidate was successful. However, Mr. Hanna continued to support me when I was a candidate for Congress and while we were perhaps not as friendly as we were before there was no real hostility between us."[35] Foraker's biographer, Everett Walters, also pointed out that amicable relations between the two men survived the patronage dispute. Hanna pushed hard, even going so far as to tell Foraker that he would not be able to return to Cleveland if another of his appointments was rejected because of the political embarrassment he would incur; but when Hanna failed to convince Foraker, he did not appear to have considered it a great breach in their relationship.[36]

At the Republican convention in Chicago in 1888, however, permanent damage was done to the relationship between Hanna and Foraker. It is possible that Hanna harbored ill feelings toward Foraker as a consequence of the oil-inspector business, but nearly everyone who knew Hanna well indicated that, once he took someone in as a friend, it was difficult to break the relationship, sometimes to his detriment. It would almost certainly have taken something much bigger than Foraker's failure to appoint Bayne as oil inspector to cause a permanent rift. At the convention of 1888, Foraker worked behind the scenes on behalf of a possible Blaine candidacy, deceiving Hanna, Sherman, and the Ohioans who supported Sherman. As Thomas Beer observed, it was Foraker's behavior at the convention that caused the real tension between the men: "The quarrel swelled in a flare of suspicion, and the alliance of Hanna and Foraker ended with the last day of the convention in 1888."[37]

For his part, Sherman had doubted Foraker's loyalty for some time before the convention and, according to Croly, tried to get Hanna to press Foraker about it. As it turned out, Sherman's concerns about Foraker were well founded. Prior to the convention, there was wide speculation in both the Ohio press and elsewhere that Foraker was possibly interested in becoming a candidate himself or was a secret supporter of Blaine. For his part, Foraker appeared to be motivated by a number of factors that prevented him from being as loyal to Sherman as he could have been before, and during, the convention. First, there was the suggestion, prior to the convention, that if Blaine were to throw his name into the ring, he would easily win the nomination, and there was a sense that the popular Governor Foraker would make a very good running mate for Blaine. Second, Foraker appears to have been miffed that it was Hanna, and not himself, who was given the job of managing Sherman's campaign at the convention. Of course, he should not have been jealous. If he was agitating behind Sherman's back for Blaine, as Sherman suspected, it would have made no sense for the senator to have Foraker lead his effort at the convention.[38]

Suspicion about Foraker continued as the convention began. As Morrow reported,

> There was friction among the delegates-at-large soon after their arrival in Chicago. Foraker was not at heart a friend of Sherman and among the Ohio delegates was openly accused of treachery. I know on one occasion word was taken to Foraker at his room in the Grand Pacific Hotel that at a meeting of Ohio delegates then being held some doubt was expressed as to his fidelity to Sherman's interests. Foraker came into the meeting before it was over, his face flushed and his eyes glaring. Springing upon a table he vehemently denied that he was secretly opposed to Sherman and denounced those who had questioned his integrity. "The man,"

he said, "from Ohio who comes here pledged to Sherman and proves false will go home in an ice box."[39]

Despite this performance, however, doubt about Foraker's allegiance still lingered.

James Blaine was not even in the country at the time of the convention. He was traveling with Andrew Carnegie in Scotland when the Republicans convened in Chicago. Furthermore, Blaine made it quite well known that he did not want the nomination, so, in theory, that left the field wide open. At the outset of the convention, Sherman seemed to have a real chance. However, there were many influential Blaine supporters in Chicago who hoped he would change his mind. In addition, Sherman was far from the only candidate in line to take up the mantle from Blaine. As Moos wrote, "Never before in the history of presidential conventions had so many candidates received votes. Before the decisive eighth ballot nineteen names were entered."[40]

Sherman was nominated by William McKinley on Friday, June 22, the first day of balloting. Nominating Sherman was originally to have been Foraker's job, but Sherman's mistrust of Foraker caused him to take the honor away from the governor and give it to McKinley. This was in part, no doubt, because Sherman was worried about a repeat of the 1880 convention when James Garfield became a viable candidate after his nomination of Sherman. The possibility must have seemed all the more real to Sherman where Foraker was concerned, since he doubted the man's loyalty.

Despite Sherman's caution in having McKinley, and not Foraker, place his name in nomination, it seemed as if history might repeat itself in 1888. After McKinley's speech for Sherman, he began to collect a small number of votes on each successive ballot. It is possible that it was at this moment that Hanna realized that McKinley might, one day, be an Ohio presidential candidate who could actually win. Beer notes that, at the convention, "an accident displayed Major McKinley favorably to Marcus Hanna. A distinct faction, made up of men from every part of the country, approached him with a suggestion that he let himself be nominated."[41] McKinley demurred, but the seeds were planted.

Sherman held the lead through each of the first three ballots, but with each successive ballot, his vote total decreased. As Hanna biographer Thomas Edward Felt observed, "As had been feared, Sherman's following was too Southern in flavor to inspire much faith in his prospects for election."[42] Support from southern Republicans meant very little, of course, because in the post-Reconstruction decades, the Republican Party had very little traction in the South. As McKinley biographer H. Wayne Morgan put it, "On paper, Senator Sherman's chances were excellent. . . . Yet the Senator's strength was his weakness, for he stood against the field. His support came largely from the South and was a token only, since it promised him no electoral votes as a candidate."[43] Republican candidates had to have solid northern and western support to be viable candidates who could win the presidency after winning the nomination. Sherman's only significant northern support came from Ohio and, thanks to Foraker, even this was in some doubt. Years later, McKinley and Hanna showed that they had learned this lesson as they lined up not only the support of the southern delegates they needed to win the party's nomination but also campaigned hard to win delegates from other regions to demonstrate McKinley's strength for the coming general election.

On Saturday, June 23, McKinley addressed the convention during the fourth ballot, when he once again received votes. H. H. Kohlsaat, a Republican newspaper man, wrote that McKinley did what he could to quash the discussion of his possible candidacy before it could get started. McKinley rose, Kohlsaat reported, to address the convention and said, "I am here as one of the chosen representatives of my State. . . . I cannot with fidelity to John Sherman, who has trusted me in his cause and with his confidence; I cannot, consistently with my own views of personal integrity, consent or seem to consent to permit my name to be used as a candidate before this convention."[44] McKinley, a very ambitious politician, was certainly internally giddy at the stir he was causing. He understood, however, that it was not his time and that appearing overeager could kill his presidential career before it got started. There is no doubt that while Hanna remained loyal to Sherman throughout the convention, he was watching McKinley carefully and considering the possibilities. The two men thus emerged from the convention much closer than they had been in the past. James Ford Rhodes observed, "The Convention of 1888, when they both supported Sherman, increased the mutual attachment. Each saw qualities in the other that drew them together and, as both were working for the same end, they were now in complete sympathy."[45]

After the fourth ballot on Saturday morning, things suddenly took a very bad turn for Sherman, when one candidate, New York senator Chauncey Depew, dropped out of the race. As Moos wrote, "Depew dropped out and 58 of New York's votes went to Harrison, who jumped from 94 to 217, just 18 behind Sherman. After the fourth ballot the story that Blaine would be a candidate on the fifth ballot buzzed the convention."[46] The Blaine rumor prompted a recess over the weekend, while his forces waited to hear from him in Scotland. During this recess, Blaine's opponents also jockeyed for position. Hanna, who was Sherman's point man at the convention, did what he could to assess the senator's chances and found they were not very good.

In Hanna's communication with Sherman, his statements suggest that while he remained loyal, he also tried to convince Sherman that, if he was going to lose in the end, it might be better to throw his support behind another viable Ohio candidate. The other viable Ohioan Hanna had in mind was William McKinley. While he wrote to Sherman that he did not advise the senator to step aside, he continually made reference to the fact that many at the convention felt McKinley was the only viable candidate who could prevent a rush to nominate James Blaine, whose distant shadow darkened the convention. Sherman observed the tradition of remaining away from the convention as a potential nominee, so communicating to him by telegram, Hanna wrote,

> The Blaine movement will develop this afternoon and I feel sure will get votes in the Ohio delegation. . . . Many of your best friends say that the only way to prevent a Blaine nomination is to wire me to announce your withdrawal and let McKinley come in. . . . I do not advise this and it should only be done as a last resort.[47]

His wording was very careful, but it seems Hanna was trying to get Sherman at least to consider the possibility of withdrawing without actually asking him to. Hanna seems to be gently attempting to persuade Sherman of the futility of his cause without slapping the senator in the face with it.

While Hanna appears to have been subtly trying to encourage Sherman to step aside, it was not because he wanted him to quit so McKinley could become the party nominee. If there had been another Ohioan with a chance, Hanna would certainly have made the same argument.

Of utmost importance to Hanna, it seems, was to ensure the best possible chance for an Ohioan to get the nomination. At that point in the convention, it looked to Hanna that the only viable Ohioan was McKinley. Hanna was more blunt in a later telegram, writing, "The Blaine move is to be made on the next ballot. We think McKinley the only man who can defeat him. Who do you advise? Can Ohio afford to lose the opportunity? I regret the situation but fear I am right."[48] Again, Hanna's prime motivation was to win the nomination for an Ohioan—any Ohioan.

Before the convention began, Hanna supported Sherman because he thought Sherman was good for Ohio, business, and the country. As Sherman's chances at the convention began to disintegrate, Hanna seemed quite ready to support McKinley for the same reasons.

Sherman was not receptive to the suggestion that he step aside for the good of Ohio, however. He wired back to Hanna that he would not make room for McKinley. Sherman wanted very badly to be president in 1888, as he had in 1884. As H. Wayne Morgan writes of Sherman, "It was no secret that he had 'the presidential fever in the severest form. . . .' It was a crucial year for John Sherman; his presidential aspirations would mature now or never, for his strength was at its apogee and his age would prevent future contests."[49] To his credit, Hanna accepted Sherman's response and remained loyal to the senator. There is no evidence that the McKinley movement, such as it was, was engineered by Hanna, and there is even less evidence that McKinley would have acquiesced to such a movement.

In his communication with Sherman, Hanna reiterated his loyalty to the senator. As Felt observed of the communication between the two men: "Hanna had told him only a few hours before that he would 'die in the last ditch if you say so,' and now it seemed he was saying so."[50] Hanna's suggestion of McKinley as a candidate died on Sherman's say-so but, unfortunately for the senator, his candidacy soon died too.

As for McKinley, it is impossible to know what his real desires were—if a massive Garfield-like groundswell happened and gave him the nomination in 1888, he no doubt would have accepted it—but his actions indicate that he very clearly understood he could not make an outward show of desiring the nomination or do anything that made it appear he was trying to get it. His efforts on Sherman's behalf were highly regarded by many at the convention. As H. Wayne Morgan wrote, "McKinley's conduct was lauded everywhere; once again he emerged safely from a sordid fight. . . . McKinley attracted the notice and praise of prominent men."[51] McKinley handled a difficult situation well, supporting Sherman and improving his reputation at the same time. His actions in 1888 certainly burnished his reputation and helped him in future campaigns.

While Hanna was busy communicating with Sherman as the convention was in recess over the weekend, Foraker was observed meeting with Blaine's supporters at their headquarters at the Grand Pacific Hotel. Morrow wrote, "I saw Foraker leave . . . at one o'clock in the morning where he had been in conference with some of Mr. Blaine's friends. He told me and other newspaper correspondents that Ohio was likely to go to Blaine in a body. When this statement was printed in Ohio newspapers Foraker took occasion to deny that he had ever made it."[52] Despite his denial, there was plenty of evidence that Foraker was working Blaine's side of the fence.

It was over this weekend of waiting and speculating that Foraker made the move that seems to have shattered his relationship with Hanna permanently. On Saturday afternoon, as Hanna was exchanging telegrams with Sherman, Foraker announced that he had done all he could for Sherman and was officially switching his allegiance to Blaine. Foraker's statement was an attempt to frame his switch as acceptance of the political reality that Sherman could not win, but Foraker's support of Sherman was in doubt throughout the convention. Foraker's decision was an unfortunate move for both Sherman and Foraker because Blaine once again made it known, through a telegram, that he did not want the nomination. This shifted the focus back to the remaining candidates. Since Ohio's own governor was now on the record as no longer supporting Ohio's favorite son, the last nail was hammered into the coffin of Sherman's candidacy.

Years later, Foraker avoided the fact that he had walked away from Sherman and aligned himself with Blaine when he talked with J. B. Morrow after Hanna's death. Instead, Foraker portrayed Hanna as a corrupt influence peddler, taking a racially tinged parting shot at Hanna when he was no longer around to defend himself:

> I had always been Mr. Sherman's friend. . . . When we arrived
> in Chicago to attend the convention McKinley, Charles Fos-
> ter, Mr. Hanna and myself occupied double rooms. In those

days Mr. Hanna believed that business methods should be employed in obtaining the results he sought in politics. A great many colored delegates from the South, as is their custom, had tickets to the convention which they desired to sell. They brought these tickets to our rooms at the hotel and Mr. Hanna in the presence of all of us bought them. I protested against such conduct, saying that it would bring scandal upon us all and hurt Sherman's cause. Mr. Hanna and I had a spirited discussion over the matter and it resulted in my leaving the rooms and seeking apartments on another floor.[53]

With this statement, Foraker provided an excuse for both his break with Hanna and the distance he put between himself and the Sherman effort at the convention, with no suggestion of the treachery that Hanna, Sherman, and many in the Ohio delegation believed he was guilty of. Rather, he suggested it was Hanna who was guilty of duplicity.

Morrow, as was his custom, commented on Foraker's version of events parenthetically. He wrote,

I was at the convention in 1888 and know Senator Foraker brought great scandal to the Ohio people who were there and to the delegates by his secret work with Mr. Blaine's friends. He was one of the delegates-at-large from Ohio and was chosen to present Mr. Sherman's name to the convention, but it was understood that his heart was not in Sherman's candidacy. . . . My understanding of events at that time was that Mr. Hanna became thoroughly angered at what he thought was Senator Foraker's bad faith. That Senator Foraker left the rooms which he and other delegates-at-large occupied at the hotel is true. I remember the incident very distinctly but that he went to another floor because of his outraged feelings over Mr. Hanna's bargaining with Southern delegates can't be believed by me.[54]

Morrow refuted Foraker's statement firmly, and he was not alone in doing so. According to the statements of others present at the convention, Foraker's version of events lacked credibility.

Regardless of the truth of the changes of duplicity against Foraker, or of corruption against Hanna, perhaps the most compelling explanation of the collapse of the relationship between Hanna and Foraker came from Thomas Beer, who suggested that much of it was ultimately due to a difference of style:

> Foraker and Mark Hanna were made to quarrel. The rich man from Cleveland accepted political theatricalities as so much chaff. There had to be processions, all these speeches, and "a lot of gas" about precedence. It amused him. He liked a phrase much used in conversation by Rutherford Hayes, "the hurrah boys." Mr. Foraker accepted chaff as something else. He felt that a bit of parade and circumstances was becoming to him, at this time, as Governor of Ohio and as Joseph Benson Foraker. He was imposingly designed; he spoke with force and certainty; he had regulated the Republican machine of lower Ohio to an extraordinary smoothness of operation. Mr. Hanna's lack of dignity annoyed him.[55]

Beer's observation is a good one. Hanna was a pragmatic businessman, for whom results were the most important issue. For Foraker, however, there was a certain theatrical instinct that influenced his behavior. It was one reason that, for Hanna, it was important for the Republican Party to move beyond waving the bloody shirt, while Foraker was less willing to do so.

The split between Foraker and Hanna had a profound impact on the subsequent behavior of both men, their careers in politics, and the Republican Party in Ohio, which was fractured by the dispute. As Croly wrote, "There resulted one of the most extraordinary factional fights offered by the history of American politics."[56] Neither man sacrificed bigger party goals to attack the other; but, as Croly observed, "Nevertheless at almost every critical point of Mr. Hanna's subsequent career he was embarrassed and at times almost defeated by the personal ill feelings consequent on his rupture with James B. Foraker."[57] Despite the ample evidence the dispute was entirely of Foraker's making, he never accepted responsibility. Further, the consequences of the break seem to have been much more frustrating to him than they were to Hanna, given his failure to attain his ultimate goal, the presidency.

What is certainly true is that Foraker had to work hard to alienate Hanna, given what many people said about how trusting Hanna was of his associates and how forgiving he was even when his trust was abused. One of his attorneys, James Dempsey, offered a typical assessment of Hanna's relations with his associates: "Mr. Hanna despised treachery, yet it was the hardest thing in the world to make him believe that anyone was false to him. There were a lot of fellows in this city who fell over him to his face but who abused his confidence when his back was turned. He found that out afterward but forgave them. He was a man of most extraordinary generosity. There was no malice in him."[58] Dempsey's statement is consistent with many of the comments made about Hanna by his contemporaries after his death in 1904. While some of these statements seem to paint a picture of Hanna as a surprisingly gullible man, he was almost certainly also forgiving of people for pragmatic reasons. Hanna was focused on big goals, so forgiving rivals for inconsequential transgressions in the name of attaining larger goals was entirely within his character. For his relationship with Foraker to have been ruptured permanently, Hanna must have felt the damage could never be repaired as he could never again trust Foraker.

Benjamin Harrison emerged as a compromise candidate after Blaine removed his name from consideration. Real support for Sherman never materialized, and Harrison slowly gained momentum, finally earning enough votes on the eighth ballot. When Harrison won the nomination, Hanna accepted the loss of his candidate with grace. As Beer wrote, "Marcus Hanna contented himself by reflecting, 'Well, Harrison was born in Ohio, anyhow!'"[59] Harrison eventually won the election in 1888 in one of just four presidential elections in U.S. history in which the winner took office without a plurality of the popular vote. Hanna, ever the loyal Republican, worked for Harrison's election, though not with the enthusiasm he showed for Garfield. His role was confined to Ohio, where he took on the responsibility of raising money in northern cities like Cleveland and Toledo.

As usual, Hanna was very effective, raising many thousands of dollars for Harrison's campaign and the Republican Party. Croly described him as a fundraiser in a new era of political campaigning in which Republicans saw the issue of protective tariffs, which manufacturers favored, as a way to get manufacturers to donate to the Republican cause. Croly wrote, "From being a generous contributor he passed by easy gradations into the position of being an able collector of campaign funds from his business associates."[60] Charles

Dick estimated that Hanna raised about one hundred thousand dollars for Harrison.[61]

During the four years of Harrison's presidency, Hanna was effectively pushed into the national political wilderness. Marginalized by Harrison, Hanna focused primarily on his business career. Through this time, however, Hanna's ultimate desire, to help an Ohioan to the White House, never lessened.

CHAPTER FOUR

The Wilderness Years, 1888–92

or several years after the election of 1888, Mark Hanna remained primarily a businessman, though he was also heavily involved in Republican politics and, increasingly, in the career of William McKinley. Most interesting about his burgeoning relationship with McKinley is the disparity between the description of the relationship as told by contemporaries of Hanna and McKinley and the image that Hearst's journalists and other critics tried to paint later. The negative press view was of Hanna as a Warwick-Svengali, controlling the actions of a naïve, malleable McKinley, but that image does not square with the picture painted by people who knew Hanna and McKinley. H. H. Kohlsaat, who was close to both men, noted in his autobiography the affection Hanna felt for McKinley. Kohlsaat wrote, "There is an impression that Mark Hanna controlled William McKinley. That is not so. His attitude was always that of a big, bashful boy toward a girl he loves. It was not the power that it brought Mr. Hanna that made him fight for McKinley's nomination and election; it was the love of a strong man for a friend who was worthy of that affection."[1] McKinley was not, according to Kohlsaat and others, a simple man under the spell of the smarter, more talented Hanna.

Andrew Squire, one of Hanna's attorneys, said, "My recollection is that Mr. Hanna became greatly attached to Mr. McKinley in the campaigns of 1888 and 1892."[2] This comment suggested a one-sided relationship, but not the kind of one-sided relationship about which Hearst's reporters wrote. Margaret Leech was one of the

first historians to dispel the Hearstian myth that McKinley was controlled by Hanna:

> In choosing McKinley as the object on which to lavish his
> energies, Hanna had not made a purely rational decision.
> He had been magnetized by a polar attraction. Cynical in
> his acceptance of contemporary political practices, Hanna
> was drawn to McKinley's scruples and idealistic standards,
> like a hardened man of the world who becomes infatuated
> with virgin innocence. That his influence ruled McKinley
> was the invention of the political opposition, of young Mr.
> Hearst's newspapers in particular. Hanna, on the contrary,
> treated McKinley with conspicuous deference.[3]

Leech's interpretation has been backed by other McKinley scholars,
such as Lewis Gould and H. Wayne Morgan. Despite this scholarship,
however, many journalists continued to misperceive the relationship
between Hanna and McKinley well into the twenty-first century.

Historian Paul Glad argued that it was McKinley's performance
at the 1888 convention that endeared him to Hanna: "McKinley's
evident sense of honor, his insistence on sticking by his word, and
his devotion to his party won him many friends in 1888. None was
to be more important to him than Mark Hanna. . . . Hanna could
appreciate honor and loyalty when he saw it, and he was ready to use
his considerable wealth in the interest of just such a man as McKinley."[4] Glad correctly asserts that Hanna and McKinley's relationship
was strengthened by what happened at the 1888 convention. Glad's
concluding sentence on the subject, however, missed the mark: "Thus
without taking the initiative himself, the Major received support from
one of the shrewdest, most canny politicians of his time."[5] Hanna was
certainly a canny and shrewd politician, but the sentence has a tone
suggesting that McKinley lucked into his relationship with Hanna
and, thus, the political good fortune that followed. A more accurate
view is that McKinley made his own luck. Other biographers, like
Leech or Gould, argued that McKinley was a very skillful politician in
his own right, and he understood very well the implications of what
he did, or did not, do at the convention in 1888. What is certainly
true is that in 1888 the two men began to develop a close working
relationship that helped put McKinley in the White House.

In the fall of 1889, Hanna traveled to Washington, DC, to help McKinley, who was still a congressman, in his campaign to become the Speaker of the House. The trip marked Hanna's first serious foray into Washington politics, and while there, he canvassed members of the House trying to drum up support for McKinley.[6] Theodore Burton reported, "Mr. Hanna . . . took an active part with Mr. McKinley's friends in McKinley's candidacy for the Speakership. I do not know that he was influential, but he was certainly active. . . . Mr. McKinley was a very active candidate for Speaker. No one except those who were close to him ever knew how anxious Mr. McKinley was for an office when he went after it."[7] McKinley failed to win the Speaker's election, but he was subsequently appointed by the winning candidate for Speaker, Thomas Reed, to be the chairman of the House Ways and Means Committee. In the short term, McKinley's appointment to that leadership position identified him with a very unpopular bill that led, in part, to his defeat in 1890. Losing his seat in Congress, however, ultimately opened the door to new political opportunities and much greater help from Mark Hanna.

Foraker was the Republican candidate for Ohio governor in 1889, but he had to deal with some convention-related backlash from Hanna and Hanna allies like Congressman Benjamin Butterworth before he secured the nomination. As Morrow wrote, "Certain it is that in the following year—1889—both Butterworth and Mr. Hanna were aggressively against Mr. Foraker's third nomination for governor. Foraker, nevertheless, was nominated but defeated. Thereafter there was no outward sign of friendship between Foraker and Hanna. On the contrary, it was generally understood that they were political enemies."[8] So, although his friends all reported that it was hard to become Hanna's enemy, Foraker accomplished that very role in 1888, and it did not take long for him to feel the repercussions. His actions forever changed his relationship with Hanna and created an enduring fissure in the Ohio Republican Party.

The Midterm Election of 1890 and a Career Change for McKinley

When McKinley lost his seat in Congress in 1890, it was not a sign of any particular weakness on his part so much as it was the consequence of an unfortunate confluence of circumstances. First, it is important to note that, in Ohio, many Republicans, including Governor Foraker, were swept out of power by the Democrats in 1889. One of the first things the Democrats did, as the new majority party, was to redraw the boundaries of the state's congressional districts. McKinley's district was redrawn with boundaries that left him with no chance of winning reelection in 1890.[9]

Second, McKinley was not the only Republican to fare badly in the election—many Republicans across the nation were defeated, and the party lost control of the House, thanks in part to a tariff bill with McKinley's name on it. As a congressman, McKinley was very outspoken about the importance of protecting American industry from foreign competition. Protectionism remained a central tenet of his political philosophy through most of his political life—he even pursued it as the central theme of his 1896 presidential campaign until William Jennings Bryan and the populist wave that supported him forced McKinley to address the currency question.

In 1890, tariff legislation known popularly as the McKinley Bill was a major campaign issue. The bill was a revision of much of the country's code of protective tariffs. It lowered tariffs on some goods and raised them on some others. The legislation was originally sponsored by McKinley, but the final version of the bill bore little resemblance to what he introduced, thanks largely to action in the Senate.

Unfortunately for McKinley and the rest of the Republican Party, the bill became politically unpopular because, as Margaret Leech wrote, "The bare threat of the new rates had been sufficient excuse for sharp traders to mark up their goods. Prices continued to mount long before the effect of the tariff could be felt, and regardless of whether or not it would increase the cost of the merchandise."[10] This opportunism by merchants benefited Democratic candidates all over the country who played on fears that tariffs were the cause of inflation. The consequence, according to Sherman's aide, Jacob C. Donaldson, was that McKinley and many other Republicans were defeated when "the whole country, almost, rejected the McKinley tariff law at the polls."[11]

On the night he was defeated, McKinley assessed the wave of negative feeling about protection and argued that his policies—and those of the Republican Party—would be vindicated in the end. He wrote of this feeling in an editorial for the *Canton Repository* in which he argued, "Protection was never stronger than it is at this hour. . . . Passion and prejudice, ignorance and willful misrepresentation are masterful for the hour against any great public law. . . . Increased prosperity, which is sure to come, will outrun the maligner and the vilifier."[12] For his part, McKinley was very positive and seemed to believe sincerely that his defeat in 1890 was little more than a minor obstacle on his path to political greatness.

McKinley was right, of course. The loss of his seat in Congress was far from the death of his career. In fact, it was an opportunity. His defeat in the congressional election allowed him to stay home and concentrate on Ohio politics. At home, he benefited greatly from a sense of outrage around the state about the fact that he was the victim of aggressive political maneuvering by the Democrats. On the day after his defeat, he was widely lauded in Republican newspapers around the state as a victim of political dirty tricks, thanks to the gerrymandering of his district by the Democrats. The tariff that bore his name was undoubtedly part of the wider defeat of Republicans in 1890, but in Ohio, McKinley was viewed as something of a political hero. Historian Margaret Leech wrote, "The injustice of the gerrymander and McKinley's gallant fight were the theme of the Republican newspapers of Ohio. They declared that his campaign had made him the next governor, and their praise and prophecy were echoed by the party press outside the state."[13] The newspapers' predictions were correct. In 1891, McKinley became a successful Republican candidate for governor.

1891–92: McKinley Becomes Ohio's Governor

Late 1891 and early 1892 was a very busy period for Mark Hanna, William McKinley, John Sherman, and Joseph Foraker, four men who defined much of both Ohio's and the country's Republican politics of the last decade of the nineteenth century. In 1891, McKinley was elected governor of Ohio, and the Republican Party retook control of the state legislature. It was, as Herbert D. Croly noted, the "first substantial triumph of Mark Hanna's political career."[14] Next, in 1892, John Sherman was reelected to the United States Senate, overcoming an upstart campaign by Hanna's new political nemesis, Foraker.

By 1891, Hanna was fully committed to McKinley. From his perspective, McKinley's loss in 1890 was nothing to worry about in the long term. Almost immediately, according to Croly, Hanna encouraged McKinley to run for governor. As Croly wrote, "He evidently argued that inasmuch as the legislation with which McKinley's name was associated had been disapproved by public opinion, it was just as well for McKinley to retire from a region of political action in which he had incurred unpopularity, and to continue his career in some other part of the political battlefield."[15] McKinley agreed and decided to run for governor.

Hanna fully understood how important it was for McKinley to win the governor's race if he was going to continue his career in politics. When McKinley lost his congressional district, he got the political equivalent of a free pass. His loss was plausibly explained by partisan redistricting by the state legislature that made it all but impossible for McKinley, or any Republican, to win the seat, the unpopularity of the "McKinley Tariff" notwithstanding. If, however, McKinley lost the governor's race, it would be a clear signal that he did not have the support of voters in his own state. If he was not able to summon the support of his fellow Ohioans, it would certainly send a signal to his fellow Republicans that McKinley was not ideal presidential timber. With that in mind, Hanna did as much as he could, especially financially, to support McKinley's effort.

While Hanna did much for McKinley in 1891, however, he focused more of his efforts on electing state legislators friendly to John Sherman for his upcoming reelection campaign in 1892. McKinley had a relatively clear path to the Republican gubernatorial nomination in 1891. Joseph B. Foraker had been out of the governor's office for two years, and his sights were set elsewhere, namely, on John Sherman's seat in the Senate. While this was good for McKinley, it did not bode well for John Sherman. Foraker's push for Sherman's seat was no idle threat as, for a while, it seemed as though he would retire Ohio's senior statesman.

Hanna was still very loyal to Sherman, and, because of the looming threat from Foraker, he was much more hands-on in running Sherman's campaign than he was McKinley's. Croly characterized his efforts for McKinley this way: "He undoubtedly took much more pains to secure Mr. McKinley's election than he did in the case of an ordinary Republican candidate; but his efforts for his friend were confined chiefly to raising money. He could trust the State Committee to work hard for the regular candidate for governor."[16] In Sherman's case, the challenge was greater, and Hanna took the job very seriously. The crusty old senator, who was not well loved, was faced with a popular younger opponent who, with his cronies, controlled much of the Republican Party in southern Ohio.

Before Sherman could be reelected to a new term in the Senate, the Republicans had to retake control of the state legislature. This was prior to the passage of the Seventeenth Amendment to the U.S. Constitution, so it meant that senators were still chosen by the state legislatures. A Democratically controlled legislature would never have allowed Sherman to remain Ohio's senator.

It is difficult to know what mattered more to Hanna—making sure his old friend Sherman kept his job or making sure Foraker did not get it. As Everett Walters, a Foraker biographer, wrote, "During the campaign the Sherman group was agitated over Foraker's threat; Hanna took over personally. . . . Still a friend of Sherman, Hanna wished to see him defeat Foraker. Too, he felt that Sherman should be returned to the senate as a reward for his long service."[17] One of Hanna's close friends and advisers, James H. Dempsey, was a member of the law firm that represented Hanna. Dempsey made the point that in running Sherman's reelection campaign in early 1892, Hanna had two reasons for working so hard for Sherman. First, he said that Hanna "worked day and night and spent his money to elect a Legislature in November 1891 which would return Sherman to the Senate. This he did unselfishly and because he thought the country needed Sherman's services."[18] This was, no doubt, because Sherman shared Hanna's probusiness orientation and felt that government and business needed to work together. Foraker stood for a different set of Republican issues than did Sherman. Foraker, while younger, harkened back to the party's earlier days and was not above waving the bloody shirt.

However, it was more than issues that made Hanna such an enthusiastic supporter of Sherman. According to Dempsey, Hanna also worked so hard for Sherman because "of Foraker's conduct at the Republican conventions of 1884 and 1888, when he pretended to be Sherman's friend, Hanna believed Foraker to be treacherous."[19] While Hanna might have been forgiving of many transgressions, as his friends attested, he was unwilling to overlook those of Foraker. To Hanna, these were damaging not only to Sherman but to the Republican Party. Few things were more important to Hanna than the party.

Hanna played an integral role in helping Sherman keep his seat in the U.S. Senate in 1892. As James Dempsey argued, "Mr. Sherman was re-elected but he would have been defeated if Mr. Hanna had not helped him."[20] Sherman was handicapped in his run for reelection by a number of factors, including his age and his unapproachable personality. Dempsey referred to him as an "iceberg."[21] McKinley biographer H. Wayne Morgan made a similar observation, when he assessed Sherman's attempt to win the presidential nomination in 1888: "Despite his longevity and ability, Senator Sherman was simply not popular."[22] Foraker was simply more of a man of the people than Sherman could ever hope to be.

Sherman's reelection in 1892 began with the state legislative election in Ohio in 1891. If Sherman was to retain his seat, Hanna first had to make sure that the Republicans won control of the legislature. As Donaldson reported, many of Sherman's old friends voiced support for his reelection, but few were willing to get involved. Without the efforts of Hanna, particularly in the Cleveland area, the legislature might not have been reclaimed by the Republicans. As Donaldson stated, "Throughout the campaign, Mr. Hanna was by all odds the most conspicuous and useful man among our leaders. We carried the state in November."[23] Following the legislative election, Sherman, with Hanna's help, focused on lining up votes in the state legislature for the Senate vote, which would take place in January when the new legislative session began. Donaldson related that "during the campaign when Mr. Sherman's political life was in constant jeopardy Mr. Hanna was our chief adviser."[24]

Foraker's push for the Senate was strong, and for a time it looked as if he might pick off enough of Sherman's supporters to win. Before the state legislature convened, Sherman's aide, J. C. Donaldson, predicted that Sherman could count on fifty-three votes in the Republican house caucus. To win there, he needed at least forty-seven votes. In the end, Sherman ended up with exactly the fifty-three votes Donaldson predicted he would get, but reporting only the final tally glosses over the drama in the middle. There were many ups and downs in the fight, and, as Donaldson related, "The situation was bad, almost desperate, and the result so much in doubt that Mr. Sherman left his place in the Senate and appeared in Columbus to work in person for himself."[25] Sherman might have come to Ohio "to work in person for himself," which was not the normal practice for the time, but without Hanna to fight for him, Sherman would likely have been retired.

Hanna's task was complicated by the fact that many of the Republican legislators he helped elect to the state house proved to be unsupportive of Sherman's candidacy, several of whom were from his own home turf. As Donaldson reported,

> Some of the members on whom we relied as being for Sherman announced that they proposed to vote for Foraker. This was especially the case in Cleveland. In that city Mr. Hanna had openly and vigorously worked for Mr. Sherman and the business men were back of him. He had thrust his hand into the nomination of candidates for the General Assembly and all who had been chosen had assured him they would vote for Sherman. You can imagine his amazement and anger when he learned soon after the election that several of the Cleveland members-elect were counted on by Foraker and his managers. Mr. Hanna got after them and one or two went into hiding. Several of them were ruined by their perfidy.[26]

No doubt, Hanna viewed the legislators' actions as extensions of Foraker's treachery. In addition to being angry that his best-laid plans were endangered, it was also outrageous to Hanna that Foraker was able to have such an influence in the northern Ohio—Hanna's home turf of Cuyahoga County. Foraker was from Cincinnati—southern Ohio—and the preexisting regional rivalry was, no doubt, exacerbated by the other, bigger differences that existed between the two men. Faced with this mutiny, Hanna took personal charge and went to Columbus to oversee the vote.

Taken literally, Donaldson's comment about men going into hiding may seem overly dramatic, but he was not the only one to report it. It was well known that Hanna was very angry at the thought that he was being betrayed, and the men about to vote for Foraker were urged to hide so Hanna would not be able to persuade them to reconsider. Hanna, however, did not take their disappearances lying down. As Croly described, "Three of the Cleveland representatives, who had gone into hiding, were unearthed and forced into line."[27] According to James Dempsey, he was the one who Hanna asked to track them down. Dempsey reported that Hanna was very annoyed to find that

> three members of the legislature from Cleveland . . . had been induced by Foraker's friends to go into hiding. These

men had promised to vote for Sherman but were preparing to reject their pledges. Their conduct caused Mr. Hanna to send for me and ask me to find them. Detectives had failed to discover where they had gone. . . . I met Frank De Hass Robison, who was associated with Mr. Hanna in the street railway business, and he boastingly admitted that he knew where Spencer, Parker and Porter were. Mr. Hanna sent for Robison and soon showed him that he was working against the best interests of the State.[28]

It would, no doubt, have been entertaining to hear Hanna explaining things to Robison.

Dempsey's explanation of why he included the story of the wayward Cleveland legislators in his account of his relationship with Hanna is instructive. He included it, he stated, because he wanted to "illustrate Mr. Hanna's activity and zeal in this campaign."[29] Indeed, Hanna seems to have demonstrated a great deal of "activity and zeal" for every campaign in which he was involved. One wonders what the three state representatives who tried to hide from Hanna thought about his "activity and zeal."

Hanna's zealousness was not the consequence of a simple drive to win elections. Rather, it was energized by his view that government, the Republican Party, and the good of society were inextricably bound together. He sincerely believed it when he argued that by acting against Sherman, Foraker's supporters were acting against the "best interests of the State." Hanna waited until relatively late in life to dive into politics full time, but when he did, he did it because he believed that politics could, and should, be part of improving society.

Understanding Hanna as a man who had a vision of the benefits of a marriage between business and politics contributes to the conclusion that it was not Sherman's personality that made Hanna such a willing, and effective, advocate for him. Rather, it was the fact that Hanna thought Sherman was a better voice for the kinds of policies he supported than Foraker would have been. Similarly, it was not McKinley's personality—though Hanna and McKinley clearly liked each other— that prompted Hanna to support McKinley's campaigns as strongly as he did. Rather, it was the ideas McKinley stood for—and the not insignificant fact that he was an Ohioan—that made Hanna work so hard for him.

For his part, Sherman was at least initially grateful for Hanna's help in 1892. As Donaldson reported, "Mr. Hanna was the vigor and the intellect of that great battle and Mr. Sherman always felt that he owed his success on that occasion to Mr. Hanna's energy, enthusiasm and power as a leader of men."[30] Sherman sent a letter to Hanna expressing his gratitude. He wrote, "Now, after the smoke of battle is cleared away, I wish first of all and above all to express to you my profound gratitude and sincere respects for the part you have taken in the recent Senatorial canvass."[31] At the time of the election, anyway, Sherman seemed to appreciate the role Hanna played in his success.

As Croly observed, however, a similar thank-you to Hanna failed to make it into Sherman's autobiography. Sherman's two-volume memoir, titled *Reminiscences,* was published in 1895 and 1896, a time when Hanna's help in his reelection should have been very fresh in Sherman's mind. The volumes were also published, as Croly mentioned, before Sherman was asked by McKinley to become his secretary of state, a move that made it possible for Hanna to take Sherman's seat in the Senate. Had the books been written after Hanna took his seat, Sherman might have refused to credit Hanna for his reelection in 1892 if he was angry because he felt he had been shoved aside, but the timing precluded that explanation. More likely, Sherman, a proud man, was unwilling to cede too much credit in his autobiography to someone else for his political success.[32] If Hanna noticed the slight, he made no public comment and gave no sign that he held the oversight against Sherman, whom he held in high esteem.

In terms of feuding partners, Foraker was unique in Hanna's political world, especially considering the fact that they were from the same party. Hanna could be dismissive, even cruel, toward people who disagreed with him, as was the case with the prosilver Republicans who bolted the party in 1896. For the most part, however, Hanna overlooked differences with fellow Republicans in the name of larger party goals. Foraker was one of the few men with whom Hanna maintained an openly hostile relationship, and Foraker had to work hard to earn Hanna's ire—it took a long while and serious treachery on Foraker's part before Hanna wrote him off.

The Presidential Election of 1892

In 1892, Benjamin Harrison was the incumbent president and, as such, had a leg up over all the other competitors in the Republican

Party, although many Republicans tried to blame Harrison for economic problems and other issues that made the Republicans generally unpopular and led to their congressional losses in 1890. Harrison, like Sherman, was not a warm or well-liked man, and he was most certainly not Mark Hanna's favorite person. As Congressman Theodore Burton reported, "I don't think Harrison ever liked Mr. Hanna and I am sure that Mr. Hanna reciprocated the feeling."[33] While Hanna did nothing overt to damage Harrison's career, he likewise did little to further it.

Despite his successful work raising money in 1888, Hanna was "left out in the cold" by Harrison, as he had been by Foraker in Ohio. Harrison, who was prickly under the best circumstances, did not follow through on any of Hanna's patronage requests.[34] While it may have been true, as Burton asserted, that Harrison simply did not like Hanna, it is also likely that Harrison felt it was wise strategically to keep Hanna from gaining too much traction.

After all, by 1888, it was clear that Hanna was intent on being involved in presidential politics and preferably on behalf of an Ohioan. Harrison's claim on the Republican nomination in 1892 was tenuous, given the way he was elected in 1888, and he certainly felt Hanna was never going to be an ally to him the way he was to his fellow Ohioans. It would not have made much sense for Harrison to add to Hanna's prestige by letting him control any patronage.

Whatever Harrison's reasons were, however, Hanna did not appreciate being ignored. As Charles Dick related,

> When the election was over Mr. Hanna was so far forgotten or his efforts so far overlooked that every recommendation which he made to the Harrison administration was wholly disregarded. . . . Mr. Hanna had been turned down on everything he asked for but the final straw was added when he requested the appointment of an old friend as lighthouse master out at the end of the Cleveland breakwater; even that was refused. Well, this hurt Mr. Hanna's pride and made him feel that Mr. Harrison was unappreciative, ungrateful, and unresponsive.[35]

Harrison may not have wanted to build Hanna's stature in the party, but all he did was ensure that Hanna would be very unenthusiastic when it came time for him to run for reelection.

In 1892, after earning Hanna's enmity by turning down his patronage requests, Harrison then asked Hanna to serve as the treasurer of the Republican National Committee. Hanna had, after all, demonstrated his aptitude for raising money on numerous occasions, and he could have greatly assisted Harrison in his reelection campaign. Despite his loyalty to the Republican Party, Hanna declined this honor. Historian Ralph Martin suggested Harrison made the offer to "swallow Hanna within the Harrison framework and thereby minimize any McKinley threat at the 1892 convention."[36] Hanna may have believed that Harrison was trying to marginalize him and McKinley, he may have simply been irritated, or both. Regardless of the reason, he refused to work for Harrison in 1892.

While there was no overt movement to remove Harrison as the party's candidate in 1892, there were many who were ready to move in if it seemed possible to unseat him. Just as he did throughout the 1880s, James G. Blaine added drama to the convention when, only three days before it was to begin, he resigned as Harrison's secretary of state, and each man complained publicly about the performance of the other.[37] Blaine was elderly and in poor health, but that did not prevent his supporters of old from responding with enthusiasm to the thought that he might make another run for the presidency. In the end, Blaine was not much of a factor at the convention; in fact, he died eight months later, but that there were many Republicans receptive to an alternate candidate could not have been reassuring to Harrison.

For his part, John Sherman made it clear that he was not a presidential candidate in 1892 and officially released Mark Hanna to work on McKinley's behalf, if the governor was to challenge Harrison for the nomination. According to H. Wayne Morgan, McKinley was the most popular man in the Republican Party.[38] For his part, Hanna was ready to promote McKinley in Minneapolis if the opportunity presented itself. As Charles Dick put it, "Mr. Hanna was not a Blaine man; he felt that the solution or the safety of the situation demanded the nomination of a new man and that man was McKinley."[39]

Hanna took his cues from McKinley in Minneapolis, and while McKinley clearly wanted to run for president as some point, he was cautious about appearing too eager in 1892. As Croly wrote, "Under the circumstances, the plan was adopted of keeping the McKinley candidacy above the surface but in the background. No attempt was made to secure the election of delegates pledged to McKinley. . . . But preparations were made to bring McKinley forward in case Mr. Harrison's renomination proved to be difficult."[40] Caution was wise. While Hanna would have enjoyed seeing President Harrison lose the nomination, it was not politically advantageous for McKinley to appear eager to supplant him.

McKinley attended the convention as one of Ohio's four delegates-at-large, along with W. M. Hahn, Asa Bushnell, and Joseph B. Foraker. Hanna was not a delegate to the convention in 1892, but he nevertheless established an unofficial McKinley headquarters at the West Hotel, near the convention. This was the culmination of a significant amount of groundwork he conducted for McKinley prior to the convention. Hanna gathered information from contacts in several regions of the country, measuring how much support existed for McKinley. Hanna's contacts led him to conclude that there was particularly strong support for McKinley in the Midwest and the South.[41]

As J. B. Morrow reported, Hanna also made "an open and spirited campaign for McKinley" in the early days of the convention.[42] Hanna's McKinley headquarters was open only for a couple of days, but its closure "did not prevent Mr. Hanna from electioneering among the delegates and especially among those from the west."[43] Thomas Beer wrote that Hanna worked for several days "gathering opinions" about a possible McKinley candidacy. In the end, Hanna did not make any serious moves on McKinley's behalf, largely because McKinley was cautious about his doing so. Hanna's own canvass of the delegates found McKinley would not be able to pull off a challenge. Making an attempt and failing would have tarnished what was, up to that point, McKinley's sparkling reputation. Still, while Hanna expected Harrison to be renominated, he remained prepared for the possibility that McKinley could emerge as a competitor for the nomination. He had McKinley badges printed and engaged in negotiations with Blaine supporters to see if they would be willing to come on board with a push for McKinley when Blaine made it clear he was not running. All the while, McKinley maintained a very clear public position that he was not interested in seeking the nomination.

Historians H. Wayne Morgan and Thomas Beer both credited Hanna with making sure that McKinley avoided what would inevitably have been a thorny political situation. As Beer related, Hanna was asked if McKinley would support the candidacy of former House Speaker Thomas B. Reed for president. If he did so, Hanna was told, Reed would make McKinley his secretary of state. Earlier in American history, holding the position of secretary of state was a common steppingstone to the presidency, but no president since James Buchanan had followed that path. In addition, it seemed unlikely Reed would be successful. As Beer reported, Hanna did not try to get McKinley to take Reed's bait because "he knew—he had been listening to the delegates—that this listless, discouraged convention would nominate Benjamin Harrison once more."[44] It was highly unlikely that either Reed or McKinley would be able to take the nomination away from Harrison, and McKinley positioned himself as being opposed to any attempt to do so. Both Hanna and McKinley concluded it was politically efficacious for future campaigns to *appear* to be loyal to the incumbent president, rather than to try to take advantage of his obvious weakness.

McKinley was elected the permanent chairman of the convention, giving him responsibility for managing the rest of the meeting. In his speech accepting the honor, McKinley reiterated his support of protective tariffs. As Moos reported, McKinley said, "We stand for the protective tariff because it represents the American home, the American fireside, the American family, the American girl and the American boy, and the highest possibilities of American citizenship. We propose to raise our money to pay public expenses by taxing the products of other nations, rather than by taxing the products of our own."[45] Moos also pointed out that many of the subsequent speeches at the convention lauded the concept of protective tariffs and praised McKinley for being their champion.[46] This very vocal enthusiasm for the tariff was surprising, given its general unpopularity in the 1890 election. It was the McKinley Tariff, after all, that was primarily responsible for the Republicans' loss of Congress. McKinley and the speakers who echoed him were clearly building a foundation for the future, beyond 1892.

McKinley was certainly ambitious, but he was also a very skilled politician. He knew an open attempt to win the nomination in 1892—which Hanna's canvassing told him would fail—would hurt him in future campaigns. Even if he thought it was possible to wrest the nomination from Harrison, there was a strong feeling that no Republican would be able to win the general election in 1892, due in large measure to the highly unpopular McKinley Tariff. If McKinley won the nomination but lost the presidential election, it could be fatal for any future aspirations for the White House. Most of McKinley's biographers painted the picture of a man who was exceedingly cautious when it came to his own career. He had a reliable sense of what was good and bad for him, and he trusted his own counsel above that of others, including Hanna. Despite the popular image of McKinley as Hanna's lapdog, there were many instances in his relationship with Hanna when McKinley reined in his wealthy friend. In 1888, he resisted the groundswell of support for him because he feared that, if he failed to get the nomination, his disloyalty to Sherman would hurt his long-term reputation within the party.

In 1892, McKinley understood there was little to be gained from a dark-horse candidacy in his name when the Republicans had no real chance of winning the election. At the same time, he let Hanna operate independently on the fringes, promoting his name among the party regulars, not for 1892 but for future campaigns. For his part, McKinley remained aloof from the effort, ruling against attempts to push for his nomination from his perch as permanent chairman of the convention and refusing to address the convention as a possible candidate.[47]

In a very real way, the convention of 1892 marked the beginning of McKinley's 1896 campaign. There is almost nothing in the way of recorded communication between Hanna and McKinley to know exactly what their strategy was in 1892, but McKinley's behavior at the convention supports the idea that he liked the attention but was not ready for a campaign. Much of McKinley's public performance at the convention in Minneapolis was a show of downplaying the efforts of Hanna and his other boosters. As J. B. Morrow wrote, "McKinley had pledged himself to Harrison and ostensibly felt some embarrassment over the energy of his friends. . . . Mr. McKinley told me at the close of the convention that he would not have accepted the nomination and that he kept a close watch on the balloting in order to prevent it if at any time conditions had been favorable for his selection."[48] At the same time, however, McKinley certainly understood the future value of having his name mentioned with such frequency and enthusiasm.

When it came time to vote, Harrison's renomination was easily secured by a group of loyal friends, known as the "Twelve Apostles." They were led by Harrison's managers at the convention, James S. Clarkson and Louis T. Michener. As Morrow wrote, "There was no chance for

Mr. McKinley at any stage of the proceedings," but in all likelihood, that was perfectly fine with McKinley.[49]

In a classic preemptive strike, the Twelve Apostles organized a meeting of all the convention delegates who came to Minneapolis with instructions to vote for Harrison on the first ballot. This group constituted a majority of all the delegates at the convention, so the meeting turned into an enthusiastic rally for President Harrison that made the outcome of the convention a fait accompli.[50] As Morrow elegantly explained, "Enough delegates assembled to affect a nomination and the meeting was conclusive in its results."[51] It proved to be a hollow victory, however, as McKinley foresaw.

Harrison was an unpopular Republican president running for reelection at a time when the Republican Party was, if only temporarily, very unpopular, and he suffered the consequences. He was blamed for much that was done during the first two years of his presidency when he went along with the Republican majority in Congress. Thomas Reed, the very powerful Speaker of the House, was responsible for most of the legislation that Harrison was blamed for, including a growth in federal spending that led to the first-ever "billion-dollar Congress," in which Congress appropriated a billion dollars in spending for the first time, creating a powerful issue for the Democrats. Tariffs, the economy, and the billion-dollar Congress were all issues in Harrison's reelection campaign. In addition, he was distracted throughout the campaign by his wife's illness. She died from tuberculosis in October, right before the election. Harrison lost the election in 1892 to the resurgent Grover Cleveland, and the Democrats retained their majority in Congress.

In February 1891, prior to his defeat of Harrison in 1892, Cleveland made his opinion on the gold-versus-silver issue very public with his "Silver Letter." In it, he tried to make it clear where he stood and to bring the Democratic Party into line behind him. As one Cleveland biographer wrote, his Silver Letter was "a declaration to his fellow Democrats that he had reentered public life with a firm determination to see that the Democrats fought the election of 1892 with a sound-money platform and a sound-money candidate."[52] It was a position that had consequences for William Jennings Bryan's campaign in 1896, as it gave ammunition to both Bryan's detractors within his own party and to the Republicans. Cleveland's second administration was marred by one of the country's historic financial "panics," which was the most severe economic crisis in United States history until the Great Depression struck in 1929. While Cleveland was not a candidate for reelection in 1896, in large part because the panic occurred during his administration, the tough economic times did great damage to the hopes of any Democrat seeking the presidency that year.

McKinley's decision not to push his own candidacy in 1892 proved to be one of the wisest choices any politician has ever made. When economic panic arose in 1893, the Democrats took the full blame, ushering in a thirty-year period of Republican dominance beginning with the congressional elections of 1894 and the presidential election of 1896.

Although Hanna may have wanted to build a wave of support for McKinley at the convention in 1892, the fact that the tide was stemmed was the best thing that could have happened to the man who many people thought looked physically like the second coming of Napoleon. When the convention adjourned, many delegates having only grudgingly given their support to Harrison for an election most thought the party would lose, they left with the confidence that, in four short years, the country would be tired of Democratic leadership and ready to return to the party of Lincoln, under the leadership of someone like William McKinley.

CHAPTER FIVE

The Hearst Effect on the Hanna-McKinley Legacy

ark Hanna has a bimodal legacy. To historians, he was a loyal and, occasionally, marginalized lieutenant to William McKinley. In the opposition press and in the popular perception of him that survives to this day, he was a sinister power behind the throne. The explanation for this lies in the fact that Hanna was a much easier target than McKinley, both in reputation and appearance, which left him open for more than his fair share of abuse. Hanna was very different from McKinley, and he was a lightning rod for the press, a way to attack the heroic, likable McKinley by proxy.

Those who disliked McKinley's politics were in a difficult position when it came to criticizing him because he was such a popular figure, widely regarded as a man of attractive features and personality. Not only was he a war veteran, but he had profound personal tragedies in his life that made even the harshest denizens of the press reluctant to attack him directly.

As Lewis Gould wrote, "When people spoke of McKinley in his prime, they used such words as 'dignity,' 'kindness,' and 'understanding.' The tragedies of his personal life . . . closed off his private life from the public, who saw him as an example of marital devotion and appropriate reserve."[1] McKinley was seen as a devoted husband, caring for his wife, Ida, who was sickly to begin with and was further crippled by grief over the death of her two children. One daughter, named Ida like her mother, died at the age of six months in August 1873. She was a sickly baby whose birth was very traumatic for her mother, and both mother and daughter spent the child's brief life in illness. Two years later, in 1875, the McKinleys' older daughter, Katie, contracted typhoid fever and died at the age of three.

Hanna had no such tragedy in his personal life. McKinley was seen as a thoughtful, compassionate attorney, working in his early career not on behalf of the corporate titans he was accused of being a lapdog to but for striking coal miners in the Massillon, Ohio, the strikes occurring during the 1870s. Hanna was on the opposite end—an owner of mines perceived, however inaccurately, as one of the men forcing other men to toil in the pits for low pay at great danger to themselves. Hanna was a peacemaker in those strikes, but that fact was easily disregarded by muckraking journalists looking for a demon.

McKinley, known widely as "the Major," was a hero of the Civil War, a man who nobly sacrificed to fight for the Union cause. Hanna, on the other hand, paid for a replacement and stayed home to watch over the family business, only joining the army at the end of the war. From Hanna's perspective, it was necessary for someone to stay home while his brother went off to war because his father was in poor health and incapable of running the family business. His family asserted that it was a difficult choice for Hanna to stay home and meet his familial responsibilities. It was easy for reporters, however, to see a man who was afraid to meet his patriotic obligation. To them, Hanna was like so many other men of privilege who took the easy way out.

McKinley, a handsome man viewed by many as having the bearing of Napoleon, was caricatured, but not with the same cruel tone as the drawings of Hanna. McKinley was fortunate to avoid the worst treatment in 1896, when the full force of the criticism was aimed at Hanna, such as in the Homer Davenport cartoon below, where the grotesquely drawn Hanna is depicted with a Napoleonic hat, donning a McKinley mask. McKinley also avoided the worst the cartoonists had to offer in the 1900 campaign, when Hanna remained a favorite target and was joined by Teddy Roosevelt, whom the cartoonists portrayed as a selfish, spoiled child with poor self-control.

McKinley, a careful keeper of his own image, was a difficult target for William Randolph Hearst and his attack dogs, who included men like writers Arthur McEwen and Alfred Henry Lewis and cartoonists Homer Davenport and Frederick Opper. McKinley's public image was of a man free of scandal who loved his wife and exuded warmth.[2]

FIGURE 5.1. Is my hat on straight? Cartoon by Homer Davenport, *New York Journal*, November 11, 1896, 1

FIGURE 5.2. Wolf in sheep's clothing. Cartoon by Homer Davenport, *New York Journal*, October 18, 1896, 1

He was more than happy to let the more vicious criticism in the press fall on Hanna. As Gould reported, McKinley kept a file of the Davenport cartoons that amused him the most. Cruel treatment in the press wore on Hanna, but as a loyal lieutenant, he preferred to receive the criticism if it meant McKinley avoided it.

H. Wayne Morgan, a McKinley biographer, addressed what was said—and misunderstood—about the relationship between Hanna and McKinley:

> Hanna's relations with McKinley were widely misunderstood in his own time. Cruel caricatures lampooned Hanna, among the first to treat with organized labor, as a huge bloated creature feeding off workingmen. McKinley, who had proved his integrity and ability during twenty-five years in public life, was the money on Hanna's string. Many—and not only Democrats—imagined that Hanna was the master, when in fact he was the loyal lieutenant; that McKinley was the tool, when in fact he planned and approved the strategy that brought him victory. But those who watched them closely saw that Hanna was the subordinate. . . . He was seldom informal and never familiar with McKinley, treating him with respect and deference in private as well as in public. Hanna often said that his association with McKinley, whose inflexible morality he admired, made a better man of him; without McKinley's steadying influence, Hanna might have become merely another party boss, like his Eastern contemporaries.[3]

Hanna never become a party boss, despite claims to the contrary by historians and journalists who, unable to prove he was a boss in the same mold as William M. Tweed, Thomas C. Platt, or Matthew Quay, tried to create a new kind of bossism—that of "national boss"—for Hanna.

In addition to the differences of physical appearance and personality between McKinley and Hanna that made Hanna a better target, Hanna was also much easier to attack because of the foundation that was laid during the press wars of the 1880s with Edwin Cowles and the subsequent willingness of the Democratic press in Cleveland to follow Cowles's negative model. Before the campaign even began, Hearst sent reporters to Cleveland to learn from and exploit Hanna's already negative reputation in his hometown. It was easier to make

Hanna the symbol of everything that would be wrong with a McKinley presidency than to attack McKinley directly.

Of course, the fact that the harshest coverage was reserved for Hanna does not mean that the image of McKinley in the Hearst press was flattering. He was portrayed as a weak-kneed pawn of Mark Hanna, a servant to the tyrant intent on crushing the common man, rather than the tyrant himself. Later historians who worked to rejuvenate McKinley's image, such as Margaret Leech, H. Wayne Morgan, and Lewis Gould, saw him as a critical link between America's past and its future as the country teetered on the precipice of becoming an industrial giant involved in international politics.

These historians objected to both suggestions of the press: that Hanna controlled McKinley and that the Republicans, led by Hanna, were intent on grinding the common man into dust. The evidence they bring to bear suggests that neither characterization was true, but the reporting and the cartoons of the day created a very strong popular image that endures to this day in modern reporting.

The press was important in the 1896 campaign, important in a different way than it is today. In 1896, newspapers worked openly with the political parties and were important parts of candidates' supporting casts. Today, political parties are much weaker and less significant to most people than they once were. The press is now the primary source of information about elections for majority of the public. The news media now serve as the major link between the voters and the political process because the links between the parties and the people have become so weak. The Internet shows promise as a link between the people and the political process, but even in 2008, the Internet was still in its childhood as a political player. In 1896—and 1900—many newspapers openly aligned themselves with either McKinley or his opponent, William Jennings Bryan, although there were many Democratic newspapers that were quieter in 1896 and 1900 than usual because they did not strongly support Bryan.

On McKinley's side, for example, was his home-state newspaper, the *Cleveland Leader*, formerly Mark Hanna's biggest critic. J. B. Morrow became the editor of the *Leader* in 1894. He wrote, "I was a zealous McKinley man. . . . The *Leader* became a thick and thin McKinley newspaper and printed everything that was available in Mr. McKinley's interests."[4] This did not mean, however, as Morrow insisted, that either McKinley or Hanna tried to control what was printed in the *Leader* or any other newspaper. According to Morrow, "Mr. Hanna was not a man to ask favors of the newspapers and never, so far as I could see, cultivated any one. I was editor of the *Leader* throughout his entire public life and I do not think he ever asked me to do him a political favor. He never made any suggestions as to the policy of the paper; never wanted anything printed and never attempted in any way to dictate to me or to any one else as far as I knew."[5] Hanna may not have asked Republican newspapers like the *Leader* for any favors, but that was because he did not need to ask for them. After all, it was unlikely that the *Leader* or any other Republican newspapers would do anything to derail McKinley.

Important eastern publications that favored McKinley included the *New York Tribune,* which was published by Whitelaw Reid, who was such a dedicated Republican that he left the newspaper business in 1892 to run as Benjamin Harrison's vice-presidential nominee; the *New York Times,* which was a Republican newspaper before Adolph Ochs decided at the turn of the twentieth century to make his newspaper the leader in the objective-news movement; and the *New York Evening Post,* published by E. L. Godkin, another Republican-leaning newspaper man. Just as there were strong pro-Republican media, there were also many Democratic-leaning newspapers in New York and along the East Coast, such as the *New York Sun* and Joseph Pulitzer's *New York World.* Despite the fact that there was no shortage of Democratic press outlets in the East, however, very few of them received the news of William Jennings Bryan's nomination for president with enthusiasm. Some traditionally Democratic papers, in fact, were quite harsh in their treatment of Bryan. The ill-feeling for him extended from newspapers to many members of the clergy and many in academia.[6]

In 1896, the only major eastern newspaper that supported Bryan was William Randolph Hearst's *New York Journal.* The Democrats of the East were, for the most part, Democrats of big business. As an outspoken advocate of the free coinage of silver, Bryan was nominated by both the Democrats at their convention in Chicago and, later, by the Populist Party. All of this was anathema to the probusiness Democrats of the East, like the incumbent president Grover Cleveland. While Bryan was strongly supported by Democratic and prosilver Republican newspapers in the Midwest and West, his media allies in the East were few and far between.

Hearst owned the *New York Journal,* a newspaper he bought and quickly turned into one of the strongest in the city by engaging in a cutthroat battle for circulation with Joseph Pulitzer. Among the tricks employed by Hearst, similar to Hanna's steps when he bought the *Cleveland Herald,* was to hire away as many of Pulitzer's staff, at exorbitant salaries, as he could. This maneuver infuriated Pulitzer, much as it had Edwin Cowles when Hanna did it, and precipitated a circulation war of monumental proportions in New York, launching the age of "yellow journalism." The phrase was coined as the circulation battle escalated to the point of the two publishers' stealing each other's cartoonists. When Hearst lured the creator of the "Yellow Kid" cartoon strip away, Pulitzer created another comic with a character who always wore yellow: thus, the phrase "yellow journalism" was born.

Hearst came from a western Democratic family. After a very successful career as a prospector and mine owner, his father, George Hearst, got into politics. In the last years of his life, George was a Democratic senator from California, so William Randolph Hearst's ties to western Democratic ideals were strong. When William Jennings Bryan won the Democratic nomination, he was the first Democratic presidential candidate since 1860 to hail from a state west of Pennsylvania. Hearst was new to the East when Bryan was nominated. He had no natural links with Tammany Hall, the New York Democratic machine that refused to endorse Bryan, but he did have strong ties to the wing of the party that supported Bryan the most enthusiastically.

The issues that concerned southern and western Democrats were very different from those that mobilized eastern Democrats. As Hearst biographer David Nasaw wrote,

> Bryan was not only too young and too inexperienced, he was an outspoken opponent of the trusts and monopoly and too committed to agrarian issues and constituencies to win votes in the cities. His pledge to increase the money supply, deflate the currency, and lower prices by coining silver was anathema to Eastern businessmen and bankers. In the days following Bryan's nomination, Eastern party leaders and newspaper publishers, aghast at the theft of their

party by Western Populists and "free silver" radicals, withdrew all support from Bryan.[7]

When this happened, William Randolph Hearst, the recent transplant from the West, was left as a lifeline for Bryan. When he threw his support behind Bryan, it made the eastern Democratic establishment wonder if Hearst had any sense. Dismay over Hearst's decision to support Bryan also extended to some of his staff.

When Hearst decided to support Bryan, it was against the advice of some of his top editors and managers, who felt that it would be a financial disaster because many advertisers threatened to pull their business if Hearst's publications campaigned for Bryan. Even Alfred Henry Lewis, one of the writers subsequently responsible for some of the most virulent attacks against Hanna and McKinley, was opposed to the decision to support Bryan. Lewis had come to dislike Bryan during his brief career as a member of Congress, but it did not stop him from savaging Hanna and the McKinley campaign. Of course, not everyone in Hearst's organization was opposed to supporting Bryan. For instance, the fiery Scots journalist Arthur McEwen was in favor of supporting Bryan, and he had a significant influence on Hearst's ultimate decision to do so.[8]

According to Hearst's official biographer, Cora Older, during one meeting about what the Hearst newspapers' position should be during the campaign, "Hearst said little. Absent-mindedly he tapped on the window pane while the editors argued. When McEwen advanced his arguments for supporting Bryan, Hearst's gray-blue eyes brightened. After the conference was over Hearst quietly asked McEwen to write an editorial announcing that the *Journal* declared for Bryan and Sewall."[9] After that, Hearst's newspapers became Bryan's loudest allies.

Outside Hearst's organization, the response was unambiguously negative. As Older wrote,

> When the *Journal* declared for Bryan, Pulitzer cheered up. At last, Hearst had made a disastrous mistake. Now the San Francisco men would walk back home. Hearst's own staff agreed with Pulitzer. Editors' conferences were like funerals. They thought their contracts worthless. Deepest of all in gloom was Business Manager Charles M. Palmer. No other paper in New York, or in the entire East supported Bryan. Hearst was called a traitor to his class. To

think of a man born in the purple supporting Bryan. Advertising was withdrawn from the *Journal*. Sane business men would show this young demagogue from California that he couldn't foist a long-haired lunatic like Bryan on the nation and bring about ruinous inflation.[10]

Like Bryan, Hearst was a maverick, though the men were of very different personalities. Bryan was pious and well spoken, while Hearst was socially awkward and morally challenged at times. Further, Hearst was not a strong supporter of Bryan's outspoken advocacy of the free coinage of silver. In the newspaper war he was fighting to win, however, Hearst had a vision, and Bryan fit into it nicely.

Despite the dramatic reaction of the naysayers and his own misgivings about the silver issue, Hearst made a full commitment to Bryan. As Older described, "Hearst was only thirty-three, beating his way along through a maelstrom of business disapproval, but in the storm he sought no safety."[11] Hearst commented about his decision to support Bryan in his publications many years later. He said that the *New York Journal* was "like a solitary ship surrounded and hemmed in by a host of others, and from all sides shot and shell poured into our devoted hulk. Editorial guns raked us, business guns shattered us, popular guns battered us, and above the din and flame of battle rose the curses of Wall Street crowd that hated us. . . . Advertisers called on me and said they would take out every advertisement if I continued to support Bryan, and I told them to take out their advertisements, as I needed more space in which to support Bryan."[12] Hearst's word, of course, is the only account of whether he actually ever told angry advertisers he was happy to have their space for more Bryan news, but he clearly acted with something other than the immediate financial health of his newspaper in mind. His business manager, Charles M. Palmer, reported that the paper was losing one hundred thousand dollars a month due to the decision to support Bryan.[13]

When Hearst jumped in with Bryan, he did so with both feet. As David Nasaw described, "With unmatched energy and skill, Hearst concentrated his newspapers' resources on the task of winning voters to Bryan by ridiculing his Republican opponents."[14] Hearst offered, on the pages of his newspapers, to make matching contributions for Bryan's campaign dollar for dollar and ran an appeal for Bryan campaign funds on his papers' editorial pages.

Hearst had reporters and illustrators on the trail with Bryan continuously. During the campaign, his papers were filled, day after day, with material in support of Bryan and attacking McKinley, though in truth the attacks were usually against Hanna as a surrogate for McKinley. McKinley's tremendous personal popularity was exalting to Hanna, but it also meant that he got most of Hearst's venom during the campaign of 1896 and the subsequent years of McKinley's presidency. As the Republican nominee, William McKinley was a target for the Democratic press, but, as stated previously, he was a popular man with a benign image that was very difficult to attack. Rather than vilify McKinley personally, a tactic that could have backfired, Hearst and his staffers chose to attack him indirectly, suggesting that he was little more than a puppet in the hands of Mark Hanna who was, in turn, depicted as the embodiment of the evils of big business, doing the bidding of "the Trusts."

Hearst published a free weekly edition about the campaign, and he started the evening edition of the *New York Journal* at this time as a way of publishing more about the election; much of that material took the form of aggressive treatment of Hanna.[15] As Older described, "Day after day, week after week, Julian Hawthorn, Alfred Henry Lewis, Arthur McEwen, and Henry George attacked Hanna, the trusts and Wall Street. McKinley, whose personal debts had been underwritten by Hanna and some of his friends, was called the 'Syndicate-Owned Candidate.'"[16] The attacks, while generally suggesting that McKinley was the wrong man for the job, did not attack him in a mean-spirited way. The vast quantities of venom were reserved for Hanna.

The question, of course, is what motivated Hearst to support Bryan in such an enthusiastic way? Since Bryan did not have the support of the eastern Democratic establishment, he seemed to have little chance of winning, and, on the surface, it made little sense for Hearst to expose his New York newspaper to criticism and trouble with advertisers. Some cynics no doubt believed that Hearst supported Bryan because the Hearst family fortune was based in mining. Bryan advocated the free coinage of silver; therefore, the Hearst family must have stood to gain millions from their silver mines. Hearst biographer Nasaw debunked this claim, pointing out that the Hearst family had far greater interest in gold mines than it did in silver mines and that, if Bryan's plan were to come to fruition, the family actually stood to lose a great deal of money.[17]

More plausible is that Hearst understood that if no other publishers endorsed Bryan while he did, it would open the door to greatly increased circulation as people sought news about the candidate. Herbert Croly, for example, saw Hearst's decision to take Bryan's side and to cover the Republicans in very negative terms as a symptom of Hearst's quest for circulation:

> The peculiar malignancy of these attacks was due partly to certain undesirable innovations which had recently appeared in American journalism. Mr. William R. Hearst was beginning his career as a political yellow journalist. He was the first newspaper publisher to divine how much of an opportunity had been offered to sensational journalism by the increasing economic and political power of American wealth; and he divined also that the best way to use the opportunity would be to attach individual responsibility to the worst aspects of a system. The system must be concentrated in a few conspicuous individual examples, and they must be ferociously abused and persistently vilified. The campaign of 1896 offered a rare chance to put this discovery into practice, and inevitably Mr. McKinley and Mr. Hanna, as the most conspicuous Republican leaders, were selected as the best victims of assault.[18]

To Croly, Hearst attacked McKinley and, particularly, Hanna for financial gain—nothing more or less.

According to Bryan's biographer Louis Koenig, Bryan was in part responsible for convincing Hearst that he could make money as the only eastern publisher supporting him. Koenig wrote that after Bryan was nominated,

> Among the first reporters to reach Bryan was Willis J. Abbot, his friend on the Hearst staff. Bryan, painfully aware that the press would be arrayed overwhelmingly against him, grasped at this straw of potential support. . . . They discussed the fact that while Abbot's employer, Hearst, had up to this point opposed free silver, he was aspiring to build up a great newspaper in New York City, the *Morning Journal*. Willis was seized with the inspiration that since most, if not all, important New York and Eastern papers would oppose silver, the *Journal*, if it supported the cause, might in one jump become the leading

Democratic paper of the East, with the joyous prospect of a
swift rise in circulation. Bryan was titillated by the plan . . .
and . . . he helped Willis prepare a comprehensive telegram to
Hearst. Hearst soon threw in with the silver cause.[19]

Circulation did, in fact, go up a great deal due to the newspaper's support
of Bryan. As the only major paper on the East Coast supporting him,
huge numbers of copies of the *Journal* were shipped to New England,
Pennsylvania, and Maryland. Many others subscribed to the paper by
mail. As Hearst biographer Cora Older wrote, "The business office
of the *Journal* despaired. But into the circulation department came a
deluge. . . . Never did a newspaper make such rapid growth."[20]

When the *Evening Journal* was born during the campaign, it quickly
ballooned to a circulation of more than five hundred thousand readers.
Following the campaign, Hearst tried to make the most out of the fact
that he was the lone publisher in the East brave enough to stick his neck
out for Bryan. As Older wrote, "Hearst's losses were appalling, and yet
he would not yield to fear. This steadfastness and courage established his
popularity with the masses."[21] Of course, as Hearst's authorized biographer, Older was inclined to put a glowing sheen on his reputation. Hearst's
decision to support Bryan was a business choice to try to exploit a niche
no one else was filling. He lost money, but it helped him build readership
for the *New York Journal,* the most prominent publication in his chain.

The shallowness of Hearst's commitment to free silver was evidenced
by the fact that, after the campaign of 1896, he quickly retreated from
his advocacy of bimetallism. In fact, he started to reject Bryan's requests for space to publish prosilver articles. Koenig reported that
"Abbot, explaining one rejection by the Great Chief of a proffered
Bryan article on silver, pointed out that while the gains in circulation
were gratifying, it was now necessary to coax back the advertisers
that had been driven away. 'Personally,' Abbot added soothingly, 'I
think other qualities of the paper repel advertisers, but Hearst is inclined
to charge all to the silver issue in which he never was a believer.'"[22]
Older's praise for Hearst's courage and conviction aside, his choice to
support Bryan appears to have been a coldly calculated business decision, and when Bryan ran a second time in 1900, Hearst endorsed
him again and was his most active supporter in the press.

William Jennings Bryan's most important supporter in 1896 and
1900 was unambiguously William Randolph Hearst. Not only did Hearst

support him unequivocally on the pages of his newspapers—during the campaigns, if not between them—he started two new newspapers, first the evening edition of the *New York Journal,* and, on July 4, 1900, at the beginning of Bryan's second campaign, the *Chicago American* to fight for Bryan. For all the talk of biased news today, it does not hold a candle to the freewheeling days of the campaigns of 1896 and 1900. Fox News may, in fact, have a strong predilection for conservative politics, and the *New York Times* may lean a little to the left; but they bear no resemblance to the hardball partisan politics that used to fill the pages of America's great newspapers.

The enduring image of Hanna from the cartoons of Homer Davenport and Frederick Opper is of a corpulent man, controlling a childlike McKinley. For Davenport, Hanna was usually dressed in a suit covered with dollar signs. Opper often depicted him as McKinley's nursemaid. The only figures bigger than Hanna in the cartoons were the malevolently drawn titans of Wall Street, usually combined in one behemoth, labeled "the Trusts," as can be seen in the Opper cartoon (see figure 5.3) from the 1900 election.

Cartoonist Homer Davenport, originally hired by Hearst to work for his *San Francisco Examiner,* went east to the *New York Journal* and spent much of his time there antagonizing Mark Hanna. When, in 1898, a book of Davenport's cartoons was released, the *Journal's* editorialist Arthur McEwen commemorated the publication with a column, writing,

> It is a fine, large book, beautifully printed and bound, and will give malign pleasure to the anarchistic hordes whose efforts to undermine the foundations of our Christian civilization render Presidential and Senatorial elections so annoyingly expensive. We have President McKinley's word for it that the best citizenship of the country, regardless of party, was made happy by the triumph of Senator Hanna at Columbus, and it is certain that nobody who shared the President's pure joy in that notable victory of sound money can take satisfaction in this book, which is largely devoted to making Mr. Hanna's life miserable by telling the truth about him. . . . Davenport's Hanna is not a surface portrait. The photograph of the President's closest friend and ablest co-worker shows a well-groomed, shrewd-faced, presentable person. Yet the caricature so hits off his characteristic points

FIGURE 5.3. "If Willie is a good boy, and minds Papa and Nursie, they will try to let him keep the pretty house until he is eight years old." Cartoon by Frederick Opper, *New York Journal*, 1900, 1

of feature and build that the stranger on seeing the breathing Hanna, bustling, assured, self-approving and contented, recognizes him instantly and perceives the justification for the jowls, the physical grossness, the aspect of moral obtuseness and the dollar-mark convict suit of the cartoons.[23]

Horace Traubel, who is best known for a multivolume biography of the last years of Walt Whitman's life, wrote the foreword for Davenport's second book of collected cartoons. Traubel exuded praise for Davenport:

Davenport is not personal either in motive or effect. He may incidentally take account of the personal equation, but if he does so it will be out of deference to and not by the sacrifice of a supreme principle. He is above, in the free air, and below, with roots, as well as on the earth, with its ravaging trade and the flare of its foppery. That is no doubt why Bryan has said in a letter to me: "Davenport stands at the head of his profession." Davenport does not live at the point of his pen. He lives up his arm, in dynamic sympathy.[24]

Davenport's image of Hanna in a suit covered with dollar signs remains an iconic view of the man to this day, though Bryan biographer Koenig was less than effusive in his comments about Davenport. Koenig wrote, "A circus hand in his youth, Davenport drew with a free line and with telling force but was handicapped by the utter bareness of his imagination. Left to himself, he was apt to produce some variation of the American eagle and depended on resourceful editors to keep him supplied with ideas."[25] Whoever supplied the ideas, however, the cartoons by Davenport and, later, Frederick Opper continue to inform America's image of Mark Hanna.

Unsurprisingly, Hanna and his allies did not see Davenport or the rest of the Hearst machine in the same glowing light as did McEwen and Traubel. Hanna's chief antagonist in print was Alfred Henry Lewis. Hanna's biographer Croly was offended on Hanna's behalf about how Hearst's and other Democratic publications treated him. Croly wrote,

> The personal attack on Mark Hanna was begun somewhat before Mr. McKinley's nomination. . . . Later the personal attack upon him was reduced to a system. For a while Mr. Lewis appears to have been stationed in Cleveland in order to tell lies about him. He was depicted as a monster of sordid and ruthless selfishness, who fattened himself and other men on the flesh and blood of the common people. This picture of the man was stamped sharply on the popular consciousness by the powerful but brutal caricatures of Homer Davenport. Day after day he was portrayed with perverted ability and ingenuity as a Beast of Greed, until little by little a certain section of public opinion became infected by the poison.[26]

To Croly, the portrayal of Hanna was an unacceptable perversion of a dedicated public servant.

Homer Davenport was for a time a very famous man, made wealthy by his work as Hearst's cartoonist. At the height of his career, he made twenty-five thousand dollars a year, the same as the president of the United States.[27] He was a passionate horseman who owned and bred horses. He became very interested in Arabian horses when he saw them at the Chicago World's Fair in 1893. His money and fame eventually allowed him the opportunity to take an odyssey of a trip to the Syrian desert in search of a full-blooded Arabian horse to bring back to the United States.[28] He was one of the first American breeders of Arabian horses. Fame and money were not enough to prevent him from getting pneumonia, however, which killed him at the age of 45.[29]

What effect, if any, did harsh treatment in the press have on Hanna? He claimed, for the most part, to be immune to criticism from the press. J. B. Morrow wrote, "Persons who did not know him thought him to be arrogant and selfish because they had seen him so described in public print. It can be said that Mr. Hanna pursued his course regardless of local criticism and so far as I know never took occasion to deny any untruth that was printed about him."[30] However, the treatment Hanna received at the hands of the much more partisan press of the Gilded Age was brutal and unrelenting, and he was not as immune as he liked his critics to believe.

While there were few cracks in Hanna's public persona, comments he made to friends and associates showed that he was piqued by the intense criticism he received in the press, despite his understanding that it was motivated by partisanship in an era of subjective media. The ceaseless negative coverage he received in the Democratic media very clearly had an impact on him. While it may be true, as Morrow argued, that Hanna did little or nothing to counteract the negative coverage he received in the press, he was not entirely immune to it. His personal secretary, Elmer Dover, spoke generally of Hanna's feeling about the press in an interview after his death: "He liked the newspapers to approve of what he had been doing; he liked to have his public conduct indorsed [*sic*], but he did not care to have his personality conspicuous in the public print. . . . He did not like to be condemned unjustly nor was he pleased with complimentary articles which he knew were not true."[31] Senator Nathan B. Scott of West Virginia, who served in the McKinley administration for a time as the commissioner of internal revenue, related a story of how hurt Hanna was by the attacks in the press. He was particularly hurt by the hands of the cartoonists, like Homer Davenport and Frederick Opper, who portrayed him in an extremely unflattering light. Scott said, "I'll never forget one morning during the campaign of 1896 when Hanna handed me a New York paper containing a cartoon of himself pictured as a huge monster, clad in a suit covered over with dollar marks, smoking an immense cigar, and trampling under foot women and children until their eyes protruded from the sockets and their skeleton forms writhed in agony. After I had looked at it for a moment he said to me, 'That hurts.'"[32] Hanna might not have responded publicly to the vitriol heaped on him by the press, but it did not go unnoticed by him.

The exaggeration of his physical appearance seems to have been particularly hurtful to Hanna, as an anecdote from J. B. Morrow demonstrated. Morrow told the story of yet another political cartoon that was no less negative in assuming that Hanna was the real power in the White House, but which put him in a much more positive personal light. Morrow said,

> He asked me if I had recently seen a cartoon in a publication called *Life,* in which he was represented as an English gentleman, tall and robust, and McKinley was pictured at his side as a page dressed in a short coat and knee breeches. The title of the picture was "Buttons." The cartoon pleased Mr. Hanna immensely. His pleasure was not because McKinley was represented as a serving boy, but the humor of it appealed to him. Moreover, it was so different from the ordinary cartoon to which he had been accustomed. He had been represented during the campaign of 1896 as a brutal boss, covered with dollar marks, and here was something approaching decency which he rather enjoyed.[33]

His protests to the contrary notwithstanding; Hanna was clearly affected by the things that were written and, especially, drawn about him. When the image was less unattractive, as in Morrow's story, the underlying message, though unchanged, was less hurtful to him. Understanding the impact he had on Hanna, Davenport once drew a cartoon aimed directly at Hanna's anger about the way he caricatured him.

FIGURE 5.4. Mark Hanna as he is and as Davenport made him. Cartoon by Homer Davenport, reprinted in "The Personal Narratives of Homer Davenport: An Interview with the Famous Cartoonist," *Pacific Monthly*, December 1905, 524

FIGURE 5.5. As he would like to be cartooned. Cartoon by Homer Davenport, reprinted in "The Personal Narratives of Homer Davenport: An Interview with the Famous Cartoonist," *Pacific Monthly*, December 1905, 525

According to Croly, the attacks in Hearst's publications were so brutal and unfair in Hanna's own estimation that, for a time, he wanted to take legal action. In 1896, he considered filing libel suits against William Randolph Hearst and his reporter Alfred Henry Lewis, but backed off when he was convinced that a public reaction was exactly what Hearst and Lewis were hoping for. Legal action would have allowed them to claim Hanna was exactly what they said he was: a bully who used fear and intimidation to make sure his point of view was the only one that mattered. Croly wrote of Hanna's treatment by Hearst and other Democratically oriented media outlets in some detail: "He became the victim of a series of personal attacks, which for their persistence, their falsity and their malignancy have rarely been equaled in the history of political invective. Mark Hanna was quoted and pictured to his fellow-countrymen as a sinister, corrupt type of the Money-man in politics—unscrupulous, inhumanly selfish, the sweater of his own employees, the relentless enemy of organized labor, the besotted plutocrat, the incarnate dollar-mark."[34] The picture of Hanna that bothered him so much had great staying power. This image of him, crafted in an era of partisan journalism, endured beyond the presidential campaigns of 2000 and 2004.

A large part of the problem with the news media's coverage of politics is that reporters, producers, and editors often have a very limited sense of history. For many, studying history means looking back through their archives to see what happened ten, fifteen, or maybe as much as thirty years ago. When a newsmaker like Karl Rove repeatedly brought up William McKinley and the election of 1896 during the campaign of 2000, it is likely that most reporters did a quick Internet search on McKinley, found references to Mark Hanna, and made the most of an interesting version of events—an American president working at the behest of a shadowy money man who put him in office. The parallels between Hanna-McKinley and Rove-Bush were irresistible regardless of the facts.

Such comparisons were certainly relevant because Rove himself invited them by bringing up the McKinley era so often. However, if reporters were going to report the comparisons, they owed it to their readers and viewers to do so responsibly by actually learning something about the fin-de-siècle Republican and Democratic parties they compared to the modern versions and about Hanna and McKinley.

The stories of 1999 and 2000 treated the Republican Party as if it had been always the party of big business. They also treated the Democratic Party as if it had been always the party of enlightened, progressive leadership. Painting the Republican Party of 1896 and the Republican party of 2000 with the same brush ignored the history of the party before 1896 and during the years in which Teddy Roosevelt occupied the White House. Neither party is the same as it once was, but few modern journalists, who are charged with the responsibility of making sense of politics for the rest of us, seem to be aware of the differences when they refer to the past in a misguided effort to make sense of the present.

Having assessed coverage of the campaign of 1896 from the perspective of many of the journalists who covered it in 1896 and from the perspective of journalists who looked back at it from the campaign of 2000, it is appropriate to examine the real campaign of 1896, the subsequent presidency of William McKinley, and the role Mark Hanna played in each.

CHAPTER SIX

The Campaign of 1896—
The Issues, McKinley, and Hanna

he presidential campaign of 1896 is one of the most examined elections in United States history. In 1896, the country faced big questions in both the domestic- and foreign-policy arenas. Domestically, the country suffered from a severely depressed economy begun by the Panic of 1893. The causes of the panic were complicated, though the triggering event is generally considered to be the collapse of the National Cordage Company in May 1893. Creditors called in their loans to the company on the suspicion that it was failing, and it became a self-fulfilling prophecy. When the company, whose stock was very actively traded at the time, failed, it set off a stampede of financial panic. The subsequent failures of many other businesses and banks accelerated the rapid decline of the economy. Low public confidence in the government and the economy was a major issue as the value of the gold-based currency dropped. Some elements of the population, particularly the farmers who made up a large part of the Populist movement, clamored for the government to put more money in circulation, backed by the more plentiful metal, silver. The farmers argued that there simply was not enough money for them to pay their bills and prevent losing their farms to the banks. On the other side, the business community feared that rapid inflation would result from artificially increasing the amount of currency in circulation by switching away from a gold-only standard.

Even as the campaign was occurring, many people sensed its historical importance because it constituted a fight over substantive ideas about the economy and the future of the American people. In fact, the campaign of 1896 provided one of the most superheated debates on issues in American political memory. Judging from the mass rallies that took place on behalf of both candidates in 1896, it is clear that many citizens were energized by the currency issue that William Jennings Bryan focused on almost to the exclusion of any other issues, and it became the dominant policy debate of the campaign. But before Bryan took over the campaign's agenda, McKinley was ready with a policy agenda of his own. Although he was forced by Bryan to address the currency issue, he stubbornly held on to his own issues; by the end of the campaign, Bryan addressed them, only to find he was doing too little, too late.

In 1896, the United States also faced questions of foreign policy that involved specific concerns and a broader uncertainty of what the country's role in the world should be. As the nineteenth century drew to a close, many in the United States debated whether the country should take its place as a world power, influencing global politics, or should remain relatively isolated from international affairs. In more specific terms, the country faced a growing question of what to do, if anything, about the oppressive rule of Cuba by the Spanish government. The yellow press, particularly the newspapers of William Randolph Hearst and Joseph Pulitzer, sensationalized Spain's treatment of the Cubans and pressured the government, suggesting America had a moral obligation to help the downtrodden people of the island country.

The incumbent Cleveland administration wanted to avoid war with Spain, in large measure because the business community, to which it was closely linked, wanted peace. Cleveland's diplomatic efforts were received with outrage by many critics in the press. During the campaign of 1896, William McKinley favored Cleveland's approach and leaned against a greater international role for the country. Before William Jennings Bryan's nomination as the Democratic candidate, McKinley planned to make protectionism his major issue in the election. While the farmers and Populists blamed the panic on the currency situation, McKinley and many in the business community blamed foreign competition for America's economic woes. Early in the campaign, McKinley's team dubbed him the "advance agent for prosperity," hoping to sell his economic ideas. As the campaign wore on, Bryan's nearly exclusive focus on the currency question forced McKinley to address the issue in great detail, but even then he continued to talk tariffs.

McKinley's enthusiasm for tariffs, which he saw as a way to protect American industry, became a part of his legacy that critics often cite as one of his many flaws. In an article from 2002, an interesting argument was made about the Bush administration's tax plans. The article was written by Robert S. McIntyre, director of the group Citizens for Tax Justice. McIntyre used his "Taxonimist" column in the political monthly the *American Prospect* to express concern that the Bush administration would push for a national sales tax, known as a value-added tax (VAT), to allow for the reduction, or even elimination, of the graduated income tax. He wrote,

> Prior to the twentieth century, except under Abraham Lincoln, the federal government relied almost entirely on regressive consumption taxes to pay its bills. This system of high taxes on the poor and middle class and hardly any tax burden on the rich and powerful reached its apotheosis under Republican President William McKinley, who worked with GOP political boss (and Karl Rove hero) Mark Hanna to raise consumption taxes to almost 50 percent on many ordinary commodities in the 1897 tariff bill.[1]

McIntyre's basic objection to sales taxes as regressive, in which the rate of taxation is the same for everyone, regardless of ability to pay the tax, is a common argument against so-called "flat" income taxes and national sales taxes. After all, having to pay 9 percent sales tax on a jug of milk at the grocery store represents a much larger proportion of the real income of someone who makes minimum wage than it does for someone who makes seventy-five thousand dollars a year. The power of McIntyre's argument, however, was diminished by his poor use of McKinley as an example of someone who supported regressive taxes. The image of McKinley and Hanna that McIntyre presented was the same inaccurate image that was popularized by the Hearst newspapers.

What McIntyre referred to in his piece was the Dingley Act of 1897, which was tariff legislation. During the Gilded Age, Democrats typically objected to tariffs, while Republicans typically supported them.

McKinley might be fairly labeled a protectionist, but he lived in an era when tariffs seemed necessary to protect American industry in a world that was quickly opening to international trade. Furthermore, McKinley was far from the most rabid protectionist that the Republicans had to offer. The real driving force behind the Dingley Act was the leaders of the Republican Congress, not McKinley as McIntyre asserted in his piece. If anything, McKinley served as a restraint on the final legislation. Three major biographers of McKinley—Margaret Leech, H. Wayne Morgan, and Lewis Gould—were of one mind on McKinley's position on the Dingley Act: he was reluctant to get involved at all and wanted to make sure that reciprocity clauses were included in the legislation to lessen the backlash the act could otherwise be expected to generate.[2]

Reciprocity clauses ensured that if other countries allowed certain American goods to enter their borders without being assessed damaging tariffs, then the United States would allow that country's goods to enter at a similarly low tariff rate. If anything, McKinley tried to slow down the eager protectionists among the Republican ranks in Congress. As Gould observed, "For McKinley the specific rates in the Dingley Act were less important than the possibility for negotiating reductions in the future, which the reciprocity clauses offered."[3] Furthermore, though McIntyre's analysis would seem to indicate otherwise, the tariff act was not very controversial after its passage. Unlike the McKinley Act, which cost the Republicans dearly at the voting booth in 1892, the passage of the Dingley Act coincided with the country's emergence from the depths of the economic Panic of 1893, and the Republicans were quite happy to take credit for the economic recovery and suffered few recriminations for the new tariffs.

As for his insinuation of "Karl Rove hero" Mark Hanna into the discussion of the Dingley Act, there is little or no evidence presented by any of the three previously mentioned biographers that Hanna was involved in any significant way in the Dingley Act's passage, either at the president's behest or on his own. In his biography of Hanna, Herbert D. Croly noted that there was simply no evidence about what Hanna's role might have been: "Senator Hanna, of course, warmly approved the changes proposed by the bill, but just how much influence he had upon its details cannot be traced by any public indications. He was not a member of the Finance Committee, and not once did he open his mouth during the public discussion of the schedules."[4] Croly quoted Foraker as giving great credit to Hanna for his role in the passage of the Dingley Act in the Senate; but that is about the only evidence that Hanna took any action to ensure its passage, and anything Foraker said about Hanna must be consumed with caution. Any influence Hanna may have had was behind the scenes, so it is a mystery as to why McIntyre referred to him. The only reason, it would seem, and this is evidenced by McIntyre's turn of phrase, referring to Hanna as "Karl Rove hero," was to continue to link Rove with the worst historical picture of Mark Hanna. Whatever may or may not be true about Karl Rove—and history will be his true judge—there are simply no grounds for painting Hanna with the brush that McIntyre painted him with.

The campaign of 1896 was of a kind not often seen in the era of politics dominated by television, in which the public was actively engaged in enthusiastic efforts by supporters of both candidates.[5] It was also a campaign in which the clashing of serious ideas about policy dominated the battle between McKinley and Bryan.

A persistent image of the relationship between Hanna and McKinley, presented by the nineteenth-century press and reiterated by modern journalists, was that Hanna controlled everything McKinley did as a candidate and as president. However, rather than Hanna's profiting tremendously from his relationship with McKinley, Croly argued that he sacrificed much to devote himself to McKinley's success, which is further evidence that belies the argument that he was motivated by personal greed. Croly argued that Hanna sincerely believed that McKinley's election to the presidency guaranteed a return to economic prosperity for the nation. The biographer characterized Hanna's decision to retire from business and devote his full energy to politics as a personal sacrifice for the betterment of the country:

> For fourteen years he had been a business man with incidental political interests. Now that business prosperity itself was dependent in his opinion on the political triumph of his party, and the work of nominating his friend was reaching a critical phase, Mr. Hanna decided to become a politician with incident business interests. He decided to sacrifice his own business career and his chance of greater personal wealth to

the opportunities and responsibilities of an increasing participation in politics.[6]

What many journalists reported about Hanna's alleged control of McKinley bore little resemblance to scholarly research on the relationship between the two men. Gould, for example, wrote,

> Because he had so many friends, McKinley faced the charge that he had no firm convictions and that he gained affection and popularity by being weak and compliant. . . . Buttressing the apparent impression of McKinley as the instrument of the will of others was his friendship with the Cleveland industrialist Marcus A. Hanna. . . . The relationship was easily caricatured in contemporary cartoons, and the notion lingers that Hanna made McKinley president when, in fact, the politician used the businessman to reach the White House. . . . McKinley needed the organizational skills and fund-raising ability that Hanna brought to politics. Their intimacy was always a political rather than a personal one, however; there were lines of behavior that Hanna knew he must never cross.[7]

In Gould's interpretation of McKinley's presidency, Hanna was a far less important figure in that administration than the public perceived him to be. The public's perception of him, of course, came from the news media. Even coverage of Hanna in the Republican press emphasized his powerful influence in the administration, and modern conservative journalists cautioned about drawing too many parallels between the two eras.

In 1919, several years after the deaths of McKinley and Hanna, a poem, famous in its time and notable for its criticism of the two men and for its adulation of William Jennings Bryan, was written by a poet from Springfield, Illinois, Vachel Lindsay. The poem, "Bryan, Bryan, Bryan, Bryan," was a romanticized lament for Bryan, the president who would have been if not for Mark Hanna. Author Mark Harris wrote what he described as an "interpretative biography" of Lindsay, called *City of Discontent*. In it, he described the moment in which Lindsay, traveling with his mother, was inspired to write about Bryan and the campaign of 1896:

He thinks back to the past, to the times when in the midst of people there were rejoicings within him, and everybody felt rejoicings, and then it fled and the mood of the instant was gone: he might write of the time when Bryan came and the world seemed about to take one forward step and then it never took it because Bryan went away on the railroad and the mood was not sustained. If one could write a great Bryan poem full of all the shouting and the hopeful singing and the cheering! Then every time a person needed to he could pick up the poem and get in a Bryan mood again.[8]

Later, still traveling with his mother, Lindsay read a newspaper account of Woodrow Wilson's return from Europe at the end of World War I and his announcement that he would travel across the country to promote his plan for the League of Nations. Harris wrote, "Wilson will go to the people because the people's servants in Washington are no longer a part of the people, because something happens to a man when he becomes a senator, and he forgets his October promise. . . . And Vachel thinks now of Bryan who lost yet never really lost, lost only the office McKinley won the office and McKinley is forgotten and Bryan but beginning to be remembered, and McKinley lived in the office and Bryan lived and still lives in the heart and brain of the people in mankind."[9] For Lindsay, Bryan was an idyllic figure, a martyr to the realities of the political system. One biographer of Lindsay, Ann Massa, wrote of Bryan and Lindsay's poem about him:

No definitive historical decision has been handed down on Bryan's political acumen and intellectual ability. . . . Certainly, in 1896, the apparent lack of an informed and practical structure behind his rhetoric made his power to convince coterminous with his presence. His speeches were even more unspecific and emotional than was usual in American presidential campaigns. Nevertheless, the Cross of Gold Speech, and Bryan's presence had a comforting and inspiring impact on millions of Americans. . . . Lindsay saw and heard him in Springfield in 1896 and reproduced his impact.[10]

For Lindsay, witnessing the Bryan of 1896 was a glorious moment of his youth. When Lindsay wrote the poem many years later, in 1920, Bryan was no longer the charismatic thirty-six-year-old he was during the campaign of 1896.[11] To Vachel Lindsay, the campaign of 1896 represented both great promise and everything that was wrong about politics and America. In the fourth stanza of his poem, Lindsay reiterated a Hearstian view of Hanna's campaign tactics, repeating the still-fresh impression that without Hanna's demagoguery, spreading fear and cash around the country, McKinley would never have been president. Lindsay wrote:

> July, August, suspense.
> Wall Street lost to sense.
> August, September, October,
> More Suspense,
> And the whole East down like a wind-smashed
> Fence.
>
> Then Hanna to the rescue,
> Hanna of Ohio,
> Rallying the roller-tops,
> Rallying the bucket-shops,
> Threatening drouth and death,
> Promising manna,
> Rallying the trusts against the bawling
> Flannelmouth;
> Invading misers' cellars,
> Tin-cans, socks,
> Melting down the rocks,
> Pouring out the long green to a million workers,
> Spondulix by the mountain-load, to stop each
> Tornado
> And beat the cheapskate, blatherskite,
> Populistic, anarchistic,
> Deacon-desperado.[12]

Like the pages of Heart's newspapers, Lindsay's poem was full of accusation and anger that Hanna had hijacked the election. Like Hearst's journalists and many journalists in 2000, Lindsay gave Hanna too much credit. There is a sense of outrage in Lindsay's writing—how could Hanna lure these voters out of their rightful camp? In the sixth stanza, Lindsay wrote of Hanna's power over McKinley:

Where is McKinley, Mark Hanna's McKinley,
His slave, his echo, his suit of clothes?
Gone to join the shadows, with the pomps of that Time.
And the flame of that summer's prairie rose.

Where is Cleveland whom the Democratic Platform
Read from the party in a glorious hour,
Gone to join the shadows with pitchfork Tillman,
And sledge-hammer Altgeld who wrecked hispower.

Where is Hanna, Bulldog Hanna,
Low-browed Hanna, who said: "Stand pat"?
Gone to his place with old Pierpont Morgan,
Gone somewhere . . . with lean rat Platte.

Where is Roosevelt, the young dude cowboy,
Who hated Bryan, hen aped his way?
Gone to join the shadows with mighty Cromwell
And tall King Saul, till the Judgment day.

Where is Altgeld, brave as the truth,
Whose name the few still say with tears?
Gone to join the ironies with Old John Brown,
Whose fame rings loud for a thousand years.

Where is that boy, that Heaven-born Bryan,
That Homer Bryan, who sang for the West?
Gone to join the shadows with Altgeld the Eagle,
Where the kings and the slaves and the troubadours rest.

While Lindsay has faded from memory for most Americans, he was very well known in his day, touring the country and giving dramatic readings of his work. His characterization of McKinley as Hanna's slave and suit of clothes reiterated many people's perception of the relationship between the two men. The sixth stanza made Lindsay's impression of Hanna clear. Lindsay played on a common memory of Hanna, that he was the Neanderthal of American politics, a bully who stole the election from Bryan with brute force so he could install his puppet in the presidency. However, the image Lindsay invokes does not withstand scrutiny.

William McKinley served two terms as Ohio's governor, from 1891 to 1895. During his time as governor, the Republican Party's strength was rebuilt in the Buckeye State. As governor, McKinley oversaw a restructuring of the state's tax system and the creation of a state labor-relations board. Also as governor, McKinley experienced a personal crisis that had a significant impact on his legacy if not his political career. In 1893, he was bankrupt and owed roughly one hundred thirty thousand dollars to creditors, due to the actions of a disreputable friend who used McKinley's name to guarantee loans for failing business ventures.

It was a potential public-relations disaster, and McKinley's initial, if short-lived reaction was to tell his friends that he would retire from politics and work as a lawyer to repay his debts. It was the type of event that would have ended the careers of many other politicians, but not many politicians were as well liked, locally and nationally, as McKinley. He was viewed by many as the potential savior of the Republican Party. His friends convinced him not to resign and arranged a syndicate to repay his debts. With the efforts of a group of men led by Canton lawyer William R. Day; Cleveland banker Myron T. Herrick; H. H. Kohlsaat, a Republican newspaper man from the *Chicago Times-Herald* (and a confidant of many prominent turn-of-the-century Republican politicians); and Mark Hanna, McKinley was bailed out of his personal financial crisis and a possible career-ending public-relations disaster. It is important to note that the syndicate was not created by Hanna, who was not even in Ohio when the crisis broke. If McKinley's success was owed to someone other than himself, it was owed to many.

In one sense, the bankruptcy that nearly ended McKinley's career had little practical impact. If anything, his financial troubles made him more of a man of the people at a time when most were experiencing financial difficulty, due to the Panic of 1893. For many voters, McKinley's financial troubles made him more human.

From a historical perspective, however, his bankruptcy and the fact that he was bailed out by wealthy friends were damaging to his legacy. There were continual derisive references to the bailout in the cartoons of Homer Davenport on the pages of William Randolph Hearst's newspapers, which usually depicted McKinley with collar and chain around his neck with the phrase "Syndicate" written on the collar; or with a ball and chain around his ankle, referring to the money paid by his friends to

FIGURE 6.1. A man of Mark. Cartoon by Homer Davenport, *New York Journal*, 1896, 9

pay his debts. The ball and chain, in addition to the fact that McKinley was always depicted as a young child, subservient to the powerful adults of business and finance, contributed greatly to the lasting impression of McKinley as a president who was never his own man.

At the time, the role Mark Hanna played in the campaigns and the presidency of William McKinley was lauded by supporters of the Republican Party and lambasted by its critics. He clearly contributed in a significant financial way to McKinley's gubernatorial campaigns, though his efforts on John Sherman's behalf were a distraction. Hanna's "real" role and impact have been debated through the years by a number of historians, much as McKinley's legacy has been a subject

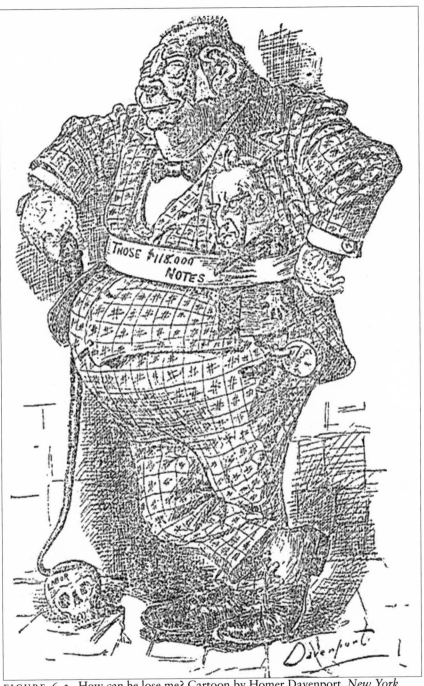

FIGURE 6.2. How can he lose me? Cartoon by Homer Davenport, *New York Journal*, October 18, 1896, 1

for disagreement. Many of the first scholars to write about McKinley's presidency were clearly influenced by his bad press and were dismissive of his administration, suggesting he was a captive of his powerful keeper, Mark Hanna, who in turn did the bidding of titans who controlled "the Trusts." Later scholars, like Leech, Morgan, and Gould, argued convincingly that McKinley was a crafty politician who was his own greatest asset. These historians all argued that McKinley knew how to bring Hanna into the circle when it suited him and to push him out when it was advantageous to create some distance. Despite this more positive academic view of McKinley, the twenty-fifth president's image that survives in popular culture is of a weak man controlled by Hanna and the political opportunists Hanna represented. The evidence, however, shows that McKinley was a skilled politician who made his reputation as a public man and member of Congress long before Mark Hanna became an important political ally.

Even during the campaign of 1896, which Hanna is widely credited with masterminding, McKinley was very much in charge. As Stanley Jones wrote,

> The popularly accepted picture of Hanna's domination was not true. Though McKinley did leave to Hanna the immensely complicated and exceedingly arduous task of organizing the campaign and though he usually deferred to Hanna's judgment in this area, he himself retained control of the general structure and program. Nothing was done without his approval. Hanna raised money, hired men, set up headquarters offices, bought literature, with the same drive and skill that he managed his business. He was confident of his mastery of that kind of operation, but he never ceased to defer to McKinley's mastery of the grand strategy of politics.[13]

Accusations about Hanna's use of McKinley to do the bidding of other powerful politicos simply do not hold up to scrutiny.

Just as some people in 1896 thought Hanna was too powerful, there were others who felt he received far more than his fair share of the credit for McKinley's success. Some of the most biting comments were from fellow Republican Joseph Foraker, Hanna's rival from Ohio, who diminished the importance of Hanna's performance as the chairman of McKinley's 1896 campaign:

I did not realize that this office and this work had given him the prominence and the influence he had acquired, for at that time it seemed to me that, with the New York *World*, the New York *Post*, the Philadelphia *Times*, the Philadelphia *Record*, the New York *Sun*, and fully one-half the leading Democratic and independent newspapers of the country bolting Bryan and supporting McKinley, his election was assured from the start, and that he would have been successful even if there had not been anything extraordinary done by the National Committee. In fact, I never had the slightest doubt from the day Bryan was nominated on a free silver platform about his defeat but people generally did not stop after the election to analyze conditions and apportion credit. All who were in responsible relation to the campaign, and especially Mr. Hanna, the Captain-General of the whole organization, were given unqualified praise for what had been accomplished. This made him at once a great man before the country and a leader of unusual influence in his party.[14]

Foraker resented Hanna's national prominence, but there was truth in what he wrote. McKinley did have a tremendous advantage with the press in 1896 because many Democratic newspapers chose not to support Bryan. As Jones pointed out, McKinley benefited rhetorically from the fact that many media outlets consistently referred to those who supported a currency based on the value of gold as "sound money men," leading readers to the natural inference that anyone who supported a bimetal standard or some other currency plan were something less than "sound."[15] In addition, McKinley also had a huge financial advantage, thanks to the wealth and resources of the people who supported his campaign.

It is unnecessary to rely on the testimony of a man like Foraker, who clearly disliked Hanna, for evidence that McKinley was his own man, however, in large measure because Foraker was also highly critical of McKinley. Despite his attempt to diminish Hanna's importance in McKinley's election to the White House, Foraker also tried to paint a picture of McKinley as a man under Hanna's spell. When he spoke to journalist J. B. Morrow after Hanna's death, Foraker tried to reinforce the popular version of the relationship between McKinley and Hanna:

During the last years of his life our relations were cordial but, of course, the old friendship was never renewed. He was a Senator from Ohio, Mr. McKinley was the President and Mr. Hanna got whatever he asked for and when he asked for a place and met with objection I am rather inclined to think that he compelled McKinley to give it to him. I was present on one occasion when the appointment of A. T. Wimberly, of New Orleans, for collector of the port was being discussed by President McKinley and Mr. Hanna. Mr. McKinley said he could not appoint Wimberly. Mr. Hanna shook his fist under the nose of the President and said: "You have got to. I have promised Wimberly that he should have the office and you must give it to him." And Wimberly got it.[16]

In making this statement, which he certainly knew was going to be source material for a book about Hanna, Foraker took the opportunity to paint McKinley as the weak-kneed little boy and Mark Hanna as the bullying, mean-spirited political kingpin in Davenport's cartoons.

There are many examples of McKinley's independence, however, that make Foraker's assertion difficult to accept. Most of Foraker's statements reflect bitterness about his failed relationship with Hanna and jealousy about the relationship between Hanna and McKinley. The sense of "what if" is palpable in Foraker's words. Despite the fact that Foraker rose to the U.S. Senate before Hanna did and was incredibly influential in his own right throughout his career in Ohio, in the U.S. Senate, and in the Republican Party, he never got over his anger that McKinley, and not he, became president.

Throughout McKinley's four years as governor, one of the most important aspects of his future run for president was making sure he remained popular in his home state. While Hanna worked hard to get McKinley elected and reelected governor, it is important to understand that McKinley was just as keenly aware of the importance of being a popular governor as Hanna. Charles Dick, who was an Ohio delegate at the 1892 national convention, was asked by McKinley and Hanna to become the chairman of the state Republican Party following the convention. Dick did not want to take the job but he was urged by both McKinley and Hanna to take it. Dick said,

> I went first to see Governor McKinley. He urged me to accept and asked me to see Mr. Hanna, which I did the next day. The reasons both urged were that the campaigns from 1892 down to 1896 must be conducted with a view to bringing about McKinley's nomination in 1896. McKinley spoke of it and so did Mr. Hanna. That was the inducement which led me to take the chairmanship and to give up everything else but my office as county auditor—this preliminary campaign looking into Mr. McKinley's nomination.[17]

McKinley had many allies in his effort to ensure his viability for 1896, though it is important to understand that he was his own best ally, no matter how much credit Hanna deserves.

McKinley was not an unwitting fool who became president thanks to the self-serving action of men who wanted someone in the White House they thought they could easily control. Rather, he was a careful politician who knew how to get the most out of the men devoted to his cause. Croly noted this in his biography of Hanna when he wrote, "No account of the promotion of his candidacy would be correct which understated the essential part played by Mr. McKinley himself. He had many friends and acquaintances among the Republican leaders in all parts of the Union, and he, himself, had established certain alliances which were of the utmost value to his personal cause. No important step was taken without consulting him, and his counsel and cooperation were indispensable to the success of the enterprise."[18] Croly gave credit to the men who helped McKinley reach the pinnacle of power. Of course, he gave special credit to Hanna, but in his book, Croly was also careful to laud men like Charles Dick, Joseph P. Smith, and Charles Dawes. At the same time, he understood none of it would have been possible without McKinley's political acumen.

McKinley's biographers focused even more than Croly on McKinley's ability to get men to do what he wanted them to, painting the image of a man who was a skillful political handler. Gould saw Hanna as important to McKinley but always under McKinley's control. Gould wrote,

> McKinley's ascendancy in his dealings with Hanna was characteristic of his management of people generally. "He had a way of handling men," said Elihu Root, "so that they thought his ideas were their own." Listening more than he talked,

patient with those who bored him, McKinley moved toward his objectives steadily and unobtrusively. "He was a man of great power," Root continued, "because he was absolutely indifferent to credit. His great desire was 'to get it done.' He cared nothing about the credit, but McKinley always had his way." From such men as Elihu Root, William Howard Taft, and John Hay, the president secured exemplary service and enduring respect. Whether they were his critics who assailed him or his friends who idolized him, most men who knew McKinley recognized that he kept the core of his personality away from public view. The private McKinley had a strain of stoicism and reserve that made him a cold and, on occasion, ruthless figure. He had ambition and a sense of his own destiny, traits that he usually kept well hidden . . . The Major could use and discard people when it suited his purposes.[19]

Gould's purpose was not to paint a picture of McKinley as a kind of malevolent puppet master, much like the image of Hanna projected by Hearst's journalists, but to strengthen the case that McKinley was more than capable of taking care of his own political fortunes. It was true, as Croly argued, that "there were limits which a candidate cannot exceed in working on behalf of his own nomination,"[20] but he never argued that meant McKinley gave up control of his own destiny. In the estimation of Croly, Gould, and other latter-day biographers, Hanna did McKinley's bidding, not vice versa.

Most telling of McKinley's independence were the moments during the campaign when he made important decisions in direct opposition to Hanna's advice. For instance, according to H. H. Kohlsaat, there were regular meetings in Cleveland between him, McKinley, Myron Herrick (a Cleveland banker), and Hanna throughout the year before the campaign. Kohlsaat wrote that at one such meeting, Hanna was sent east by McKinley to recruit two major Republican power brokers, Thomas C. Platt of New York and Matthew Quay of Pennsylvania, to McKinley's team. After he returned, Hanna was asked by McKinley to report on the discussion. Kohlsaat wrote:

> Hanna said: "They want a promise that you will appoint Tom Platt Secretary of the Treasury, and they want it in writing. Platt says he has had an experience with one President

(Harrison) born in Ohio and he wants no more verbal promises." McKinley was smoking a cigar. He threw his head back and let the smoke curl up for a moment or so, then got up and paced the little room for a few minutes; finally, facing Hanna, Herrick, and me, he said: "There are some things in this world that come too high. If I cannot be President without promising to make Tom Platt Secretary of the Treasury, I will never be President." Hanna remarked: "New York and Pennsylvania will clinch the nomination—with the votes already in sight." McKinley said: "I can't do it, Mark." "Well," sighed Hanna, "we have got to work harder to make up that big block of votes, but we will get them!"[21]

McKinley may have feared being accused of impropriety or he may not have trusted Platt and Quay or he simply did not want to be beholden to the two men. Whatever his reason, McKinley flatly rejected a deal to make Platt a cabinet secretary. In one decision, he rejected the advice of the man who was alleged to control his every move and rejected the advances of two men with great influence in the Republican Party.

At this meeting, a McKinley campaign slogan was born. Purportedly, McKinley proposed using the slogan "The Bosses against the People." Further discussion ensued, and it was changed to "The People against the Bosses."[22] The incident made very clear that McKinley was in charge and not Hanna. Jones wrote, "The McKinley group did not yet consider Hanna to be a political boss, and in relationship to McKinley, they never believed he played such a role."[23]

Another telling incident was the decision in 1896 to run McKinley's campaign from the front porch of his house. The "Front Porch Campaign of 1896" has attained an almost legendary status in American political lore, but it is often misunderstood. First of all, there was nothing particularly brilliant or unique about running a front-porch campaign. Garfield did the same in 1880 out of financial necessity, as did many other candidates in the nineteenth century. It was considered unpresidential and unseemly for candidates to stump around the country in the quest for votes.

Second, and more important, is the fact that Hanna did not make the decision to campaign from home. He worked on developing the strategy to campaign from home, but it was McKinley's choice to stay in Canton. Croly wrote,

One of the major necessities of the campaign as a whole was the adoption of some measure which would counteract the effect of Mr. Bryan's personal stumping tour. . . . Of course the countermove was to keep Mr. McKinley's ingratiating personality as much as possible before the public; but the Republican candidate cherished a high respect for the proprieties of political life and refused to consider a competing tour of his own. It was arranged, consequently, that inasmuch as McKinley could not go to the people, the people must come to McKinley.[24]

McKinley was motivated not only by a sense of "propriety," as Croly suggested, but also by a clear understanding on his part that he could not energize audiences in the same way Bryan could. Myron T. Herrick, an intimate of the campaign, reported that McKinley said, "I might just as well put up a trapeze on my front lawn and compete with some professional athlete as go out speaking against Bryan. I have to think when I speak."[25] Charles Dawes's biographer Bascom Timmons reported a similar comment from McKinley to Hanna about campaigning on the road against Bryan. Hanna reportedly told McKinley that if he did not leave his front porch and take to the campaign trail like Bryan, he would lose. McKinley did not accept Hanna's advice and replied, "I will not try to compete with Bryan. I am going to stay here and do what campaigning there is to be done. If I took a whole train, Bryan would take a sleeper; if I took a sleeper, Bryan would take a chair car; if I took a chair car, he would ride a freight train. I can't outdo him and I am not going to try."[26] Dawes, who was a good friend of William Jennings Bryan in addition to being an intimate of the McKinley campaign, understood Bryan's crowd appeal and wrote in his journal that he felt McKinley made the right decision.

In agreeing with McKinley's decision, Dawes was almost alone among prominent Republicans like Hanna. McKinley had a reputation as a good speaker who addressed hundreds of thousands of people in his political career. But McKinley felt firmly that he should not try to compete with Bryan at what Bryan did best, and Dawes understood the wisdom of McKinley's decision.

McKinley was also motivated to stay home in Canton by the poor health of his long-suffering wife, Ida. He did not want to leave her behind or compel her to travel with him.[27] His obvious concern for his wife worked well for him with the press and the public, who saw him as a caring and devoted husband.

For many reasons, McKinley campaigned from his front porch in 1896, but none of those reasons involved "minding" Hanna. McKinley did not do Hanna's bidding; rather, Hanna did his. McKinley was a master politician and the captain of his own ship. A good captain knows how to delegate, and McKinley delegated much to his executive officer, Mark Hanna.

Of course, none of the foregoing should be taken as argument that Hanna was unimportant. One historian who did a particularly good job in understanding both McKinley's strengths and the importance of Hanna in McKinley's success was Hanna's brother-in-law, the Pulitzer Prize-winning historian James Rhodes. Rhodes, was careful to acknowledge the contributions of both men in the victory of 1896. He gave credit to both McKinley's aptitude and to circumstances which, while not great for the country, were fortuitous for McKinley. He wrote,

> Yet it was not Hanna's work alone that won the prize. McKinley, in capacity and manner, was well fitted for the White House; moreover, since 1893, affairs had been working his way. The panic of 1893 had been followed by a commercial crisis and business was extremely bad. The Republicans ascribed the evil condition to Democratic success and to the avowed promise of a reduction of the tariff. The tariff was reduced during the summer of 1894 and the autumn elections for Congressmen showed a complete change in public sentiment. It was natural that a distracted public should turn to the arch-protectionist for relief. McKinley was reelected Governor of Ohio in 1893 by an increased majority and in geographical and all other respects was an available candidate.[28]

Rhodes was careful not to lower Hanna to as servile a position as Gould did, but he still made it very clear that McKinley was an important part of his own success. To Rhodes, the two men formed an effective team. Rhodes wrote, "But McKinley's and Hanna's relations were so intimate that Hanna might be called an alter-ego. What one could not do, the other could. McKinley knew the men in public life through and through, and Hanna learned how to manipulate conventions and secure delegates."[29] Rhodes's description of the relationship between Hanna and McKinley is particularly apt. No one is elected president on his own. To see McKinley and Hanna as teammates who needed each other does nothing to diminish either man. It is possible to acknowledge, as Rhodes did, that McKinley was an effective politician and manager while also acknowledging that without Hanna, and crucial others like Charles Dawes, his career might have taken a very different turn.

It is possible that Gould underplayed Hanna's influence over McKinley, but if he did, he was in agreement with several other prominent McKinley biographers in doing so. These include H. Wayne Morgan and, before him, Margaret Leech. All three writers concluded that McKinley was a very talented politician in his own right and that Hanna was a complement to his skill, not a substitute for it.

Gould argued that McKinley was his own man, not a pawn of Hanna and the trusts whose interests Hanna allegedly represented. Gould suggested it is much more appropriate to see Hanna and McKinley as partners, rather than to see Hanna as the puppeteer and McKinley as the puppet. As he observed, Hanna was a "force in Ohio politics for more than a decade" before McKinley's election to the White House in 1896, and a major stepping stone to the White House was becoming Ohio's governor. It is entirely possible McKinley would have been unable to succeed in Ohio, or in national politics, without the help of Hanna, but it is just as likely that Hanna would have been failed to be part of a successful presidential campaign if he had a candidate other than McKinley. After all, he tried and failed twice with Sherman. The two men formed a winning team, a model that has often been repeated in American politics.

Biographer Margaret Leech wrote eloquently of the contributions made by both men to the successful campaigns of 1896 and 1900:

> Together these two made one perfect politician. In the foreground was the zealous protagonist of his party's causes, the speaker who could inspire faith in well-worn platitudes, the moralist who spurned commitments, the diplomat who avoided unpleasantness. Behind him moved the practical businessman, whose brain was unclouded by muzzy ideals; the clever organizer, who could push and publicize, make deals and raise money; the blunt and bad-tempered fighter. . . .

On the candidate's behalf, Mark Hanna pulled the powerful strings of money and organization and publicity. "He
has advertised McKinley," Theodore Roosevelt would ex-
claim, "as if he were a patent medicine." McKinley was like
a talented artist who needed an impresario, a press agent,
and an angel. In Mark Hanna, he found all three.[30]

Leech argued that, during the campaigns, McKinley and Hanna were
indispensable to each other, but she did not assert that this meant
McKinley was somehow a captive of Hanna. In fact, she argued quite
the opposite when she wrote that, in Washington, McKinley was close
to a long list of men that did not include Hanna. Instead, his confidants
were people like William R. Day, Myron Herrick, and the young Charles
Dawes. Leech wrote of what she viewed as a rather one-sided relationship with Hanna in a sympathetic tone:

> Hanna was outside this circle of intimacy. He belonged in
> the category of politicians who respected McKinley's ideal-
> ism, but were perpetually amazed at the revelation, finding
> it strange as well as admirable. These men did not possess
> the key to McKinley's inmost sentiments. In love and con-
> fidence, he gave them less than he received. Because Hanna
> gave so much, McKinley appears the colder and poorer man
> in his personal relationship with the frank, profane, cheer-
> fully ignoble realist who was so useful to his fortunes.[31]

To Leech, Hanna was an important part of McKinley's success, but he
was never viewed by McKinley as Warwick, and the politically savvy
president kept him at a careful distance. Gould echoed this sentiment, writing, "For all this reputation of being McKinley's Warwick,
Hanna's power depended on influence that the president wished for
him to have."[32] Hanna may have had great influence, but rather than
lead McKinley, he was a senator from Ohio.

George B. Cortelyou was McKinley's personal secretary and, in that
capacity, behaved very much as the first presidential press secretary.
After McKinley's assassination, Cortelyou served in Teddy Roosevelt's
administration as both the secretary of the Department of Commerce
and Labor and the secretary of the treasury. Cortelyou wrote of the
relationship between Hanna and McKinley:

Mr. Hanna was a very able politician. I think, however that McKinley was the best politician of his day—I mean that he was an extraordinary politician in the best meaning of the description. He was shrewd and diplomatic. While he had no vociferous arguments with men with whom he differed, nevertheless, he usually had his way and was far more resolute and courageous than the public thought he was. Mr. Hanna was what might be termed an organization man. He believed thoroughly in rewarding the party workers and held that an organization could be maintained in no other way. It sometimes happened that Mr. Hanna and President McKinley differed about matters pertaining to patronage. It must be understood, however, that no Republican Senator asked for so few personal favors as did Mr. Hanna. He rarely requested an appointment on his own behalf. After an election he would have a good many obligations but they were not his obligations. They were the obligations of the party.[33]

Cortelyou's account, along with the accounts of many of McKinley's intimates, clearly demonstrates that McKinley was in charge of his own presidency.

CHAPTER SEVEN

The Campaign of 1896—
The Nomination of William McKinley

hile some historians have either under- or overestimated Mark Hanna's importance to William McKinley's success, he was certainly a part of it. It is undoubtedly true that Hanna dedicated himself completely to McKinley's presidential aspirations. He was so determined that McKinley get the nomination in 1896 that he quit his "real job" of running the large Rhodes-Hanna family business and ceded control of it to his brother Leonard in January 1895 so that he could devote his full energies to politics.

For the rest of his life, nine short years, politics was Hanna's full-time job. During the year and a half leading up to the Republican convention in St. Louis, Hanna worked hard to help McKinley win the presidential nomination. Hanna wanted to have the nomination assured before the delegates gathered in St. Louis for the convention, and cultivating a strong relationship with southern Republicans was a large part of his plan. While southern voters were largely unimportant for Republican presidential candidates in the general election at a time when the South was solidly Democratic, the southern states sent delegates to the convention, and their votes counted as much as the delegates from other regions of the country in the nominating process. Southern delegates could be an important part of pushing a candidate over the top; in working hard to recruit them, Hanna was determined to make the Republican convention of 1896 one of the most undramatic in history.

With that goal in mind, Hanna took up part-time residence in Thomasville, Georgia, where he took a five-year lease on a house. The house gave him and his wife a place to escape the cold Cleveland winters and relax, but the purpose of renting it was really to give him a staging ground for the effort to recruit southern Republicans. McKinley joined Hanna in Thomasville, and Republicans from all over the South, black and white, were invited to the house to meet and take the measure of the governor. It was a very successful strategy, for it gained McKinley the support of a large share of would-be delegates and gave him a nice cushion, well in advance of the national convention. As Croly related,

> When it was all over he [Hanna] could reasonably count upon having obtained for the benefit of his guest a considerable majority of the Southern delegates to the Republican Convention of 1896. . . . The work was so well done, that although frantic efforts were subsequently made by able and unscrupulous Northern politicians to stem the tide in favor of McKinley in the South, they had small success. Mr. Hanna and Mr. McKinley had put a correct estimate on the situation in that part of the country. They had nothing to offer in return for the delegates that could not be offered on behalf of another candidate—viz. the Federal offices in the event of success—but they divined that personal attention means much to Southerners; and they used most effectively the knowledge.[1]

The Thomasville "headquarters" also worked well with McKinley's desire to downplay his presidential candidacy in the early days of it, when he continually made public denials that he was running. Going down to Thomasville allowed McKinley the pretense of a vacation while he was, in fact, making political allies.[2]

Hanna's southern strategy was effective, though not without controversy, especially with regard to race, which McKinley referred to in a letter to Hanna before he went to Thomasville. It is an early example of McKinley's making clear to Hanna that McKinley was, ultimately, his own man. He wrote, "We can never give our consent to a practice which disenfranchises any of our fellow citizens. I believe that the time is coming when the injustice will be corrected, largely by the people of the South themselves, but in the meantime we cannot abate our insistence upon the exercise of constitutional rights."[3] On another occasion, McKinley wrote to a Georgia Republican, Walter H. Johnson:

> Information has reached me that the old slander is being revived in the South that because of my earnest advocacy of protection I feel no interest in the political welfare of the masses of your State, black as well as white. Any one at all acquainted with my record in Congress knows how unjust these reflections upon me are. . . . I think it can be fairly claimed that no member of Congress was ever more active in support of every measure guaranteeing to those Republicans of the South equal rights and privileges with those of any other section. I am told these charges go still farther and insinuate that I favor the organization in the Southern States of a new Republican party composed of largely white men and controlled by white leaders. Such insinuations are utterly without foundation and do me grave injustice.[4]

He sent this letter to Colonel Alfred E. Buck, a Republican leader in Georgia whom McKinley later named as a diplomat to Japan, to give to Johnson. In his cover letter to Buck, McKinley wrote, "Enclosed I hand you a letter for Mr. Walter H. Johnson . . . who is, I am told, expected to visit every district in Georgia and will doubtless be confronted with the base charge that I am not in sympathy with the colored Republicans in their struggle for equal rights and recognition."[5] Later in the year, as the Republican delegates gathered in St. Louis, Hanna was once again accused of buying the votes of African American delegates, as he was in 1888, but nothing could be proved and the accusations did no harm to McKinley's nomination.

In addition to seeing the importance of lining up the southern delegates, Hanna and McKinley also understood they faced an organized attempt among some Republican Party bosses to prevent McKinley from sweeping through the convention in St. Louis. Chief among the bosses who opposed McKinley were Thomas Platt and Matthew Quay, who were angry about being rebuffed by McKinley when they asked for consideration in return for support of his candidacy. Quay, Platt, and others hatched a plan that involved a number of so-called favorite-son candidates who would arrive at the convention with regional support, thus dividing the votes of the delegates and making it impossible for McKinley to win an early victory. As previous conventions showed, once multiple ballots were taken, seeming front-runners, like John Sherman or James G. Blaine, could fall by the wayside and lose nominations to people like James Garfield and Benjamin Harrison. Favorite-son candidates were ready around the country, including the Speaker of the House, Thomas Reed from Maine; Matthew Quay from his home state of Pennsylvania; Senator William Boyd Allison from Iowa; and Senator Shelby M. Cullom from Illinois.

McKinley had a high national profile and was considered popular among voters, but without the nomination, that popularity would be meaningless. Both Hanna and McKinley understood how conventions could spin wildly out of control once delegates were gathered together, and they wanted to quash the favorite-son candidates before they ever got to St. Louis. As a consequence, they engineered efforts at state conventions around the country to make sure as many delegates as possible were committed, or "instructed," for McKinley before they traveled to Missouri.

The Man in Evanston — Charles Gates Dawes

Ultimately, the state that played the decisive role in defeating the favorite-son strategy was Illinois. It was here that the McKinley campaign's greatest effort was concentrated, but neither McKinley nor Hanna had much to do with it. This was an important point in the campaign because if the Illinois delegation had not emerged with instructions for McKinley, the course of events at the national convention might have been much different. Winning in Illinois gave the McKinley campaign energy to carry the day at other state conventions and have a safe, favorite-son-proof majority in place for St. Louis. The credit for success in Illinois properly belongs to Charles Dawes, a young man who lived in Evanston, Illinois, and is one of the most accomplished, and yet unrecognized, Americans.

Charles Dawes was born and raised in Marietta, Ohio. Dawes's father, Rufus Dawes, was a veteran of the Civil War, where he rose to the rank of brevet brigadier general; served one term in the United States House of Representatives from 1887–89; and was a friend and supporter of William McKinley. Rufus Dawes, who was a merchant in Marietta, Ohio, between stints in public service, lived until 1899 and passed his support of McKinley to his son Charles.

Charles Dawes moved from Ohio to Lincoln, Nebraska, in 1887 to begin practicing law. While in Lincoln, he became friendly with young William Jennings Bryan, who also moved to Lincoln in 1887 to practice law. The two men had offices in the same building and, in their free time, engaged in public debates about the merits of a currency based on the gold standard versus one based on a bimetal standard of silver and gold. As one Dawes biographer, Charles Leach, reported, his debates with Bryan inspired Dawes to learn as much as he could about currency, banking, and national and international finance. His research culminated in a book, *The Banking System of the United States, and Its Relation to the Money and Business of the Country,* published in 1892, that put him in good stead for a lifelong career in banking and finance.[6]

While in Lincoln, Dawes also became friends with John "Black Jack" Pershing, who would go on to command the allied forces in World War I. At the time, Pershing was the commander of the ROTC unit at the University of Nebraska. His connection to Pershing later facilitated Dawes's entry into the army during World War I at the age of 50, where he quickly rose from major to brigadier general and was given command of the allied supply lines.

After a celebrated case in which he represented the Lincoln Board of Trade in a lawsuit against "discriminatory freight rates," Dawes moved to Evanston, Illinois, in 1895, where he bought and sold the Northwestern Gas Company, which made him a millionaire by the age of thirty. With his financial future thus secured, Charles Dawes became attracted to politics. His entrée into politics was as the coordinator of McKinley's nomination effort in Illinois.

Later in life, after his time with William McKinley, a career in banking, and his stint in the army, Dawes served as vice president of the United States under Calvin Coolidge; won the Nobel Peace Prize for his work as the head of the Dawes Commission, which worked on German war reparations following World War I; served as the U.S. ambassador to Great Britain for President Herbert Hoover; and rounded out his career in public service as the president of the Reconstruction Finance Corporation in the administration of Franklin Roosevelt. He wrote nine books during his life and was also a talented musician. One of his compositions, "Melody in A Major," written in 1912, became a hit when Carl Sigman added lyrics to it in the 1950s. The resulting new song was called "It's All in the Game" and quickly became a pop-music standard, the best-known version of which hit number one on the charts when it was recorded by singer Tommy Edwards in 1958.

In the 1890s, Dawes was still new to Illinois, where politics was controlled by machine-like organizations, both Republican and Democratic. Chicago had one Republican machine, ostensibly headed by Mayor George Swift, and a separate one in Cook County, where Dawes lived. County Republican politics were controlled by William E. Lorimer, known as the "Blond Boss." Lorimer did not know Dawes and was not prepared to accept him, the new kid in town, as a mover and shaker. Despite being new and unwanted by the establishment, however, Dawes was energetic and quickly became well connected by working quietly behind the scenes.

William Lorimer aspired to be as powerful in Illinois as Quay and Platt were in their home states of Pennsylvania and New York, but that level of authority eluded him. Since McKinley was closed out of the states controlled by strong political bosses, he saw Illinois as a chance to make a splash in a large state. Illinois had the third highest number of delegates of any state at the time. A victory there would give the campaign much needed prestige.[7] The urgency to win in Illinois was further heightened after McKinley lost his bid to have the national convention held in Chicago. Quay, Platt, and other party forces hostile to McKinley saw to it that St. Louis was awarded the convention. Following this development, McKinley thought it all the more important to win big in Illinois.[8]

While many give Hanna credit as the architect of victory in 1896, the fact that it was McKinley who ultimately shaped the campaign strategy that emphasized the need to win in Illinois is a clear sign that Hanna was not the only architect. As Dawes's biographer Bascom Timmons wrote, Dawes found McKinley to have a much better understanding of political reality than Hanna. To Dawes, Hanna was naïve about the power that Platt, Quay, and other bosses wielded.[9] In December 1895, Dawes wrote in his journal, "December 23. Arrived at Columbus and met Governor McKinley at his rooms at the hotel. He is urging me to more aggressive measures in Illinois, and Hanna rather advises against it."[10] Ultimately, McKinley's opinion determined the strategy for Illinois, which is further evidence of the fact that McKinley was his own best campaign adviser, not Hanna.

Dawes was heavily involved early in McKinley's effort well before his thirtieth birthday. After doing some early work for McKinley in Nebraska, North Dakota, and Wyoming in 1894, McKinley and Hanna tasked Dawes with the job of winning Illinois—thanks in no small part to lobbying on Dawes's part to be involved in the campaign. On October 22, 1894, Dawes wrote to Joseph Smith, one of McKinley's close aides:

> Relative to our conversation as to the best method of doing effective service in Major McKinley's interests in this state, and adjoining states, I again repeat that in this part of the country, an active organization in his interest should be maintained. Such an organization we made in this state this summer, and I think both you and the Governor noted the good effects of it during your trip through the state. The people are for McKinley—85% of them—and nothing can take the support of Nebraska, Kentucky, the Dakotas, and Wyoming, from him in the National convention except the machine politicians. . . . I do not think that the machine men can do it, but to be forewarned is to be fore-armed and there is no use in running any risk of not having those states represented by delegates put there for one purpose—to stay with McKinley.[11]

Throughout 1894, Dawes communicated about the efforts of the campaign to line up delegates in states like Wyoming, Nebraska, and North Dakota.[12] Hanna responded, writing, "I note all you say in reference to matters connected with the Governor's interests in the west and am glad to feel that he has such an energetic and devoted friend."[13] Hanna added, "We are depending upon your organization for your state and will be glad to co-operate with you in any adjoining territory that you may find missionary work to do."[14] On March 10, 1895, Dawes wrote in his diary about McKinley's and Hanna's approval of his work: "During the year 1894 I met with Major McKinley in Columbus, Ohio, and also in the fall at Lincoln. In his interests I did considerable work among the politicians of Nebraska, Wyoming, and North Dakota. In January of this year I met M. A. Hanna of

Cleveland, and with him had a conference over McKinley's plans to secure the nomination for the Presidency. My plan of enlisting support for McKinley is being followed in the West, and Mr. Hanna has given my work full endorsement."[15] Dawes elaborated further, writing, "Hanna is in full charge of the McKinley campaign throughout the entire country. He wrote me yesterday that McKinley would soon visit him at Thomasville, Georgia, where they would meet many people. He said things looked very favorable in the south. He has asked me to look after matters in Illinois. McKinley seems to be the coming man."[16] While Hanna may have given his endorsement to Dawes, the record clearly shows that the two men did not see the situation in Illinois the same way.

Dawes was frequently on a different page than Hanna. To his credit, Hanna allowed Dawes to prove him wrong. Dawes's biographer Charles Leach wrote of the campaign in Illinois, "Hanna visited Chicago to look over the Illinois situation and came to the conclusion that wresting an endorsement for McKinley there from Cullom was impossible. Dawes believed otherwise. He believed it so strongly that Hanna gave him permission to go ahead and see what he could see, do what he could do. There was no organization to elect Dawes formally to the job. He simply took command with Hanna's sanction."[17] In Illinois, Senator Shelby Cullom, a man whose popularity was at least partly due to the fact that he bore a physical resemblance to Abraham Lincoln, was supposed to be the state's favorite-son candidate. He was believed to have the popular support of Republicans throughout the state. For this reason, both Hanna and McKinley worried about their chances. Dawes, on the other hand, saw Cullom as vulnerable and assured the Ohioans the state could be won. While Dawes was ultimately proven right, it was not easy, especially in the beginning.

Dawes's chief rival, the Blond Boss Lorimer, was ostensibly a Cullom supporter, though he really wanted the state's at-large delegates to leave Springfield as uncommitted and under his control so he could play the role of power broker at the convention. Lorimer and his cronies had no desire to let Dawes become a power broker in his own right, and they resisted him with all of their resources. As Bascom Timmons noted, "The ruthlessness of the machine Dawes had set out to wreck was soon manifest. McKinley supporters, in search of meeting places, found all available halls rented for weeks in advance, by the opposition, and standing empty. All vehicles for hire were somehow engaged elsewhere."[18] If Dawes was to bring Illinois into the McKinley column, he had to figure out a way to defeat Lorimer's influence. Working behind the scenes, Dawes worked to build a group of McKinley supporters from around the state that would challenge Lorimer's organization. Hanna commented on Dawes's efforts to build a McKinley organization to challenge the Cook County machine: "If they are willing to undertake to raise a purse for our campaign expenses I certainly have no objection to that and would be glad of the help. I believe, as I stated before, that the start of the boom about the time of their banquet will make it irresistible until the [Illinois] convention is held. If we can't have the help of the County crowd this is decidedly the best basis for an organization for us."[19] Within two weeks of being given the job of winning Illinois, Dawes had campaign organizations in each of the 102 counties in Illinois.[20] On February 3, 1896, Dawes wrote in his journal, "Met Hanna at his office. Said he would stand back of me in any fight I decided to make. . . . The Governor agrees that we must fight. He gives me full authority."[21]

Dawes was aided in his effort by McKinley, who made his only campaign speech out of Ohio at the Marquette Club in Chicago to mark the first national holiday observing Lincoln's birthday. As Timmons noted, the appearance was a great success because it made McKinley seem very appealing to many Illinois Republicans. Timmons wrote, "The man who was, perhaps, the most charming of modern Presidents was never more irresistible."[22]

Even as Dawes was leading the campaign in Illinois, Hanna called on him for further assistance in the West. Hanna wrote, "The details of this campaign are growing so that it will be impossible for me to keep in touch with each individual state and if you can assume this responsibility it will be a great relief."[23] Hanna followed this entreaty a few days later with a request for financial help from McKinley supporters in Chicago: "it is absolutely necessary that we must have some help from some of our Chicago friends. A very fierce attack is being made against our lines in the south and it will require all of our available funds to protect us against this on-slaught."[24] Hanna commented on the campaign-fund problem in a later letter to Dawes, when he wrote, "I am in receipt of a letter from C. A. Vaughan, President of the Cook Co McKinley Club . . . asking me for financial assistance. This seems a startling proposition to me, coming from a large city like Chicago. And while I do not want to discourage them or offend them, I do not see how I can spare any means for that work unless absolutely necessary."[25] Fortunately for Dawes, he was not alone in Illinois and had the help of some people who were far better known than he. Dawes's major ally in Illinois was Major General John McNulta, a Civil War veteran who was thirty years Dawes's senior. McNulta was much better known in Illinois Republican circles than Dawes, and he helped to expand McKinley's network to include members of Mayor George Bell Swift's Chicago machine.[26] Though Swift supported McKinley, like most Republicans in Illinois, he did not know Dawes at all. His ties to the effort came through McNulta. The fact that he did not know Dawes made for an interesting moment as the delegates to the state convention gathered in Springfield.

Throughout the state, Dawes oversaw efforts to win delegate elections at first the county and then the congressional-district levels. He was advantaged particularly by the fact that Cullom's supporters had little respect for Dawes or his abilities as an organizer, which allowed him several sneak-attack victories. Notable successes included winning first a county in Senator Cullom's home district and then winning the senator's district itself. Leach wrote, "They kept on smiling at his efforts until they awoke suddenly on the last day of March to find, in the Seventeenth Congressional District convention at Decatur, that Cullom had lost his own district. Its two delegates to the National convention were instructed to vote for McKinley."[27] While Dawes handled Illinois, which Hanna and McKinley saw as crucial to the success of the broader campaign for nomination, Hanna focused on the national effort. He wrote to Dawes, "Please send me by return mail, or as speedily as possible the official call for the Republican State Convention of Illinois. Also please send calls for your District Conventions, where same have been issued. . . . We are anxious to know who our friends are in several districts. . . . Please give us this information in detail at once, or as rapidly as possible for we want it in order to prepare a correct roster for the National Convention."[28]

As the state convention approached, Dawes's forces had already captured many of the state delegation's votes for McKinley, and Hanna continued to encourage and push Dawes. He wrote, "I agree entirely with you as to the necessity of ringing resolutions for McKinley at your State Convention. If you carry things, as I believe you will, do not fail to have strong resolutions instructing the delegates, adopted."[29] Hanna continued to focus on the bigger picture, leaving much of the fight in Illinois to Dawes. On March 12, he wrote to Dawes, "We desire to send at least one good McKinley newspaper regularly each day from now until the St. Louis convention to the address of every delegate and alternate elected to that Convention from the State of Illinois. Please send us the name and post office address . . . of each delegate . . . as rapidly as possible on the selection of your delegates."[30]

By March 13, six weeks before the convention, Dawes was full of confidence and expecting victory. He wrote to McKinley, "The machine has 'unconditionally surrendered.' They had nothing left to surrender so far as that is concerned; but the notification of their desire to now assist us in our work for instructions is at least an evidence of the thoroughness of the victory of the people. You will receive instructions in the State Convention, and in fourteen, if not all, of the fifteen . . . districts. This result is in no way dependent upon the attitude of Senator Cullom."[31]

As April, the month of the state convention, arrived, however, Hanna and the national campaign remained nervous about Illinois. Despite the overwhelming success of Dawes's efforts, on April 7 Hanna wrote to Dawes to encourage him to press harder: "Every day brings fresh encouragement to our cause, and we hope soon to see a radical change in the situation in Illinois. . . . Cullom will be left outside the breastworks if his friends don't look out."[32] Not only did Hanna continue to remind Dawes—almost certainly unnecessarily—of the importance of total victory in Illinois, Joseph Smith did also, writing,

> I have a decided conviction that old Cullom is going to fall so hard that he will hurt himself more than McKinley when at last he does tumble. Still, there is one thing I want to say in the profundity of my political wisdom. Illinois has some of the most adroit and cunning political schemers on this continent. . . . I have never seen their equal in duplicity and scoundrelism. If you can get a few districts to thump into Cullom pretty vigorously within the next two weeks, we will have a good deal less trouble with Quay, and on April 15th may knock Bradley out in Kentucky. . . . It is very important to keep pounding away at Cullom through your

County conventions. Don't lose another one from now until April 15th, whatever the cost or trouble.[33]

While Dawes worked in Illinois, McKinley's national organization kept a close eye on what he was doing and frequently offered suggestions. Smith followed up his letter about "scoundrelism" with another just a week later, writing,

> You will perhaps think me something of a nuisance in my frequent suggestions, but I am excessively anxious about Illinois because I know something of the unscrupulous character of the men you have to face. The more enthusiasm you have at your State Convention the better things will go. One excellent way to evoke this (although you may think it a trivial matter) is by striking badges, mottoes, banners, etc. which catch the unthinking, who of course, seldom read much of anything. Enclosed I send you one of the handsomest McKinley badges I have seen and I would respectfully suggest that you get a lot of them for the Illinois State Convention to be worn by delegates from Cook County and other parts of the State.[34]

At stake at the state convention were four at-large delegates whom McKinley's supporters wanted instructed to vote for him. On March 14, Dawes wrote in his diary, "Our organization is rapidly being reinforced by recruits anxious to come in with the winner. While we will not relax our efforts, the battle is practically won and McKinley will be nominated with Illinois supporting him. Almost every county in the State is falling into line. . . . We are directing this week all our force against the enemy's weakest spot."[35] On the same day, he wrote to McKinley, "Several prominent Republicans have been to see me recently to discuss who shall go as delegates at large. . . . Our friends in the convention will be numerous enough to instruct, and for the present the fight must come before the principle—for McKinley—not for any particular individuals for delegates."[36] As March drew to a close and Dawes prepared for the state convention in Springfield, Hanna wrote to him, encouraging him not to let up: "Cullom seems to be ugly so we must give him a thrashing. Do you think it advisable to try and get the Cook County delegates to come out jointly and declare for McKinley? Talk with McNulta about it."[37]

A few days later, Hanna exhorted, "It looks to me as if brother Cullom was determined to stay in the race, unless he made his own conditions, which at this time seems improbable. I note that Mr. [James] Aldrich claims that my interview, which I suppose is the one you sent out at Chicago, is manifestly incorrect, which, according to the papers is confirmed by Mr. Lorimer; therefore we must keep up our fight, and make them eat their words."[38] Aldrich, a congressman from Chicago, was a vexing problem from the perspective of McKinley's national campaign. In mid-April, Joseph Smith wrote to Dawes,

> A friend who knows him very well has written me that Congressman Aldrich ... who seems utterly lost to common decency, and who is perhaps bitterly mortified by the ill success which has attended his efforts for Speaker Reed, is behind the A.P.A. movement against Major McKinley. He is, I am told, in consort with some of the most beastly characters in the country, low blackguards who have no character or standing anywhere that they are known, and only go about the country traducing and vilifying good men because they can't use them. If you could get on to some of his work in Chicago I would have it exposed in the most vigorous and unsparing manner. He ought to be drummed out of the community if he persists in his present course.[39]

In this letter, Smith referred to the American Protective Association (APA), the anti-Catholic organization that tried to brand the McKinley campaign as pro-Catholic, which frequently put the campaign in the awkward position of having to deny being pro-Catholic without alienating the Catholic vote, which they hoped to get. Hanna wrote to Dawes about Aldrich soon after Smith did, writing, "I am in rec't of yours of the 15th inst. and had wired you about the A.P.A. business. We have it straight that your man Aldrich is the manager of this business and Illinois and Michigan are the objective points of operation. I had a man from Michigan here yesterday and we will shape things up on that state and trust in you and friends to do the same in Illinois."[40]

A year before, McKinley engaged in an exchange of letters with a man from New York named T. C. Evans, who wrote to McKinley with concern about the religion issue. McKinley responded, "The United

States guarantees religious freedom to every citizen. I believe in that guarantee, and believe that every man has a right to worship God according to the dictates of his own conscience."[41] Still, he was sure in the letter to point out on multiple occasions that he was a Protestant. For example, he wrote, "One day I am charged in Boston with being a Catholic, and another day with being a member of the A.P.A. I am neither."[42] Before sending the letter to Evans, McKinley wrote to his cousin, William McKinley Osborne, "I received a letter a day or two ago from a Mr. Evans in Boston, to which I have written a reply. I do not know Mr. Evans, nor how much attention I should pay to his letter, whether it deservers the reply which I have made. . . . I think it is sound in every particular and expresses just what I feel."[43]

Throughout the campaign, McKinley found himself on the defense against the anti-Catholic group. In one letter to the president of the Indiana chapter of the APA, McKinley wrote, "Replying to your inquire, I beg to say that Mr. James Boyle, who was my private secretary during my entire two terms as Governor of Ohio, and is still with me in that capacity, is not a Roman Catholic. He is a life-long member of the Protestant Episcopal Church."[44]

Hanna worked his own connections to deal with the APA threat. One of those connections was Moses Handy, the editor in chief of the pro-McKinley newspaper the *Chicago Times-Herald*. In response to Hanna's claim that the newspaper was paying insufficient attention to the threat represented by the APA, Handy wrote to Hanna,

> So far from underestimating the importance of the A.P.A. I believe that we have more to fear from the treachery of a few officials of that organization, apparently in the pay of the combine, than from any other source. The idea that I intended to convey to you was that I thought it was a mistake for those immediately surrounding the Governor, and particularly those of his official household, to make defensive explanations. I agree with you that the best way to fight the thing is by the dissemination of correct information through the membership of the organization.[45]

Smith followed up on the APA problem once again on April 22, complimenting Dawes on his handling of the issue and commenting on the *Times-Herald*'s coverage:

> I beg to say that I agree with you regarding the policy you have pursued in the A.P.A. matter. It is causing us a great deal of trouble on account of the solicitude of our friends, but that very solicitude indicates they are looking after it in their respective localities, and I am consequently not panic stricken over it. It seems to me that the general course of the Times-Herald is right, but they ought not to have made the serious mistake of magnifying Lynton by publishing his portrait and giving their columns to the publication of A.P.A. matter. What they ought to do is expose the scoundrelly conduct of Congressman Aldrich who has done everything in his power in this matter to belittle, slander, and humiliate Major McKinley. . . . I read your letter to Mr. Hanna on the A.P.A. matter and he approves of your course.[46]

Hanna, meanwhile, remained in contact with Dawes, often via multiple daily telegrams, throughout the Illinois campaign. On April 14, Hanna wrote to Dawes in response to news of a McKinley victory in the congressional district of Joseph Cannon, the future Speaker of the House. Hanna wrote, "I am in receipt of your telegram about Joe Cannon's district, I have just telegraphed him to go to John Chamberlain's and have a 'cold bottle' at my expense. This victory is very significant and may help Uncle Shelby to a conclusion."[47]

Dawes was fully committed not only to McKinley's cause, but to proving himself as a political force. His style was different from the Blond Boss, Lorimer, but his ambition was no less. Dawes prepared for the state convention with enormous focus because there were four at-large delegates at stake, and he wanted them to be instructed for McKinley. Lorimer, his major opponent for control of Republican delegates in Illinois, wanted them uninstructed so he could control their votes at the national convention.

The McKinley campaign wanted the at-large delegates instructed to vote for McKinley because it understood the powerful effect such an outcome would have on other states as they held their own conventions. In attaining this goal, McKinley and Hanna put their trust entirely on the shoulders of Charles Dawes.[48] Their trust was well placed. Prior to the state convention, from January through April, Dawes's campaign organization saw to it that 90 out of the 102 counties in Illinois instructed their delegates to vote for McKinley. On the eve of the convention, Hanna wrote to Dawes, exhorting, "This is the 'battle royale' of the campaign and the most important convention. Instructions for McKinley means nomination sure. Get our boys enthused!"[49] Throughout the state convention, Hanna was in continuous communication with Dawes by telegram, exchanging information and encouragement.

At the convention, Dawes played political hardball to make sure that two primary goals were accomplished. These were getting the at-large delegates instructed for McKinley and burnishing his reputation. To accomplish both of these objectives, Dawes believed it necessary that he be seen as the undisputed leader of McKinley's campaign in Illinois.

Dawes encountered some difficulty when a former secretary of state of Ohio, Samuel Taylor, came to Springfield as an observer. Taylor complained to McKinley that Dawes's strategy was flawed. He felt that winning the at-large delegates was not enough. He wanted McKinley's supporters to dominate every aspect of the Illinois convention to send the country a signal of McKinley's strength.[50] Taylor was not alone in wanting to dominate the convention. The Chicago Republican machine, led by Mayor Swift, also wanted to take control of the convention in order to assert its own power versus that held by its enemy in the Cook County machine, the Blond Boss.

For Dawes, both Taylor's interference and Swift's ambition were unwelcome developments. He worried that a battle for control of the convention could start a chain reaction that would benefit Senator Cullom. While Swift's machine supported McKinley, Dawes did not believe Swift's organization was strong enough to beat Lorimer and his machine. To head off a potentially disastrous fight, Dawes first convinced John McNulta that Swift should not try to make a power play, knowing Swift would listen to McNulta. Next, he went to see John R. Tanner, who was the de facto Republican candidate for governor. He would be a controlling force at the convention, and Dawes wanted to make sure that he would allow McKinley's supporters a chance for an up-or-down vote to instruct the at-large delegates for McKinley.

Dawes feared that Lorimer and Cullom's supporters would try to adjourn the convention without taking a vote to instruct the at-large delegates. This would allow Lorimer to play the part of power broker in St. Louis. Dawes convinced Tanner that if he refused to promise McKinley's supporters the chance to hold a vote on instructing the delegates, then

McKinley's supporters might challenge Tanner for control of the convention. Dawes's actions followed advice Moses Handy gave to Mark Hanna on April 22. Handy wrote,

> Things are lining up for a pretty fight at Springfield. What I am trying to impress upon our people is that however large our majority may be we cannot afford to give the opposition the benefit of a single doubt nor to leave anything to chance. We are going to lack leadership on the floor of the convention. On the other side there will be thorough organization and every man will be at his post ready to obey orders. Our programme ought to be cut and dried. I have seen many conventions overwhelmingly for one candidate handed over to another by machine leadership. Tanner promises fair play, but we ought not to presume on that. Let him once feel that he is out of the woods and he would knife McKinley in a minute. The scheme now is to keep him on the anxious seat until the last. If we succeed in doing that we are all right, for he is an arrant coward. On the eve of the convention we will raise the spectre of Uncle Dick Oglesby's candidacy, just to scare him and make him understand that he has got to play fair by the men endorsed for McKinley as well as for those for Tanner.[51]

Dawes followed Handy's advice to perfection. Though Tanner would almost have certainly won such a fight, it was not a chance he wanted to take. He promised Dawes that there would be an opportunity to vote on instructing the at-large delegates.

With that promise from Tanner, Dawes next went to a meeting of McKinley's supporters and argued forcefully that there should not be an effort to wrest control of the convention from Tanner. Leach reported the following exchange from the meeting:

> As the meeting began, Dawes leapt up, and in a rasping, high-pitched, nervous voice, proceeded to tell those present that if any action were taken it would be by accredited delegates. He hammered on the table as he spoke and he shook his fist at them. "Who is that young man?" Mayor Swift of Chicago asked one of the delegates.
>
> "That's Charlie Dawes," Swift was told.

"And who is Charlie Dawes?" Swift demanded.

"Why," the delegate scratched his head, "I guess he's running this thing for McKinley."

The meeting melted and there was no serious opposition to Dawes as McKinley leader in Illinois thereafter. The other McKinley delegates likewise "guessed" that he was managing the campaign, and they looked to him for direction from that time until McKinley was elected.[52]

Regardless of the veracity of the details of Leach's recounting of this conversation, Dawes emerged from that meeting as the undisputed leader of the pro-McKinley effort. Bascom Timmons reported Dawes's speech at that caucus. Dawes said, "The anti-McKinley minority in this convention is not going to fox us into a position where, after state candidates are nominated and delegates at large chosen, a tired convention can be tricked into adjournment without voting Presidential instructions. This is the time for decisiveness, not hesitation. There are not going to be any more caucuses. That's the way it is going to be; and if you, Mayor Swift, don't like that procedure, you can get the hell out of here."[53] Swift did not get the hell out, but he did accede to Dawes's wishes.

The days of the convention were filled with political intrigue as Dawes worked hard, going from one delegation to another to keep enthusiasm for McKinley at a fever pitch. In the end, Lorimer was prevented from adjourning the convention prematurely, and the four at-large delegates were instructed for McKinley, along with all but a very few of the district delegates. Dawes endeared himself to William McKinley for the rest of the future president's life.

Dawes's accomplishment was enormous. The Republican machines, both in Cook County and at the state level, opposed McKinley, and the campaign needed a savvy strategist to pull off the victory. Hanna was not the man for the job. Dawes's accomplishment in Illinois was all the more remarkable for the fact that he was new to Illinois and relatively unknown to the state's Republican leaders. When the state convention was over, Joseph Smith wired Dawes, "Thank God we can all retire in peace. You have proven yourself a hero and a general."[54] Following his triumph, Dawes wrote in his journal, "Received a beautiful letter from Governor McKinley, which shows at least that he knew what I had accomplished for him. . . . Even after two years of work in his behalf, this expression of appreciation from him touched me with its earnestness and sincerity."[55]

In the letter Dawes referred to, McKinley wrote, "I can not close the day without sending you a message of appreciation and congratulation. There is nothing in all of this long campaign so signal and significant as the triumph at Springfield. I can not find words to express my admiration for your high qualities of leadership. You have won exceptional honor. You had long ago won my heart."[56] McKinley held Dawes in such high esteem that he became a member of McKinley's inner circle with few equals. Timmons asserted there was no one, other than Hanna, with more responsibility and authority in the 1896 campaign than Charles Dawes. By the end of the campaign in Illinois, Dawes could truly say he had done what Joseph Smith advised him to do in a letter in March: "Whoop it up and don't sleep any."[57]

The victory in Illinois had the effect McKinley and Hanna hoped it would: other states that were choosing their delegates for the national convention started to line up in the McKinley camp. After Illinois, McKinley won the majority of the delegates from Vermont. This was an important victory because Vermont was in the heart of the territory controlled by two would-be favorite-son candidates: Thomas Platt from New York and Speaker Reed from Maine. Winning Vermont belied the eastern bosses' claim that they would control the region. Following that victory, the McKinley campaign also scored big wins in Arkansas, Indiana, Kansas, Michigan, and Wisconsin. As Timmons wrote, "The McKinley band wagon was rolling."[58] And it was rolling, thanks in large measure to the contributions of Charles Dawes and thus to Mark Hanna's and William McKinley's recognition of Dawes's talents.

The Convention in St. Louis

When they arrived in St. Louis just after a devastating tornado that carved a wide swath through the city, the McKinley forces were virtually assured of victory, despite the claims of angry bosses like Thomas Platt, who came to St. Louis advocating for Levi P. Morton, New York's governor. Platt's bravado aside, the McKinley campaign was confident of victory. Control of the convention was firmly in the hands of McKinley and Hanna from the moment it began.[59] The only drama at the convention occurred largely behind the scenes as Hanna and a group of campaign insiders focused on drafting the party platform. One issue that was a subject of debate and backroom negotiation among the members of the platform committee was the party's position on which standard—gold or bimetallism—the currency should be based. This issue later became the central focus of the general-election campaign.

Those involved in writing the currency plank included Hanna; Myron Herrick, from Ohio; Henry C. Payne, from Wisconsin; Melville Stone, the general manager of the Associated Press; William Merriam, the former governor of Minnesota; Vermont senator Redfield Proctor; and H. H. Kohlsaat. Kohlsaat was a strong advocate of keeping the currency on the gold standard, and he wrote extensively of the process of crafting the plank in his autobiography. He reported that all the men meeting to write the plank were strong gold men.

The currency plank that McKinley agreed to before Hanna came to St. Louis, however, failed to mention gold specifically and only indicated support for the current standard. The current standard was gold, but Kohlsaat, especially, wanted the word *gold* in the platform. Hanna was coy with Kohlsaat and other gold advocates, like Henry Cabot Lodge. He was aggressive with both Kohlsaat and Lodge, chastising them for refusing to compromise on the wording of the plank. In reality, Hanna also wanted to include the word *gold* in the plank, but he worried about public perception and wanted to make the inclusion of the word look like the result of an unavoidable compromise. Kohlsaat reported Hanna's reaction to Lodge's attempts to influence the wording of the platform:

> Without any preliminary greeting Mr. Lodge said: "Mr. Hanna, I insist on a positive declaration for a gold-standard plank in the platform." Hanna looked up and said "Who in hell are you?" Lodge answered: "Senator Henry Cabot Lodge, of Massachusetts." "Well, Senator Henry Cabot Lodge, of Massachusetts, you can go plumb to hell. You have nothing to say about it," replied Mr. Hanna. Lodge said: "All right sir; I will make my fight on the floor of the convention." "I don't care a damn where you make your fight," replied Hanna.[60]

Out of concern that the stronger wording would precipitate a bolt from the convention by prosilver Republicans and thereby endanger McKinley's nomination, Hanna appeared to be stubbornly fighting for milder language in the platform. Ultimately, a platform using the word *gold* was adopted. In its final form, the plank read as follows:

> We are therefore opposed to the free coinage of silver, except by international agreement with the leading commercial nations of the earth, which agreement we pledge ourselves to promote; and, until such agreement can be obtained, the existing gold standard must be maintained. All of our silver and paper currency must be maintained at parity with gold, and we favor all measures designated to maintain inviolably the obligations of the United States, and all our money, whether coin or paper, at the present standard, the standard of the most enlightened nations of the earth.[61]

When the words "the existing gold standard" were written into the platform, the battle lines for the campaign of 1896 were drawn.

In the aftermath of the decision on the gold plank, several men involved in writing it took credit for including the word *gold,* especially Kohlsaat. Ultimately, though, it was McKinley's decision to make. No doubt, the issue was irritating to McKinley, who did not consider it to be nearly as important as his soon-to-be opponent William Jennings Bryan did. For McKinley, protectionism was much more important. As Hanna wrote in a letter to the *Philadelphia Press* following the Illinois Republican Convention, "The tariff is by popular esteem the chief issue between the parties, and Major McKinley, sound, able, and convincing on all public questions, is its chief and most distinguished exponent. His name is a synonym for patriotism and protection, and he has been aptly described as the 'Advance Agent of Prosperity.'"[62]

Currency was not an area of expertise for McKinley, and he relied on the advice of the members of the committee, as well as others like Charles Dawes. It is important to understand, however, that the final decision to include the word *gold* was not made until Mark Hanna spoke on the telephone with McKinley who did not attend the convention, as was customary for a presumptive nominee, and got his approval. As historian Stanley Jones explained, "When McKinley assented to this fundamental alteration in the platform, he understood clearly the significance it would have in the strategy of campaign politics."[63]

There was a vocal, but ultimately inconsequential, group of prosilver Republicans from the West, led by Colorado senator Henry M. Teller, at the convention. Teller made an emotional speech to the delegates about the platform. He said, "I cannot subscribe to it, and if it is adopted I must, as an honest man, sever my connection with the political organization which makes that one of the main articles of its faith."[64] Ultimately, the vote on the plank was 818½ to 105½, which was an even larger majority than the vote for McKinley, who received 100 votes more than he needed for nomination on the first ballot.

Following the vote to adopt the platform, Teller was joined at the dais by Senator Frank Cannon of Utah, who read what amounted to a manifesto for the supporters of silver at the convention. Teller was later singled out for praise by William Jennings Bryan in his autobiography of the 1896 campaign, writing, "His standing in, and long connection with, the Republican party, together with his great ability and high character, made him the acknowledged leader of the silver Republicans. At St. Louis he was at the head of the revolt against the Republican platform, and his withdrawal from the party cost the Republican candidate thousands of votes."[65] Bryan's praise for Teller and other Silver Republicans aside, Cannon was jeered throughout his speech, and as he and Teller led a group of twenty-one delegates out of the convention, the other delegates screamed for them to go. As Jones reported, "When the silver men reached the main door at the rear of the hall, the delegates watching their departure were in a frenzy, shouting, singing patriotic songs or the words of 'Goodbye, my lover, Goodbye.' One of the delegates from Ohio, Mark Hanna, was observed standing on a chair, his face contorted with anger, as he screamed, 'Go! Go! Go!'"[66] With that bit of drama, the convention was basically over.

The last important business was to nominate Garret Hobart, a relatively unknown businessman and lawyer from New Jersey who was closely aligned ideologically with McKinley and Hanna, as the vice-presidential candidate. New Jersey Republicans, who had recently made significant gains in their state, were eager to put one of their own on the national stage. According to most reports, he was handpicked by Hanna and was quickly nominated by delegates who wanted to balance the ticket, headed by a midwesterner, with an easterner. As Croly related, "Mr. Hobart was well known to Mr. Hanna, and in all probability his nomination had been scheduled for some time. It was practically announced in early in June. He was a lawyer and a businessman with an exclusively local reputation; and if he did little to strengthen the ticket he did nothing to weaken it. He proved to be a useful coadjutor both during the campaign and after the election."[67] During the campaign, Hobart remained at home in New Jersey, campaigning from his home, much as McKinley would do in Canton, Ohio, supporting the gold standard and McKinley's protective tariff.[68]

If Hanna handpicked Hobart, however, it was Charles Dawes who took credit for Hobart's easy nomination. In his journal, Dawes wrote, "Together with Herrick called on Tanner and arranged to have Illinois cast her vote for Hobart for Vice President as far as Tanner controlled same. . . . Had many conferences with Hanna and others during all the week relative to the Vice Presidency, and devoted much time to matter. Definitely arranged Illinois matter. . . . Hobart was nominated for the Vice Presidency. I think the position taken by Illinois practically settled the question of the Vice-Presidency."[69] Dawes's biographers, Leach and Timmons, both concurred with Dawes's assessment of the situation that his leadership of the Illinois delegation put Hobart over the top and gave Hanna the nominee he wanted. Once again, Hanna owed much to Dawes's political acumen.

As the convention wound down, Mark Hanna was treated to a standing ovation and lauded as a conquering hero. This enthusiasm was due largely to the fact that most of the delegates believed that the Democrats were in such dire straits, due to the poor state of the economy, that winning the general election was little more than a formality. Once Bryan got the Democratic nomination and the campaign intensified, many Republicans revised their understanding of the campaign, but in St. Louis enthusiasm abounded.[70]

This enthusiasm was recorded in the official proceedings of the convention:

> A general call from all parts of the Hall was then heard for Mr. Hanna, who finally yielded to the entreaties of the audience and arose and said: "Mr. Chairman and Gentlemen of the Convention: I am glad that there was one member of this convention who has the intelligence at this late hour to ascertain how this nomination was made—by the people. What feeble efforts I may have contributed to the result, I

am here to lay the fruits of it at the feet of my party and upon the altar of my country. [Applause.] I am ready now to take my position in the ranks alongside of my friend, General Henderson, and all the other good Republicans from every state and do the duty of a soldier until next November." [Great applause.]

At the end of the convention, Hanna was the overwhelming choice to be the chair of the Republican National Committee. As chair, he was given formal responsibility not just for McKinley's campaign, but for the electoral fortunes of the entire party.

When Hanna returned to Cleveland, he was met by a large crowd at the train station. In the crowd, Hanna met the eyes of an old friend, A. B. Hough, and shouted, "'Hello Hough!' Then inflating his chest he pointed to himself with mock pride and added: 'Big Injun! Me Big Injun!'"[71] In the brief speech he gave to the large crowd, however, Hanna was a model of humility. According to Croly, these were his words:

> Mr. Chairman and Fellow-members of the Tippecanoe Club: This unexpected and almost overpowering reception robs me of what little power of speech I had left. I had little idea that anything I had done entitled me to such distinguished consideration. True, I have been for a number of months associated with a cause dear to the heart of every honest Republican in Ohio and every patriotic citizen of the United States. I entered upon that work because of my love for William McKinley. No ambition even for honors such as are being accorded to me on this occasion prompted me. I acted out of love for my friend and devotion to my country. I lay no claim to the honors you have accorded to me. I could have done nothing without the people. All I have done is to help the people in gaining a result upon which they were united—the ascension to the presidency of William McKinley.[72]

The Democrats' surprising nomination of William Jennings Bryan at their convention in Chicago and his ability to make the election an emotional referendum on the currency made the campaign much more difficult than Republicans anticipated at the end of their convention.

Hanna's reputation, however, was nevertheless established by the end of the 1896 convention.

Bascom Timmons argued that Hanna received more credit at the time than he really deserved: "After the St. Louis convention, he was to rank incomparably the greatest political manager ever to come on the national scene. The Hanna legend would grow lustier and lustier; soon he would be said to have his hands on wires he never touched, and to have accomplished feats he never attempted."[73] Timmons did not accuse Hanna of self-aggrandizement, but he also clearly felt that Hanna was overly praised. As a biographer of Charles Dawes, Timmons no doubt felt the man from Evanston deserved more credit than he got.

In truth, Hanna and Dawes both made very important contributions to the campaign, and Hanna certainly understood Dawes's value as a member of the team. At the same time, the overarching strategy of the campaign, the decision to have two campaign headquarters—one in Chicago and one in New York—and many other critical decisions were made by Mark Hanna. He was, as Croly wrote, "not merely the nominal head of the campaign. He was the real leader of the Committee."[74] As such, it was up to him to decide who he would depend on to see the campaign to a successful conclusion, and he recognized Dawes as a great talent upon whom he could rely.

The Enduring Legacy of Campaign 1896: Linking 1896 and 2000

One of the first stories to draw attention to parallels between George W. Bush and William McKinley was a story in *USA Today* by reporter Jill Lawrence, who suggested that there were stylistic similarities between McKinley's front-porch campaign, in which he refused to travel from Canton and, instead, brought the campaign to him, and the early days of the Bush campaign. As Lawrence pointed out, in the days before Bush officially declared his candidacy, Republicans, largely organized by Karl Rove, streamed to Austin for an audience before their potential standard-bearer. Meanwhile, Bush publicly declined to declare his candidacy, saying he had a job to do in Texas.[75]

Another early story to address parallels between the Bush campaign and the 1896 campaign of William McKinley was a lengthy piece in the *Washington Post* by David Von Drehle. The article contained an analysis of the Bush campaign that suggested it was modeled on the McKinley campaign of 1896. Like the Lawrence piece, Von Drehle was careful in how he characterized Rove's interest in McKinley, and he offered a positive assessment of McKinley's administration and his partnership with Hanna. In doing so, he distinguished himself from many of his colleagues by showing his historical research. He wrote, "Democrats would complain that McKinley was a mere puppet of moneybags Hanna . . . but historians generally believe they were a well-matched team of two strong men."[76] In support of this statement, Von Drehle quotes historian H. Wayne Morgan, an expert on McKinley and the Gilded Age.

Unlike much of the reporting about parallels between the campaigns of 1896 and 2000, Von Drehle's piece deserves praise for presenting an accurate description of the relationship between McKinley and Hanna and for accurately noting Karl Rove's interest in the McKinley era. According to Von Drehle, it was not idolization of Hanna that made Rove so interested and outspoken about the 1896 campaign, but, rather, his interest in it as a realigning election that began a long period of Republican dominance.

Von Drehle's article was not responsible for creating the spurious notion that Rove idolized Hanna, but it was one of the first to draw national attention to Rove's interest in the McKinley era, and Von Drehle coined a phrase that other reporters picked up in their own stories: "McKinley Mania." The mania, as Von Drehle described it, meant that "Republicans from K Street to Austin are dusting off their history books and boning up on bimetallism. . . . The party of Lincoln and Reagan has gone dizzy over William McKinley."[77] It's not clear how many Republican politicians became smitten with the presidency of William McKinley, but in 1999 and 2000, many reporters brought up the memory of not only William McKinley but of Mark Hanna as well.

An editorial in the *Cleveland Plain Dealer* about the Bush campaign efforts in Ohio in 1999, for example, considered "McKinley Mania." The editorial noted that Rove often remarked to reporters that the McKinley administration marked the beginning of a long period of Republican dominance:

> Backed financially by Cleveland millionaire Mark Hanna, McKinley spent much of the 1896 general election campaign against William Jennings Bryan speaking to voters from his front porch in Canton, promising a "full dinner pail" if he became president. . . . The McKinley fan in the Bush

organization is top strategist Karl Rove. . . . McKinley, he
said, recognized Republicans had to look to working-class
voters and immigrants to build a lasting electoral majority
and change the political landscape, which had been characterized by divided government.[78]

The editorial is accurate in its explanation of Rove's stated opinions
about the importance of McKinley for the fortunes of the Republican
Party at the turn of the twentieth century. Its characterization of Hanna
as a major financial backer of McKinley is also accurate. Hanna donated one hundred thousand dollars to McKinley's campaign in 1896,
helped him significantly with his gubernatorial campaigns, and organized his fundraising from others. Hanna was far from McKinley's
only backer, however, as the story suggests. For example, a total of at
least $3.5 million from other donors was contributed to McKinley's
1896 campaign.

One column by a conservative, Paul Greenberg, offers criticisms of
Bush and his campaign style and makes comparisons to McKinley based
on a less-than-flattering analysis of McKinley. In his column, published
in *Jewish World Review* in June of 1999, Greenberg wrote a scathing indictment of George W. Bush as an intellectually bankrupt candidate. He
wrote, "He's been doing so well without issues and ideas, why should
he risk them? A prudent presidential candidate will avoid anything that
smacks of ideology. And the surest way to avoid ideology is to avoid
ideas. His father's son, George W. should have no difficulty with that
assignment."[79] It was a strong indictment from a dedicated conservative
who might have been expected to support George W. Bush.

For Greenberg, the problem went deeper than Bush or Campaign
2000. He noted the lack of ideas and ideology on either side, dating
back a full century to the campaign of 1896:

> In 1896, William Jennings Bryan stumped the whole country,
> covering more than 13,000 miles in 14 weeks, delivering 600
> flamboyant speeches in 29 states in that pre-jet America. He
> scarcely left a county seat unscathed. And what good did
> it do him? His opponent, William McKinley, stayed home
> on his front porch in Canton, Ohio, mouthed respectable
> niceties, neither impressed nor frightened anyone, and was
> elected. . . . So if Bush the Younger is looking for a model,

he might do worse than study the watershed campaign of '96. In some ways, it was the beginning of the modern, issue-less campaign and the end of ideology in American politics. With an occasional exception, the ideologues—The Gold-waters and McGoverns—have been losing ever since.[80]

Greenberg's interpretation of the campaign of 1896 is not accurate. The campaign of 1896 was rich in ideas on both sides. It is true that Bryan personally ran the more energetic campaign of the two candidates, but he had little choice. He supported ideas that scared most people with money in the United States; as a consequence, he had little campaign money in comparison to William McKinley. A three-and-a-half-month campaign on the road was his only alternative. That McKinley did not want to engage in such a campaign does not mean he was without ideas.

The impact of Greenberg's column would have been negligible if not for the fact that other journalists ran across the column and cited it in their own, more mainstream publications. For example, David Von Drehle referenced the column in his "McKinley Mania" piece. Von Drehle wrote, "Last month, conservative columnist Paul Greenberg used 1896 as a stick to beat Bush for lacking substance."[81] What made Greenberg's quote irresistible, perhaps, was the fact that it was a negative opinion from a conservative voice. Modern, "objective" journalism has many conventions, but few are as important as providing two sides to every issue and replacing the run-of-the-mill "dog-bites-man" story with an eyebrow-raising "man-bites-dog" story. In Greenberg's comments, Von Drehle had both. Greenberg, of course, was not the only critic of Bush, Rove, and the parallels with the McKinley campaign.

In December 1999, Jonathan Alter, a reporter for *Newsweek,* wrote about the campaign of John McCain. In doing so, he addressed the question of what the word *reform* meant to Republicans. He wrote, in part,

> Reform. It's such an old concept for the Grand Old Party that it's almost new. The way one reads that party history is central this season, as the Republicans struggle to redefine themselves. Karl Rove, the canny architect of George W. Bush's campaign, is especially interested in the last turn of the century, when the afterglow of the Civil War was wearing off and the party of Lincoln was at loose ends. A brilliant

political strategist named Mark Hanna packaged William McKinley as a perfect vessel to conserve the business gains of the Industrial Revolution. Rove sees Bush as doing the same for our own technology revolution. His tightly scripted plan is reminiscent of Hanna's in 1896, when he had McKinley campaign from his front porch in Canton, Ohio.[82]

In this passage, Alter made at least two serious errors of fact that hurt the effectiveness of his point. First, it was McKinley's choice to campaign from his front porch, not Hanna's. Second, Hanna did not package William McKinley. Alter was probably playing off a comment by Teddy Roosevelt, who said Hanna sold McKinley like a "patent medicine" during the campaign of 1896. If McKinley was packaged, however, it was not by Hanna alone. Ultimately, McKinley was always in charge, and much of the campaign was run by other important players like Charles Dawes, while Hanna focused on raising money in New York. For instance, Dawes was in charge of the campaign's finances—the money Hanna raised—and he wrote frequently to both Hanna and McKinley with updates. On August 1, 1896, Dawes wrote to McKinley:

> In the first place, we have the system established under which our contracts will be let and our business transacted. No contract is made by this Committee without my approval and no contract is let without being subjected to competitive bids. . . . I have a book which shows the total outstanding contracts and liabilities of the Committee and I have served notice on all concerned that the minute the sum total of these contracts exceeds the money in my hands, or assured to me by responsible parties, the expenditures must cease.[83]

Alter's piece contained other questionable conclusions. He wrote, "But the conservative Business First theme didn't hold. When McKinley ran for re-election in 1900, he chose a hot-blooded veteran of the Spanish-American War as his running mate. One congressional leader fretted that only a heartbeat stood between that madman and the White House."[84] First of all, his characterization of McKinley's campaign of 1896 as "conservative Business First" was a debatable choice. While McKinley had many allies in the business community, he was also the favorite of the urban working class on election day.

When Bryan began his populist campaign, he expected to woo both farmers and the industrial working class. He won many farmer votes, but he had more trouble with the working class, many of whom were immigrants. Bryan's explanation for what was to him a surprising lack of support from urban voters was that the McKinley campaign had intimidated them. From the perspective of the McKinley campaign, they had merely appealed to the workers with a message that a healthy business community was good for employers and employees alike. The campaign also went to great lengths to print voluminous quantities of campaign materials that spoke to workers in each of several different languages, including Swedish, Yiddish, and German. Second, McKinley did not choose Teddy Roosevelt, the "hot-blooded veteran of the Spanish-American War"; he was foisted on McKinley by leaders of the Republican Party, some of whom wanted him out of New York in 1900 and some of whom wanted to embarrass Hanna who did not want Roosevelt on the ticket. The congressional leader Alter quotes was none other than Hanna.

One article that appeared during the 2000 campaign that should have been better written and better researched was by Nicholas Lemann who, as the dean of the Columbia University Graduate Journalism School, is both an academic and a writer for the *New Yorker* magazine. In his article about George Bush, Lemann addressed Rove's interest in McKinley in a section focused on George W. Bush's rather light political resume:

> George W. Bush's ascension would represent the apotheosis of an ordinary man. Karl Rove has a riff, which he gives to anybody who will listen, entitled "It's 1896." Every national political reporter has heard it, to the extent that it induces affectionate eye-rolling when it comes up. "It's 1896" is based on Rove's reading of the work of a small school of conservative revisionist historians of the Gilded Age (that is, historians who love the Gilded Age), one of whom, Lewis Gould, taught a graduate course that Rove took at the University of Texas. Here's the theory, delivered at Rove's mile-a-minute clip: "Everything you know about William McKinley and Mark Hanna"—the man elected President in 1896 and his political Svengali—"is wrong. The country was in a period of change. McKinley's the guy who figured

it out. Politics were changing. The economy was changing. We're at the same point now: weak allegiances to parties, a rising new economy."[85]

In this passage, Lemann gives readers every reason to doubt Rove's version of events by besmirching the reputation of Lewis Gould and the "small school of conservative revisionist historians" to which he allegedly belongs.

Lemann later wrote that it was reasonable to compare the two eras, but that conclusion was obscured by the condemnation offered in what he had already written. Lemann does some of the same things writers with less reason to worry about the facts—both conservative and liberal—did when assessing the Bush campaign in 2000. First, while he quotes Rove saying that the conventional wisdom about McKinley and Hanna was wrong, Lemann reinforces that conventional wisdom in the same sentence when he identified Hanna for readers as McKinley's "political Svengali."

Second, Lemann also does his best to counter Rove's argument that McKinley was his own man, at least as responsible as Hanna for the start of an era of Republican hegemony, by calling the credentials of Rove's sources into question. Instead of merely referring to the fact that Rove's interest in McKinley peaked when he took a class with Lewis Gould, now a professor emeritus of history at the University of Texas, Lemann instead referred to Gould derisively as a conservative revisionist historian. First, it is worth noting that Gould denies being a conservative.[86] Second, revision is merely the act of changing or updating something. The term *revisionist,* however, connotes a very different kind of exercise, in which changes are made to fit the past to a current agenda. It is a term that has taken on a pejorative meaning. But if the word is used correctly, the historians who worked to clarify the records of presidents like Harry Truman and Dwight Eisenhower were revisionists. It does not mean that they played with reality to create positive stories about Truman and Eisenhower to fit a specific agenda but that they used historical records, as they became available, to correct previously misleading pictures of those men. Similarly, Gould and other historians who reexamined McKinley's presidency were not trying to fit a specific political agenda, but to set the record straight. It should also be noted that work of the historians who revised our image of McKinley was released over the span of half a century. It is hard to imagine a shared agenda by these historians, as Lemann's comment suggests.

Unlike the *Washington Post* reporter, David Von Drehle, who portrayed H. Wayne Morgan's version of McKinley's presidency—which is similar to Gould's view—as the mainstream view of McKinley's presidency, Lemann instead chose to diminish Gould as a scholar. Gould and other scholars, like H. Wayne Morgan and Margaret Leech, who have written of McKinley's merits as a politician and a president, are simultaneously painted by Lemann with a brush that makes them look more like highly motivated political operatives than historians.

To call Lewis Gould a conservative revisionist historian is to diminish him and others who have similarly reassessed McKinley's presidency as authorities in the eyes of Lemann's readers. This is inaccurate. When Gould's major work on McKinley, *The Presidency of William McKinley,* was published in 1981, reviewers in *Presidential Studies Quarterly,* the *Journal of American History,* and the *American Historical Review* all praised Gould's efforts in contributing to our understanding of the McKinley presidency, and none of them labeled him as a revisionist with a political agenda, as Lemann does.[87]

For example, Louis W. Koenig, himself a highly respected presidential scholar and biographer of McKinley's opponent, William Jennings Bryan, reviewed Gould's book in *Presidential Studies Quarterly.* He wrote, "Gould's study will stand at the front of the McKinley literature, for it is admirably researched, insightful, and sure-footed in analysis and argument. It presents the case for McKinley convincingly and with a fullness and sophistication that will make this study a lasting contribution to our knowledge of presidential power and presidential leadership."[88] Similarly, writing in the *American Historical Review,* Vincent P. DeSantis, of the University of Notre Dame, argued that Gould's book was an important contribution:

> He has written a splendid book about McKinley's Presidency that supersedes the other accounts of this administration in analysis and perception. Gould's book has the virtues of being tightly and clearly written, deeply researched in both American and European sources, and balanced on topics he has examined. While he does not make McKinley a great

president, he does make him a figure of higher importance and interest than he has usually been. . . . One might disagree with Gould here and there in the book, but overall it is a fine performance and will, I believe, be the standard work on McKinley's presidency for years.[89]

In a very positive review essay, Richard Welch, of Lafayette College, differed with Gould's assessment of McKinley's record on domestic policy, but he soft-pedaled it so much, it is difficult to see it as a major criticism:

> It is in the realm of McKinley's domestic policy concerns that one can perhaps feel a measure of strain in Gould's claims for the significance of the McKinley presidency. The McKinley administration was not without a policy on tariff and monetary questions nor for the problems of industrial combination, the civil service, and the relationship of the Republican party to black Americans. It is not clear, however, that McKinley's leadership here represented either a significant change or a major contribution in the evolution of the modern presidency. Whatever one's judgment on that score, Gould has demonstrated conclusively that students of the political and institutional history of twentieth-century America must begin their investigation not with the ebullient Theodore Roosevelt but with the presidency of the pious, platitudinous, and important figure of McKinley.[90]

Welch found room to critique Gould, as no project is without room for improvement, but he couched the critique in language that leaves readers with the overall impression that Gould made a major contribution to our understanding of history. Welch certainly did not make the assertion, as Lemann did, that Gould was on the fringe of scholarly understanding of the McKinley presidency.

Lemann's characterization was both inaccurate and harmful. A journalist, especially a scholar-journalist, writing a piece he had to know would be influential with both readers and other journalists, should have been more careful in what he wrote. It is not a requirement of Lemann's several jobs that he be an expert on Mark Hanna, William McKinley, the Spanish-American War, and the Gilded Age.

At the same time, however, he should not have given his readers the impression that he is an authority on these matters when he clearly is not. He besmirched the work of a respected historian and ignored the work of others to report instead an out-of-date, inaccurate view of McKinley's presidency.

Lemann's inaccurate analysis of McKinley's presidency continued when, later in the article, he assailed the actions of McKinley before and during the Spanish-American War:

> Lewis Gould has noted hopefully that McKinley is rising into the middle ranks of Presidential greatness, but the main event of his Presidential term, the Spanish-American War, caught him flat-footed. George W. Bush represents the hope not so much of a redirection of the federal government as of another Republican restoration, one that would put the White House back in the hands of the party of business and—by bringing suburban, female, and minority voters into the Republican coalition—perhaps do so for a good long time.[91]

Here, Lemann did not write a handwringing piece about the doom and gloom of a possible Republican hegemony, but at the same time, he incorrectly dismissed the presidency of McKinley, who built a new coalition of Republican voters.

What did Lemann mean when he wrote that the Spanish-American War caught McKinley "flat-footed?" Did he mean that he was surprised when the war came along? Did he mean that McKinley was unable to respond and lead the military when the war began? Did he mean that McKinley was unable to lead the country as a newly victorious world power when the war was over? None is true. War had been brewing for years, under the leadership of President Cleveland. There was nothing surprising about it. It is true that McKinley resisted going to war with Spain and, in so doing, resisted tremendous pressure from the press, the public, and the Congress. This resistance is a well established fact, and both he and Mark Hanna received voluminous criticism in Hearst's newspapers because of it. As Richard Welch wrote in his review of Gould's book in the *Journal of American History,* McKinley forever changed the presidency with his forceful leadership before and during the war. Welch wrote, "Gould breaks new ground in his careful description of McKinley's role as commander-in-chief during the war years and his efforts to make the White House a command post. McKinley cannot claim rank as a master strategist, but in his determination to center military and diplomatic authority in the executive branch and restrict congressional initiative in foreign affairs he offered a model for many later presidents."[92] McKinley's slowness to engage in military conflict with the Spanish was not due to a lack of awareness that a crisis was brewing. The crisis was already well on the way to being at full boil during the last year of Cleveland's presidency, and Cleveland did not favor going to war with Spain either.

CHAPTER EIGHT

The Campaign of 1896—Battling Bryan

n his responsibility as chairman of the national committee, Mark Hanna was given complete discretion in appointing an executive committee to assist him in running the campaign. The campaign had an eastern headquarters in New York, which was rather minimally staffed and existed mainly to give Hanna a base of operations for his fundraising efforts. The lead roles there were played by Hanna; McKinley's cousin, William McKinley Osborne; and Cornelius N. Bliss, who was the treasurer of the Republican National Committee. Bliss was a longtime president of the American Protective Tariff League, which made him a supporter of William McKinley's favorite issue, and later became McKinley's secretary of the interior.

McKinley's western headquarters was in Chicago, which quickly became the nerve center of the campaign. Because William Jennings Bryan's appeal in the East was perceived to be minimal, Hanna believed that the real fight for the presidency would take place in the West, which was home to many farmers and silver mines. Both were constituencies inclined to support Bryan over McKinley.

There was no southern campaign office. The South was considered out of play for a Republican candidate, and, despite the report by historian Stanley Jones that the campaign pumped some money into the South to attract gold Democrats and Populists who did not support a bimetal standard, there was never a serious effort to win votes in the South.[1] When the votes were counted, the only southern state McKinley won was Kentucky, which he took by just a few hundred votes. Every other southern state, including the states that embodied the tension that resulted in the Civil War, went for Bryan, along with a border southern state with its own tumultuous Civil War history, Missouri.

The importance of having a McKinley headquarters in Chicago was magnified when Bryan also chose the city for his headquarters. He wanted to have his headquarters there because it was "the source of his triumph and well removed from the Senators who advocated a campaign of mild discourse and a benign slurring of the issues."[2] The importance of the western campaign made the choice of who was to be in charge of the Chicago operation incredibly important.

Hanna was expected to appoint an Illinois man to his executive committee, and it was further expected that man would play a leading role in running the western campaign. The Illinois delegation, under the control of the Blond Boss, Lorimer, elected a man named T. N. Jamieson as the state's member of the National Committee, a deliberate snub of Charles Dawes, despite his obvious contributions to McKinley's nomination. Since Jamieson was Illinois's man on the committee, it was assumed he would be Hanna's choice for his executive committee.

Another possible candidate was H. H. Kohlsaat, but Hanna chose neither Kohlsaat nor Jamieson, opting instead to give the post to the young genius of the Illinois campaign, Charles Dawes. As Margaret Leech reported, Hanna did this because he "knew and approved, also, his methods of working with little talk, no personal publicity, and direct action toward a given objective."[3] Hanna clearly understood how valuable Dawes was to the team. Henry Payne, a member of the goldplank committee at the convention from Wisconsin, was put in charge of the Chicago office. Payne was presumably given the job because he had a reputation as an effective campaigner, but he was not the most important member of the Chicago staff. That distinction belonged to Dawes, in large part because of his talent but also because Payne was attacked by organized labor forces as being antilabor.

The importance that McKinley and Hanna assigned to the western campaign was further evidenced by the caliber of the people who rounded out the Chicago staff. Others based in the campaign offices at the Auditorium Building on Michigan Avenue included Albert Cummins, who would soon be elected governor of Iowa; William Merriam, the former Minnesota governor who also served on the gold-plank committee; Charles Dick from Ohio, who succeeded Mark Hanna in the

U.S. Senate and was the secretary for the western campaign office; Perry Heath, an Ohioan in charge of the campaign's publications, an enormous job of major importance in a campaign of information and education; William Hahn, the former chairman of the Ohio State Republican Committee, who ran the speaker's bureau, coordinating hundreds of McKinley surrogates, many of whom were paid by the campaign, who went around the country, speaking in a variety of languages; and William R. Day, one of McKinley's closest friends. When McKinley gave up his legal career for the U.S. Congress, Day became his adviser of legal, political, and personal matters.[4] Day was a lawyer from Canton who later became a judge and served on the Supreme Court.

It is difficult to overemphasize the importance of Day's role in McKinley's political success. When McKinley found himself bankrupt in 1893, it was Myron Herrick and Day, not Mark Hanna, who quickly jumped to action and organized the bailout that saved both McKinley's personal finances and his political career. McKinley had been led astray by a friend, Robert L. Walker, a manufacturer and generous donor to his congressional campaigns. In 1892, Walker encountered financial difficulties and asked his influential friend McKinley, then governor of Ohio, to endorse some loans for him. This made the governor legally responsible for repaying the loans. McKinley, feeling a debt to Walker, signed blank documents and left it to Walker to fill in the amounts. At first, McKinley thought Walker's loans totaled seventeen thousand dollars, which was the total of all McKinley's assets. It became apparent quite quickly, however, that Walker had indebted McKinley to the tune of one hundred thirty thousand dollars.

Faced with this personal financial crisis, McKinley's initial, embarrassed response was to tell his friends he was retiring from politics so he could work to repay his debts. The problem was initially faced without Hanna, who was out of the state on business. The fund created to raise the money to repay McKinley's debt was headed by three trustees, men who were significant players throughout McKinley's political career: William R. Day, H. H. Kohlsaat, and Myron Herrick. The McKinleys gave these men control of all their assets and left them to handle the situation.

As Kohlsaat reported in his autobiography, "Governor McKinley never knew who contributed the money. The list of subscribers was refused him later when he asked for it, declaring he would pay them back with the money he saved out of his salary as President, and turned over to Mr. Herrick, who made some fortunate investments, which gave McKinley's estate some $200,000."[5] Hanna, who arrived shortly after the crisis broke, helped these men raise money from all over the country to pay McKinley's debts and allow him to remain in office as governor of Ohio. Kohlsaat, who liked to claim as much credit for every aspect of McKinley's success as he could, chose to mention little about William R. Day. In his autobiography, he made only one reference to Day's role: "Judge Day, who handled the matter in Canton . . . told me that not one single claim was filed against the estate."[6] Kohlsaat's faint acknowledgment aside, McKinley depended heavily on Day as an adviser.

Day remained intimately involved in McKinley's career following the bankruptcy. In a meeting following the Democrats' nomination of William Jennings Bryan that included Herrick, Hanna, Kohlsaat, and Day, McKinley continued to discount the importance of the currency issue. He simply could not believe it was an issue that would energize the electorate, and he expected that Bryan would be unable to continue to push it as the centerpiece of his campaign. McKinley biographer Charles Olcott described the discussion this way, "Someone said, 'The money issue is a vital thing,' to which McKinley replied, 'I am a Tariff man, standing on a Tariff platform. This money matter is unduly prominent. In thirty days you won't hear anything about it.' Judge Day remarked laconically, 'In my opinion, in thirty days you won't hear of anything else.' And so it proved."[7] Day's biographer Joseph McLean suggested that the exchange and Day's accurate prediction demonstrated Day's skill as an adviser and political strategist to McKinley and also showed, in that particular important circumstance, that "Day had his ear closer to the ground than did the Major."[8] Later, Day served a critically important role as the first assistant secretary of state. McKinley turned to the trusted Day when it became clear that his secretary of state, John Sherman, who had been given the position to free up his seat in the Senate for Mark Hanna, was not capable of doing the job. From the middle of 1897 through 1898, Day was ostensibly the secretary of state, seeing the McKinley administration through the crisis with Spain.

The Currency Question—A Matter of Standards

For a few days after the Republican convention ended and before the Democrats nominated William Jennings Bryan, Hanna and the others in McKinley's inner circle felt a sense of relief and a degree of comfort about the upcoming general election. Immediately after the Democratic convention, when the fiery orator Bryan grabbed the nomination, the Republicans were encouraged and felt even more certain the road to the White House would be relatively easy.

Unlike the Republican convention, which began with McKinley as the prohibitive favorite, there were better than twenty possible nominees when the Democratic convention began in Chicago. The favorite was a prosilver congressman from Missouri named Richard "Silver Dick" Bland. However, Bryan spoke last when the convention was considering the currency plank for the party platform, and he electrified the crowd, beginning a short, dramatic rise to the party's nomination. The only member of McKinley's inner circle who predicted Bryan would be the eventual nominee was his old friend from Lincoln, Charles Dawes. McKinley and Hanna both assumed it would be Bland.[9]

While the Republicans were initially happy with the Democrats' choice of Bryan, it quickly became clear they had a fight on their hands, centered on a complicated issue that was subject to emotional appeals. In the West and South, Bryan appealed to farmers, silver miners, and silver-mine owners. In the more densely populated, industrialized East, his appeal was far lower. The Midwest was difficult to predict, for while there were many farmers in that section, it was also McKinley's home base, and the Ohio governor was very popular. What Bryan needed to do in the Midwest and the East was convince the working class, the immigrants who worked in factories, that the Republican did not have their best interests at heart. To Bryan, the gold-based currency limited the amount of money in circulation and disproportionately affected people on the lower end of the economic spectrum. Allowing money to be based on silver, which was much more plentiful, would put much more currency in circulation.

On the other hand, the Republicans—and many eastern Democrats—felt that converting the country to a bimetal standard through the free coinage of silver would have a disastrously inflationary effect. The currency standard issue was a very old one, dating back to the earliest days of the country's existence. For several decades after the passage of the Coinage Act of 1837, the country's currency was based on a bimetal standard, with a ratio of sixteen to one, meaning a dollar coin contained 371.25 grams of silver or 23.22 grams of gold.[10] The bimetal standard gradually fell out of favor, and it was eventually eliminated by the Coinage Act of 1873 that put the country on a gold-only standard. There was an immediate outcry from those who felt that a gold-only standard limited the amount of money in circulation in a way that had negative consequences for the national economy.

In response, Congress passed the Bland-Allison Act in 1878, which compelled the Treasury Department to buy two to four million dollars worth of silver each month and gave it the option of minting it into money or issuing silver certificates. Bryan wrote of Bland, one of the bill's sponsors, "His name is known among students of the money question in every civilized nation, and his faithful and continuous labors in behalf of the restoration of bimetallism have given him a warm place in the hearts of his countrymen."[11] In 1890, the Congress passed the Sherman Silver Purchase Act, which compelled the Treasury Department to buy four-and-a-half-million ounces of silver each month, paid for by the issuance of treasury notes. Neither law, however, put the country back on the bimetal standard that existed under the Coinage Act of 1837.

By the election of 1896, there were essentially two sides to the standards debate. On one side were those who argued a gold-only standard was bad for the country because the limited supply of gold in the world meant there was far too little currency in circulation. This, they argued, stifled economic growth and, especially, drove down the prices for farm goods. Those who favored remaining on the gold standard argued that if the country adopted a bimetal standard and minted more money, it would have a disastrously inflationary effect by increasing the amount of currency in circulation with money based on a so-called inferior metal.

Economics is an imprecise science, and the currency question, like many complicated economic issues, had ample evidence for advocates of both sides to draw upon in building their cases for the American public. Both sides felt they were waging "campaigns of education" to teach voters the "truth" about the issue. In 1896, as the country was mired in an economic slowdown that affected millions, a real, substantive policy debate was conducted by candidates who believed firmly in their respective positions.

On the gold, or "sound money," side, were the majority of Republicans and many eastern Democrats. For years before McKinley ultimately agreed to the wording change from "maintain our present standard" to "the existing gold standard should be preserved" in the Republican platform, he tried to remain silent on the currency question, for fear of alienating western Republicans, emphasizing protectionism instead. A few years earlier, as his prospects as a presidential candidate were growing, McKinley was heavily pressured to take a position on the currency question, prompting him at one point to speak in favor of a bimetallic standard, with the ratio of gold-to-silver coinage to be determined by an international agreement.[12]

This was a compromise position advocated by many moderates who felt bimetallism was a good idea but that it was too risky for the United States to adopt by itself.[13] In 1892, the Republican Party's platform contained a plank supporting a bimetal standard based on international agreement. Hanna, who was always a firm supporter of the gold standard, understood the political sensitivity of the subject and agreed with McKinley's unwillingness to engage in a debate on the subject, especially before the 1896 convention. In an election where the South was already lost, it was important not to alienate Republican voters in the West if at all possible. Ultimately, McKinley and his advisers decided it was necessary to take a position that clearly aligned them with the powerful interests across the country that feared the consequences of a bimetal standard, and the platform language advocating the gold standard was adopted.

Elements of the Democratic and Populist Parties supported the bimetallism side, along with a new party, created by the American Bimetallic League, known as the Silver Party. The prosilver advocates benefitted from the bestselling writings of William "Coin" Harvey who, three years before the campaign of 1896, said, "I look for some man like old Abe Lincoln to turn up or be the result of the new conditions now forming. The country is now staggering along like a man depleted of half his blood, and will continue to do so until silver is added to our metallic money as it existed prior to 1873."[14] William Jennings Bryan was Coin Harvey's Abraham Lincoln.

While Bryan certainly benefited from having William Randolph Hearst on his side, he gained more from the writings of Harvey, who sold hundreds of thousands of copies of his books. Bryan's biographer, Louis Koenig, wrote, "The highest note on Bryan's political harp, the silver question, was gaining ever-widening popularity thanks to a sudden new phenomenon. A stupendous venture in mass education was afoot, launched by William H. Harvey of Chicago, author of an enormously popular pamphlet, *Coin's Financial School.* . . . Seldom, if ever, has a publication educated so vast a public on a serious political issue."[15] Bryan, himself, was effusive in his praise of Harvey. He wrote, "The argument was in dialogue form, and the book aptly illustrated. The discussion was so elementary as to enable a beginner to master the principles involved. It is safe to say that no book in recent times has produced so great an effect in the treatment of an economic question. . . . Notwithstanding the number of publications issued by him, he found time to deliver many lectures and to take part in several debates."[16] Harvey felt the currency question was as serious an issue in 1896 as slavery was prior to the Civil War and felt his pamphlet was to the free-silver movement what *Uncle Tom's Cabin* had been to the abolition movement.[17] The parallel between the Civil War and the free-silver movement were frequently echoed in the speeches of William Jennings Bryan. In his famous "Cross of Gold" speech, for instance, Bryan said the silver issue was a battle of brother against brother and father against son, just like the Civil War.[18]

Campaign Finance in 1896—Funding the Campaign of Education

When Bryan was nominated and the men of the McKinley campaign—Hanna chief among them—saw the raw emotional appeal both he and the free coinage of silver held for voters, they felt they would have to "teach" voters why Bryan was wrong, and they conceived a campaign of education. Trying to educate voters cost a great deal of money in 1896, not unlike today. The media were different, but it does not mean they were free; and McKinley's campaign, with Mark Hanna as the fundraiser-in-chief, was far better at raising the necessary money to conduct an educational campaign than Bryan's. Does this mean that Hanna—and, by proxy, McKinley—did something untoward or unethical in raising and spending money? Furthermore, does it mean that Hanna deserves credit for singlehandedly getting McKinley elected? The available evidence does not support an affirmative answer to either question.

In a modern-day organizational chart of the McKinley campaign of 1896, Mark Hanna's name would unquestionably be at the top. As a consequence, he was depicted as Warwick and Svengali, drawn in

FIGURE 8.1. Honest money. Cartoon by Homer Davenport, *New York Journal*,
September 12, 1896, 1

political cartoons in pro-Democratic publications as a puppet master, a nanny, and a grotesquely overweight tycoon who controlled William McKinley. He was portrayed as a ruthless fundraiser, who pressured donors to give millions of dollars to the campaign. He was painted as a disingenuous demagogue who pressured voters to choose McKinley by making them fear that life as they knew it would come to an end if Bryan were elected president. How much truth was there in these accusations?

From the campaign of 1896 through the rest of his life, Mark Hanna was often depicted in the political cartoons in pro-Democratic publications wearing a suit covered with dollar signs. This image apparently originated not with Hanna but with Thomas Platt, who reportedly came to the convention in St. Louis with a large amount of money he intended to use to grease the way for Levi P. Morton to get the Republican presidential nomination. A political cartoonist drew an image of Platt arriving at the train station with a suitcase covered in dollar signs. Following the convention, other cartoonists adopted dollar "marks" and covered Mark Hanna with them in all of their drawings.[19] Thus the image of Hanna as "Dollar Mark" was born.

Few cartoonists used dollar marks quite as effectively as Homer Davenport did for Hearst, and few writers attacked Hanna with quite as much ferocity as Alfred Henry Lewis, who wrote for Hearst. In one column about Hanna and the labor unions, Lewis wrote:

Scene—Waldorf

Reporter—Do you expect to elect McKinley, Mr. Hanna?

Hanna—McKinley will be the next President. We can't win one way we will win another.

> As ruthless in politics as in business, as careless of public, as of private right, by fair means or foul, by hook or by crook, Mark Hanna wages his war and proposes to land his man. . . . McKinley is of no present or future consequence. Hanna is casting the shadow in this campaign. The candidate is swallowed by the manager. The Canton mute is merely a syndicate's entry for the White House stakes.[20]

Herbert D. Croly traced the beginning of Lewis's aggressive treatment of Hanna to an article published in the *New York Journal* in early

FIGURE 8.2. What further use can Hanna have for a charter of rights? Cartoon by Homer Davenport, reprinted in *The Dollar or the Man? The Issue of the Day*, ed. Homer Davenport and Horace L. Traubel (Boston: Small, Maynard, 1900), 30

1896. As Croly wrote, the article was presented as an interview with Hanna that never actually took place. It made him "appear as a fool and a braggart. In a letter to the owner of the *Journal*, Mr. Hanna protested vigorously against the misrepresentation, but without effect. Later the personal attack upon him was reduced to a system."[21] More often than not, the attacks were centered on the issue of money.

During the general-election campaign, Hanna's attention was primarily focused on his self-appointed fundraising duties, leaving the details of strategy and mechanics to men like Charles Dawes. To raise the money he felt was necessary, Hanna needed access to the nation's financial titans, many of whom were in New York. Access came, in part, due to his friendship with John D. Rockefeller. As children, Hanna and Rockefeller, who had relocated to New York by the time of the campaign, went to school together in Ohio. While most of the New York money world did not know much about Hanna, Rockefeller knew him well. This helped introduce the little-known Hanna to the money men, but Hanna also understood that he had to mend fences with the eastern politicians with whom he had butted heads during the nomination battle.

The most important of these was Thomas Platt, who controlled the state Republican Party in New York. Hanna reached out to Platt during his first campaign trip to New York, in late July. During this visit, the two men met and ironed out their differences. In a letter to Levi P. Morton, his erstwhile presidential nominee, Platt wrote, "When you come to think of it, there was nothing else for Mr. Hanna to do except to recognize the regular Organization of the Party in this state or any other State, and particularly in *this* State, at *this* time, when it was evident to the wayfaring man . . . that the Republican Party has continued confidence in its present management, and desires them to remain in control."[22] Hanna was a pragmatist. Though Platt had been bothersome during the nomination phase of the campaign, he understood that winning in New York was critical to winning the election and that having Platt as an ally was critical to winning New York.

Hanna worked tirelessly to raise money for the campaign. He also gave generously from his own coffers. According to Croly, he was the sole source of funds for the effort to win the Republican nomination. Croly wrote, "Early in 1896, when the demands upon him became very heavy, he cast about for some means of shifting the burden. . . . But further reflection convinced him that to collect a fund for the purpose of nominating a candidate was a different thing from collecting an election fund. The appeal in the former case had to be made on personal rather than party grounds. So he made up his mind to pay the expenses himself."[23] Hanna's detractors could—and did—argue that he was trying to buy the presidency single-handedly. If he was trying to buy the presidency for McKinley, it was not an unprincipled grab for power. Rather, it was because he believed in McKinley as a person and in what he stood for. As Croly wrote, Hanna loved McKinley as a man. He admired the politician. Whenever he had an enthusiasm, he could communicate it. He could make others believe in McKinley as he did. He could impart his own energy of affection and conviction to the whole movement on behalf of his friend's nomination. He himself was the kind of American citizen whom McKinley could represent only. . . . The restoration of the Republican party to power and the election of McKinley assumed in his eyes the character of a patriotic mission.[24]

Hanna felt that, in supporting McKinley, he was doing what was best for the country. Certainly there were many who disagreed that his ideas were the right ones. The critics may have had merit, but it is incorrect to attack Hanna's motives as something sinister.

For the first two months of the general election campaign, Hanna was greatly frustrated in his efforts to raise money, and Charles Dawes, playing a key role in the Chicago headquarters, pressured him to raise more. In a telegram to Hanna in July, Dawes wrote, "The demands upon this committee for literature, speakers and assistance is enormous. In accordance with your directions the system of expenditure of funds has become perfected. The system of collecting funds, in view of demands upon us here becomes of vital importance. The prevailing impression that money will be easily raised leads each individual to evade or lessen his just subscription. The situation should be impressed upon eastern men."[25] In addition to whatever financial difficulties they might have had as a result of the Panic of 1893, Hanna's trouble with the "eastern men" was due, in part, to the fact that it took time for the eastern money men to warm up to him. It was also due to the fact that, in the early stages of the race, few people gave credence to Bryan's campaign.

Bryan simply was not viewed as a serious threat to win the presidency by many in the East. He had very little support among eastern Democrats or Democrats across the country who owned property or the powerful Democratic newspapers of the East. Though Bryan gave his formal acceptance of the nomination he had received in New York, it lacked energy and was negatively received by the crowd in attendance and by the press. Following the speech, Bryan let himself be talked into abandoning plans to make a two-week tour of the East, on the grounds that the campaign simply did not have the funds to pay for it. Of course, it looked as if he was admitting he had no chance in that part of the country. In addition to that tacit admission, Bryan also made a blunder that haunted him throughout the campaign.

In explaining why he chose to give his famously lackluster speech accepting the Democratic nomination at Madison Square Garden instead of his adopted hometown of Lincoln, Nebraska, Bryan said he chose New York "in order that our cause might be presented first in the heart of what now seems to be the enemy's country, but which we hope to be our country before the campaign is over."[26] It was not quite "rum, Romanism, and rebellion," which sank James G. Blaine in the last stages of Campaign 1884, but according to Koenig, the phrase was "ripped out of context and pointed to incessantly as proof of his hate and fiendish intent toward the propertied class."[27]

Just a week after Bryan gave his tepid acceptance speech at Madison Square Garden, Bourke Cockran, the "champion Democratic orator of the East," gave a speech to a full house at Madison Square Garden that was full of contempt for Bryan. As Koenig described,

> Unlike Bryan, Cockran spoke without notes, in a pugnacious speech of unbridled accusation and insinuation. The country, he said, would not "consent to substitute for the Republic of Washington, Jefferson, and Jackson the Republic of Altgeld, Tillman, and Bryan." The country would not accept "the fantastic dream of Populism." Cockran, who made Bryan's performance seem a model of the innocuous, defined "Bryanism" as "a conspiracy between professional farmers who want to pay low wages and unreconciled slaveholders who would like to pay no wages."[28]

Of course, Bryan's words were not enough to cause a groundswell of opposition from his party by themselves.

President Grover Cleveland opposed Bryan's position on the currency issue and refused to support him. There was so much enmity against Bryan among some Democrats, especially probusiness Democrats from the East, that it prompted them to form a breakaway party, known as the National Democrats. Nine hundred delegates held a convention in Indianapolis after the Democratic convention in Chicago. After being turned down by the incumbent, President Grover Cleveland, they nominated Illinois senator and former Civil War general John

Palmer for president and a former Confederate general from Kentucky named Simon Bolivar Buckner for vice president.[29] The historic reality is that the Panic of 1893 and William Jennings Bryan's push for silver-backed currency drove business leaders to the Republicans as much as anything McKinley or Hanna might have done to attract them.

This splinter party proved costly to Bryan, as splinter parties often do. The splintering of the Republican Party by Teddy Roosevelt's Bull Moose Party in 1912, for example, cost William Howard Taft his re-election. The National Democrats won only 133,000 votes, but they got enough in Kentucky, Buckner's home state, to cost Bryan those votes, and about fifteen thousand ballots were declared invalid in Minnesota after voters who were confused by the two Democratic tickets ruined their ballots. Most of them intended to vote for Bryan.[30]

Bryan returned to the East Coast later in the campaign, and while he continued to receive the cold shoulder from the eastern Democratic establishment, he drew large, friendly crowds when he spoke. As Bryan continued to draw big crowds to his speeches, even on the East Coast, those who feared his economic ideas began to worry that he might win. It was at this point that Hanna's efforts to raise money for the campaign began to bear fruit.

While Charles Dawes was not technically in charge of the western campaign office, it was largely his operation, especially where issues of campaign finance were concerned. In his journal, Dawes wrote of the early days of the general-election campaign:

> July 20: Hanna expects me to be responsible for *all* funds spent in the campaign.

> July 21: Simply overwhelmed by applicants for positions under the National Committee. Worked at getting matters in running order. Somehow it looks as if in Hanna's absence, the whole burden it to be on me.

> July 24: Worked hard getting our work systematized. The labor attack on Payne is throwing the responsibility more upon me. I propose that as far as I am connected with it, the campaign in the West shall be run honestly, and upon strict business methods.

> July 29: Met Committees, etc., in afternoon. Matters are now running more systematically at headquarters. I make

all departments work through me in ordering and have adopted our Akron Gas Company system largely.[31]

Dawes was given financial responsibility for the campaign, a little more than a month before his thirty-first birthday, August 27, 1896.[32] In a letter to McKinley, dated August 1, 1896, Dawes addressed his concerns about the campaign's coffers: "While the interest of business men is greater, in our contest, it is more difficult for them to spare the money for subscriptions. I am in daily consultation with Ellsworth, Allerton, and others, in reference to this part of our work. It is very important that we shall have our funds, before we spend them."[33] Dawes, who knew Bryan well, felt from the early days of the campaign that great resources would be necessary if McKinley were to win.

Dawes's concern about funds continued to appear in his journal throughout the first weeks of the campaign. For example, in late August, Dawes wrote, "August 24: The outlook for money for campaign purposes for the committee is very poor. Our plans will have to be cut down. August 28: The outlook for funds to run the campaign is very poor."[34] Dawes's mood matched that of Hanna. In a letter to McKinley, his cousin William McKinley Osborne wrote from the New York headquarters, "Mr. Hanna feels very cheerful to-day about the situation so far as the party is concerned. He is somewhat disturbed, however, over financial matters at Cleveland."[35]

Croly reported that, through the first half of August, Hanna was greatly discouraged by the cool reception he received from the New York financial world. Things started to change in the latter days of August and into September as the New York financiers became more familiar with Hanna and accepted the fact that the midwesterner McKinley was the Republican nominee and not Levi P. Morton, as many of them had wanted. When they made this adjustment, they opened their purse strings to Hanna.[36] One factor that made it possible for Hanna to turn the corner was the very large donation of two hundred fifty thousand dollars he received from Standard Oil.[37]

The tone of Dawes's journal entries brightened considerably as the campaign turned the corner into mid-September. Dawes wrote:

> September 9: The disbursements for National Committee for printing and expenses are very large. Drew on Cornelius N. Bliss for $50,000. Received contributions of $20,000

during day—$15,000 from C.R.I.&P Railroad and $5000 from O. F. Aldis. Have now received as a committeeman nearly $300,000 since the campaign opened.

September 11: At lunch with Mr. Hanna who handed me an envelope containing 50 one thousand dollar bills—being the contribution of a railroad to the Republican campaign fund. Deposited a check for a similar amount from another source. These will be the largest contributions of the campaign.

October 1: Am beginning to feel the wear and tear of the campaign a little. Hanna sent me $35,000 for fund, and I drew for $50,000 more, and received contribution of $5,000 more during day. The election is going to be a tremendous landslide in our favor.[38]

In the October 1 entry, Dawes succinctly connected money with victory. Were other Republicans as confident as Dawes? Not according to Bryan biographer Koenig, but his evidence for this is suspect. He wrote, "October: The campaign in high gear. The 'enemy' in alarm. A projection of the *New York Herald* gave Bryan 237 electoral votes, 13 in excess of victory. Mark Hanna was doleful. Shaken by anticipations of defeat, he commanded his lieutenants to 'Quit blowing and saw wood.' Senator Jones fanned Republican alarm by predicting that Bryan would carry thirty-six of forty-five states."[39] Koenig offered no documentation for his quotes of Hanna and Jones, and the *Herald* was a Democratic newspaper. The observation is interesting, but dubious. Without the source of Hanna's quote, it is impossible to verify. What is definitely true is that Hanna frequently spoke of his confidence to newspaper reporters, and that confidence was frequently published, even on the pages of Hearst's newspapers. Hanna certainly worried about the election until the moment McKinley was declared the winner, but the lack of a cited source makes Koenig's characterization of Hanna as doleful in early October difficult to prove.

Still, the contrast of Dawes's confidence and Hanna's possible lack of it is interesting. If, in fact, Dawes was sanguine about McKinley's chances and Hanna was worried, what would it say about the alleged architect of McKinley's campaign? Would it simply mean that Hanna was, by nature, a worrier? There is evidence to support this conclusion, such as when Hanna tried to convince McKinley that he would lose to Bryan if he did not leave his front porch to go out on the stump. But it could also mean that Dawes, who managed the day-to-day operation of the campaign from Chicago, was simply more qualified to make a judgment about where and how things were going. That would be further evidence of Dawes's importance to the campaign.

One of the great controversies of the election was the estimates of how much, exactly, the Republican side spent to get McKinley elected. Dawes's diary was peppered with financial statements that offer some information, but for some researchers, they raised as many questions as they answered. On September 26, Dawes prepared a statement for Hanna that indicated the campaign had raised $570,329.71 and spent $523,441.92. On October 8, he prepared an estimate of the remaining cost of the campaign for Hanna that totaled $322,427.11. On October 13, he followed his cost estimate with another financial statement in which he reported that the campaign had collected $940,000.78 and spent $869,461.07. Presumably then, Dawes was estimating a total campaign expense of $869,461.07, plus the $322,427.11 he predicted was necessary for the rest of the campaign. This comes to $1,191,888.18. However, only one more financial statement was reproduced for public consumption in Dawes's journal, and it was dated November 21, well after the campaign was complete. In that statement, Dawes reported total campaign expenditures of $3,562,325.59, which was more than three times the total amount he estimated the campaign would cost with less than a month to go.

With a large gap between financial statements in Dawes's journal, from October 13 to November 21, large questions remain about financial issues. Why did expenses so far outstrip Dawes's October 8 and 13 reports? Where did the tremendous influx of cash between October 13 and November 21 come from? We know the bulk of the money came from New York because that was where Hanna did the bulk of his fundraising and there were also several reports in Dawes's journal of receiving drafts from the Republican National Committee's treasurer, Cornelius Bliss; but there was no detail about the original sources of money. These kinds of gaps in information, at a time when there were no federal campaign-finance reporting requirements, made it easy to make accusations about Hanna's motives and methods.

The bulk of the contributions to McKinley's campaign in 1896 came from the eastern United States. Critics railed about Hanna's methods, but in reality, there was nothing particularly outrageous or even unique about them. Many claims have been made that the amount of money was unprecedented, but even that may not be true. An enormous amount of money was raised, for example, by Benjamin Harrison's 1888 campaign. In 1888, the major issue was protectionism, with the corporate forces of America lined up against Grover Cleveland, whom they perceived to be weak on protection.

Just as the country's economic titans were stirred up in 1896 by fears of skyrocketing inflation if the free coinage of silver was allowed, they were also animated by Harrison's campaign manager, Matthew Quay, who stirred their fears about the danger of unchecked foreign competition. As Allan Nevins, a biographer of Grover Cleveland, wrote, Harrison benefited from Quay's solid connections to the business community. Nevins wrote that Quay was

> expert in the process known, after a phrase incautiously used by Quay, as "frying the fat" out of the business beneficiaries of the party. Quay shortly enlisted the aid of John Wanamaker, who became head of a large committee of business men, covering the whole country. . . . The Republicans also possessed an immense advantage in the vigor and astuteness of the high-tariff associations supporting them. There were half a dozen of these bodies, all supported and largely officered by the keenest business men of the period.[40]

Perhaps the only important difference in fundraising between the Harrison and McKinley campaigns was that in 1896 Charles Dawes kept better financial records than Quay, who allegedly destroyed many of the financial records of that campaign.[41] The lack of precise records makes it difficult to compare the two campaigns, but it is clear that McKinley's campaign was hardly path-breaking in raising and spending large amounts of money.

It is true that Hanna was the figure most responsible for raising money in the 1896 campaign and that he used a wide variety of tactics to do so, including trying to generate public concern about Bryan's fiscal principles. When a twenty-first-century reporter like Slate.com columnist Jacob Weisberg writes that Hanna "ran a sophisticated, hardball campaign that got McKinley to the White House," it is true, but within limits.[42] One problem for understanding Hanna's legacy, however, is that, despite Dawes's meticulous records, there are to this day many conflicting reports about just how much money the campaign raised. As we have seen, Dawes's official estimate from the books he kept in the campaign's Chicago headquarters was $3.5 million. Many of the ideas were certainly Hanna's, but many others were Dawes's and others' in the campaign organization. Furthermore, the execution of the ideas fell largely to Dawes and the rest of the Chicago staff. It was the scale of his efforts that brought most of the criticism to Hanna's feet. The campaign of education envisioned by Hanna required large amounts of money to finance.

Once Hanna convinced the giants of corporate America that McKinley was their man, he was able to use a system of assessment that asked corporations to give donations based on a percentage of their assets. Banks, for example, were asked for a contribution equal to one-fourth of a percent of their capital.[43] Hanna has often been singled out by critics for this allegedly outrageous tactic, but he was not the first to do so. For example, Matthew Quay used very similar methods managing the effort for Benjamin Harrison. The difference between the money raised in 1896 and that raised for Harrison was a matter of volume, not method. In 1892, for example, Harrison's reelection campaign raised an estimated $1.5 million. If Hanna can be accused of anything, it is of taking an established method of raising money and implementing it more efficiently.

But is that something for which to criticize Hanna? It is important to remember that it was an issue, and not necessarily Hanna, that motivated the dramatic increase in donations. Once eastern financiers were convinced they could trust McKinley, they put their resources behind him because they greatly feared the consequences of a Bryan presidency. The donors making the decision to give money to the McKinley campaign were shrewd businessmen. They were not duped by Hanna into giving money by a demagogic appeal that the sky was falling. They arrived at their dim view about the free coinage of silver long before Hanna made his dunning calls. These were "sound-money" men, and once they believed McKinley was likewise, they opened their wallets.

While the Republican press and Hanna biographer Croly wrote of Hanna's fundraising efforts in a positive light, there were many detractors. On one hand, Croly wrote admiringly, "Mr. Hanna always did his best to convert the practice from a matter of political begging on the one side and donating on the other into a matter of systematic assessment according to the means of the individual and institution."[44] On the other hand, journalist Matthew Josephson saw Hanna's efforts very differently. In his book *The Politcos,* he wrote, "But Mark Hanna was a political generalissimo of genius, risen suddenly from the councils of the leading capitalists, to meet and checkmate the drive of the masses by summoning up the berserk fighting power latent in his class."[45] Josephson further argued that Hanna's genius (albeit an *evil* genius, from Josephson's perspective) was in convincing the ruling class that its very way of life would be threatened if Bryan became president. He wrote, "There came into use, in greatly expanded form, the device of the political assessment upon corporate wealth used in 1888. . . . Thus a war chest equal to all demands was gathered by Hanna, a sum which Croly modestly estimates at $3,500,000 (as officially recorded), but which other estimates have placed at from $10,000,000 to $16,500,000. Never had politicians wallowed in such a golden stream as now poured forth for them, and which increased in abundance up to the closing days."[46] In a footnote, Josephson elaborated further: "The expenditures in the final days of the canvass throughout the country for getting out the vote are never officially recorded or made public. Croly does not include these in his estimates."[47] Croly's response to critiques, like Josephson's description of the amount raised, was dismissive.

Croly wrote, "Although the amount of money raised was . . . very much larger than in any previous or in any subsequent campaign, its total has been grossly exaggerated. It has been estimated as high as $12,000,000; but such figures have been quoted only by the yellow journals and irresponsible politicians."[48] One of the reasons for the controversy about how much money Hanna did or did not raise stemmed from the fact that there was no legal requirement to make exact records public.

There was no Federal Election Commission at the time, and none of the regulations that compel today's candidates to file regular reports about how much money they raise and spend was in existence. In addition, there was no law in 1896 limiting the amount of money that could be raised or spent.[49] Croly wrote, "The question of political ethics involved in by the collection of so much money from such doubtful sources, if it ever was a question, has been settled. American public opinion has emphatically declared that no matter what the emergency, it will not permit the expenses of elections to be met by individuals and corporations which may have some benefit to derive from the result. But in 1896 public opinion had not declared itself, and the campaign fund of that year was unprecedented only in its size."[50] Hanna was accused by critics, who often referred to him as "Dollar Mark," as doing something untoward and, quite possibly, illegal. In reality, what Hanna did was play the game better than anyone had before. It is easy to accuse him, with hindsight, as Bill Bradley did in his book *Time Present, Time Past* of doing something that forever tainted American politics, but is it fair?

One unresolved issue of note was the discrepancy between Dawes's reported figure of $3.5 million raised and the much higher figures many detractors claimed. Josephson, for example, placed the figure at between $10 and $16.5 million. With no citations in his text to support his assertion, Bryan biographer Louis Koenig wrote that while the official Republican total was $3.5 million, "The amount actually spent by local and national committees approached $16,000,000."[51] In his journal, Dawes reported a postelection conversation he had with his friend William Jennings Bryan. Bascom Timmons wrote of the conversation, "When Bryan and Dawes met for the first time after the election, Bryan asked: 'Charley, how much did you fellows spend to beat me?' 'We spent $3,562,325.59,' said Dawes. Bryan was amazed. 'Why, Tom Lawson told me he saw Pierpont Morgan give Hanna a check for five million dollars!'"[52] Undoubtedly, one of the reasons the amount of money raised by McKinley's campaign was often wildly inflated was because of the coverage Hanna's New York fundraising efforts received in the *New York Journal*. For example, the following chart appeared in the *Journal* in August 1896. It showed readers not how much money had been donated by well-heeled supporters but how much those supporters were worth. Casual readers, however, were no doubt confused. While McKinley did not raise half a billion dollars, he did raise millions.

Bryan, on the other hand, raised considerably less than even the official figure of $3.5 million, because he and his wing of the Democratic Party had far fewer deep-pocketed friends. Koenig, who wrote that such donors were "as scarce as hen's teeth," reported that while there were rumors of big donations from wealthy silver-mine owners

HALF A BILLION BACK OF McKINLEY.

List of Some of the New York Millionaires Who Have Combined to Carry New York for the Candidate of the Hanna Syndicate.

The following is a list in part of the members of the Union League Club Committee that has been appointed to provide funds to combat the free silver sentiment. Each man is possessed of great wealth and control of much more:

Name.	Occupation.	Wealth.
JOHN D. ROCKEFELLER	Manufacturer	$125,000,000
CORNELIUS VANDERBILT	Railroads	$100,000,000
C. P. HUNTINGTON	Railroads	$60,000,000
J. PIERPONT MORGAN	Banker	$25,000,000
JOSEPH MILBANK	Banker	$20,000,000
ANDREW CARNEGIE	Manufacturer	$20,000,000
WILLIAM D. SLOANE	Carpets	$15,000,000
JOHN SLOANE	Carpets	$15,000,000
DAVID DOWS	Banker	$12,000,000
HERMAN O. ARMOUR	Provisions	$12,000,000
BRAYTON IVES	Banker	$10,000,000
JOHN H. STARIN	Transportation	$10,000,000
GEORGE BLISS	Banker	$8,000,000
SAMUEL THOMAS	Contractor	$7,500,000
CHARLES L. TIFFANY	Jeweller	$7,000,000
LE GRAND B. CANNON	Railroads	$6,500,000
HENRY H. COOK	Financier	$6,500,000
SETH M. MILLIKEN	Manufacturer	$6,000,000
JAMES A. BURDEN	Capitalist	$5,000,000
JOHN G. MOORE	Banker	$5,000,000
EDWARD D. ADAMS	Banker	$5,000,000
GEORGE F. BAKER	Banker	$4,500,000
CORNELIUS N. BLISS	Dry Goods	$4,500,000
M. C. D. BORDEN	Manufacturer	$4,000,000
WILLIAM BROOKFIELD	Manufacturer	$3,750,000
WILLIAM C. BROWNING	Clothier	$3,500,000
CHARLES T. COOK	Jeweller	$3,500,000
JOHN H. DAVIS	Broker	$3,250,000
JAMES H. HARPER	Publisher	$3,250,000
CHARLES B. FOSDICK	Banker	$3,250,000
MARCELLUS HARTLEY	Jeweller	$3,250,000
AUGUSTUS D. JOUILLARD	Dry Goods	$3,000,000
CHARLES LANIER	Banker	$3,000,000
EDWARD H. PERKINS, JR.	Banker	$3,000,000
FREDERICK D. TAPPEN	Banker	$3,000,000
WILLIAM H. WEBB	Shipbuilder	$3,000,000
ALFRED VAN SANTVOORD	Steamboats	$3,000,000
CHARLES A. PEABODY	Railroads	$2,500,000
JAMES A. GARLAND	Banker	$2,250,000
WOODBURY LANGDON	Dry Goods	$2,250,000
THOMAS L. JAMES	Banker	$2,000,000
JOSEPH H. CHOATE	Lawyer	$2,000,000
WILLIAM S. HAWK	Hotels	$2,000,000
WHITELAW REID	Editor	$2,000,000
WASHINGTON E. CONNOR	Banker	$2,000,000
TOTAL		$552,250,000

FIGURE 8.3. Half a billion back of McKinley. *New York Journal*, August 3, 1896, 8

Subscription Blank.—Fill in and Send with Contribution.

(*Date*)_____

*To*_____

*I hereby subscribe the sum of $*_____
*to the New York Journal's fund for the education of
the voters of the United States.*

(*Name*)_____

(*Address*)_____

[The Journal would like the full names and addresses of subscribers, but
agrees to use only initials or pseudonym when requested.]

FIGURE 8.4. Subscription blank. *New York Journal*, September 12, 1896, 12

who stood to benefit if Bryan's free-silver plan came to fruition, such
people actually donated very little. In fact, the largest single donor of
cash to Bryan's campaign was Hearst, who ran an ad campaign in his
newspaper in which he promised to match a portion of every dollar
donated to Bryan. Hearst ultimately funneled forty thousand dollars
to Bryan, though the value of his support for Bryan's campaign in his
newspapers amounted to far more.

Joseph Foraker, who supported McKinley but never hesitated to
criticize Hanna, expressed skepticism of Dawes's and Croly's total
and suggested Hanna used the money to expand his personal power.
He wrote, "The campaign funds so raised and disbursed by Mr. Hanna
were estimated at the time to amount to six or seven millions of dollars; but Mr. Croly states in his life of Mr. Hanna, apparently speaking
from the official record, that the total sum amounted to only about
three and one-half millions of dollars. Assuming that this statement is
correct, though I know there are many would challenge it, the amount
was sufficiently large to make a very popular man out of any distribu-
tor of it, no matter how unselfishly he might use it."[53] Where did the
large figures reported by people like Josephson, Koenig, and Foraker
come from? Was there any factual basis for them?

In modern campaign-finance parlance, there is more than one way to donate to a candidate. One way is with cash donations directly to candidates and political committees. Another way is with in-kind donations, which are donations of goods and services to candidates. A well-heeled interest group, for example, might donate staffers or polling services to a campaign. Under twenty-first-century campaign-finance law, the values of those in-kind donations have to be reported to the Federal Election Commission just as cash donations are reported. Just as there was no law requiring that cash donations be reported in 1896, there were no regulations requiring the reporting of in-kind donations either.

There were many in-kind donations made to the McKinley campaign whose value increased the amount of money raised by the campaign considerably. For example, railroad companies made large in-kind donations to the Republican campaign in the form of subsidized travel for delegations from around the country to visit McKinley's front porch. At the time, it was a commonly held view that it was cheaper to travel to Canton than it was to stay home. Clearly, these discounts had as much of a positive impact on McKinley's campaign as a cash donation handed to Mark Hanna in a white envelope, but the railroads did not prepare public statements about the value of such subsidized travel, and the campaign did not report receiving that value.

Another example of in-kind donation was press coverage. It is important to remember that the campaign of 1896 took place during an era of partisan press. The support that William Randolph Hearst gave to Bryan is well documented; but McKinley likewise received support from Republican newspapers and from some of the men behind those newspapers, such as H. H. Kohlsaat and the one-time presidential candidate Whitelaw Reid, editor of the *New York Tribune*. Both Kohlsaat and Melville Stone, the manager of the Associated Press, were part of the committee that drafted the gold plank in the Republican Platform of 1896, and Reid consulted with McKinley extensively about the plank, writing to him and Mark Hanna with suggestions and revisions as the Republicans gathered in St. Louis for their convention.[54] Reporters for Republican-leaning media outlets greatly subsidized the McKinley campaign effort, just as Hearst subsidized Bryan's efforts. In McKinley's case, reporters were stationed in Canton, while in Bryan's case, they traveled with him on his train back and forth across the country.

While it is possible to come up with hundreds of other examples of in-kind donations, it is also important to remember two things in general. First, both sides received in-kind donations, so it is not fair to condemn one side for receiving them. It is not as if the Bryan campaign piously turned down the friendly coverage it got from Hearst's newspapers or Coin Harvey's books, for example. In fact, that coverage was actively solicited by Bryan. In the 1900 campaign, Bryan implored Hearst to start a newspaper in Chicago so he would have a powerful media presence in the Midwest, and Hearst followed through for him.

Second, it is undoubtedly true that, just as McKinley received many more cash donations than Bryan, he also received many more in-kind donations. The reason for the discrepancy, however, is what is most notable. Again, this was a campaign centered on an issue of great importance to many people. Unfortunately for Bryan, there were more well-heeled people on McKinley's side of the issue than Bryan's. Maybe that reality should inspire a discussion about how important money ought to be in American political campaigns, but it does not mean that there was a conspiracy to defeat Bryan. It was, in fact, quite an open effort to beat him.

It was the issue, and not anything unusual about Mark Hanna's powers of persuasion and manipulation, that lined up the vast majority of America's wealthy on McKinley's side. Hanna and McKinley were, in fact, impediments to raising money for the Republican effort in the early effort. Only after the Rockefeller showed confidence in both men and only after William Jennings Bryan began to appear as a serious threat to win the election did the captains of industry begin to contribute to McKinley's campaign in an energetic fashion.

What All That Money Was For

The McKinley campaign, as envisioned by Hanna and implemented by Dawes and other lieutenants, was heavily dependent on printed material in English and in several other languages. The volume of printing was overwhelming, as Dawes often alluded to in his journal. The printing and distribution were coordinated by Perry Heath, and according to many different sources, the campaign produced in excess of one hundred twenty million copies of 275 different pamphlets, the vast majority of which came from the western headquarters in Chicago and were shipped around the country to state Republican committees for distribution.

Dawes wrote to McKinley of Heath's efforts in the campaign: "The pressure on Mr. Heath has been something terrible, and yesterday I was afraid he was going to give way under it. He is feeling much better today, and is going to be all right. I cannot speak too highly of his efficiency and good common sense."[55] Dawes's last financial statement indicated that the campaign spent roughly $469,000 on printing.[56]

In the first months of the campaign, the pamphlets were nearly all about the sound money issue, with remarks from McKinley, members of Congress, and experts on finance about the folly of a bimetal standard. Later in the campaign, the subject matter of the pamphlets grew to include more material about McKinley's favorite issue, protectionism. The pamphlets were produced in several different languages, including English, German, Yiddish, Spanish, Italian, French, Norwegian, Danish, and Dutch. In addition to the pamphlets, the campaign produced original stories for publication in friendly newspapers. The campaign also reprinted friendly newspaper articles for mass distribution. In some cases, they mailed entire friendly newspapers around the country. For example, the *Cleveland Leader* was used extensively during the campaign. Cleveland journalist and Hanna archivist J. B. Morrow reported, "When McKinley's campaign for the nomination opened in earnest, with Mr. Hanna in charge, some seventeen hundred copies of the *Leader* were sent out under Mr. Hanna's orders to all parts of the country. This fact was not known to me at the time but I afterwards learned that Mr. Hanna had obtained the names of leading citizens in several hundred congressional districts throughout the west and that he had ordered the *Leader* sent to each of these men for a period of three months."[57] Finally, the campaign also produced massive numbers of pictures, cartoons, handbills, buttons, and posters. According to Croly, the most popular poster was a picture of McKinley with the caption, "The Advance Agent of Prosperity."[58]

While the campaign, as envisioned by Hanna, was designed to leave all printing responsibilities to the Chicago office, William McKinley Osborne wrote to McKinley of trouble with that arrangement and urged for more printing to be done in New York in order to better facilitate the distribution of literature on the East Coast:

> There seems to be a terrific demand for literature everywhere. According to the plans laid out at Cleveland this was not to

be the place where literature was to be sent out. Chicago was to be the place. Experience thus far shows, however, that we must prepare literature here. We can not get any from Chicago, although we wrote for a supply ten days ago. I have had printed here Mr. Blaine's speech on the Bland-Allison Bill. Probably you saw the reasons put out in the papers why we printed it. We have contracted for a million copies. I spoke with Mr. Hanna over the long-distance telephone today.... I told him we must print matter here. There is an intense feeling everywhere, and much interest in this money question, and we have got to furnish the literature that will enlighten the people.[59]

Likewise, the Bryan campaign, largely subsidized by Hearst, also relied heavily on printed material, despite the three thousand speeches Bryan gave from July to November. His campaign train, on which Bryan reported he traveled 18,009 miles, was loaded with printed campaign material that was thrown from the train "at every town, village, railroad crossing, and farmhouse" and included pamphlets and copies of Hearst's *New York Journal*.[60] So, although Bryan was clearly deficient in funds, he was nevertheless able to get his message out.

One of the logistical challenges of the McKinley campaign was how to keep the candidate, who refused to travel, in front of the voters. Rather than taking the campaign on the road, the campaign had to be brought to McKinley. This effort was managed from the Chicago office, and during the course of the campaign, the parade of delegations to McKinley's front porch in Canton was continuous, facilitated, as already noted, by the subsidized travel offered by friendly railroads.

Each delegation went through basically the same routine. A delegation arrived at the train depot in Canton and was met by an official from the campaign. The campaign official spoke to the leader of the delegation; found out what remarks he planned to make; suggested some revisions if necessary to keep the statement in line with the campaign's message; and sent a runner ahead of the delegation so McKinley would know exactly what was going to be said, thus giving him time to prepare his response. Day after day, hour after hour, delegations came to McKinley's house. By the end of the campaign, the grass in his yard was worn away, the plants were trampled, and his front porch was severely damaged by souvenir seekers who dismantled it piece by piece. Reporters wrote stories about the appearances, and the campaign saw to it that news stories of the events were disseminated to regions around the country where they would have the desired positive effect on the campaign.

Throughout the front-porch campaign, McKinley spoke the party line on sound money and the gold standard, but he also stuck to his guns on the issue he was truly passionate about, protectionism. The campaign effectively linked both gold and protectionism with patriotism. The potent symbol of the American flag was closely linked to McKinley throughout the campaign.[61]

Hanna was credited with tying McKinley closely to the flag from the beginning of the campaign at the convention in St. Louis when he arranged for buttons with the image of the American flag on them to be distributed as McKinley campaign buttons. Later, millions of flags were bought and used in McKinley rallies and parades around the country.[62] According to Jones, the appeal to patriotism was particularly effective with upper-middle-class conservative Democrats and Republicans, and when Hanna arranged for a national flag day at the end of October, the Democratic Party was put in a terribly awkward, no-win position. Jones wrote,

> After Hanna issued the call for a national flag day in terms that made it at the same time a demonstration for McKinley, the Democratic Chairman, Jones, and Bryan attempted to neutralize the effect of Hanna's action by asking Democrats to join the demonstration as a tribute to the flag and the flag alone. This gesture by the Democratic Party had no effect whatever. It was inevitable that some ardent Democrats would resent the display of the flag in connection with the McKinley-Hobart campaign and in anger would tear down flags that were so used. As soon as the Democrats became principals in such incidents, the Republicans pointed to their actions as further proof of the lack of patriotism among the Democrats.[63]

In hindsight, of course, there was no reason to believe that Bryan was any less patriotic than McKinley.

In fact, both men felt they advocated agendas that were in the American public's best interest, but the since the Civil War, the Republicans

FIGURE 8.5. Last charge of the Buncombe brigade. Cartoon by Homer Davenport, *New York Journal*, October 31, 1896, 1

had waved the bloody shirt and associated the Democratic Party with secession. It should be noted that Democrats in the South also waved the bloody shirt to rally their supporters, and historian H. Wayne Morgan argues that they did so even more effectively, and for a longer time, than the Republicans.

Since McKinley was a Union veteran of the Civil War, it was not a long stretch when Hanna and the Republicans took the initiative and worked to portray McKinley as more American to voters (especially those in the East, Midwest, and West) than Bryan. However, Hanna endeavored, effectively, to so without overtly waving that bloody shirt, as Republicans did in previous campaigns. Hanna wanted the campaign to show that the Republicans were more than the victors of the Civil War, and for that reason, waving the bloody shirt was never a centerpiece of the campaign; but by claiming the American flag as a Republican symbol, voters made the connection themselves.

During the campaign, Bryan clung steadfastly to free silver as the centerpiece of his campaign. He did this to his detriment in the East, where he was already at a serious disadvantage. The currency question simply did not appeal to laborers or immigrants, whom he needed to peel away from the Republicans, as powerfully as other issues, like the use of injunctions by employers to prevent strikes and the income tax. Koenig observed, "In the eyes of his foes, Bryan was committing an enormous blunder. Mark Hanna, McKinley's campaign manager, rejoiced in the discovery that Bryan's 'talking silver all the time and that's where we've got him. And Joseph B. Foraker, another Republican potentate of Ohio, declared triumphantly, 'Mr. Bryan made himself by one speech and now he has unmade himself by one speech.'"[64] Bryan made free coinage the predominant issue of his campaign because he believed in what he was saying, but that did not mean everyone did.

While the issue was initially very potent for Bryan, developments in the world gold market during the campaign suddenly sapped the issue of its strength and emotion. Suddenly, and quite suspiciously to some observers, the amount of gold in the U.S. Treasury increased dramatically during the campaign, thanks to an influx from Europe.[65] This had the effect of putting more money into circulation and raising farm prices. While it was inflation, the progold side found it acceptable since it did not involve the coinage of silver. In a way, it was affirmation of what Bryan was saying—more money in circulation was good for the economy. Unfortunately for Bryan, it was done without silver and without him. As Koenig observed, "How could Bryan sound his notes of woe and reform when his rural audiences could see in the distance the outline of the very prosperity his campaign was promising?"[66] Undoubtedly, the sudden increase of gold in circulation and in wheat prices had an impact on his campaign. Koenig wrote,

> One political analyst was convinced that the sensational rise in wheat prices cost Bryan Minnesota, North Dakota, Iowa, California, and Oregon. It overwhelmed the silver issue and seemed automatically to vitiate the contention that gold had depreciated every other commodity. The wheat price rise was the consequence of crop failure in India and a sudden increase in the production of gold resulting from the discovery of new deposits in the Klondike, South Africa, and Australia, made operational by the cyanide process. *The validity of Bryan's quantitative theory of money was demonstrated—unfortunately for his own political welfare—before*

his election, rather than after, and to his opponent's profit. (emphasis added)[67]

It was much harder to make a possible currency shortage compelling to voters, and when gold became more plentiful and the financial straits of farmers suddenly lessened, Bryan was put in a very difficult position.

Later in the campaign, when speaking to eastern crowds, Bryan talked about other issues besides silver, but it was too little too late, and he lost in all the northeastern states and by a considerable margin in most. Despite the fact that he had the support of every major labor leader except Samuel Gompers of the American Federation of Labor, he never truly won rank-and-file labor over to his cause, largely because he failed to address issues that were important to urban workers until it was too late to do him any good.[68] In addition to the fact that he failed to address issues that were popular with workers, Bryan also failed to respond—either positively or negatively—to McKinley's true favorite issue, protective tariffs. While McKinley campaigned heavily on sound money, he never gave up on tariffs, and protective tariffs were a very popular issue with urban workers. By refusing to engage with McKinley on the issue, Bryan gave the Republican and his campaign the chance to appeal to them unimpeded on an issue that resonated with them.[69]

Despite Bryan's tactical blunder in deciding which issues to emphasize and his considerable disadvantage in fundraising, the election was much closer than one might have expected. Part of this may have been due to the fact that Bryan had such energetic support from William Randolph Hearst, who began an evening edition of the *Journal* in the middle of the campaign to help Bryan.

In part, Bryan's relative success in the campaign was almost certainly due to the energy and enthusiasm of his campaign. According to Bryan's bookkeeping, he logged over eighteen thousand miles and gave three thousand speeches during the campaign. In the end, McKinley won the popular vote by roughly six hundred thousand votes. He received 7.1 million votes, while Bryan received roughly 6.5 million votes. Bryan won more states than McKinley, twenty-six to twenty-one, but in the Electoral College, McKinley received 271 votes to Bryan's 176.

Both campaigns were fortunate to have remarkably enthusiastic support among rank-and-file voters. The reported level of passion in the electorate in 1896 is but a faded memory in nearly every modern election. Dawes's biographer Charles Leach described the enthusiasm of the campaign by comparing it to the much more sedate election of 1928. The 1928 campaign, he pointed out, had its own high level of controversy, thanks to the fact that Al Smith, the Democratic nominee was the first-ever Catholic presidential nominee, but was far less energetic than 1896. It was no coincidence, of course, that the campaign of 1928 was the first to avail itself of the country's first truly national medium, radio. As early as 1928, broadcasting demonstrated its impact on American politics. Leach wrote,

> Contrast the 1928 campaign (controversial because Al Smith was Catholic), with men and women voters—the women of course did not vote in 1896—sitting at home and listening to speeches by the two candidates broadcast by radio, to the doings of 1896—the enthusiasm, the night rallies when men marched in oilcloth capes, to prevent drippings from the kerosene torches on poles over their shoulders from ruining their clothes. Every boy able to walk took sides, and they fought like little devils, those youthful adherents of McKinley and the supporters of Bryan, while their elders were almost as rabid. The Middle West was aflame. It set its own self afire, but the fire had to be kept at white heat. What a job it was for the campaign managers of both sides![70]

One of the most fascinating aspects of the campaign of 1896 was the enthusiastic involvement of the devotees of the newest craze of the day, bicycling. Bascom Timmons wrote of what would, no doubt, be viewed by today's observers as a bizarre spectacle:

> The McKinley and Hobart Wheelman's League came to Canton. Battalions of wheelmen, two and four and six abreast, most in suits of pure white, faced in red, or in white capes with huge magenta collars. Bicycle floats, with McKinley and Hobart riding in tandem in the lead, Bryan and Sewell in second. Marchers followed the floats, carrying bicycle rims with pictures of McKinley and Hobart in the circles. They performed intricate mass-formation rides. In front of McKinley, they dismounted, raised their front wheels in salute. Their spokesman addressed the candidate: "The wheeled hosts of

the nation came to avow their allegiance to you. . . . Our bond of brotherhood is our wheel; not a mere toy or simple source of pleasure, but a great commercial auxiliary, the acme of mechanical skill in the evolution of vehicles." McKinley replied: "In this country of inventions, I doubt if any means of locomotion was ever so favorably received. Rapid transit in this novel form depends largely upon a single condition, good roads (loud applause and ringing of bicycle bells), and I am for them. There are 800,000 bicycles being produced each year. The bicycle has beaten the best time ever made by a running horse."[71]

Until the highly energized campaigns of 2004 and 2008, the level of excitement attending the campaign of 1896 would have been something hard to fathom in the unenthusiastic, uninteresting campaigns of the 1990s. The year 1896 was a time when political campaigns were a form of high entertainment. Now, in an era when we are besieged by entertainment from all sides, campaigns are often ignored by all but the most politically engaged among us.

Dawes, the linchpin of the western campaign, was brimming with confidence on the day before the election, November 1:

> The campaign, one of the most notable the country has every passed through, is drawing to a close. I write this on Sunday evening, before the eventful Tuesday. I am so confident of victory, and have always been, that I cannot even contemplate defeat as a possibility. It has been a great privilege to be connected with the campaign as one of the Executive Committee; and I have appreciated and, I think, improved my opportunities for gaining political knowledge and experience. I have kept my hands clean, and finish the campaign with a clear conscience.[72]

Given Dawes's early concerns about money, it is difficult to accept totally that he was always confident of victory, but it was also clear that Dawes was not writing his journal solely as a cathartic exercise: he was writing with future audiences in mind.

Unfortunately for Bryan, Dawes's confidence was well founded. McKinley won and took office with a majority of Republicans in both the House and the Senate. At the beginning of the Fifty-fifth Congress, the margin in the House was 206 Republicans to 124 Democrats, with 22 Populists, three silver Republicans, and one member of the Silver Party. In the Senate, the margin was 44 Republicans, 34 Democrats, five Populists, five Silver Republicans, and two members of the Silver Party. McKinley won fewer states than Bryan, but he won the states with the most electoral votes, such as New York, New Jersey, Pennsylvania, Ohio, Indiana, Illinois, Michigan, and Wisconsin. Koenig argued that Bryan's defeat could easily have been victory if he had won the electoral votes of California, Oregon, Kentucky, North Dakota, Indiana, and West Virginia by gaining a total of just 19,436 more popular votes in those states.[73] While many losing presidential candidates have similar experiences, those tantalizing statistics were more than enough to stoke the anger of Bryan's supporters.

Following the election, there were many Bryan supporters, including Bryan himself, who cried foul. While Bryan did not accuse McKinley's side of voter fraud, as many of his supporters did, he reprinted newspaper reports of "coercion, direct and indirect" of voters in his book.[74] His suggestion, made through the reprinted comments of friendly journalists, was that the McKinley forces strong-armed voters who would otherwise have supported Bryan. For instance, laborers were frightened into voting for McKinley by employers who told them that, if Bryan won, the companies they worked for would be driven out of business by Bryan's dangerous economic policies.

Ignatius Donnelly, a Bryan soldier from Minnesota who began his career as a Republican but also ran for office as a Democrat and as a member of several other parties, lamented the fact that laborers had not flocked to Bryan: "We had a splendid candidate and he made a gigantic campaign; the elements of reform were fairly united, and the depression of business universal, and yet in spite of all, the bankrupt millions voted to keep the yoke on their own necks! I tremble for the future."[75] It is difficult to assess the veracity of accusations like this because political ideology gets in the way. To supporters of Bryan, who believed in his ideas, telling workers that they would lose their jobs if Bryan won was the worst kind of political fearmongering. To supporters of McKinley and, more importantly, opponents of Bryan, they were telling workers the way of the world. Unfortunately for Bryan, the message of his opponents was just compelling enough to derail him in some critical states.

Hanna's postmortem of the campaign was much different. At a postelection party at the Republican Club in New York on November 10, 1896, he said,

> At first it was difficult to diagnose the situation, but it was soon discovered that we would have on our side a solid phalanx of patriotic citizens. The conclusion was also reached that under the influence of education we could leave the result to the people. The position of our party was misunderstood by a large class of people, particularly the farmers. The poison had been well distributed by our opponents, and the work of eradicating it was by no means easy. The work of education was first begun from the Chicago headquarters among the farmers of the states of the Middle West. Our literary bureau had documents prepared by the best minds, and 2,000,000 of these were distributed. Besides, we supplied what is known as patent insides and plate matter to 13,000 weekly newspapers. Even with this work it was found that many farmers did not understand the money question, and an army of "colporteurs" were sent into seven states of the Middle West.

In addition to talking about the mechanics of the campaign in the speech, Hanna also talked about Bryan as an opponent for McKinley:

> When Bryan was first nominated I was with my chief. I told Gov. McKinley that he would be a hard man to beat. I was familiar with the situation in the Middle West, and I pointed out the difficulties that would have to be overcome. Governor McKinley replied that, notwithstanding that, he had the greatest faith in the loyalty and integrity of the American people. Looking back over all this, it must be admitted that Bryan made a great canvass. . . . Matters began changing our way, although I was being accused of almost everything—particularly with raising the price of wheat. . . . In conclusion, I want to say that I have a soft spot for the sound-money Democrats. They frequently consulted our wishes, and finally word was passed along the line to "vote for McKinley."[76]

At the end of the event, Hanna was lauded by General Horace Porter, a Congressional Medal of Honor winner from the Civil War, who, suggested that, by refusing to join McKinley's cabinet, Hanna "refused to become a King in order to remain a Warwick."[77]

CHAPTER NINE

Mr. Hanna Goes to the Senate

fter a year of attacking Mark Hanna, the Democratic press might have shifted much of its focus from him if he simply returned to Ohio and went back to monitoring politics from that remote location. Hanna, however, was not interested in returning to Cleveland. He retired from his business career when he began running the McKinley campaign in earnest, and he harbored no desire to return to the family business. Many assumed he would take a position in the McKinley cabinet, but he had no interest in that either. There was speculation that Hanna might be McKinley's secretary of treasury or, more appropriately for the dispensing of patronage, the postmaster general. After the campaign, William McKinley wrote Hanna a letter of thanks, imploring him to join the cabinet:

> We are through with the election, and before turning to the future I want to express to you my great debt of gratitude for your generous life-long and devoted services to me. Was there ever such unselfish devotion before? . . . Now to the future. I turn to you irresistibly. I want you as one of my chief associates in the conduct of the government. From what you have so frequently and generously said to me in the past, I know that you prefer not to accept any such position, but still I feel that you ought to consider it a patriotic duty to accept one of the Cabinet offices.[1]

McKinley clearly wanted Hanna around, as is reflected by a letter from Whitelaw Reid to McKinley about his forthcoming cabinet. He

wrote of Hanna, "Your remarks about Mr. Hanna were purely tentative; and as to him anyway, no other human being can judge half as
well as yourself. Knowing Mr. Hanna's tried ability and devotion, and
the entire confidence you have reposed in him, I have felt pretty sure
of two things; that as the time for going to Washington approached,
you would not like to leave him behind, and that he would not like to
shrink from whatever you wished."[2]

Hanna, however, did not want to join the cabinet, as McKinley wished
him to do. Hanna had many reasons for resisting this entreaty, however. First, he was sensitive about his portrayal in the press, and he
worried a cabinet appointment would be seen as a political payoff. Although he was never averse to dispensing such payoffs, he worried about
the effect receiving one would have on his reputation and McKinley's.
Russell Alger, McKinley's first secretary of war, reported to Hanna's
old nemesis Foraker why Hanna did not want to join the cabinet: "I
called upon Hanna. I asked him if he was going into the Cabinet, and
he said no. In the first place it would look as though he was getting
from President McKinley a compensation in way of office for his services, and in the next place he could not afford the time to leave his
great business to go to Washington permanently, as he would have to
do to fill any place in the Cabinet; unless as he said to me, I had your
place, which will occupy less time than any other."[3]

In addition to these concerns, it is also true that Hanna simply did
not see much personal opportunity in being a cabinet secretary. He
wanted to be more than a political manager, and to him that meant he
needed to win a prestigious office of his own.[4] It is likely that McKinley, the president who always kept an eye on his legacy, knew what
Hanna really wanted when he wrote the letter. His very public letter
to Hanna may well have been designed to give McKinley some cover
for what was about to happen. McKinley made it clear to Hanna in the
letter that, while he wanted his advice in Washington, Hanna had to
hold some sort of office—he could not have Hanna hanging around
the White House appearing like a political hired gun.[5]

McKinley sent a final, resigned, written statement to Hanna on
February 18, 1897:

> It has been my dearest wish ever since I was elected to the
> Presidency, to have you accept a place in my cabinet. This

you have known for months and are already in receipt of a letter from me . . . written a few days after the election. . . . I have always hoped and so stated to you at every convenient opportunity, that you would yet conclude to accept the Post-master-Generalship. You have so often declined and since our conversation on Tuesday last, I have reluctantly concluded that I can not induce you to take this or any other Cabinet position. You know how deeply I regret this determination and how highly I appreciate your life-long devotion to me.[6]

From this, one can clearly see that McKinley valued Hanna and wanted him close. What cannot be determined from the only two written communications on the subject is whether McKinley preferred to have Hanna in the cabinet because he thought it was the best use of Hanna's skills or because he wanted to ensure that he was Hanna's boss. Just as Hanna worried about the impact negative media coverage of him on McKinley, McKinley worried about it too. He also, as events in coming years would show, worried about Hanna's occasionally impulsive, overly enthusiastic behavior.

For many years, Hanna had expressed a desire to hold an office, but it was not a cabinet portfolio that he wanted. Rather, he wanted to serve in the United States Senate. In a conversation with Jim Dempsey, Hanna expressed this desire as early as 1892. In his statement following Hanna's death, Dempsey reported,

> During our conversation Mr. Hanna said: "Jim, there is one thing I should like to have but it is the thing I never can get." I asked: "What is it?" He replied: "I would rather be a Senator in Congress than have any other office on earth." He spoke with great feeling, telling me that I was the only person to whom he had ever expressed this wish. I remember that I said to him: "If you feel that way why don't you go to work?" To this Mr. Hanna replied: "Jim, I could no more be elected to the Senate than I could fly." This Conversation occurred on January 3, 1892.[7]

McKinley referred to Hanna's desire in his February 18 letter. He wrote, "You have said that if you could not enter the Senate, you would not enter public life at all. No one, I am sure, is more desirous of your success than myself, and no on appreciates more deeply how helpful and influential you could be in that position. It seems to me that you will be successful, and I predict for you a most distinguished and satisfactory career in that greatest of parliamentary bodies."[8]

The problem was that when McKinley was elected president four years later, there was no open Senate seat in Ohio. For Hanna to become senator, it meant either John Sherman or the newly elected James B. Foraker, Hanna's nemesis, would have to be moved out of the way. Moving Foraker out of the way was out of the question; but Sherman was aging, and he had cabinet-level experience, having served as Rutherford Hayes's secretary of treasury.

Sherman's term in the Senate was to end in March 1899, but McKinley wanted Hanna in Washington, and he wanted him there in an official capacity sooner than that. For his part, Hanna certainly did not want to wait. Even if he was willing to wait, Hanna knew he was not guaranteed victory in an election in Ohio because he had many enemies even within his own party and he was far from the "Boss of Ohio," which many in the press painted him to be. Even getting appointed to fill out the remainder of Sherman's term was a challenge for Hanna.

The difficulty stemmed from the fact that the man who had to appoint him was Ohio's Republican governor, Asa Bushnell, an ally of Foraker. Hanna opposed Bushnell's first nomination to become governor in 1895, and Bushnell remembered the slight. In his book *Notes of a Busy Life,* Foraker reported a conversation with Hanna on the question of appointing Sherman to the cabinet and Hanna to the Senate. Foraker wrote that he was surprised to hear of the plan and even more surprised to hear that Hanna and McKinley already viewed both appointments as a fait accompli. Foraker clearly believed that Sherman was being moved out of the Senate chiefly to make room for Hanna. When Russell Alger wrote to Foraker in February 1897, much of his agenda was to convince Foraker of the sincerity of McKinley's appointment of Sherman to the State Department. Recounting his conversation with Hanna, Alger writes,

> I asked him about his plans for the Senator-ship, and he became quite reticent. He said, "Of course I would like to go to the Senate because that would be the voice of my State instead of the President. I would like to go there," he said, "as

the associate of Governor Foraker and should recognize his leadership, as the senior Senator because he is always ready in the field of debate, and as we all know, an excellent man to associate with." He however expressed very grave doubts about Governor Bushnell appointing him. . . . From there I went to Canton and met a most cordial reception. . . . I asked him (McKinley) concerning Hanna and the Senatorship. He said he had understood it had been stated that he appointed Senator Sherman to his Cabinet, for the purpose of making a place for Mr. Hanna. That was absolutely untrue. He had looked the field over and decided that he wished Senator Sherman in the place, and appointed him without even consulting Hanna, and that the one had absolutely no connection with the other. At the same time, he said of course he would be gratified "if Governor Bushnell would see his way clear to appoint Mr. Hanna, as you know our personal relation," "and then I feel as though Hanna had fairly earned the recognition."[9]

Alger's communication has the feel of a propaganda effort, designed to persuade Foraker, but it did not work.

According to Foraker's version of events, reported in his autobiography, he remained entirely uninvolved in the matter, but he made a point of writing that he thought Hanna was not qualified to be a senator at the time and that he did not think Sherman was a good choice for secretary of state, largely because of his failing health. He reported expressing his concerns about Sherman to Hanna, but that Hanna was determined to move forward. Foraker wrote, "'A man convinced against his will is of the same opinion still.' I discovered that I was arguing with exactly that kind of a man, and was glad when it came time to tell him I would think the matter over more carefully, find out what the Governor might be willing to do, end my call and get away."[10] Foraker reported having a similar discussion with McKinley that ended in much the same way.

Despite Foraker's claim that he had nothing to do with the drawn-out process of appointing Hanna or with the disputed election of Hanna to a term of his own in 1898, a passage in his book belies that claim and shows how deep his resentment of Hanna went:

> This is a disagreeable chapter in Ohio politics, not only be-
> cause of the embarrassments caused by the plan . . . but also
> because of the unfortunate results that followed, so far as
> Mr. Sherman was concerned. Governor Bushnell's friends
> and all my friends were displeased with the proposition.
> Mr. Hanna's attitude during the campaign of 1889 and his
> rather boastful proclamation given in a New York inter-
> view, that he was entitled to credit for having defeated me
> and "driven me out of politics," followed by his opposition
> to my candidacy for Senator in 1891–2 were still fresh and
> rankling in the warlike minds of thousands of good Repub-
> licans, who were not afraid to battle. To all such the propo-
> sition seemed like a piece of impudence and effrontery. As
> I now recall those troublesome days, the Governor and I were
> about the only ones who kept our temper and tried ear-
> nestly to bring about some satisfactory result.[11]

Foraker continued, suggesting that he and Bushnell finally gave in and
let Hanna take Sherman's seat in the Senate to serve the greater good.
He wrote, "At last we reached the conclusion that, while Senator Hanna
had no claim on either Governor Bushnell or myself for such recognition, yet in view of the President's desires and the importance of having
harmony in the party at home and with the administration at Washington, it was better to yield. Thereupon, February 21st, Governor Bushnell
wrote Hanna to that effect, thus ending what Mr. Croly says was for Mr.
Hanna an 'agony of suspense.'"[12] Clearly, Foraker was much more intimately involved in this process than he might have liked to appear, consulting with Bushnell about how to resolve the Hanna situation.

Though McKinley made his strong preference known to Bushnell,
the governor kept Hanna waiting many months before he finally came
to Washington for McKinley's inauguration in March of 1897 and
gave Hanna his commission. Hanna and McKinley must have been
frustrated by the delay, and Hanna wrote to McKinley of an incident he felt was making Bushnell delay the announcement that he
would appoint Hanna. Hanna wrote about the newspaper publication of a letter detailing plans to make Sherman the secretary of state,
thereby clearing the way for Hanna to become senator: "The effect of
the headline of the *Cincinnati Enquirer* gives Bushnell an excuse for

resenting this afront which is about what you might expect."[13] In late February, Bushnell had sent a letter to Hanna, as Foraker indicated, that demonstrated his intention to give the seat to him. It included an explanation for waiting so long to make the appointment:

> When Senator Sherman announced his intention of accepting the portfolio of the State Department in the Cabinet of President McKinley, I deemed it best to make no announcement as to my action in the matter of appointing his successor until the vacancy actually existed. However, the interest of the people and their anxiety to know what will be done has become so evident that it now seems proper to make the definite statement of my intentions. I, therefore, wish to communicate to you my conclusion to appoint you as the successor of Senator Sherman when his resignation shall have been received.[14]

Even after he had received the letter, though, Hanna still doubted Bushnell would actually appoint him to the Senate. He remained anxious about it until the governor handed him his commission in the lobby of the Arlington Hotel in Washington the day after McKinley's inauguration, March 5, 1897. It is difficult to say with certainty if the reason Bushnell waited so long to follow through with the appointment was that he was waiting for Sherman to leave office or if he was waiting for a different reason. It is possible, for instance, that he wanted to give Foraker the opportunity to take his oath of office first, making him Ohio's senior senator.[15]

Later, after Sherman's dismal performance as secretary of state, Hanna and McKinley were accused of manipulating Sherman into leaving his Senate seat to make room for Hanna. Foraker, for instance, implied this in his autobiography. However, there is no evidence that when he accepted the portfolio of secretary of state, Sherman felt he was being shoved aside. Later, after his disastrous tenure in that position and as his mental and physical health deteriorated, he expressed bitter sentiments about the move, but it is impossible to know how much of that thinking was his own and how much he was influenced by others.[16] Captain J. C. Donaldson, Sherman's longtime aide, wrote a statement following Hanna's death that made it clear he did not feel Sherman was manipulated out of his Senate seat:

In 1897, Mr. Sherman expressed to me his desire to return to the Senate, should the Republicans of the state desire it, and asked me to assist him in ascertaining the drift of sentiment. . . . Immediately, a Cabinet appointment began to be discussed, and very many of his tried and true friends urged him by letter to round out his career in the Cabinet. I was doubtful of the wisdom of his abandoning the race for the Senate, but I never ventured a suggestion, further than to assure him that I thought he could be elected. I could see by Mr. Sherman's letters, that he was not averse to a Cabinet appointment, and finally, on the invitation of President McKinley, did accept the Premiership—which called forth the letters handed to you—and was accepted, I am sure, without any pressure whatever, on Mr. Hanna's part. . . . He was always recognized as a stanch friend of Senator Sherman. I make this statement in refutation of the charge that Mr. Hanna had manipulated Mr. Sherman, against his will, out of the Senate.[17]

There were no positions in government viewed as being more prestigious than secretary of state. It was often seen as a stepping stone to being president. Sherman had given up his presidential ambitions, but he was certainly aware of the symbolic importance of the job. He was no doubt honored by the idea of rounding out his public career with the appointment.

Once he was given the appointment to replace Sherman in the Senate, Hanna had to worry about the upcoming election to

FIGURE 9.1. A tight squeeze. Cartoon by Homer Davenport, *New York Journal*, November 4, 1897, 1

serve out a remaining year of Sherman's term and another six years of his own. Since this was before the passage of the Seventeenth Amendment to the Constitution and the direct election of senators, Hanna first had to make sure a friendly group of state legislators was elected in Ohio in 1897. Hanna seemed to be in complete control when the state's Republicans gathered for the convention in Toledo in June.[18] During the campaign that followed, Hanna and his allies worked to get him the endorsement of the Republicans in eighty-four out of Ohio's eighty-eight counties, and, according to Croly, "His candidacy dominated the campaign and either overawed or included all other issues."[19] During the campaign, Hanna traveled the state extensively and spoke on his behalf for the first time to sell himself to Ohioans. Croly wrote, "The voters of Ohio had much more reason in the fall of 1897 to be curious about Mr. Hanna than to have confidence in him. He was one of the best advertised men in the country, but the people did not know him. While they had read a great deal about him in the newspapers, their reading probably misrepresented him and predisposed them against him."[20]

Hanna campaigned with great enthusiasm, and, in October, McKinley returned to Ohio to aid the campaign by appearing in Cincinnati and Canton.[21] McKinley remained very involved in the campaign through its completion, making appeals to people in and out of Ohio to support Hanna. He tried unsuccessfully, for example, to get Carl Schurz, a highly-respected progressive Republican who served as President Hayes's secretary of the interior and as a one-term senator from Missouri during the Reconstruction, to speak in Cleveland on Hanna's behalf.[22] McKinley also coordinated efforts to bring errant Ohio Republicans into line. For instance, the president got Representative Charles Grosvenor to put some friendly pressure on Ohio state senator J. L. Carpenter. Grosvenor wrote to Carpenter, "The President called my attention to the article in the Columbus correspondence of the Cincinnati Commercial Tribune of yesterday morning, which arrived here today, headed 'Carpenter, the Sphinx.' I could make no explanation about it except to say to the President that you were a Hanna man; that you talked so during the campaign and that I could not conceive of any possibility that could have changed you."[23]

On the other side, Democrats, including William Jennings Bryan, came from around the country to participate in the campaign as well.[24]

This was much more than a run-of-the-mill state-legislative campaign, for it was a referendum on Mark Hanna, a rehash of campaign 1896, and a preview of 1900. The campaign appeared to work out well for Hanna. In November, the Republicans won majorities in both houses of the Ohio legislature, and the vast majority of those newly elected and reelected legislators pledged to support Hanna in his bid to remain in the U.S. Senate. Charles Dick, who eventually succeeded Hanna in the Senate, explained the situation this way: "The State Convention met at Toledo that year and endorsed him with enthusiasm. I think resolutions endorsing him had been or were adopted by eighty-four of the eighty-eight counties in Ohio. There was no candidate against him; no other candidate was thought of during the progress of the campaign. After the election in November Mr. Hanna on the face of the returns would be elected by a majority of fifteen."[25] While Hanna's return to the Senate seemed to be a fait accompli, in truth his reelection was far from certain.

The vote for Ohio's seat in the U.S. Senate proved to be much closer than the returns in the state-legislative election might have indicated, as Dick explained:

> There were seven bolters and finally on joint ballot he had a majority of one. But he should have had a majority of fifteen, as I remember it. The opposition developed immediately after the election. I might say the plotting, so far as the bolters were concerned, began before the election. . . . The fifteen majority melted away. The organization of the Legislature went against us. That was a very severe shock and ordinarily would have indicated Hanna's defeat. We lost the Senate and the House both.[26]

Congressman Theodore Burton, another Hanna ally, described the effort to defeat Hanna in this way: "I went to Columbus in January 1898 to do what I could for him when he was a candidate for Senator. I was there throughout the contest and a more desperate conspiracy was never organized against a public man in this country than he had to face at that time. The conspiracy of Catiline was a patriotic agreement among ladies and gentlemen for the public interest as compared with the combination which attempted to beat Mr. Hanna."[27] Setting aside Burton's overly dramatic analogy between Hanna's difficult election and the alleged misdeeds of Catiline in 62 BCE that ended in his bloody death, Burton was correct when he asserted that there was a concerted effort to prevent Hanna from being elected. There were two main causes of the "conspiracy" that led to Hanna's surprisingly close fight in the Senate election. The first was the behavior of Foraker and his allies. The second was the behavior of another resentful Ohio Republican, Robert McKisson, mayor of Cleveland.

At the state Republican convention in 1895, prior to McKinley's successful presidential campaign, Hanna and McKinley ran into significant opposition from a coalition led by Foraker, the "boss" of Cincinnati politics; George Cox; and A. L. Conger, a businessman from Akron whom Foraker frequently supported in opposition to Hanna-backed candidates as a delegate to Republican conventions. At the 1895 convention, Hanna and McKinley lost their handle on the state Republican Party. They lost control of the party's gubernatorial nomination when Asa Bushnell was nominated against their wishes; and they lost control of the endorsement of candidates for other statewide offices, such as the post of state auditor they hoped to win for Charles Dick. Moreover, the convention also took what Croly described as an unprecedented step when it endorsed Foraker as the state's next senator. This upheaval in the Ohio Republican Party did not end up damaging McKinley, but the story was different for Hanna. Croly wrote, "The outcome was generally interpreted as a victory for Mr. Foraker; and Mr. McKinley's opponents in other states used it to cast doubt upon McKinley's ability to go to the Convention with the united support of his own state. In the end the consequences of the defeat were, however, much more serious to Mr. Hanna than they were to Mr. McKinley."[28] Bushnell became governor despite Hanna's opposition, which was evidence that Hanna was not, in fact, the boss of Ohio politics, and he did not forget the fact that Hanna had tried to prevent his nomination. The consequences Croly wrote of were Bushnell's reticence in appointing Hanna to the Senate in 1897 and the closeness of the Senate election in 1898.

The candidate whom Hanna's antagonists supported in opposition to him in the 1898 election was Robert McKisson, who had his own reasons to dislike Mark Hanna. When McKisson decided to run for mayor of Cleveland in 1895, he asked Hanna for his endorsement. McKisson, then a member of Cleveland's city council, was not supported by the city's business community; and when he went to see Hanna, seeking his endorsement, Hanna told him, "Young man, you have yet to win your spurs." Despite Hanna's open opposition to the young man's mayoral campaign, McKisson won the election and became Cleveland's mayor, which is clear evidence that Hanna was not even the boss of Cleveland politics. As Thomas Beer observed, "The truth is that Mark Hanna's control of Cleveland was never so absolute as legend asserts, and Robert McKisson was then able to begin the contrivance of a personal machine for his own ends."[29]

Despite his victory, McKisson harbored a grudge against Hanna, much as Bushnell did. According to Charles Dewstoe, who was the postmaster of Cleveland at the time of Hanna's death, "When Hanna was a candidate for Senator . . . McKisson and his friends united with the Democrats to defeat him."[30] Many of Hanna's supporters were incredulous that McKisson was the man whom his opponents rallied around in the Senate race because they viewed him as a man of low character. Congressman Theodore Burton said, "McKisson in some respects, politically at least, is a degenerate and was egotistical enough to believe that he could organize a movement in Cleveland that could destroy Mr. Hanna."[31] Nevertheless, McKisson was the man whom the rebellious Republicans supported in a campaign organized in Columbus by Charles Kurtz.[32] The Republicans who allied with the Democrats to unseat Hanna included Foraker, Asa Bushnell, George Cox, and Kurtz.

An Ohio state senator, James R. Garfield, son of President James A. Garfield, was in charge of the effort in the state senate to make sure Hanna retained his seat. Garfield said, "From Cleveland we made various inquiries regarding all the members of the legislature and from the inquiries concerning the leaders of the Cuyahoga county delegation, Burke, Bramley, and Mason, we were convinced there would be an attempt to bolt the caucus nomination of Senator Hanna and precipitate the fight. That afterwards came on."[33] Hanna set up camp in Columbus and personally worked to make sure that the Republicans, many of whom he campaigned to elect to the state legislature in the first place, voted for him. As the drama intensified, Croly reported that "Columbus came to resemble a medieval city given over to an angry feud between armed partisans. Everybody was worked up to a high pitch of excitement and resentment. Blows were exchanged in the hotels and on the streets. There were threats of assassination."[34]

Rumors abounded that legislators were held hostage by the forces of both Hanna and McKisson. Some of the reports had more truth than others. One such story was related by Major Estes G. Rathbone, a friend of Hanna's who later become deeply embroiled in a postal scandal in Cuba that generated significant tension between Hanna and McKinley during the reelection campaign in 1900.

Rathbone told the story of a legislator-elect from Union County named John E. Griffith. Weeks before the legislators gathered in Columbus to vote, McKisson's allies met with Griffith's wife and gave her one thousand dollars in return for her husband's vote. The trouble for Griffith was that the Union County Republicans had instructed him to vote for Hanna. According to Rathbone, when Griffith and his wife got to Columbus, they were spirited away to McKisson's headquarters at the Southern Hotel and kept under a twenty-four-hour guard. When Rathbone and Hanna's allies got word that Griffith did not want to vote for McKisson, someone was sent to the Southern Hotel and, before McKisson's forces "knew it, Griffith and his wife were in our carriage and were being driven rapidly to the Neil House." The Neil House was Hanna's headquarters, and Griffith and his wife were kept there, "practically under lock and key," until it was time for him to cast his vote for Hanna. Rathbone reported having an hours-long discussion with Mrs. Griffith in which he advised her that "there was only one way open to her husband and that was to keep the thousand dollars and vote for Mr. Hanna."[35] Ultimately, Griffith voted for Hanna. The record is unclear about what he did with the thousand dollars.

According to Charles Dick, once the Democrats and the insurgent Republicans decided to work together for McKisson, "Every species of boodle and corrupt politics known in any campaign was indulged in. Money and offices, threats and debauchery were resorted to in the campaign against Mr. Hanna. I doubt if there is in the history of the country anything quite like it, anything quite so bad."[36] In just one example of many, James R. Garfield related a story about one legislator from Cleveland who turned against Hanna:

> Bramley admitted . . . that his real reason for opposing Mr. Hanna was that his extensive contracts with the city of Cleveland for brick and for paving would be cut off if he did not follow McKisson and that McKisson and his machine could ruin his business. I talked with him frankly and

he admitted that he had pledged himself to support Senator Hanna before the election and that the situation was very embarrassing to him at that time. He said he would be damned if he voted for Senator Hanna and he would be damned if he voted against him. "I am between the devil and the deep blue sea," he declared. He said that McKisson refused his public contracts under the McKisson administration, but that I was convinced if he voted for Senator Hanna and McKisson tried to ruin him the citizens of Cleveland would not permit such a thing to happen. Bramley replied that McKisson had him where it was impossible to do anything except to oppose Mr. Hanna.[37]

Of course, Hanna's opponents were not the only ones accused of high jinks and shenanigans.

FIGURE 9.2. What a difference being appointed and being elected to the Senate. Cartoon by Homer Davenport, *New York Journal*, October 28, 1897, 1

The senator's allies were also accused of playing dirty in order to keep Hanna in office. Hearst and his reporters were, of course, particularly outspoken in their criticism. The most famous accusation—famous because it was featured prominently on the front page of the *New York Journal*—made against Hanna and his allies involved a newly elected legislator from Cincinnati named John Otis. Otis may have made a particularly appealing subject for Hearst because he was a Silver Republican. While the scandal was splashed across the front page of Hearst's and other opposition newspapers, it apparently had little impact on public opinion where it mattered most, Ohio. Most of the public in his home state supported Hanna. Nevertheless, the story remains a black mark on Hanna's legacy.

According to Charles Dick, the trouble began when Major Rathbone told Dick that he had been contacted by a New York businessman named C. C. Shayne. Shayne seemed to be genuinely outraged at the notion that Republican representatives would vote for anyone other than Hanna. Shayne wrote to McKinley, arguing, "The renegated Republicans in Ohio, like the renegades of the Revolution, will be placed on the black list by the American people. It is a crime for a man to be elected by the people for a purpose and then violate it, by working directly against his constituents." Shayne promised McKinley that "those representatives who were elected and instructed to vote for Senator Hanna who have deserted him will be buried so deep by the condemnation of an indignant people that they will never be heard of again politically."[38]

Shayne claimed he had influence with some legislators from the Cincinnati area and that he could help recruit some pro-Hanna votes. In another letter to McKinley, Shayne wrote, "I received a telegram from Cincinnati this morning, stating that Otis had just sent you the following telegram: 'For the best interest of Ohio and the Republican party, I shall cast my vote for Mark A. Hanna for Senator, both for short and long term.' This is just as I expected after batteries had been brought to bear upon him. Others will follow him."[39]

Shayne put Rathbone in contact with a man in Ohio named Henry M. Boyce who would act as a go-between. Dick, who was careful in his statement to distance himself from any personal involvement in the matter, said he told Rathbone to look into the matter. Eventually, the contact led to Otis who, in addition to being a newly elected representative, was also a pharmacist with a failing business. According to Dick, after he put Rathbone in charge of the matter, he had nothing further to do with the situation. He said, "The next thing I heard about it was that an effort was being made to have Boyce, S. D. Hollenbeck, and Rathbone arrested for trying to bribe Otis and a great sensation was sprung in Columbus and the State concerning the matter. When it was sprung it made a terrible sensation. The newspapers played it up in big type and the situation was very menacing, indeed, to Mr. Hanna's cause."[40] Like Dick, Rathbone denied any wrongdoing in the Otis matter.[41]

Many of the people who gave statements about Hanna after his death were his friends and political allies, so it is not surprising that they spoke supportively of the senator. Many of them denied money was used to bribe anyone for his vote. Representative Burton's denial was typical. He said, "I never saw any evidence of the use of money in Columbus and don't believe any money was used corruptly."[42] Throughout his career in politics, Hanna was accused of using money to grease the skids. His opponents always made the charge, and his friends always denied it.

Given Hanna's determination to win and his willingness to play by the rules as they existed, money may have changed hands during the campaign, but if it did, it is important to remember the context. If Hanna engaged in such behavior, that was the way the game was played on both sides. To Hanna, he was not breaking the law: he was playing by the rules of the game. This is difficult to judge from the perspective of a post-Progressive, post-Watergate, post–Iran-Contra, post-Whitewater, post–war-on-terror world. As James R. Garfield observed, in a tone that was at once disapproving and understanding, "In the matter of offices Mr. Hanna always considered it the proper thing to promise political patronage for political services. He held that to be good politics and he paid his political debts in that way. I have no doubt that he made promises in advance. I think that in municipal affairs that is the way in which he carried on his political business. And he always kept his political promises."[43] Later in his statement he continued, "The Senator was a man of wonderfully big heart and it was a very great pleasure to be with him. But I always felt that he lacked ideals, politically. He had been brought up in the school of practical politics. He was an absolute believer in the

Republican party. The idea that civil service reform had anything to do with practical politics didn't appeal to him. He said you had to take human nature as it came. . . . I mean that Mr. Hanna hadn't ideals in the sense that he felt there was any use in attempting to improve practical political conditions."[44]

In the case of his Senate victory in 1898, however, Garfield, along with all of Hanna's close associates, denied that Hanna sanctioned the granting of favors and the distribution of money to get the votes he needed for the Senate. Garfield said, "Mr. Hanna was in a most trying position. He was stronger than I had ever seen him. Men came to him, his personal friends, men whom he had known all his life and insisted that the public exigencies required that he should shut his eyes to some things. But he declined to do it."[45] Garfield's claim fit well with other reports about Hanna: he would do anything for the Republican Party, and some of it may well have violated the law, but he never broke or bent the law for personal gain.

For many, this may be a distinction without a difference, but it made sense to Hanna. For Hanna, loyalty to the Republican Party was paramount to everything else because the party stood for ideas that were good for the country. The disruption caused by his opponents outraged him because he perceived it as damaging to the party. Garfield explained Hanna's anger in this way:

> The Senator told me once that these men got around him like leeches and insisted that Grosvenor and others had promised them this or that. The thing which disgusted Mr. Hanna with that Legislature was that men who had promised their constituents they should vote for him would come around and demand offices. Some of them were given offices. John J. Sullivan was made a United States District Attorney, but with no promise beforehand. Leland was made a judge in Indian Territory. Voight was made collector of customs at Cincinnati; I don't think there was any bargain. I would have known it if there had been. Voight promised me to vote for Mr. Hanna and nothing of that kind was ever mentioned.[46]

It was impossible at the time to figure out exactly what really happened. It is even more difficult today to figure out what happened. Garfield said, "I never have been sure as to what some of the men who called themselves Senator Hanna's friends really did do. . . . At that time I knew nothing definite and I know nothing today."[47]

While Garfield vouched for Hanna but not necessarily for his friends, Charles Dick went farther. He said, "Of course I have heard a great deal said about the use of money during that whole proceeding. I do not believe a cent went to any of the seventy-three who voted for Mr. Hanna. I don't believe one of that number ever received a dollar directly or indirectly to vote for Mr. Hanna."[48] Dick reported a conversation he later had with President McKinley. He said, "Mr. President, there isn't anything in Mr. Hanna's election from start to finish that is not honorable, clean and justifiable," and he again denied that money changed hands for votes.[49]

Time and again through his career in politics, Hanna showed that he hated nothing more than a turncoat. As men elected to the Ohio legislature who pledged to support Hanna continued to turn up saying they opposed him, Hanna's incredulity turned to intense anger. As Garfield said, "They were afterwards called the traitors."[50] As the vote in the state legislature approached, the chances of Hanna's retaining his seat began to look rather grim.

Hanna, of course, was not without resources. It is helpful, for example, when you are good friends with the president of the United States, a man who was also personally very influential in Ohio politics. McKinley was very concerned that Hanna might lose the Ohio seat. He informed Hanna that he had written a letter to a member of the Ohio House imploring the man to vote for Hanna because "I want no failure on my part to result in your defeat, which I would regard as a great calamity."[51] In his journal, Charles Dawes related a tale of McKinley's personal involvement in the drama in Columbus. On January 8, 1898, Dawes wrote,

> The President read me a letter which at the request of a large number of Hanna's friends from Columbus, he was writing to Jones, the Stark county member of [the] Ohio House, who announced that he would vote against Hanna contrary to the instructions of the convention of the people who nominated him. This letter he sent by a special messenger (an army man) to Columbus, with instructions to Jones to fulfill the people's commission entrusted to him. It was splendid evidence of the President's loyalty to his friend, Mr. Hanna.[52]

In this letter, McKinley wrote that voting against Hanna would "inflict upon the Republican Party of Ohio an injury which it will require long years to heal—will shock the moral sense of all parties and shake confidence in party conventions and the binding force of popular elections. It is not a case of personal preference. The party has spoken and the people of Ohio have ratified its action at the polls. Nothing remains for the Republican Representative but to register with fidelity the people's choice."[53]

Why was McKinley so invested in Hanna's Senate career? One obvious reason was that McKinley certainly felt a debt to Hanna, whose efforts were in large part responsible for putting him in the White House. McKinley also wanted to make sure his loyal supporter stayed in the Senate to guard the administration's interests. However, to a very real extent, Hanna's reelection in Ohio was seen by many as a referendum on McKinley's administration. Hanna received a telegram from Russell Alger, for example, who wrote that even Hanna's old rivals in the Senate were concerned for his political survival. Alger wrote, "Senators Quay and T. C. Platt were at my house yesterday. All said your defeat would be a national calamity. It is already cropping out in Maryland and the chances are if you are defeated New York and Pennsylvania will politically go to pieces."[54]

In the end, Hanna's tactics—whatever they really were—and his allies carried the day. McKisson and his coalition of Democrats and rebellious Republicans were defeated, and Hanna retained the seat in the Senate. On January 11, Dawes wrote in his journal, "The news of Mr. Hanna's victory . . . was received. I was greatly pleased," and, in theory, the drama was over.[55] Of course, where Hanna was concerned, the drama was never over. On the other side, Alfred Henry Lewis summed things up for the opposition press. He wrote, "The opposition to Hanna was utterly disorganized by the history of yesterday, and, practically speaking, went into joint session today somewhat like a routed army might take up some battle it could not avoid. The Hanna line was firm, and it carried victory before it. There is nothing like 'the cohesive' power of plunder, nothing like coin of the realm to stiffen a line of battle."[56] While his place in the Senate was assured, the debate about how he managed to hold the seat raged on, as opponents and the Democratic press continued to cry foul. For his part, Hanna, ever solicitous of and devoted to McKinley, wired the president, "The triumph of party principles in Ohio today is recognized by Republicans everywhere as a merited endorsement of your administration and I congratulate you sincerely."[57]

Croly, ever Hanna's advocate in print, wrote, "He triumphed only because he represented the will of his party, and enjoyed the confidence of the Republican rank and file in his leadership. If he had not gone upon the stump, if he had not made a favorable impression upon his hearers, and if he had not created a genuine public opinion in his favor, his political career might well have ended in January, 1898."[58] In this assessment, Croly left out an important postscript that remains a stain on Hanna's record to this day.

The Democrats in the Ohio legislature saw things quite differently from the way Croly described them, and they convened a special committee to investigate wrongdoing in the election. The only Republican appointed to the committee was James R. Garfield who, when Hanna was reelected, wired McKinley that "the future of our party in Ohio is brighter than for many years past. The mask has been removed and the people have decried and condemned the disloyal members who sought its ruin. We congratulate you."[59] Garfield largely refused to participate in the committee's activities. The conclusion of the Ohio committee was that Hanna and his associates violated the law in the process of getting him elected to the Senate and the evidence was forwarded to the U.S. Senate for its consideration. Skeptics in the press assumed Hanna would encounter little resistance there. In the *New York Journal*, Arthur McEwen wrote with obvious sarcasm,

> Since his election to the Presidency Mr. Hanna has procured the subsidiary honor of a seat in the United States Senate. Seditious persons who, strange to say, appear to be numerous in the Ohio Legislature, accuse him of having obtained his seat by purchase and have carried the matter to the Senate, which, of course, will ignore so feeble an attempt to annoy a man in whom his party sees itself reflected, and whose wealth, political influence and social position constitute a sufficient answer to any facts of which he does not care to take cognizance. Since to unseat Senator Hanna for bribery would be to deliver a blow at the permanence of the existing form of government, every defender of our civilization can

be counted on to come to his aid, should need arise, against the sinister spirits who love to disturb settled conditions.[60]

McEwen's prediction was correct. In the Senate, a committee controlled by his fellow Republicans exonerated Hanna. His career as a senator continued, but accusations of wrongdoing remain a part of his legacy well over a century later.

A few months later, in June 1899, the newly reelected Hanna returned to Columbus to manage the administration's interests at the Ohio Republican Convention, where he faced a party that was still divided into factions friendly to him and to Foraker, dating all the way back to their split in 1888. Hanna triumphed. In reporting to McKinley about the convention, Myron Herrick wrote,

> Senator Foraker came in at the close of Congressman Kerr's speech, which, by the way was one of the best I have ever heard. There was wild applause calling him to the front. After he had spoken there were many calls for Mr. Hanna, at which the anti-Hannites called the loudest, saying among themselves that they would call him out and show him up in contrast with Senator Foraker. Mr. Hanna appeared, and, it is needless to say, was in every way equal to the occasion. He made a speech which while it caught well with the crowd, was superior to Foraker's, and was received with greater enthusiasm. His enemies had been banking upon his so-called unpopularity, and had made much of this, but at the adjournment there was a decided reaction in favour of Mr. Hanna.[61]

Following his speech there and a convention that went much the way Hanna and McKinley wanted it to go, Hanna, who suffered continually from rheumatism, received congratulations from many people around the country, including McKinley, who wrote, "I hope you have recovered from the fatigue of the convention. The nominations made on Friday seem to be well received in Ohio and throughout the country. . . . Every bit of information I have had indicates that the convention was a great one and its spirit that of harmony," and he added a handwritten postscript reading, "Everybody compliments you upon your . . . speech before the convention, for all of which I rejoice and am glad."[62] To McKinley, Dawes wrote, "Of course the Ohio outcome was most gratifying, and helpful to the situation everywhere. It was a demonstration of the growing strength of the administration within the party lines, and will have the proper culmination in a large majority in the state in the fall."[63]

For his part, Hanna wrote to McKinley, "I went to Columbus—stood my trial before the party—under charges from Kurtz. Received a favorable verdict and am now prepared to state that the Administration controls the situation in Ohio. Geo Cox showed his appreciation of what had been done for him and is your friend. I think we have buried all carcasses which were offending the nostrils of the public and can now feel ourselves safe from another epidemic."[64] Following his victory with the Ohio Republicans, Hanna took a trip to the warm sulfur springs in Aix-les-Bains in western France for treatment of his rheumatism.

In a personal letter to McKinley that reflected the depth of their friendship, Hanna wrote, "I have been here a week and am sorry I cannot report much progress in getting rid of my rheumatism. The doctor says it is a very stubborn case and I must not get discouraged. He says—'You Americans want to do everything in a hurry.'"[65] Always worrying about McKinley, Hanna also commented on a recent shake-up in McKinley's administration—the naming of a new secretary of war. Hanna wrote, "Well, I see Alger has resigned and Root appointed. I am glad you are relieved and that Root would accept—he is a splendid fellow and will be a comfort. I can't help feeling sorry for Alger and his family. I do hope he will not make the fight for the Senate as I am afraid he would lose and there would be more humiliation."[66]

CHAPTER TEN

The Country Goes to War

ark Hanna served in the Senate throughout William McKinley's four-and-a-half eventful years as president. During that time, the country went to war with Spain, McKinley was reelected to a second term, the Republicans were established as the majority party in America for the next three-plus decades, the president was assassinated, and the legend of Mark Hanna's power continued to grow. As is true with all legends, there was more myth than reality in the story. One such pervasive myth was that when the Ohioans moved to Washington, Hanna made the decisions and that McKinley did what he was told. There is ample evidence to show this was not true, and perhaps none more compelling than the fact that Hanna was far from McKinley's closest friend in the capital city.

Hanna Moved to Washington,
but Dawes a More Frequent Guest in the White House

Mark Hanna was obviously part of William McKinley's inner circle, both before and after his election to the Senate. When he first came to the Senate and was looking for a residence in Washington, McKinley invited him to live in the White House until he found a place. The headlines of the *New York Journal* trumpeted this news as further evidence, as if more evidence were needed, of Hanna's control of McKinley. A front-page story read, "Having made Mr. McKinley President, and feeling a proprietary interest in him and all the perquisites of

FIGURE 10.1. All the comforts of home. Cartoon by Homer Davenport, *New York Journal*, January 26, 1898, 1

the office, the Senator doubtless feels that if anybody has the right to make himself at home in the White House he is the man."[1]

In truth, however, while Hanna was an important star in McKinley's galaxy, he was not at its center. If that honor belonged to anyone, it belonged to men like William R. Day and, most especially, to Charles Dawes. This is not to say that Dawes controlled McKinley anymore than Hanna was falsely alleged to control him, but that McKinley turned to Dawes for advice and as a sounding board far more than he did to Hanna. While Hanna was in regular communication with McKinley and was clearly always keeping an eye on both McKinley's and the Republican Party's business, he was largely focused on the business of Ohio, and the vast majority of his written communication with the president dealt with matters of patronage and offering introductions of people to the president.

After the presidential election, Dawes was McKinley's confidante in Washington. Charles Leach wrote, "Although not of Cabinet rank, Dawes found himself one of McKinley's closest advisers, perhaps the closest, on an even more intimate basis than Hanna enjoyed."[2] Dawes was supremely self-confident, as demonstrated in his journal where he made frequent references to his role as the president's adviser. Although he occasionally wrote of concerns over potential embarrassment if the scope of his role as an adviser was publicized, he made no effort in his own writing—which he intended to one day become public—to downplay his influence. As Bascom Timmons explains, "Although Dawes always disclaimed ever having had any decisive influence on McKinley's decisions, he was never reticent about his own opinions."[3]

According to Dawes, his role as adviser to McKinley predated the start of the campaign. On April 3, 1895, Dawes wrote of his role as an adviser to McKinley on the currency issue: "Hanna sent McKinley my letter on the subject of silver, and [the] attitude the Major had better take. It is, perhaps, presumptuous to advise—but if you think you have common sense notions, you need not think them out of place in any company."[4] And it is clear that McKinley valued Dawes's advice on many matters, including the makeup of his new administration.

Following the campaign, Dawes was discussed as a possible nominee for secretary of the treasury, and Bascom Timmons reported that well-placed luminaries such as Judge Peter Grosscup and General John McNulta went to Canton to lobby for Dawes's appointment.[5] Dawes reportedly objected to his possible appointment, primarily because he worried his youth would be considered a liability. McKinley reluctantly agreed. Dawes was ultimately appointed as comptroller of the currency in the Treasury Department.

Dawes urged McKinley to turn to another Illinoisan, Lyman G. Gage, who was the president of the First National Bank, for his secretary of the treasury. Dawes wrote to McKinley,

> After thinking over what you said about Mr. Gage last night, I went to see him this morning, not as representing you, but stating that I believed his appointment as Secretary of the Treasury was one which would be appropriate in view of state and national conditions. . . . I was very careful not to say anything which could be construed as even a tentative offer of the position as coming from you. Mr. Gage is a man of great discretion and fully understands how great a mistake it would be, if he was not appointed, to allow a public impression to go forth that he had been offered the position. He is interested deeply in the success of your administration.[6]

According to Dawes, however, McKinley worried about appointing an Illinoisan other than Dawes, lest it appear to be a slap at Dawes, who had served his campaign so well. Dawes wrote in his diary of his discussion of this matter with McKinley on January 20:

> Of his own accord before I had mentioned the matter, McKinley asked me for my impression of Gage. He seemed surprised and pleased when I stated I had come for the sole purpose of urging his appointment. Inasmuch as he had stated to me in the past that if I did not go into the Cabinet from Illinois he would make no appointment from that State, even though I had already accepted the Comptrollership of the Currency, I think that my advocacy of Gage was a relief to him as he is so extremely sensitive in all points of honor.[7]

While Dawes had no compunction about writing of his role as McKinley's adviser, he was sensitive to the impact his role might have on McKinley if it became known how closely he advised the president-elect. On January 23, he wrote in his diary,

The Friday papers had received an inkling of my negotiations with Mr. Gage in reference to the Treasury Department and reported that the tender had been made to him. I was under great embarrassment lest it should seem that I had exceeded my authority and had made a tender for McKinley. Mr. Gage sent for me and submitted a statement he had prepared for the press in view of erroneous reports published yesterday. He embodied in this statement his affirmative answer to my query as to whether he would accept the Treasury portfolio if tendered coupling it with the statement that it had not yet been offered. This was a graceful act, and a great relief to me, as it made unnecessary any explanations. I approved the statement and it was given to the press. I wired it to McKinley.[8]

Ultimately, Gage became McKinley's secretary of the treasury and Dawes's influence in that decision was quite obvious.

It was, and still is, unusual for someone holding a comparatively low-level appointment like comptroller of the currency to have as much access to a president as Charles Dawes had to McKinley. Immediately following the inauguration, Dawes had free access to the White House and served as a dispenser of spoils for the new president, along with Joseph Smith who was an Ohio ally of McKinley's, having served in his administration as the state librarian when McKinley was governor. Lewis Gould estimated that, until his death in 1898, Smith was at least as powerful in controlling patronage as Hanna; and, especially in the important state of Illinois, McKinley did all he could to satisfy the patronage needs of Dawes.[9] Dawes wrote in his journal, "March 8. Was besieged with office-seekers for a time. Then went to White House. The President has arranged for my admittance at any time, having given instructions to this effect, saving me much inconvenience and delay."[10]

The proper characterization of Dawes as a major dispenser of patronage on behalf of the administration necessarily diminishes the role Hanna could have played in that capacity. Dawes's role, however, was rarely properly characterized during McKinley's presidency and is seldom mentioned by modern reporters in stories about the McKinley administration. For example, following the 2002 election, Paul Krugman wrote about the Bush administration's proposed changes to the federal civil-service system in his *New York Times* column. Krugman, a professor of economics at Princeton, is yet another academic who made comparisons between Karl Rove and Mark Hanna who should have been more diligent about accuracy. In his column, Krugman made a perfectly reasonable argument that one reason the Bush administration might wish to make changes in the civil service system was to create opportunities for political patronage. In making this argument, Krugman wrote,

> A few months ago Mr. Rove compared his boss to Andrew Jackson. As some of us noted at the time, one of Jackson's key legacies was the "spoils system," under which federal jobs were reserved for political supporters. The federal civil service, with its careful protection of workers from political pressure, was created specifically to bring the spoils system to an end; but now the administration has found a way around those constraints. . . . So am I saying that we are going back to the days of Boss Tweed and Mark Hanna? Gosh, no—those guys were pikers. One-party control of today's government offers opportunities to reward friends and punish enemies that the old machine politicians never dreamed of.[11]

The problem with this passage was Krugman's assumption that Mark Hanna was in charge of patronage for the McKinley administration. This was certainly not the case. In addition to having men like Dawes and Smith, McKinley was a savvy politician who understood the value of when and where to distribute patronage.

For his part, Hanna was regularly rebuffed when suggesting jobs be awarded to certain people, a trend that dated back to when McKinley was governor of Ohio. In general, Hanna had influence in patronage decisions in Ohio. He also had a good deal of influence in the South, where there were few elected Republicans to make patronage requests. In northern and western states, his influence was much less, as the administration deferred to the wishes of Republicans from those states.[12]

Perhaps the best evidence that Hanna was far from supreme in dispensing McKinley patronage comes from George Cortelyou, who served as McKinley's private secretary and de facto chief of staff before the position was invented. Cortelyou, who had ample opportunity to observe both men, felt McKinley was a superior politician and noted that Hanna never dictated to McKinley on matters of patronage or anything else. In his statement to James Morrow following Hanna's death, Cortelyou said,

> Mr. Hanna was a very able politician. I think, however, that McKinley was the best politician of his day—I mean that he was an extraordinary politician in the best meaning of the description. He was shrewd and diplomatic. While he had no vociferous arguments with men with whom he differed, nevertheless, he usually had his way and was far more resolute and courageous than the public thought he was. Mr. Hanna was what might be termed an organization man. He believed thoroughly in rewarding the party workers and held that an organization could be maintained in no other way. It sometimes happened that Mr. Hanna and President McKinley differed about matters pertaining to patronage. It must be understood, however, that no Republican Senator asked for so few personal favors as did Mr. Hanna. He rarely requested an appointment in his own behalf. After an election he would have a good many obligations but they were not his obligations. They were the obligations of the party.[13]

As William McKinley's secretary, Cortelyou was responsible for modernizing many White House operations. He later served in Theodore Roosevelt's administration as the first-ever secretary of commerce and labor, as postmaster general, and as secretary of the treasury. While serving in Roosevelt's cabinet, he was also the chairman of the Republican National Committee from 1904 to 1907 and played a key role in the reelection of Roosevelt, much as Hanna did for McKinley in 1896 and 1900. He was present for the length of McKinley's and Hanna's time in Washington and, as such, is a well-qualified witness about the relationship between the two men.

As the chairman of the Republican National Committee and as a senator from Ohio, Hanna certainly had some influence over patronage positions, but for Krugman casually to compare him with a figure like Boss Tweed was sloppy work. Tweed was a major leader of New York's Democratic machine from the 1850s until his death in 1878. To suggest Hanna was to the McKinley administration what Tweed was to Tammany Hall is so far from reality that it does not merit even being called an exaggeration. Krugman is yet another example of a writer who ignored most of what has been written about Hanna and McKinley—except for the work of journalists and strong political partisans—since his death in 1904.

Dawes did not begin his tenure as comptroller of the currency until December 1897, when his predecessor resigned. Ironically, the office was supposed to be insulated from patronage; as such, the term of Cleveland's appointee, James Eckles, extended well into McKinley's administration. Despite the fact that he lacked an official position in those early days, Dawes spent much time in the capital city. During the first year of McKinley's presidency, Dawes socialized frequently with the president and advised him heavily on a range of issues from patronage to the currency, or sound money, situation.

On the sound-money issue, Dawes contradicted the policy ideas of Lyman Gage, the secretary of treasury he played a role in appointing, and helped the president write the statements he delivered to the public and the Congress on the issue. In a journal entry from November 3, 1897, Dawes wrote about the currency question in his diary:

> In this great message you are taking the position that hereafter revenue laws must be based upon two great principles: 1st. That of protection to American industries, and of 2nd. Maintaining the present gold standard and credit of National obligations. This proposition established by the passing of the law providing for an issue and redemption department of the Treasury and your other detailed recommendations, the revenues will follow. With your policy established, the currency problem becomes simply a revenue problem. The amendment of revenue laws is simple as compared with the amendment of currency laws, considered from a political standpoint.[14]

A month later, Dawes wrote of a meeting with the president, "December 1. Was at White House most of day. Took lunch there and spent an hour with the President looking over the currency recommendations of his message. He made some slight changes in phraseology and arrangement at my suggestion. It is a great document and one which will add to his reputation."[15] In a letter to McKinley on the subject, Dawes wrote, "In accordance with your suggestion, I have given thought to the tentative proposition of your next message which you read to me at Washington. The more I think of them, the more they commend themselves, although . . . their publication will result in a form of criticism which you should anticipate to some extent in your message in my judgment."[16] Clearly, the president regularly solicited and accepted Dawes's advice on financial matters, an area in which Dawes was an acknowledged authority. However, finance was not the only area in which the president looked for advice from Dawes, who had proved during the campaign that he was a shrewd politician.

After Dawes assumed the duties of comptroller of the currency at the beginning of 1898, his official duties had little impact on the time he spent with the president. Timmons described the relationship in this way:

> Dawes's office in the Treasury Building looked out upon the White House, a scant 200 feet away. Two or three times a week he had lunch there with the President. He often joined the President and his wife for dinner as well. Dawes saw President McKinley more often than any other man in his White House office. Sometimes, when he was troubled, the President would ask Dawes to go on long slow walks with him. Sometimes they would go for rides in a one-horse trap. "The President would drive at a fast clip," Dawes wrote.[17]

One of Dawes's primary political tasks for McKinley was dispensing patronage. In reality, he played a larger role in handing out the spoils than Mark Hanna, whose efforts were often confined to Ohio. While Hanna frequently consulted McKinley on patronage matters or to seek the president's support for something in the Senate, it was always in the most deferential tone that reflected his clear understanding of the proper hierarchy of their relationship, in which McKinley was firmly at the top.

Hanna was perhaps the most aggressive in urging McKinley to lend support to Hanna's favorite issue, which frustrated the senator for much of his career in the Senate. He frequently asked McKinley to mention the issue in his annual State of the Union message to Congress, imploring him not to "forget the Merchant Marine." After the midterm election of 1898, for instance, he wrote, "I find the sentiment ripe for a move in that direction both North and South and I am going to lead the movement."[18]

The nature of the relationship is demonstrated by an obscure, but telling, attempt on the part of Hanna to get the president to support the development of a new weapon system, the Gathman artillery shell. Historian Margaret Leech reports that Hanna promoted the shell "with great energy and had persistently recommended" it to the President.[19] Hanna took up Gathman's cause through another acquaintance who had a financial interest in Gathman's shell, George W. McMullen, and Hanna lobbied, along with others, to get McKinley to help facilitate testing and adoption of the new weapon. On June 30, 1898, Hanna reminded McKinley of a meeting he was to have with Hanna, Myron Herrick, and some other supporters of the shell and requested that the secretary of the navy be present at the meeting as well.[20] After that meeting, Hanna followed up with McKinley and urged that the president pressure the military to move forward with testing of the Gathman shell, which officials were reluctant to do.[21]

As part of his lobbying effort, Hanna forwarded McKinley reading material on the shell, writing, "Mr. Gathman's letter explains the situation in the Navy Dept. They are determined the shell shall never have a chance there. O'Neil and Alger of the Navy have as much as said no and I suppose will be able to prevent any fair experiments."[22] Hanna's attorney, Andrew Squire, wrote to McKinley of the Gathman shell in glowing terms: "If this Gathman improvement is what our investigation leads us to believe it is, the United States Government cannot afford to pass it by unheeded. The Gathman shell is practically an aerial torpedo."[23] McKinley, however, seems to have not been particularly moved and, in fact, gave his friend Hanna, as well as Herrick, a verbal cuff in response to their lobbying. As Margaret Leech writes,

> One evening, in late July, when McKinley was entertaining these two intimate friends at dinner, he made an ambiguous comment on their interest in the invention. Though Herrick referred to this remark as a "jest," it had been sufficiently barbed to upset him. He stayed late at the White House, in hopes of a confidential word with the President. Failing an opportunity for this, Herrick returned to his hotel; and, before he went to bed, wrote to assure McKinley that the "moneymaking feature was the least of the considerations" that animated his interests in the weapon.[24]

When he wanted to, McKinley did not fail to make sure his friends, no matter how loyal, devoted, and integral to his career, knew that *he* was the president.

The Spanish-American War

It is difficult to say with certainty exactly how much influence Dawes had over McKinley, but there is plenty of evidence that he had the president's ear. During the buildup to the Spanish-American War, the largest foreign-policy crisis of McKinley's presidency, Dawes spoke constantly with the president and many of his other advisers, such as Assistant Secretary of State William R. Day, whom Dawes referred to as "the virtual Secretary of State," about the situation.[25] In the three months before the war with Spain began, Dawes wrote about the crisis thirty-six times in his journal.[26]

While Dawes took no credit in his journal for McKinley's caution about getting into the war, it was clear that while Hanna received much of the *New York Journal*'s criticism for the nation's failure

to engage in war with the Spanish, Dawes also preferred a peaceful solution and he had far more regular contact and, presumably, influence with the president. Dawes repeatedly praised McKinley's judgment and careful handling of the situation in the weeks before the war in his journal.

Hanna became concerned about the political consequences of not going to war as the pressure from the Congress and the press mounted. According to Koenig, Hanna said, "Look out for Mr. Bryan. Everything that goes wrong'll be in the Democratic platform in 1900. You can be damn sure of that!"[27] While

FIGURE 10.2. Idol of yellow patriotism. Cartoon by Homer Davenport, *New York Journal*, March 16, 1898, 1

Dawes did not express this sentiment in the same terms, his journal reveals a desire for peace along with praise for McKinley's judgment, if McKinley decided to use the military. When reading what Dawes wrote about a justifiable reason for going to war with Spain, one is reminded of one of the reasons the Bush administration gave for going to war against Iraq. On March 27, Dawes wrote, "Neither the President nor Sagasta desire war. But the President proposes to intervene to stop the suffering. If this purpose of relieving suffering is interfered with, he will use force and his conscience and the world will justify it. He is making a magnificent fight for peace and God grant he may succeed. He will have won a greater victory in peace than was ever won by an Emperor in war. Nothing disturbs him in his great and good resolves."[28] The next day, he defended McKinley whether the end result was peace or war. He wrote,

> He expects abuse for his efforts for a peaceful settlement of the Cuban situation, but when his policy and acts are all known to the public, they will know his true strength and moral courage. . . . War may be very near. But the President will do right. . . . There is great indignation among the more radical members of Congress at the President's message, which was not warlike enough for them. Foraker introduced a resolution recognizing Cuba's independence and a resolution declaring war was also introduced. We all want Cuban independence, but if we fight it must be for humanity's sake, not from other motives. War is a hideous wrong when used to achieve ends possible by peace.[29]

Dawes, who was a wealthy businessman like Hanna, no doubt feared the economic impact a war might have. These concerns turned out to be much ado about nothing—when the fighting started, the U.S. was able to dispatch the Spanish military quickly—but that could not have been known in advance. In addition, winning the war had the effect of making the United States an instant colonial power, inheriting Cuba, Puerto Rico, and the Philippines from Spain. The same papers that had advocated so strongly for war, along with William Jennings Bryan, who organized his own army unit for service in Cuba, responded to this by branding McKinley an imperialist.

FIGURE 10.3. And they called him Napoleon. Cartoon by Homer Davenport, *New York Journal*, April 7, 1898, 8

In the Senate, meanwhile, Hanna tried to look out for McKinley's interests. As McKinley prepared to ask for a declaration of war with Spain, Hanna acted as point man for the administration in the Senate. On April 3, eight days before McKinley made his request, Hanna wrote,

> I have been talking with some of our friends this morning, particularly Senators Platt of Conn and Spooner. They think that no more committees should go to confer with you at this juncture and that it is very important that some one man (Senator) should be so far taken into confidence and consulted before your message went to Congress that your friends in the Senate . . . be prepared to meet the situation and intelligently support your policy. In that connection, I have no hesitancy in saying that Senator Spooner should be that man and I know it will cause no jealousies among the others.[30]

Hanna was undoubtedly worried about how McKinley handled his message to the Congress about war with Spain because McKinley and Hanna received criticism from all sides on the subject of the Spanish-American War. Advocates of war—especially the Hearst newspapers—attacked them for trying to avoid war and negotiate a peaceful settlement with Spain. After the war, critics of U.S. expansionism branded them imperialists. This criticism is frequently revived today, especially in the press.

In one example, a historian from Ohio State University, Austin Kerr, was quoted in 1999 *Cleveland Plain Dealer* editorial. He was highly critical of McKinley's foreign-policy legacy, especially with regard to the Spanish-American War and U.S. intervention in the Philippines, and he urged the Bush campaign to be cautious in drawing comparisons to it. Kerr said, "The one thing I would be careful about if I were the Bush people is that McKinley was abysmally ignorant of foreign affairs. He was an imperialist of the first order."[31] In one important way, Kerr was right that, in opening the door to comparisons with the McKinley administration, Rove and the Bush campaign opened it not just to positive comparisons but to negative ones as well. For example, two years later, in a 2002 piece in the *American Prospect*, Harold Meyerson accused McKinley of being an imperialist. At the same time, he dismissed Karl Rove and drew a parallel between McKinley and George W. Bush. Meyerson wrote, "Indeed, the parallel to be concerned about is less Hanna and Rove than McKinley and Bush.

McKinley launched the American empire—conquering and coloniz-ing Cuba and a chunk of the Caribbean, Hawaii and the Philippines. Bush is the most nakedly imperial president we've had in 100 years. The second coming of Mark Hanna may be cause for concern; the second coming of McKinley is cause for alarm."[32] Meyerson's analysis con-tained a logical inconsistency. In his piece, he argued that McKin-ley was weak. On the subject of Karl Rove, Meyerson wrote, "So is Rove—as he has long wished to be—the latter-day Mark Hanna (the brain and muscle behind William McKinley who forged the coalition that made the Republicans the dominant party in the late nineteenth and twentieth centuries)?"[33] The problem is that at the same time he argued McKinley was created by Hanna, Meyerson also credited (or blamed) McKinley, not Hanna, with single-handedly launching the "American empire." This was an interpretation of history, but it was certainly not historical fact. McKinley was a very reluctant warrior when it came to Spain and U.S. expansion into international affairs.

While historian Austin Kerr's warning about the unintended con-sequences of making comparisons between Bush and McKinley was quite accurate, both Kerr and Meyerson were simply wrong in their characterizations of McKinley. President McKinley simply was not "an imperialist of the first order," as Kerr said. If he later became an imperial-ist, it was because circumstance dictated its necessity. Describing this necessity, Herbert Croly wrote, "In the end both he and Mr. Hanna became convinced Imperialists; and their Imperialism may have been due to a final understanding of the close relation between the tradi-tions of the Republican party and a policy of national expansion. A party which originated in the deliberate assumption of a neglected national responsibility cannot well avoid the assumption of new respon-sibilities, whenever such a course is dictated by a legitimate national interest."[34] It was the Republican Party, Croly asserted, that did some-thing about slavery, and it was the Republican Party, led by McKinley and Hanna, that did something to help the people subjugated by the Spanish. Croly may well have gone too far in the opposite direction of Kerr's characterization. In that passage, he painted McKinley and Hanna as sainted men who just wanted to save the oppressed people of the world. In truth, as Croly himself observed, McKinley ultimately became an advocate for war because circumstance left him little choice. Still, it was not right to brand him, as Kerr did, an "imperialist of the first order." The United States became a colonial power because of its victory in the Spanish-American War; McKinley never wanted to enter that war, but the situation left him no choice.

Kerr ignored McKinley's reluctance to begin a war with Spain. The Democrats in Congress and the Democratic press banged war drums for years, pressuring not only McKinley but his Democratic predecessor, Grover Cleveland, to go to war with Spain to save the Cubans from Spanish oppression. A popular understanding of the Spanish American-War that still persists is that the media incited the war. It is certainly true that the press, especially the papers of Hearst, fanned the flames of conflict before the war. After McKinley won election to the presidency, something Hearst tried so hard to prevent, Hearst sent a representative to ask for a meeting with McKinley to discuss his paper's "appeal for help to relieve the want and suffering in Cuba. Mr. Hearst's representative states that he—Mr. Hearst—is desirous of taking up this matter at once and through the medium of his paper making it yield a very large sum for the purpose desired."[35] Later, once war began, Hearst traveled to Cuba and tried to insert himself in the brief war.

The most famous "evidence" of Hearst's instigation of the war was an alleged exchange between Frederic Remington, who was stationed in Cuba as an illustrator for the *New York Journal,* and Hearst. Remington allegedly observed to Hearst that there would be no war in Cuba. Hearst reportedly replied, "Please remain. You furnish the pictures, and I'll furnish the war."[36] Hearst biographer David Nasaw argued that this exchange probably never took place; and, if it did, Hearst did not mean he was going to get the United States to declare war, only that fighting would break out between Cuban rebels and the Spanish. For his part, Hearst later denied that he did anything to start the war.[37] While the Remington story is probably apocryphal, it nevertheless has a life of its own, and many still believe—and teach—that the Spanish-American War was started by William Randolph Hearst so he could sell newspapers. This clearly shows that when a myth is repeated often enough, it takes on the force of truth.

As Nasaw demonstrated, the Remington story was probably untrue, but truth was seldom a top priority in the newspaper wars of the Gilded Age. Virtually every newspaper publisher in America sold newspapers with stories of questionable veracity about Cuba, and few did so more effectively than Hearst. The newspapers got tremendous mileage out of stories about the inhuman conditions that existed in Cuba under Spanish rule. In Hearst's newspapers, the tale of one young woman, Evangelina Cisneros, provided fodder for stories that sold many newspapers and whipped up public sentiment against the Spanish. Cisneros was a teenage girl, imprisoned by the Spanish because she was the daughter of a rebel leader. Hearst organized a letter-writing campaign, prompting prominent women from around the United States to implore the queen regent of Spain to release Cisneros. For days, the *Journal* featured headlines about which famous women, such as William McKinley's mother, Jefferson Davis's wife, and William Jennings Bryan's wife, had written to the queen. Hearst also cabled McKinley's wife Ida asking her to write to the queen.[38] When that failed, Hearst organized a dramatic "rescue" of Cisneros by a Hearst reporter who purportedly broke her out of jail and brought her to New York. While his detractors at other newspapers alleged that much of the Cisneros story was made up by Hearst, the criticism did nothing to deter him, and Cisneros was featured on the front page of the newspaper for weeks.[39] The predictable headline on the front page of the *New York Journal* on October 12, 1897, was "An American Newspaper Accomplishes at a Single Stroke What the Red Tape of Diplomacy Could Not," and the administration was made to look incompetent, again. Of course, it was made to look incompetent in a story that was entirely constructed by Hearst.

Hearst's *New York Journal* predictably characterized McKinley's reluctance to enter the war as obedience to his master, Hanna, who determined all administration policies. A common Hearst headline featured the charge that Hanna, with Navy Secretary John Long as his unwitting dupe, conspired to keep the country out of war. After the explosion of the USS *Maine,* for example, a lengthy piece in the *Journal* reviewed Hanna's alleged wrongdoing:

> Senator Hanna, fresh from the bargain for a seat in the United States Senate, probably felt the need of recouping his Ohio expenses as well as helping his great financial friends out of the hole when he began playing American patriotism against Wall Street money. . . . When the game was ready, Hanna said there would be no war. He spoke as one having authority. His edict meant that Uncle Sam might be kicked and cuffed from one continent to another, but that under

no circumstances would he fight. That was just the sort of talk Wall Street wanted.[40]

These accusations had no basis in reality, of course, but Hanna became the public face of an unpopular stance on war with Spain. Hanna was, in fact, an opponent of war with Spain because he feared the consequences a war might have on the country's recovery from the economic disaster of the Panic of 1893, but he did not speak publicly about his opposition. Hanna neither tried to assume control of the White House nor of the Senate in his first two years in office. His only public act during the Fifty-fifth Congress was to introduce a bill allocating funds for a government building in Cleveland.[41] While he was certainly active behind the scenes, there is no evidence to support the virulent charges made against him on the pages of Hearst's newspapers.

McKinley resisted going to war for a long time in the face of mounting pressure from the press, the public, Democrats in Congress and, eventually, the members of his own party, although men like Hanna, Dawes, and Whitelaw Reid continued to support him. Nearly a year before the war began, Dawes wrote to McKinley, "The people who are demanding immediate intervention are the very ones who would be first to blame the administration, if in following their demands for hasty and ill-considered action, evil should result. The majority of the thinking people of this country are behind you in your determination to be sure that you are right before taking further steps."[42] The following year, shortly before the war began, McKinley received a letter of support from Reid following the explosion of the *Maine:*

> The impression I got on crossing the continent was that the more intelligent classes are not greatly affected by the sensational press; but that, on a conviction that the Maine was blown up by Spanish agency, with or without the active connivance of the present Spanish authorities, there would be no restraining them. Meantime I have never seen a more profound or touching readiness to trust the President, and await his word. They really seem to feel, as every patriot must, in this crisis, a readiness to hold themselves subject to call when and where the Country needs. Conservative public sentiment will sustain purchases of ammunition and even of war-ships.[43]

It was only after the publication of a highly provocative and insulting letter written to a Spanish official in Cuba by a Spanish diplomat in Washington, Enrique Dupuy de Lôme, and the explosion of the battleship USS *Maine,* the exact cause of which remains doubtful, that war with Spain became inevitable.

The de Lôme letter was intercepted by Cuban revolutionaries and published by Hearst in the *New York Journal* on February 9, 1898. In it, de Lôme referred to a statement McKinley made about the need to proceed with caution and continue to negotiate with Spain. He wrote, "Besides the natural and inevitable coarseness with which he repeats all that the press and public opinion of Spain has said of Weyler, it shows once more what McKinley is: weak and catering to the rabble, and, besides, a low politician, who desires to leave a door open to me and to stand well with the jingoes of his party."[44] Weyler, referred to in the letter, was General Valeriano "Butcher" Weyler, the commander of the Spanish military in Cuba. The headline that accompanied the text of the letter in the *Journal* was predictably inflammatory, "The Worst Insult in the History of the United States."[45]

Shortly after the publication of the de Lôme letter, the battleship *Maine,* anchored in Havana's harbor, exploded on the night of February 15, 1898. A four-week investigation by the Navy concluded that the explosion was caused by a mine under the ship. While the report did not assign blame for the mine, the press and public assumed the Spanish were responsible, and the pressure for war reached a fever pitch.[46]

Following these actions, McKinley seemed to accept that war was inevitable and changed his previous position. He ordered the military to prepare for war. On April 21, 1898, the U.S. Navy began a blockade of Havana's harbor. The Spanish declared war against the United States on April 23, and the U.S. Congress responded with its own declaration of war four days later. The war was over by August 13, 1898. While McKinley was highly criticized before the war for not being more aggressive with Spain, he also received a great deal of criticism from detractors who criticized him for going to war with Spain and for the subsequent acquisition of Puerto Rico, Guam, and the Philippines after the war. Cuba was established as an independent country with close supervision by the United States.

McKinley was not without defenders, however, who saw his switch as a necessary acceptance of political reality. If he continued to hold out against war, he would almost certainly have done serious damage to his presidency. His own party was already divided on the possibility of military intervention, and, as Croly wrote, "Congress wanted war and had the power to declare it. The people were willing. If war had been declared, in spite of his opposition, neither Congress nor the country would have had sufficient confidence in him as the commander-in-chief of its army and navy."[47] Could McKinley have handled the situation better? It is almost certainly true that negotiations with Spain were harmed by the fact that Secretary of State John Sherman was not up to the job. As was mentioned previously, William R. Day, McKinley's confidante from Canton, was the assistant secretary of state. He stepped ably into the void, but Sherman's shortcomings made McKinley look weak to the Spanish. As the de Lôme letter showed, the Spanish did not believe the United States had the will—or, perhaps, the ability—to make war against them. What incentive did they have to accede to U.S. wishes at the negotiating table? Sherman resigned at the beginning of the war and was replaced by Day, who served through the end of the war and then stepped down to become a federal judge. He was replaced by John Hay. The administration was also criticized heavily for what was perceived as incompetent handling of the preparation for fighting by Secretary of War Russell Alger. Alger was asked to resign by McKinley after the war and was replaced by Elihu Root.

These difficulties, which were at least in part of McKinley's own making since he made what quickly came to be seen as poor personnel decisions, had little impact on the fight. The war ended quickly and successfully. McKinley was viewed favorably by the public, and none of the negative economic effects that Hanna and McKinley had feared came to be.

A century after the war, McKinley was identified by some as the president who helped establish the United States as a world power. Others, however, pointed to him as the person most responsible for making the United States an imperial power. This charge was leveled against him by Bryan during the campaign of 1900, and it continued to resonate during the campaign of 2000.

The two areas annexed by the United States that generated the most criticism of McKinley as an imperialist were the Philippines and Hawaii. The Philippines became U.S. territory during the Spanish-American War, but it was Assistant Secretary of the Navy Theodore Roosevelt

who issued unauthorized orders during his short stint as acting secretary of the Navy that started the ball rolling toward Commodore
George Dewey's eventual capture of the Philippines from the Spanish
in June 1898.[48] Roosevelt's actions were taken without the knowledge
of McKinley. The country was ceded to the United States as part of the
settlement of the war. The Philippines contentiously remained under
U.S. control until after World War II. The United States also annexed
Hawaii during McKinley's time, but it was due more to action by
Congress than by the president. The pretext was that the Navy needed
a refueling station in the South Pacific, but there were strong American economic interests in Hawaii pushing hard for annexation. None
of this is to say that McKinley was not responsible for the expansion
of U.S. territory during his presidency; but he did not act alone, and
often he had to make decisions in the wake of other people's actions.

As the fighting drew to an end, Dawes assessed the state of contemporary public opinion. He wrote to McKinley, "I am impressed with the
present strength of the sentiment in favor of the retention of at least
the best portion of the Philippines which seems to pervade all classes
of the people. As is always the case in important questions with the
public, there goes with it the desire for further information. The people are not yet ready to form their lasting opinion in this connection—nor would they have viewed with toleration any hasty attempt
on the part of the administration to settle prematurely this policy."[49] A
few months later, Dawes commented on a forthcoming statement by
McKinley on the subject of the Philippines:

> The more I have thought of your Boston address, a portion
> of which you read me, the greater is my hope that you will
> leave it as you read it to me. In many respects it will be the
> most important speech you have delivered—especially from
> the standpoint of the historian of the future. What you have
> prepared seemed to me as I heard it, the most powerful,
> conclusive, and concise statement of the nation's position;
> and in the future story of the Philippines this speech may
> serve the same purpose which your message to Congress just
> prior to the war accomplished in justifying before the world,
> the nation's position in regard to Cuba and Spain. A sense
> of the importance of the speech has grown upon me since I

left Washington, and the feeling also that what you had prepared was worthy in every way of this great emergency.[50]

While the assessment of McKinley's actions may have changed over
time to a point of view that sees him as an imperialist, Dawes points
to a public opinion in McKinley's day that approved of his actions.

Of course, all was not entirely rosy for the Republicans in 1898.
In the midterm election in November, the Republicans lost nineteen
seats in the House—although the party gained seven seats in the Senate, which was still elected by state legislatures at the time, and it won
the most symbolically important of those elections, Hanna's. However, the gains made by the Democrats were not as dramatic as they
might seem. The Democrats gained thirty-seven seats, but nearly half
of those were formerly held by the Populists, not the Republicans. In
all, Hanna and McKinley both viewed the election as a success. On
November 10, Hanna wrote to McKinley, "I have been so anxious
about the next House that [I] have not felt like crowing until we got
'out of the woods.' But now that that question is settled in our favor
we can congratulate each other. It turned out as predicted that the
House must be saved west of the Missouri River and what a victory
it was to win back so many of those states."[51] On November 15, he
wrote, "Am just beginning to fully realize the results of the recent
election. Our business interests are placed in a position of safety that
has not been enjoyed for years. That means continued prosperity and
Republican success. I am more than pleased that in the western states
where my orders as Chairman of the national Committee were carried
out that the St. Louis platform should be the issue as the foundation
and the "Administration" the super structure. We were successful to
a marked degree."[52] Hanna's comments reflect his most important
priority, no matter what projects he supported in the Senate, be it
funding for the merchant marine, the development of the Gathman
shell, or, later, the building of a canal between the Atlantic and Pacific
Oceans—and that priority was success for the Republican Party and
his friend, William McKinley.

CHAPTER ELEVEN

Election 1900

 ollowing the war, sudden control of the Philippines made the United States a country with interests in Asia. One consequence of this was the open-door policy, crafted by Secretary of State John Hay. The policy was conceived as a way to prevent nations with a colonial presence in China, such as Britain, France, Russia, and Japan, from preventing the United States from engaging in trade there.[1] Hay also reiterated the administration's support for Chinese independence following the Boxer Rebellion in 1900.[2]

As the campaign of 1900 approached, William McKinley had reason to feel his first term was a success. He counted America's China policy as a triumph of his administration. He also felt other achievements—such as the victory in the war with Spain; actions taken to make gold the permanent standard of American currency; the annexation of Hawaii; the extension of the eight-hour workday; and the passage of the naval expansion bill that would make the United States a world naval power—marked his four years as president a success.[3] Despite these achievements, however, one McKinley biographer, Margaret Leech, speculated that the president was privately pessimistic about the prospects of winning a second term, due to a variety of issues he viewed as potentially damaging. One of his concerns, she suggested, was the negative coverage he and Mark Hanna received on the pages of William Randolph Hearst's newspapers. Leech wrote of McKinley's concern that "nearly every day the New York *Evening Journal* hammered the theme that the President was the child of the trusts and the helpless nursling of Hanna."[4] According to Bascom Timmons, Mark Hanna also worried about the 1900 campaign. Hanna wrote to Dawes that Bryan would be a stronger candidate in 1900 than he was in 1896 but that "winning will 'be no boy's play this year.'"[5]

McKinley was tired when he spoke with Charles Dawes on January 29, 1900, and told him he was considering not running for a second term. Dawes wrote in his journal, "Spent some time with the President who is celebrating his fifty-seventh birthday. He reviewed the past few years of his life and his prospects. It would be a great personal relief to him not to again receive the nomination for the Presidency."[6]

While Dawes was sympathetic to McKinley, he did not see the election of 1900 as one McKinley would lose. While Dawes was the first of McKinley's advisers to see William Jennings Bryan's potential in 1896, he did not share Hanna's concern about him in 1900. In his journal, Dawes wrote on July 6, 1900, "William J. Bryan and Adlai Stevenson have been nominated for President and Vice President by the Democratic National Convention on an anti-progress platform. The Republican party will be victorious in the coming election."[7] There was little chance he would fail to win reelection. Despite various Democratic complaints about issues such as the currency situation and charges that McKinley was an imperialist, victory against Spain had left him a popular president. As McKinley decided to be a candidate for reelection, he did not spend any more time campaigning in 1900 than he did in 1896 and, rather, devoted himself to the job of being president, especially dealing with foreign policy and the continuing tension in China. Late in the campaign, Dawes commented on the president's decision in a letter to McKinley's secretary, George Cortelyou. He wrote, "I am very glad the President has decided not to make any speeches. His judgment on these things is always the best, and I hear the contrast between his attitude in the campaign and that of the other nominee most favorably and generally commented on. It is also very evident that his letter of acceptance has been read by every Republican in the Country. I go nowhere without hearing that letter discussed as the basis of our campaign."[8]

McKinley's Hanna Problem

There are few incidents that more graphically demonstrate McKinley's independence from Hanna than the way he treated him in 1900. While

McKinley was an enigmatic man and it is difficult to say with certainty how he felt about many issues, there is evidence to support Leech's observation that he was concerned about how he was portrayed in the press. His behavior, once he decided to seek reelection, suggested he really was concerned about the impact his relationship with Hanna had on his reputation.

Hanna was once again the chairman of the Republican National Committee in 1900, which made him the head of McKinley's reelection campaign. The process of reappointing Hanna, however, was more dramatic than casual observers might have expected. On the surface, it seemed obvious that Hanna would be reappointed to do what he had done four years earlier. As Herbert Croly wrote, "Everybody had assumed, as a matter of course, that he would do so. His selection for the place was only a proper recognition of his ability as a campaign manager."[9] However, when Hanna made statements about not feeling well enough to do the job again in 1900 because of his painful rheumatism, no one—most glaringly not McKinley—rushed to argue that it was absolutely necessary that he ignore the pain and once again oversee the campaign.

In fact, McKinley took his time making the formal announcement, waiting until the end of May. This was a great source of stress to Hanna, who worried both about the campaign and his relationship with McKinley. So stressed was he by McKinley's seeming lack of support that Hanna suffered what Croly described as "an attack of heart failure," fainting in his office.[10] McKinley biographer Leech characterized it as an actual heart attack and wrote that the cause of the stress was Hanna's fear that he was in danger of losing control of federal patronage that made him a power in the Senate.[11] The heart trouble was apparently not terribly serious, as he went to the theater that evening, but McKinley's lack of obvious affection was a source of great stress for Hanna.

Because both men were so enigmatic, there is not a great record of what transpired. It is possible to argue that Hanna was merely being overly sensitive to what he perceived as a lack of timely consideration from McKinley, but Croly saw it as more serious than that. He wrote, "from remarks which Mr. McKinley made to other people, it is probable that the President really was hesitating."[12] Croly's analysis of McKinley's apparent hesitancy was that it was due to Hanna's growing—and separate—status as a national political figure in his own right.[13]

Leech, on the other hand, rejected this argument out of hand, arguing that Hanna was still little known outside of Ohio, "except by sinister reputation." She elaborated, writing that McKinley was likely bothered more by a lingering scandal from Cuba involving fraud and abuse of power by politically appointed postal officials. These were officials such as Hanna's "crony," the Havana post office's director general, Estes G. Rathbone. Anxious to avoid a politically damaging scandal, McKinley sent investigators to Cuba to put an end to the corruption, regardless of who might be implicated. It was this, Leech contended, that caused him to hold Hanna at arm's length. Her assessment of Hanna's reaction to McKinley's response to the postal matter was less than complimentary. She wrote: "In earlier days of hero worship, he had gloried in McKinley's scruples. Now he was nearly sixty-two, rheumatic and cross, enamored of the exercise of power. He would always love McKinley, but the bloom of romance had faded. Scruples had lost their charm."[14] To Leech, McKinley's delay in offering Hanna responsibility for the campaign was clearly intended to send a message to rein Hanna in.

As with much about McKinley's presidency, it is difficult to say with certainty what made him hesitate, because there is a dearth of written records to which to refer. McKinley biographer Lewis Gould made an argument that contained elements of both Croly's and Leech's interpretation of events, characterizing McKinley's delay as "a quiet kind of discipline" to keep Hanna under control.[15] McKinley felt this was necessary, Gould suggested, because of Hanna's propensity to speak for the president whenever he felt enthusiastic about something, whether he was authorized to do so or not.[16] Hanna's biographer Thomas Beer wrote that Hanna's sometimes aggressive behavior caused a cooling of the relationship between the two men.[17]

In the end, Hanna was put in charge of the campaign, but the fact that McKinley exerted himself, albeit quietly, over Hanna is noteworthy because it is more evidence that it was McKinley, and not Hanna, who was the real captain of the ship. While McKinley understood the important role Hanna played in his success, he also understood that being too closely linked to Hanna could be his undoing. As Campaign 1900 approached, McKinley was nervous about Hanna and the effect the senator might have on his reputation and legacy.

By the time he was finally named chairman, Hanna was emotionally drained. When he showed up at the Republican convention in

Philadelphia, he was haggard and seemingly unprepared to lead the debate on the one campaign issue that was unresolved—who would be the party's vice presidential nominee.[18] Deciding who would replace Garret Hobart, who died on November 21, 1899, turned out to be a genuine political embarrassment for Hanna, who got precious little support from President McKinley on the matter.

Throughout the buildup to the convention, McKinley was silent as to what, if any preference he had for a running mate. Hanna supported Cornelius Bliss, but Bliss made it clear that he was not interested in the job. By the time Hanna realized that momentum was pushing Teddy Roosevelt toward the nomination, there was nothing he could do to stop it. One telling sign of Hanna's trouble in his relationship with the president was the fact that it was not he but Charles Dawes who was in regular touch with McKinley and who remained in Washington during the convention.

Dawes played a crucial role for McKinley at the Republican convention in Philadelphia, acting as McKinley's watchdog, keeping tabs on Hanna. Dawes's biographer Charles Leach wrote, "Dawes, now of real political stature, due to his close relationship to the President, was chosen a delegate-at-large in the Illinois state convention, and as such, with entry where he pleased in the convention and around headquarters, was McKinley's constant adviser. He telephoned to George Bruce Cortelyou, secretary to the president, who took the Dawes reports in shorthand, even when the President was listening silently on an extension phone."[19] No doubt, Hobart would have been McKinley's choice to remain vice president, but his death left a void that had to be filled, and both Dawes and McKinley felt it would be perilous for him to intervene in the selection of a replacement.

The process of vice-presidential selection was much different in 1900 than it is today. In the modern era, presidential candidates choose their own running mates. It is, in fact, quite remarkable that the choice of the person who could very well become president of the United States is left to one person—the presidential nominee. This was not the case in 1900, when the party bosses ran the convention and chose the nominees. If it had been left to McKinley, there were probably several men he would have been happy with, such as Cornelius Bliss, Seth Low, Andrew White, William Boyd Allison, or Secretary of the Navy John D. Long.[20] If he made an aggressive case for any of those men, McKinley may have been able to control who got the nomination, but McKinley's view, as well as the view of advisers like Dawes, whom he trusted, was that he needed to remain hands off for the sake of party harmony. This attitude ultimately led to Teddy Roosevelt's nomination.

In 1900, Teddy Roosevelt was the governor of New York, and, due to his progressive reform agenda, he was considered a nuisance by Thomas Platt and many other New York Republicans. They wanted him out of New York— what better place to park him than the vice presidency? In large measure, Teddy Roosevelt became both vice president and president because he was a burr under the saddles of powerful Republicans in his home state. Ironically, when Roosevelt was tapped to become New York's governor in 1898, it was argued on the pages of Hanna's and McKinley's great antagonist, the *New York Journal,* that Roosevelt was the party's candidate for governor to remove him as a threat for the presidential nomination in 1900. For Hanna, the idea of moving Roosevelt to the vice presidency just to get him out of the way simply was not acceptable. Croly wrote, "The Vice-Presidency might have seemed to be one of the safest offices in the government in which to confine an unsafe political leader; but Mr. Hanna had gone to Philadelphia with the intention of engineering the nomination of a Vice-Presidential candidate who would make from his point of view a thoroughly good President."[21] To Hanna, Roosevelt was unacceptable as a vice president precisely because he might become president.

In addition to the practical motives of Platt and his cronies, Matthew Quay also played a role in making sure that Roosevelt got the nomination. He wanted to ensure Hanna was saddled with a candidate he did not want. As the Republicans gathered in his home state of Pennsylvania for the convention, Quay sought revenge on Hanna because he held Hanna personally responsible for the loss of his seat in the Senate. This was despite the fact that thirty-two senators in addition to Hanna voted to prevent Quay from keeping his seat.

Quay's term as senator ended in March 1899. He had the support of the majority of the Republican caucus in Pennsylvania's state legislature for reelection, but he had some detractors within his own party, and, of course, Democrats opposed his nomination. While he received a plurality of support in the legislature, the law required a majority, and he was unable to get a majority through four months of voting, from January through April 1899.

When the state legislature adjourned without filling the Senate seat, the governor of Pennsylvania appointed Quay to fill the seat until the next session of the state legislature. The legality of this move was questioned, and it led to an investigation by the U.S. Senate's Committee on Privileges and Elections. The committee recommended against allowing Quay to fill the seat, and the recommendation was approved by the full Senate on a vote of thirty-three to thirty-two. Hanna, the most Republican of Republicans, voted against Quay, and he was publicly perceived as having cast the deciding vote, especially by Quay himself.[22]

Hanna was silent as to his reasons for the vote, leaving his biographer Croly to speculate. It was clearly an unwise move from a political standpoint because, senator or not, Quay was a political force with which to reckon. Croly wrote, Hanna "incurred the embarrassing hostility of a man who continued to be powerful in an important Republican state. When Mr. Quay's name was read aloud in the Philadelphia Convention as the member of the National Committee from Pennsylvania, the applause consumed several minutes."[23] Croly rejected the notion that Hanna voted against Quay because of preexisting bad blood between them. He also rejected the idea that Hanna was troubled by any "technical Constitutional reasons." Instead, Croly felt that Hanna decided to vote against Quay because he truly felt that the governor of Pennsylvania had "no right to fill a vacancy in the Senate with a man whom the Legislature might have elected, but instead deliberately took the opportunity of rejecting."[24] Whatever Hanna's real motive was for voting against him, the convention and the selection of the party's vice presidential nominee afforded Quay a chance for revenge.

Croly observed that if not for Platt's desire to get Roosevelt out of New York and Quay's desire to get his revenge on Hanna, Roosevelt never would have been vice president. Added to the motives of these two men was an obvious enthusiasm among the rank and file for the dynamic Roosevelt. Many in the party thought nominating Roosevelt made good political sense. As Gould observed, "The party faithful viewed Roosevelt as an excellent counterweight to McKinley. He was an easterner with western connections, he was young, and he was a symbol of Republican success in foreign policy."[25]

Unlike many Republicans at the convention, Hanna felt no enthusiasm for Roosevelt and worked to prevent his nomination. Roosevelt was a political animal with ambitions that did not fit with Hanna's worldview, and Roosevelt was not shy about criticizing both McKinley and Hanna. Roosevelt biographer Edmund Morris described a meeting Roosevelt had with the famed journalist William Allen White in the summer of 1897. Morris wrote that during the meeting, "Roosevelt spoke with shocking frankness about the leaders of the government, expressing 'scorn' for McKinley and 'disgust' for the 'deep and damnable alliance between business and politics' that Mark Hanna was constructing."[26] Roosevelt spoke all the time to anyone, according to Dawes's characterization of him, and his words no doubt reached Hanna and the White House. They certainly did nothing to endear Roosevelt to Hanna.

For his part, Roosevelt demurred repeatedly at the convention, telling all who would listen that he was the governor of New York and intended to keep that job. His denials, however, were something less than convincing. Hanna got him, on more than one occasion, to say that he was not interested in being vice president. He also tried to get Roosevelt to issue a written statement that he would not, under any circumstances, accept a vice-presidential nomination. Roosevelt was on the brink of writing such a statement, but he ultimately decided not to, in part because he was uncertain about his reelection chances as governor of New York and, in part, because he seemed to feel that if he was called by the party to be vice president, he had a duty to accept.[27] That, combined with the powerful influence of Platt and Quay, virtually assured Roosevelt's nomination.

Charles Dawes, who claimed some credit for Garret Hobart's vice-presidential nomination in 1896 because of his guidance of the Illinois delegation, was also involved in the negotiations that left Roosevelt with the vice-presidential nomination in 1900. As Timmons wrote, "With Hobart dead and the Vice-Presidency vacant in 1900, Dawes was again to play a decisive part in the selection of the nominee for that office, a part which was to have a profound influence on the course of American history."[28] Dawes left a detailed account of both Hanna's desire to prevent it from happening and his ultimate failure to do so. Throughout the drama that led to Teddy Roosevelt's nomination, Dawes played the role of McKinley's surrogate, tasked with the job of reining in Hanna.

Dawes sensed both the pro-Roosevelt momentum and Hanna's growing stubbornness about allowing him to get the nomination. Concerned about the fallout of a fight at the convention, Dawes circumvented Hanna and counseled the president that if he took any public position on the nomination short of choosing Roosevelt, whom McKinley did not really want any more than Hanna did, McKinley ran the risk of public embarrassment. Dawes related a critical conversation on the matter in his journal on June 20:

> At about noon was in Hanna's room with H. C. Payne, Senator Burrows and others. Hanna was much enraged at the fact that Quay had started a stampede for Roosevelt, and seemed about to line up the administration forces for Long. He said that, if Roosevelt were nominated "by Quay and Platt," he would refuse to be chairman of the National Committee, etc. Hanna and I had almost an altercation, since I insisted with all my power that any interference on his part for Long or anybody else would start a stampede in the West for Roosevelt and thus he (Hanna) would be playing into Quay's hands—that it was simply a trick of Quay's to take advantage of the Roosevelt sentiment and make it appear that he was a factor in it. Hanna was in such a state of mind that I arranged to have Cortelyou at one telephone and the President at another (at the White House) so that I could talk with Cortelyou and have the President hear what I said. Outlined the situation to them and received an ultimation from the President for Hanna which, at his dictation, I copied and took to Hanna.

In his diary, Dawes then related what the message from McKinley said:

> It read as follows: "The President's close friend must not undertake to commit the administration to any candidate. It has no candidate. The convention must make the nomination. The administration would not if it could. The President's close friend should be satisfied with his unanimous nomination, and not interfere with the Vice-Presidential nomination. The administration wants the choice of the convention, and the President's friend must not dictate to the convention." After the session of the convention, I took this to Hanna. He had already called a conference at Bliss' rooms at the Stratford at 10:30 p.m. to "decide whether to

make an effort to unite the convention on some other candidate than Roosevelt for Vice-President." Hanna said, however,
that he would follow the President's instructions. . . . As I
left the room Hanna whispered to me to tell the President
that he would do exactly as he had requested. Was greatly
relieved at the outcome, as nothing could have stopped the
Roosevelt movement, and the only result of Hanna's interference would have been his humiliation, and embarrassment
to the President.[29]

While Dawes felt that McKinley was saved from humiliation and
embarrassment, Hanna was certainly humiliated, no doubt feeling he
had been let down by both his president and his party. Quay had his
revenge. As Croly wrote, "The Roosevelt candidacy had developed
a spontaneous strength which astounded the candidate himself and
really did embarrass Mr. Hanna."[30] The convention was not one of
Hanna's political triumphs. As historian Margaret Leech notes, not
only did Hanna get stuck with a vice-presidential nominee he was
unenthusiastic about, his will was also at least partly thwarted in the
party platform. Leech writes of the fate of items Hanna wanted in
the platform: "A startling aftermath of the convention was the revela-
tion that the platform, as adopted, was lacking in certain declara-
tions which had been sanctioned at the highest level. . . . Whoever the
culprits were, they were not friends of Mark Hanna. They had also
contrived to water down the recommendation of his favorite project,
government subsidies for the American merchant marine."[31] After the
convention, Hanna wrote to McKinley. His words are chilling, given
the fact that McKinley had little more than a year to live. He wrote,
"Well, it was a nice little scrap at Phila. Not exactly to my liking with
my hand tied behind me. However, we got through in good shape and
the ticket is all right. Your duty to the country is to live for four years
from next March."[32]

Recapturing the White House

Unlike the convention in 1896, where Hanna's control of the proceedings was nearly total, he lost control of the issue that was of the most
importance to him in 1900. This leads to an important question: how
powerful an influence over McKinley's administration could Hanna
have been if he was unable to swing the outcome of such an important

debate and if the president was willing to muzzle him on the advice of another, much younger man like Dawes? McKinley biographer Gould praised McKinley's handling of the Roosevelt situation: "Whether by accident or by arrangement, McKinley had allowed talent to enter his government in a way that improved the party he led."[33] Croly made a similar observation, noting that, though Hanna might not have liked the "damned cowboy" being so close to the presidency, Roosevelt was, in fact a great asset to the campaign:

> If the country had not become relatively prosperous, the Republicans would surely have been defeated. But just in proportion as prosperity returned, it lost some of its value as a political issue. . . . The war had aroused national feeling and had made the people more alive to their joint national interest. . . . If the Republican ticket had not provided them with a candidate who appealed, as Mr. Roosevelt did, to their patriotic imagination and aspirations, it would have failed wholly to satisfy a widespread and vital element of public opinion. Against their own will Mr. McKinley and Mr. Hanna had called to their support the one man who could most effectively supplement their own strength with the American people—the one man who could make the ticket represent the nationalism of the future as well as that of the past and of the present.[34]

Roosevelt used his tremendous charisma to great effect during the campaign.

After the drama of waiting for McKinley to make him the chairman of the campaign and the decision to nominate Teddy Roosevelt for vice president, Hanna approached the 1900 race with the same focus and purpose he had in 1896. In fact, as Croly observed, he did not simply wish to win the election, he wanted a "victory so decisive and so comprehensive that the Republicans would be seen unquestionably as the dominant party."[35]

The campaign in 1900 went quite well. McKinley was a known, popular quantity to the voters in 1900. Because Bryan once again insisted on making the currency question a major issue, it was unnecessary for Republicans to engage in a campaign of education on the same titanic scale they adopted in 1896 when the country was swept with

Bryan-mania and McKinley was less well known. Far less money, $2.5 million, was raised and spent by Hanna in 1900, and there were even reports of money returned to donors at the end of the campaign. For example, Standard Oil donated two hundred fifty thousand dollars to the campaign and at the campaign's conclusion the company received a refund of fifty thousand.[36] While the campaign may have been easier in 1900 than it had been four years earlier, it was not uninteresting.

As he had been in 1896, Hanna was the architect of the campaign in 1900, though he was once again greatly aided by talented subordinates in both the Chicago and New York campaign offices. Croly wrote, "Early in the campaign even his intimate associates were puzzled as to his reasons for making certain moves, but their relation to the general plan was gradually unfolded. Every part of the work was well organized, and every part of the organization was thoroughly energized."[37] Late in the campaign, Dawes wrote to McKinley, "This is the critical week of the campaign—but I cannot detect anything unfavorable. The Committees are all doing well in the matter of a proper distribution of their speakers, and the rallies are keeping up the interest and efforts of Republicans everywhere."[38]

Bryan forced the sixteen-to-one plank (referring to the ratio of silver to gold currency) into the Democratic platform, and the issue was especially emphasized in the West, where it remained a popular cause. However, Bryan's campaign was not the one-trick pony it had been in 1896. The Democratic agenda was expanded in an attempt to attract groups, like labor, that had not been energized by Bryan's first campaign, and with the hope of bringing the Gold Democrats back to the fold.

At least in part, Bryan responded to the suggestions of his supporters who saw his 1896 campaign as fatally flawed. For instance, William Randolph Hearst wrote, "I have become convinced that the people do not want free silver" and suggested that if the campaign focused on silver again, Bryan would "lose the opportunity to do great good in other directions."[39] Hearst's reporter James Creelman expressed a similar sentiment when he wrote, "I have seen most of the leaders in every part of the country and they all oppose any specific form of free silver in the platform and want simply to reaffirm the platform of 1896 in general terms and devote the new platform to new issues."[40] Bryan, a true believer in sixteen-to-one, refused to drop the plank, but he understood the need to expand the campaign beyond that single issue.

Bryan defended the Democratic platform in a letter to Bradford Merrill, the editor of the *New York World*. His argued that those opposed to U.S. imperialism and opposed to the power of the trusts should also favor the free coinage of silver. Further, he argued that to abandon the silver issue would be an act of great disloyalty to the people who had supported his 1896 campaign.[41] Bryan felt so strongly about keeping the free-silver plank in the platform that he told the platform committee, via long-distance telephone, that he would refuse the nomination if the platform did not include it.[42] Still, Bryan understood that talking only gold in 1896 was not a winning strategy, and he spoke of his three issues selectively, depending on where he was. In fact, when he gave his speech accepting the Democratic nomination, he spoke at great length about imperialism and made only joking reference to the silver issue.[43] Mark Hanna responded to the speech with an eye toward exposing Bryan's political strategy. He said, "I think that that speech was put forth as a feeler and was devoted to the line it took in order chiefly that Mr. Bryan might see whether the country took the bait."[44]

In addition to silver, Bryan campaigned against U.S. imperialism and in favor of reining in the trusts. Eastern Democrats opposed both Bryan and free silver, but he did his best to appeal to them. His real problem in New York was that the Democratic machine controlled by Boss Richard Croker was intimately tied to the trusts, which he wanted to break. There was a strong feeling among his supporters that if he was able to win in New York, he would win the election, but Bryan had no relationship with Croker and had no prospect for building one.[45]

In the beginning of the 1900 campaign, Bryan's style differed from that of 1896. Believing that he would be the party's nominee in 1900, Bryan stayed away from the Democratic convention, holding with the tradition that it was distasteful to appear to be actively asking for the nomination. Likewise, he began the campaign at home in Lincoln, much as McKinley kicked off his campaign with an acceptance speech from his front porch in Canton. Bryan did not remain in Lincoln for long, however. A campaign conducted by surrogates was not to his liking, and in October he hit the campaign trail with fervor, racking up sixteen thousand miles and six hundred speeches.[46]

For McKinley's part, the situation was very different in 1900 from what it had been in 1896. He was a popular incumbent president, and the whole nation knew he led the country to a successful victory over Spain. The economy was prosperous, and while many in the Democratic Party wanted Bryan to downplay the free-silver issue, the Republicans were very interested in making Campaign 1900 an object lesson about the wisdom of their policies. The Republicans waged what Koenig characterized as a "scare" campaign, emphasizing the economic disaster that would follow if Bryan were to win. Unlike Bryan, who avoided the currency question in his acceptance speech, McKinley devoted the bulk of his speech to sound money.[47]

Anti-imperialism failed as an issue for Bryan. In large part, this was because it simply did not capture the public's interest the way sixteen to one did in 1896. There was a core group of anti-imperialists concerned about American behavior toward the Philippines, but, for most Americans, the islands were simply too far away to matter much. Koenig characterized the anti-imperialism effort as a "classic example of lofty ethical resolve articulated with masterly eloquence going for naught" because the people "lay deep in moral slumber."[48]

McKinley responded to Bryan's anti-imperialist calls with a reasoned argument against words or deeds that would add to Philippine instability. In his letter accepting the nomination to a second term, he wrote of a desire to establish an eventually independent government in the Philippines but added that it was necessary "to prepare them for self-government, and to give them self-government when they are ready for it and as rapidly as they are ready for it."[49] Other than this statement, McKinley largely refused to engage with Bryan on the issue of anti-imperialism, and it was of little consequence in the campaign.

The antitrust issue offered more opportunity for Bryan because it was a popular issue to which many people could relate. He particularly hoped it would appeal to urban voters.[50] Bryan promised that the trusts would be controlled by the federal government whenever possible. Bryan's rhetoric was potentially powerful, but McKinley and Hanna neutralized it by co-opting the issue. McKinley simply positioned himself and the Republicans as trustbusters as well. In his letter accepting the Republican nomination, McKinley declared, in a passage written by Hanna, that the Republican platform "condemned 'all conspiracies and combinations intended to restrict business, to create monopolies, to limit production, or to strain and prevent all such abuses'" and called trusts "dangerous conspiracies against the public good and should be made the subject of prohibitory or penal legislation."[51] In his response to Bryan, McKinley did much as Dawes had suggested in a letter a year before when Dawes had written to McKinley:

> On every hand there is evidence of unparalleled prosperity—in manufacturing, trade and banking. To me there seems noticeably less rash talk about trusts, and more careful and considered comment on the situation. People do not seem to want to listen to denunciation; but to proposals for remedies. And my impression is growing that general business conditions are so satisfactory that the demand will not be for hasty legislation so much as for right legislation. The position the Republican party must take must appeal to the mind, and not to the emotions.[52]

The McKinley team knew Bryan had to do better in eastern cities in 1900 than he did in 1896, hence Bryan's antitrust appeal. McKinley's rhetorical approach in his letter and throughout the campaign was designed to take the steam out of Bryan's efforts on the issue. McKinley's biographer Gould characterized his acceptance letter as "a masterful political document."[53]

Because he wanted desperately to improve his performance in urban areas, Bryan tried hard to appeal to two demographic groups: labor and ethnic voters, especially Germans, who were one of the country's largest immigrant groups. As Koenig observed, "In certain states, particularly in the Midwest, Bryan considered the German vote critical."[54]

In 1896, Hanna saw to it that the McKinley campaign appealed directly to many ethnic groups, including Germans, with pamphlets and speakers addressing them in their native languages. In 1900, however, the president's relationship with Germany and German Americans was strained. This tension was caused by the country's stewardship of the Philippines and the imperialism-expansionism issue. Some German-language newspapers published in the United States objected to the administration's actions in the Philippines, and Bryan saw an opportunity. He counted on the support of German Americans because many of them equated imperialism with militarism, and they had left Germany to avoid being drafted into the military.[55]

However, Bryan had two problems when it came to attracting German votes. First, McKinley and Hanna did not plan to give up the German vote easily—just as they did not plan to give up any group of voters easily—and they pumped tremendous resources into keeping this ethnic group in the fold. Second, while Bryan's anti-imperialism was appealing to Germans, his free-silver approach was not. They did not support his continued advocacy of the sixteen-to-one ratio of silver-to-gold currency. Bryan's attempts to win the support of the United States' largest and most influential German-language newspaper, New York's *Staats Zeitung,* were unsuccessful because of the currency issue. The newspaper's editors were pleased with his stance against imperialism but were unconvinced on the currency issue. As a consequence, Bryan was similarly unsuccessful in wooing German-American voters.[56]

Because Bryan had bobbled an opportunity with labor in 1896 to campaign to workers on themes like opposition to the use of injunctions to break strikes, he was sure to address such issues in 1900. He opposed injunctions, the blacklisting of workers, and Asian immigration. He called for the creation of a federal labor bureau and for a voluntary arbitration program to prevent strikes and lockouts.[57] In portraying McKinley as antilabor, Bryan and the pro-Bryan press had a ready target in McKinley's campaign manager, Hanna. Unfortunately for Bryan, Hanna stepped in to neutralize much of that effort.

As a mine owner, Hanna had a longstanding reputation as a man who was willing to engage with his workers, despite the way he was portrayed on the pages of Hearst's newspapers with his foot on a skull labeled "Labor" or, as in this Davenport example, crushing a labor skeleton.

Hanna's reputation as a labor crusher persisted well past his death, despite the work of historians like Lewis Gould who tried to counter the image of Hanna from Hearst's newspapers. This view of Hanna is compelling, but it does not conform to most of the recent scholarship on the McKinley era. Gould, for example, writes, "Hanna was not the swollen plutocrat that his enemies depicted; he was a capitalist who dreamed about harmony between employers and workers, and his position with McKinley was always that of a subordinate."[58] Gould did not see Hanna as a "swollen plutocrat," but despite the work of Gould and other historians, that image of Hanna endures.

Few reporters in 2000 were either aware of, or willing to accept, the assertion that Hanna "dreamed about harmony between employers and workers." Two reporters, James Moore and Wayne Slater, have published several books about Karl Rove's role in the Bush administration.

FIGURE 11.1. Where Mr. Hanna stands on the labor question. Cartoon by Homer Davenport, *New York Journal,* September 8, 1896, 12

In one of these books, *Bush's Brain,* Moore and Slater related a tale of Hanna as a crusher of the labor movement and as a man who said one thing about the importance of harmony between labor and ownership but behaved in a very different way. As evidence of this antilabor sentiment, the authors quoted from a *New York Times* article published on September 7, 1896. It was about a meeting of the New York Central Labor Union, which was an umbrella organization for unions in many different trades.

In quoting the *New York Times* story and treating it as "evidence" to be used in building a case against Hanna, however, Moore and Slater took a quote out of context and gave readers an altogether incorrect impression of history. The *Times* story was really about allegations made about Hanna by a Cleveland labor leader. It was not, as Moore and Slater presented it, a statement of fact about Hanna as a labor crusher. Specifically, the story was about a letter the New York Central Labor Union received from an official of the Cleveland Central Labor Union about Mark Hanna. In it, the official made the case that Hanna was an enemy of the labor movement. The portion Moore and Slater quoted in their book read as follows:

> The secretary of the Cleveland Central Labor Union wrote that Mr. Hanna had wrecked the Seaman's union of the lower lake regions, that he had smashed the union of his street railway employees, and refuses to allow them to organize. Further, Mr. Hanna had assisted in destroying the mineworker's unions of Pennsylvania, and had tried to break up the carpenter's unions of Cleveland by employing nonunion men on his mansion at a critical time last spring, when the eight-hour law was being put into effect.[59]

In isolation, this quote painted a very negative picture of Hanna and his treatment of union workers in Cleveland. As is, however, the quote lacked necessary background. To contextualize the events related in this quote, it is necessary to refer to an article published in the *New York Times* a week earlier, as well as to read further into the article that Moore and Slater did quote.

The earlier article, published on August 31, 1896, reported the following:

> A delegate from the Cleveland Central Labor Union, to whom the New York body had written for information about Mr. Hanna, was heard at the New York Labor Union meeting yesterday. This delegate, Isaac Cohen, had come here to solicit moral and financial aid for the strikers in Cleveland. His appeal was well received. He said that the strike had been caused by the employees asking for a Saturday half holiday.... Then Delegate Cohen said: "We will die before we go back, and that is the reason why the Cleveland Central Labor Union is drilling its members and will get them rifles." Many of the delegates moved uneasily in their chairs, and some coughed, but no one uttered a word. Then Delegate Cohen perceived that he had made a mistake, and began talking about righting the wrongs of the workingmen at the

ballot box. After speaking for some time in this strain, he said: "I can tell you about Mark Hanna. He is the most uncompromising foe that organized labor ever had. I can give you his record." "Go ahead," exclaimed several delegates.[60]

The August 31 story continued with a description of the partisan-based arguments about the appropriateness of allowing Cohen to continue to speak. In the end, the chairman of the meeting decided to wait for the formal report the delegates had already requested about Hanna's labor record from Cleveland, rather than letting Cohen continue.

The article published a week later, from which Moore and Slater drew their quote, was about the report received from Cleveland and the reaction of the New York delegates to it. The remaining two paragraphs of the three-paragraph article showed the partisan politics that were involved in the union members' debate about the Hanna report. According to the article,

> Delegate McCabe of the goldbeaters tried to prevent the meeting from taking any action on the letter. He said he did not see why the meeting should go any further in the matter, as it would only be making political capital for one party. Delegate Meiser of the bartenders said that the matter had nothing to do with politics. The Central Labor Union had asked for Mr. Hanna's record, but that did not arrive in time to be published in the Labor Day Journal, which had already been made up. Mr. Hanna had the reputation of being a labor crusher, and organized workmen were against him, not on account of his politics, but on account of his labor record. The letter was then ordered to be filed.[61]

When the article is presented in full, it seems to be a straightforward news report about a political dispute at a labor meeting. In their use of just one inflammatory paragraph, however, Moore and Slater used it as evidence of Hanna's maltreatment of labor.

Stanley Jones, who wrote extensively about the campaign of 1896, wrote also about Hanna's and McKinley's position on labor issues. He wrote, "Mark Hanna was more sympathetic toward labor, organized and unorganized, than most industrialists. The Democratic and Populist campaigners tried to develop the theme that Hanna exploited his own workers and was hostile to organized labor, but they were not able to present convincing evidence of their accusations."[62] Jones also pointed out that the Democrats had their own problems with labor. The Democratic nominee for vice president, Arthur Sewall, was accused of mistreating the men who worked for his shipping line. In his biography of Hanna, Croly suggested there was little or no evidence to support the charge that Hanna was a labor crusher and that it was based almost entirely on the assumption that a man as successful as Hanna must have treated his employees unfairly.[63] Croly wrote of Hanna's relations with unionized coal miners in the 1870s and pointed out that, while Hanna was not a champion of organized labor, he also treated workers with respect. Croly wrote, "Mr. Hanna himself, at a time when labor-unions were regarded with even greater disfavor by employers than they are at present, was friendly to the unions. John James, the secretary of the Miner's National Association in 1875 and 1876 states that 'he was the first mining operator in the bituminous fields of the United States to recognize the cardinal principle of arbitration in the settlement of wages, disputes, and the first also to recognize the Miners' National association.'"[64] Hanna remained friendly with the men who worked for him through his career in business, and, late in his political career, he became an outspoken advocate of improving relations between business and organized labor.

One columnist, Linda McQuaig, wrote in the *Toronto Star* that the Bush administration was poised to undo the progressive reforms of the twentieth century: "If the Bush presidency resembles anything, it's that of William McKinley, who occupied the White House in the late 1890s at the height of the era of unchecked corporate power. Bush strategist Karl Rove has been likened to McKinley strategist Mark Hanna, who believed government should be run by, and for, big business."[65] However, Hanna, like McKinley, had a well-documented record of working to facilitate a good relationship between business and labor. It is certainly true that Hanna wanted business to prosper, but for that to happen, he felt it was imperative that there be harmony between management and labor. The longer he was in politics, the more he worked to fulfill that goal. After McKinley's death, one of the things for which Hanna was best known was his role as a leader of the National Civic Federation, an organization devoted to improving the business-labor relationship.

If Hanna, as McQuaig asserted, "believed government should be run by, and for, big business," it was for more principled reasons than a desire to increase the size of his personal bank account. Hanna believed that the United States depended on a strong economy and that government had a responsibility to keep the economy strong. As citizens, we can take exception with this belief and argue convincingly that the government goes a little too far in helping big business in the name of keeping the economy strong, but to argue that Hanna was motivated solely by personal greed flies in the face of the truth. He surely would have contributed much more money to the Hanna family fortune had he stayed in the private sector and continued to run his many companies.

Hanna did not seek to be a leader of the National Civic Federation, but when he was pursued by men of business and labor, he answered the call because he had long been concerned about the turmoil between business and labor. Was he concerned about turmoil between labor and management because he worried about diminished profits? Certainly, but his sincerely held belief was that profits benefited owners and workers alike. Croly summarized Hanna's role in the National Civic Federation with these words: "For the first time in his public career he became a reformer, dedicated consciously to the task of converting other people to a better way of dealing with a fundamental problem; and the best of it was that his public appearance as a labor reformer was the natural, although fortuitous, expression of his life-long personal feelings and behavior."[66] It is legitimate to object to policies that seem to benefit management over labor, or vice versa, but it is inaccurate to label Hanna as a labor crusher when, in fact, he understood there was a symbiotic relationship between labor and ownership. Hanna was no idealistic revolutionary—he certainly felt the bulk of the power should lie with ownership, but at the same time, he respected workers and understood their irreplaceable contribution to the economy.

For his part, McKinley cared very much about labor and had an even stronger reputation in that area than Hanna. While it was probably not their first meeting, McKinley and Hanna became familiar with each other during a trial in Canton when McKinley defended several coal miners accused of crimes during a strike in 1876. As the head of an association of coal-mine owners, Hanna was an interested party in the case. McKinley effectively represented most of the twenty-plus defendants to not-guilty verdicts. During the 1896 campaign, McKinley walked a cautious line on labor questions, not wanting to alienate either business or labor, but there is nothing in his record to indicate a hostile attitude toward organized labor. Jones observed that McKinley always made an effort to address the concerns of labor, often engaging with members of organized labor to clarify statements he had made or to address their arguments and criticisms.[67] McKinley was not necessarily an outspoken supporter of the organized labor movement, but neither was he dismissive of, or hostile to, labor's concerns.

In large measure, the coalition that elected McKinley in 1896 and reelected him in 1900 was made up of the wealthy men of industry and the laborers who worked for them. One argument that critics of McKinley's campaigns frequently make is that workers were either coerced into supporting McKinley or duped into believing that a vote for McKinley was not in their best interest. However, as the biographies written by historians like Morgan, Gould, and Leech show, McKinley passed the most important test of electoral politics: he followed through—or, at least, tried to follow through—on his campaign promises to laborers.

As president, McKinley championed the idea of an eight-hour workday. He brought a leader sympathetic to labor's concerns, Illinois's Lyman J. Gage, into his administration as the secretary of treasury. As Gould described, "After the Haymarket Riot of 1886, Gage favored pardoning the accused participants and became an advocate of 'more friendly consultation and less inconsiderate action on the part of capital and labor.'"[68] McKinley and Hanna both professed a deep desire to move America into the industrial age by creating a partnership between ownership and labor.

After his experience as a mine owner during the violent coal-miners' strike in Massillon, Ohio, in 1876, in which William McKinley served as defense counsel for almost two dozen miners, Hanna came to feel it was important to avoid conflict between labor and management whenever possible, for the good of the economy.[69] He did not believe in the heavy-handed tactics of many mine owners. When miners in Pennsylvania threatened a strike during the 1900 campaign, Hanna stepped in and organized negotiations that prevented the strike from becoming an issue. Hanna wrote to McKinley in July, "I am working

FIGURE 11.2. Hanna—"He didn't know his business." Cartoon by Homer Davenport, *New York Journal*, August 15, 1896, 1

hard in this strike matter and don't want to leave for a moment until I accomplish something or fail."[70] Hanna largely sided with the miners and worked with the titan of American banking, J. P. Morgan, to broker a deal between the miners and ownership.[71] The strike was averted, if only temporarily, and it took the steam out of a potentially powerful campaign moment for Bryan. Leech characterized Hanna's mediation of the strike as Hanna's "single greatest contribution to the Republican cause."[72] As with the anti-imperialism issue, the McKinley campaign succeeded in co-opting an issue on which Bryan hoped to separate himself from the popular incumbent.

In addition to labor and immigrants, Bryan made a special effort to appeal to African Americans. Trying to attract their votes was an ambitious goal because the Democrats were traditionally anathema to African American voters. While Bryan was sincere in his effort, much of the Democratic Party, the dominant party of white southerners, was not as accommodating to this group. The McKinley campaign successfully appealed to African Americans in 1896 and then again in 1900.

No group pursued by Bryan was left unattended by McKinley and Hanna. While the educational efforts of the 1900 McKinley campaign were not as massive as they had been in 1896, there was still a significant volume of material distributed. Campaign publications included one hundred twenty-five million pamphlets, twenty-one million postcards, and copies of McKinley's acceptance letter in a multitude of languages, such as German and Polish.[73] In addition, just as in 1896, materials were provided by the campaign for publication in newspapers across the country. Once again, the campaign also sent out hundreds of speakers across the country as surrogates for McKinley, each armed with a briefing book produced by the campaign. McKinley's campaign was largely defined by two particularly busy—and effective—speakers: Teddy Roosevelt and Mark Hanna.

There is an odd parallel here between Roosevelt and Hanna. McKinley was seemingly reluctant to give Hanna the same level of power in 1900 that he had in 1896, but he eventually did so and most of the important decisions of the management of the campaign were left to Hanna. Similarly, Hanna was very reluctant to nominate Roosevelt for vice president, but once Roosevelt had the nomination, Hanna accepted him and understood he was of great importance to the campaign. Roosevelt quickly became a powerful representative of the re-election effort. During the campaign, Roosevelt traveled and spoke extensively, especially in the West, where he was immensely popular.

While Hanna had not wanted him, and Roosevelt was well aware of the fact, the two men cooperated quite nicely during the campaign. At the outset, Roosevelt told Hanna, "I am as strong as a bull moose and you can use me to the limit, taking heed of but one thing and that is my throat." As Roosevelt's biographer Edmund Morris reported, by the end of the campaign, Roosevelt out-traveled Bryan both in 1900 and in 1896, travelling 21,209 miles.[74] During those travels, Roosevelt gave a reported 673 campaign speeches.

Hanna did not travel as extensively as Roosevelt, but he was in as much demand as the governor of New York. His speeches were influential, and some caused new friction with McKinley. While Hanna's job was to run the campaign, he was slowly pulled into it as an active participant, responding to requests from various places around the country to speak. He had spoken with frequency in Ohio throughout his public career, but before the campaign of 1900, he had only rarely taken the podium outside of Ohio.[75] His first foray in 1900 was a speech in mid-September in Chicago. He subsequently gave a speech in New York and then another in Indiana.[76] Because he was well known nationally, once he opened the door, Hanna was deluged by requests for appearances, even though his Chicago speech showed his inexperience as a stump speaker.

Although Hanna wrote McKinley's passage about trusts in his acceptance letter, this was an area where Hanna did not always stay on message. In his speech in Chicago on September 18, just ten days after the release of McKinley's letter, Hanna said, "There is not a trust in the United States. There is a national law, and in every state there is a law against trusts. They cannot exist, and every law against trusts, national or state, has been the product of Republican lawmakers."[77] While Hanna's words could be taken to mean that trusts were not the issue that Bryan wanted to make them, there was ample evidence, and an enthusiastic Democratic press ready to use it, that trusts were alive and well. Hanna's speech gave ammunition to Bryan and his allies in the press. His spoken words seemed to contradict the statement he wrote for McKinley's letter, acknowledging that trusts were a problem that needed attention.

Margaret Leech argued Hanna's speech was the equivalent of a Freudian slip, revealing his genuine lack of regard for the regulation of business. The resultant bad publicity was annoying to McKinley because "Hanna's injudicious remark could be uncharitably construed as a correction of the President by the leering 'Nursie' of the cartoons."[78] Shortly after the Chicago speech, Hanna spoke to reporters in Cleveland and explained that he was not suggesting that there were not trust-like entities in which businesses collaborated with each other in a way that did damage to common people, merely that, in the strictest legal sense, there was no such thing as a trust in the United States.[79] Shortly after making this clarification, Hanna embarked on a speaking tour that once again highlighted his tensions with McKinley.

Hanna was approached by Republican leaders in Nebraska and South Dakota to make a tour through the area, and he found the temptation irresistible. In the case of Nebraska, it gave him the opportunity to traverse the home territory of the enemy. Hanna's personal secretary,

Elmer Dover, reported that Republican leaders in Nebraska made it clear that if they could not have Hanna, they did not want anyone, so he consented to go.[80] The invitation to travel to South Dakota gave Hanna the chance to go after a personal enemy, Senator Richard Pettigrew, who was up for reelection. Hanna's eagerness to go after Pettigrew caused McKinley discomfort, and, in turn, McKinley's reluctance to attack Pettigrew vexed Hanna.

Pettigrew was a Republican when he became a senator, but he left the party and became a Silver Republican over the currency issue. This naturally made him a turncoat in Hanna's eyes. To Hanna, party loyalty was second to none. Pettigrew was also an anti-imperialist who attacked McKinley about U.S. involvement in the Philippines. In 1899, he wrote to McKinley, "The blood of the South Dakota boys sacrificed in that contest must be laid at the door of your administration, and that impartial history must place you among the most dishonored rulers in all time."[81]

Hanna had a particularly heated exchange with the senator in the first week of June that made him especially eager to close the door on Pettigrew's career.[82] As the Congress was wrapping up its session, debate turned to a failing antitrust bill. Taking the podium, Pettigrew attacked Hanna personally, saying, among other things, that he had bribed his way into the Senate and that he was killing the antitrust bill deliberately in order to ensure large campaign contributions from big business. Hanna responded by questioning Pettigrew's sanity, and the debate escalated to the point that physical altercations between senators seemed likely.[83]

In July, Hanna wrote to McKinley and suggested a monetary attack on Pettigrew:

> Mr. E. G. Johnson has brought to my attention the matter of making a payment to the Indians of the Sisseton Reservation in South Dakota. An effort was made in the last Congress to abolish the agency on that Reservation, and it was defeated in the Senate by Senator Pettigrew. The Senator is making great claims for the Indian vote on account of this. There is a large fund in the Treasury belonging to this tribe, and it is simply a question of expediency as to when it shall be paid to them. The Indians are in need of a payment now,

and desire a payment of three hundred thousand dollars. Please give it consideration.[84]

The fact that Hanna would so openly—unusually, for him—urge the president to make such a move reflects his ire for Pettigrew.

Hanna received advice from many in Republican circles not to make the tour of Nebraska and South Dakota, which were hotbeds of Populist politics. Some suggested Hanna would be in physical danger; others suggested the trip would be a bonanza for media outlets in the area that had already made a cottage industry out of pillorying him; and still others said the trip to South Dakota would look too much like a naked abuse of power as the powerful chairman of the Republican Party carried out a vendetta against Senator Pettigrew. He ignored all of this advice, which prompted a last effort by McKinley to get Hanna to cancel the trip. The same basic story appears in the major biographies of both Hanna and McKinley.

Hanna was in Chicago when he was joined by Postmaster General Charles Emory Smith. Smith presented a laundry list of reasons that Hanna should not make the tour, which made Hanna suspicious, though Smith claimed he was speaking only for himself and other members of the cabinet. When pressed, Smith admitted that McKinley had sent him, and Hanna reportedly responded, "Return to Washington and tell the President that God hates a coward!" While the quote sounds almost too good to be true, Elmer Dover reported it was true, and Hanna made the tour of South Dakota and Nebraska in direct opposition to McKinley's wishes.

Hanna was annoyed by what he felt was McKinley's lack of confidence in him. Dover said, "They had given him the campaign to manage . . . and here was a simple matter of detail which they wanted to interfere with. They doubted Mr. Hanna's judgment and it irritated him."[85] Thomas Beer viewed Hanna's tour as a tremendous success, in large measure because most people who came out to see Hanna knew little about him. Their only prior knowledge came from critical newspaper articles and vicious political cartoons. After hearing him speak, they were unable to reconcile the media image with the "real" Hanna. Beer wrote, "The human image asserted itself against the cartoon, and in South Dakota it asserted itself at close range, since a law of the state forbade orators to speak from trains. Mr. Hanna trundled two hundred feet to a platform and spoke thence, while boys crept so near that they could smell his cigars. The demon pock-marked with dollars vanished in this sunlight; it was just a man standing there, without diamonds on his thumbs."[86] In quantifiable terms, Hanna's tour was a tremendous success. According to Dover, the crowds that came out to see the senator in South Dakota were much larger than those that turned out to see either McKinley when he toured the state in 1897 or Roosevelt when he campaigned there a few weeks before Hanna.[87] McKinley won both South Dakota and Nebraska, and South Dakota's state legislature refused to return Pettigrew to the U.S. Senate. These developments were, no doubt, gratifying to Hanna.

One additional bit of acrimony between McKinley and Hanna deserves consideration. As was often the case, Charles Dawes was right in the middle of things, playing the go-between for Hanna and the president. Like other run-ins between the two men, this last incident indicated that McKinley was concerned about Hanna and corruption, whether real or perceived.

Hanna began a written exchange on August 3, 1900, when he had Dawes deliver a letter to McKinley. In the letter, Hanna asked McKinley to intervene in a number of political matters, including concerns about the loss of patronage jobs in the Brooklyn Naval Yard; the loss of patronage jobs at a facility called Iona Island on the Hudson River because, he alleged, the man in charge, Sergeant Dugan, was giving them to Democrats; and a complaint about Secretary of the Treasury Lyman Gage's refusal to allow government-subsidized campaign travel by Treasury Department employees. The latter complaint was inspired, in part, by a letter Hanna received from Chase Lichtman, who wrote, "I can understand that if this rule is rigidly enforced it will interfere very materially with us in the campaign. At the same time I am sure our Democratic opponents will have the active, even if perforce secret, aid of every Democrat upon the Government pay roll."[88]

Hanna forwarded Lichtman's letter to McKinley and wrote, "If I cannot receive this much aid from the Administration, I do not see what encouragement there is for me and my co-laborers in this campaign."[89] He also wrote a second letter on the same day regarding the Brooklyn Navy Yard and Iona Island, suggesting each could result in the loss of votes and damage to party interests.[90] In a return letter, McKinley delivered the written equivalent of a slap on the wrist.

Hanna found the tone of the letter scolding and condescending. Everything about it irritated the senator, who regarded it as a statement for McKinley's future biographers. With regard to the question of Lyman Gage's refusal to allow government-subsidized campaign travel, McKinley wrote, "Surely there should be no travel expense paid by the Government which is not for the public service, and I am absolutely and totally opposed to any use of the public money for travel or any other expense for party interests; and in this sentiment I know you share."[91] On the subject of the Brooklyn Naval Yard, McKinley wrote, "I am sure when you know the facts you have no reason for criticism or complaint. . . . It would not be right, and I am sure you would not have the Department employ men at the Navy Yard who are not needed, nor would you have work done there that could be best done at some other Navy Yard in the country."[92] On the subject of Iona Island, he wrote,

> As to the conduct of Sergeant Dugan at Iona Island . . . I know nothing about it, but will at once make an investigation. If he is using his office for the appointment of Democrats for party purposes, he shall be called to account. This is a time when every effort will be made to have the administration do questionable things. It is a period of great temptation, just the sort that will require the highest courage to meet and resist. If elected I have to live with the administration for four years. I do not want to feel that any improper or questionable methods have been employed to reach the place, and you must continue, as you have always done, to stand against unreasonable exactions, which are so common at a time like the present.[93]

From Hanna's perspective, he was not asking the president for anything that had not been done by every preceding administration. Beyond that, Hanna was annoyed by the tone adopted by the man for whom he had many great sacrifices over the years. He was particularly galled by the fact that the letter was not handwritten by McKinley but had been dictated, which ensured that it was copied for the White House file and was a matter of public record. Hanna was so angry after reading the letter that he threw it to the floor and raved that it had been written for the president's biographers.[94]

Hanna's biographer Croly defended the president to an extent, recognizing McKinley as a leader of strong moral standing. He wrote, "Neither of these practices can be defended, and Mr. McKinley in repudiating them was contributing, as he did in so many other instances, toward the establishment of higher administration standards. . . . When such cases arose, Mr. McKinley's action in refusing indefensible demands was often admitted by Mr. Hanna to be as much for his own protection as for the President's."[95] While she did not counter Croly's high opinion of McKinley's morals, McKinley's biographer Leech observed that McKinley's writing clearly showed he was interested in establishing a clear record of upright behavior and in creating some distance from Hanna. To Leech, Hanna's assertion that McKinley wrote with his biographers in mind was right on target. It was normal procedure for McKinley to keep copies of letters in the White House file but, "in this case it seemed to indicate a nervous desire for the protection of the record. He would not ordinarily have discussed the delicate matter of campaign ethics in explicit detail on paper."[96]

By 1900, McKinley had clearly grown tired of coverage of Hanna as a corrupt political boss, just as he was tired of being portrayed as Hanna's puppet. During the campaign, McKinley was especially concerned about a postal scandal in Cuba. Hanna's friend Estes G. Rathbone, for whom Hanna had secured a patronage job in Cuba, was under arrest, and another crony of the senator, Perry Heath, had been quietly removed from his position in the postal service and shifted to a job with the Republican National Committee. In July, Hanna wrote McKinley in Rathbone's defense: "Somehow I cannot bring myself to the belief that R has done anything criminal and if there is anything of an injustice done him we will all feel sorry for it."[97]

McKinley seems not to have been impressed from this entreaty, and he responded by having his secretary, Cortelyou, write to Charles Emory Smith, the postmaster general, that "the President has no directions to give in this matter, leaving to you and the Secretary of War, who are familiar with the conditions in Cuba and with General Rathbone's relations thereto, to make such answer to Senator Hanna and give such directions as are required by the public interests."[98] What is clear from his letter admonishing Hanna is that McKinley wanted to cover his bases where Hanna was concerned. He worried about the effect Hanna's reputation had on his own, but he also understood that

Hanna was important to his reelection chances. Cutting Hanna loose was never an option, but McKinley saw no harm in creating a record that showed him disciplining his politico.

Critics of Mark Hanna argued that he was at least as motivated by a personal quest for power as he was by devotion to McKinley. Yes, Hanna was dedicated to McKinley, Leech might argue, but it was because he felt that, if McKinley were no longer president, then Hanna himself would lose much of his prestige. Those with a more sympathetic view of Hanna, like his own biographers Croly and Beer, saw Hanna as a man with scruples but who was also willing to do almost anything for the president whom he adored. In either view, Hanna was an important and effective advocate for McKinley, but he was also potentially dangerous to him. In treating Hanna as one would treat a loved but rambunctious child, McKinley wanted to have his cake and eat it too—and did. He had the devoted energy of Hanna working for him, but he was careful to insulate himself from the worst of the senator's eager overexcess.

This turned out to be a successful arrangement. Despite whatever tension there might have been between the two men, Hanna continued to work effectively for McKinley's reelection. In a report to McKinley in August, he wrote of his efforts with several constituencies:

> I had a long session today with Genl. Shaw and others of the "Grand Army" with reference to the management of the soldier element in the campaign. Of course they present many complications but boiled down they do not amount to much. Their principal object—which they will press in legislation—to establish a pension court of appeals which seems all right to me. . . . Bliss and I went to Boston to stir up the business interests, which we did most effectively. . . . We are getting along nicely with our organization both here [New York] and in Chicago.[99]

The "soldier element" proved to be a valuable campaign resource for McKinley in 1900. As Perry Heath observed to George Cortelyou, "The G.A.R. parade yesterday was along Michigan Avenue where Republican National Committee headquarters are located. In front of the headquarters on canvass, is a very large and excellent portrait of the President. It would have made your eyes rain to have noticed the veterans line up in front of that picture as they passed along, and salute with bared heads, give three cheers and a tiger for their comrade."[100] The campaign was conducted in much the same way as the 1896 campaign, with two campaign headquarters and many of the same key figures involved in running the race.

Despite his involvement in the scandal that resulted in his removal from government service, Perry Heath continued to be in charge of printed campaign material that included newspaper supplements with a circulation of nearly two million copies a day.[101] By late September, Heath reported a wide variety of published campaign materials to George Cortelyou:

> Up to this time I have gotten out about seventy different forms of documents, beside about fifteen or twenty forms of posters and lithographs, all aggregating possibly one hundred and ten million copies printed and distributed. This year we have sent documents direct to county committees. . . . This has enabled us to expedite the distribution to the greatest possible degree of efficiency. The newspaper work is I think more extensive and larger than in 1896, covering a supplement service aggregating about two million copies per week, a patent inside to practically the same extent, with a large plate service to another class of newspapers, and yet original matter weekly to nearly six thousand newspapers that afford their own type composition. . . . In all of the present work, while we are drawing contrasts and reminding the people of the times and conditions of four years ago, prophesies of Major, Governor and President McKinley as against the false prophesies of Candidate Bryan are doing us more good than almost anything else.[102]

While much of the campaign of education in 1896 was focused on the gold standard, the campaign of 1900 focused on many issues, including a rebuff of Bryan's attacks on McKinley as an imperialist. Heath wrote again to George B. Cortelyou:

> I have tried for a fortnight to induce one or two of my writers, among them Mr. Halsted, to write me a ten thousand word sketch of the President's work in the Spanish-American

war, so as to bring out his personality, and also to make it perfectly plain to the people why we are fighting Aquinaldo's banditti in the Philippines. I deeply regret that up to this time the matter has not been produced, and in a state of desperation, I wired for a copy of the book published by Haskell, Norwich, Conn., and I will have lifted out of that a sufficient amount of matter to make the point I desire to bring forward. I have also striven hard to secure a character sketch of Aquinaldo—not an abusive or ugly one, but a true statement of his life and political machinations—in order to make it clear to the people why we are trying to subjugate him and his followers.[103]

During the campaign Hearst's cartoonists continued to be Hanna's nemesis, and Hearst started his Chicago newspaper on July 4, solely for the purpose of aiding Bryan's campaign. Heath commented on the virulence of the Democratic press's attack in a letter to Cortelyou:

The abuse being heaped upon the President and Mr. Hanna in certain directions out here is simply terrible, and we all can see every day the good effect it is having upon our cause. Essentially this is an impersonal campaign, the issues all being general and vital ones, and when an opposition is compelled to resort to personal abuse of any one, especially when the opposition is led individually by one who aspires for the high office of President of the United States the opposition becomes weaker with every class. This kind of campaigning only breeds anarchists, it does not change the sentiment of thinking people. I hear every hand and from every distance most favorable comments upon the dignified position assumed by President McKinley . . . while his opponent is galloping over the country and inciting nasty personalities and groveling in the mud.[104]

Observing the election from the campaign trail, where he made speeches on McKinley's behalf, Dawes reflected much of Heath's sentiment and wrote to McKinley: "The people are intensely interested in this campaign, and the comparative quietness of 1900 as distinguished from 1896 comes from a greater thoughtfulness and from decided convictions—not from indifference."[105] The incumbent president was reelected by a slightly wider popular margin—7,218,491 to 6,356,734—and with twenty-one more Electoral College votes—292 to 155—than he had received in 1896.[106] In one of several congratulatory telegrams Hanna sent McKinley that day, he wrote, "Accept congratulations on your re-election. We fought nobly."[107] The improved numbers were not dramatically different, but McKinley won in some places, like Bryan's home state of Nebraska, that he had lost in 1896, and his continued hold on power reflected the fact that Bryan's charisma could not make up for the fact that many in the public were wary about his position on the issues, especially the currency question. McKinley also clearly benefited both from economic prosperity during his first term and success against Spain. In Congress, the Republicans retained significant majorities in both chambers. At the beginning of the Fifty-seventh Congress, the margin in the House was two hundred Republicans, 151 Democrats, five Populists, and one member of the Silver Party. In the Senate, the margin was fifty-six Republicans, thirty-two Democrats, and two members of the Populist Party. Though it would take years of Republican dominance to be identified as such, Hanna achieved his goal of establishing a Republican majority.

The party held its majority in Congress through the 1920s and only gave up the White House to Woodrow Wilson when Teddy Roosevelt fractured the Republican vote in 1912 with his third-party run for the presidency. McKinley's presidency ended all too soon in tragedy, but in November of 1900, he stood firmly at the front of a Republican government that would hold power for decades. And although he was controversial and his role was open to interpretation, Mark Hanna played a significant part in that achievement.

During the campaign of 2004, many comparisons were made to the McKinley's successful reelection campaign. Before the election, many reporters focused especially on Karl Rove's role in the campaign. In a piece that might have reminded some of conservative journalists' earlier concerns, Elisabeth Bumiller, of the *New York Times*, addressed the subject of Rove as a target for Democratic presidential candidates in January 2004.

The article included a collection of quotes from a variety of candidates such as Wesley Clark, Howard Dean, and Tom Harkin, who each asserted that the real power in the White House was Karl Rove and that Americans ought to vote Karl out of office. In the piece, Bumiller invoked the name of Mark Hanna, as reporters often did when writing about Rove's influence. She wrote, "But like Mark Hanna, the strategist and fund-raiser behind William McKinley's 1896 drive to the presidency, he has longer-term goals. Not incidentally, Mr. Rove is an avid student of Hanna's role in history."[108]

Bumiller was quite accurate when she compared the way their opponents invoked the names of Hanna and Rove:

> At the same time, invoking Mr. Rove, at least among the Democratic loyalists who vote in primaries, is a kind of code describing a president who Democrats say is manipulated by the political strategist behind the curtain. . . . Hanna's name was used in a similar way with McKinley, and cartoonists of the time often drew the president as a small boy with his strategist telling him what to do. But historians note that McKinley was re-elected in 1900, ushering in a period of Republican dominance. Mr. Rove, not incidentally, believes that Hanna's role was overstated, and that McKinley was far more politically engaged than people knew.[109]

She was right to assert that Hanna and Rove were both lightning rods for their opposition. Both Hanna and Rove made easy targets—easier, perhaps, than the presidential candidates they worked for (although Bush became a much better target of his own after the 2004 election)—for political opponents to attack.

As in earlier elections, it was not just reporters who commented on the relationship between Rove and Bush in 2004 by connecting—usually improperly—Rove with Mark Hanna. Writing about campaign finance in the conservative *Weekly Standard,* David Tell wrote, "What if the election is therefore a close one, as it was last time? And what if, in a close election, money really can make the difference—a postulate, after all, on which much of American politics has based itself at least since the time when Karl Rove's hero, Mark Hanna, was managing the fortunes of William McKinley. In that case, it looks like Bush really will be a lock."[110] Even fellow conservatives had failed to absorb by 2004 Rove's consistent denial that he did not view Mark Hanna as a hero.

One article that appeared late in the 2004 campaign described the challenges facing Bush's reelection effort. Reporter Howard Fineman made what were by that time the requisite references to Mark Hanna. Describing a campaign visit to Canton, Ohio, Fineman wrote,

> Rove was delighted. And in his world, Canton had special meaning. It's the home of President William McKinley, whose pro-business yet progressive wartime leadership made him a nineteenth century "compassionate conservative"— and whose close adviser, Mark Hanna, was the country's first famous handler. . . . Having built Bush's political career from the ground up, their shared goal now is to do what McKinley and Hanna did a century ago, but what Bush's dad failed to do: win re-election. . . . Accomplishing that will test even Rove's mastery.[111]

Fineman's identification of McKinley as a nineteenth-century compassionate conservative was unique and more admiring than most reporters covering the connection between 2004 and the Gilded Age. And, of course, the final line about the difficulty of repeating the realignment won by McKinley and Hanna was prescient.

EPILOGUE

Mark Hanna's Legacy in the Twenty-first Century

 he election of 1896 is often noted by historians and political scientists as a realigning election, in which the preponderance of popular support and the enduring allegiance of a majority of voters switch from one political party to another.[1] In realignments, the change in allegiance is permanent enough to ensure that the new majority party organizes American politics for decades. The election of 1896 gave the Republican Party solid control of American politics until the 1930s.

FIGURE E.1. Mark Hanna

FIGURE E.2. Karl Rove

Despite its historical importance, however, the election of 1896 was largely forgotten by most Americans at the end of the twentieth century until it began to appear in coverage of the 2000 presidential campaign, thanks at least in part to the fact that Karl Rove encouraged the comparison by talking to reporters about the similarities between the two eras. However, as soon as Rove compared 1896 to 2000, he lost control of his analogy. When he brought up 1896, he opened the door to comparisons between the major players in the two campaigns. George W. Bush was compared to William McKinley, and Rove was compared to Mark Hanna, often inaccurately.

Rove rarely spoke specifically about Hanna, he objected to comparisons between him and the Ohio senator, and he disagreed with those who argued that Hanna was primarily responsible for McKinley's political success. There are plausible explanations for Rove's objection to these comparisons. In part, Rove may have objected to them because the contemporary memory of Hanna—what memory exists—is very negative. He is presented often as a man who was a friend of big business at the expense of the little guy. He is generally spoken of in the popular press as a power-hungry puppet master, pushing McKinley to do his bidding. For that reason alone, Rove was probably motivated to discourage the comparisons. Perhaps Rove should have expected comparisons to Hanna when he started invoking McKinley's legacy, but that does not mean the comparisons were accurate.

Protests or not, Rove was unable to avoid comparisons to Hanna. David Gergen, a former aide to several presidents, frequently spoke of the Rove-Hanna parallel and suggested an answer in a discussion with White House correspondent John King on July 13, 2005, during the CNN program *Inside Politics*. The discussion was sparked by speculation about the Democrats' desire to use the Valerie Plame affair against Karl Rove. King and Gergen had the following exchange about the media and why Democrats were eager to knock Rove down a peg:

> John King: They are charging, with the help of the Democrats at the moment. What is it about Karl Rove that makes him such a boogeyman to the Democrats? He's more polarizing to many Democrats than even George W. Bush.
>
> David Gergen: Because he may be the Mark Hanna of our time, to go back to another historical analogy. Mark Hanna

was the adviser to William McKinley—President McKinley, who created an enduring Republican majority early in the twentieth century. And people think Karl Rove—and the most important mission that Karl Rove is on with the president is to build a durable, long-lasting Republican majority that will rule the White House, the House, the Senate, and the Supreme Court for a generation. That's what he's about, and he's been remarkably successful so far.

John King: So the Democrats see an opportunity that's perhaps motivated by their fear of his success?

David Gergen: Yes. If you discredit him, if you can take him out of action, if you can distract him, distract him before the Supreme Court fight starts, that would be progress for the Democrats.

In this exchange, Gergen repeated a mistake he made in other forums, that Mark Hanna was an aide to McKinley as president, but his observation about Rove was more apt. When Hanna is remembered in the modern context, he is remembered for a number of negative reasons, but he is also associated with a long reign by the Republican Party. Unlike his aversion to being compared to Hanna, Rove never denied the desire to reestablish the Republican Party as the majority party in American politics.

Rove was certainly uncomfortable with comparisons between him and Hanna that also compared Bush and McKinley in an unfavorable way. In political reporting from his day and from the present day, William McKinley often comes off as being less than his own man and more like a naïve child or a puppet, controlled by Mark Hanna. When modern-day reporters depicted Hanna as a master of a lesser man in stories about Karl Rove, they painted Rove—unintentionally or not—with the same brush. History will show what Karl Rove's role in the White House really was and what reputation he deserves—but it is understandable why he wanted to avoid being compared to Hanna.

On the eve of the Republican National Convention, in late July 2000, a newspaper story about the convention's historic host city, Philadelphia, referred to Rove's interest in the parallels between the McKinley and Bush eras. The reporter, James O'Toole of the *Pittsburgh Post-Gazette*, wrote, "Karl Rove, a member of George W. Bush's inner circle, loves the McKinley-Bush parallel. His thesis is that McKinley, at a time of economic change, was able to broaden the appeal of his party to appeal to immigrants and the middle class—a turn-of-another century version of compassionate conservatism."[2] Many reporters and commentators made note of Rove's self-professed interest in McKinley, the election of 1896, and the Republicans' long period of dominance that began with that election. Coverage of the connection between 1896 and 2000 and between McKinley and Bush frequently went further and connected Hanna to Rove, sometimes merely suggesting that they played similar roles, but in other instances suggesting that Rove wanted to *be* Hanna. Such assertions erred in two ways: they misrepresented the role of Hanna in McKinley's career, and they appear to have misrepresented Rove's true goals.

One of the first in the media to put in print the idea that Karl Rove not only wanted to replicate the Republicans' success of 1896 but that he wanted to be the new Mark Hanna was a conservative syndicated columnist, Jack Kelly. In his March 5, 2000, column, Kelly argued that Republicans should support John McCain because he was, in Kelly's estimation, the Republican who could beat Al Gore. His column began with this passage:

> George W. Bush strategist Karl Rove imagined himself to be a latter day Mark Hanna, the Cleveland industrialist who masterminded William McKinley's landslide victory in 1896. The old GOP strategy of attacking Democrats as the party of "Rum, Romanism, and Rebellion" wasn't working anymore. Hanna devised a new set of issues, kept tight control of his candidate to keep him on message—McKinley rarely left his front porch in Canton, Ohio—and raised gobs of money.[3]

This passage plays an important part in the birth of a political myth—that Karl Rove envisioned himself as the "new" Mark Hanna. Kelly did not write that Rove *said* he wanted to be the next Mark Hanna or that Rove *said* Mark Hanna was his idol, but the statement, phrased as Kelly wrote it, contains the seeds of similar claims other journalists subsequently made. It is true that Rove wanted to duplicate what a talented team of Republicans, including Hanna, had done in 1896. Anything that asserted more than that seems to be untrue.

In addition to his incorrect characterization of Rove's feelings for Hanna, Kelly's column contained two other errors that were common misperceptions in reports about the Bush campaign and its similarity to 1896. First, he wrote, "The fly in Hanna's ointment was Teddy Roosevelt, who Hanna had stuck on the ticket with McKinley to get him out of the way. When McKinley was assassinated, Hanna exclaimed: 'Now that damned cowboy is president.'" As we have seen, Roosevelt certainly was not put on the ticket by Hanna—Hanna did all he could at the 1900 convention to prevent that from happening before McKinley called him off. Second, Kelly wrote, "The Bush campaign began promisingly enough. He was the compassionate conservative who could reach out to Hispanics and women. And Rove, like Hanna before him, raised a ton of money."[4] However, fundraising was not Rove's main responsibility in either presidential campaign.

In 2000 and 2004, the people most crucial in the fundraising efforts were men like Jack Oliver, who was the Bush campaign's finance chairman in 2000 and its deputy chairman in 2004; and Mercer Reynolds, who was the cochair for finance for Bush in Ohio in 2000 and was the national chairman for finance in 2004. Oliver was credited, for example, with helping to raise over a billion dollars for Bush between 2000 and 2004.[5] Another man responsible for Bush's remarkable fundraising drives was Don W. Evans, a longtime friend of the president from Midland, Texas. Evans was the chair of the Bush-Cheney campaign in 2000, and he went on to become Bush's first secretary of commerce.

Many other journalists in 1999 and 2000 perpetuated a historically inaccurate picture of Hanna when comparing him to Rove. In a *Newsweek* postmortem of the 2000 campaign, Weston Kosova wrote, "Still, the comparison between Rove and Hanna, a clever, controlling kingmaker, was too obvious to ignore. Within the Bush campaign, Rove was called 'King Karl,' though usually not to his face."[6] In explaining this connection, Kosova reiterated common misperceptions of McKinley, Hanna, and the 1896 campaign:

> A self-taught student of history, Rove had studied William McKinley's 1896 "front porch" campaign. McKinley's campaign manager, Mark Hanna, had brought the great and powerful to see Representative McKinley as he sat on the front porch of his home in Canton, Ohio. Since Hanna, a

Cleveland business tycoon also known as "Dollar Mark," was the father of modern campaign finance—and its corrupting effects—and McKinley was widely regarded as an amiable dunce, the Bush campaign did not make too much of the front-porch metaphor.[7]

This passage contained a basic factual error. Kosova referred to Hanna as the "father of modern campaign finance—and its corrupting effects," much as Bill Bradley did, as we saw in the introduction. Hanna raised an enormous amount of money, but the tactics he used were not invented by him. Did he do it better than it had been done before? Perhaps. But he was not the first to use techniques, such as dunning banks and corporations, convincing them to make donations based on a percentage of their assets.

In this passage, Kosova also did something that journalists frequently do: he used rumor and innuendo to create an impression while retaining the ability to distance himself from what he wrote. Kosova did not write that McKinley *was* an "amiable dunce," rather he wrote that McKinley was "widely regarded as an amiable dunce." However, to most readers, the conclusion is the same: McKinley was an amiable dunce whose strings were pulled by Hanna. This was simply not an accurate view of Hanna's role in the McKinley campaign or administration.

After election day in 2000, references to McKinley and Hanna continued in the press, sometimes positively and sometimes negatively. Given the closeness and controversy of the election, it was inevitable that Rove's early allusions to the realigning power of McKinley's 1896 election would come back to haunt him. On November 26, 2000, a reporter for the *New York Times,* Alison Mitchell, argued that the Bush campaign had failed to live up to its self-reflexive comparison to McKinley and repeated the common error that Rove somehow saw himself as Hanna at the same time that he compared Bush to McKinley:

> Back in headier times when George W. Bush was first stepping onto the stage as the Republican Party's putative savior from the southwest, Karl Rove, the Texas governor's chief strategist, liked to draw grand parallels with William McKinley and prophesy that the 2000 election would be as historically significant as the election of 1896. Like Newt Gingrich before him, Mr. Rove, a history buff, was fascinated by

how McKinley and the political king maker, Mark Hanna, produced a new and enduring Republican majority. . . . Of course, as every poisonously partisan new day of the presidential standoff makes clear, Mr. Rove and Mr. Bush failed to create that commanding new majority.[8]

In this passage, Mitchell was careful not to write that Rove wanted to be Hanna, but following the election, other comparisons between Hanna and Rove were not as careful.

On the Fox News Channel program *The Beltway Boys,* hosted by Fred Barnes and Mort Kondracke, Rove was a subject of discussion on what they described as their year-end "awards show." In giving Rove the "award" for best political strategist, Barnes, the conservative editor of the *Weekly Standard,* expressed reservations about the magnitude of Rove's achievement:

Well, he did a good job in the campaign, but he didn't achieve what he wanted to. You've heard him talk about how recreating this new Republican majority, like William McKinley did with Mark Hanna in 1896. The trouble is, he got the working class part, a lot of low-income people voted for Bush. But he lost all the upper income elitists, you know, all the limousine liberals and folks like that. He's got to win some of them back.

Kondracke, a former editor of *New Republic,* responded, "Yes, Karl Rove wants to be Mark Hanna. It worked with Bill Clinton to, to, to run a front-porch campaign. The problem is that at the very last, you know, the last weekend of the campaign, George W. Bush went dogging it down to his ranch in, in Florida, and he very nearly lost the whole election on that account, while Al Gore was sweeping the country and, and, and campaigning hard."[9] The criticism was interesting because Barnes, a conservative, was much harder on Rove than was Kondracke, a liberal, although it was Kondracke who uttered the apparently inaccurate phrase, judging from Rove's protestations, "Yes, Karl Rove wants to be Mark Hanna." What does that mean exactly? It is certainly true that Rove wanted to create an enduring Republican realignment for the twenty-first century. However, it is not true that, had he been able to do so, Rove would say he wanted to be Mark Hanna.

Rove felt Hanna had an outsized reputation. It is unlikely that Rove ever saw himself as the new Mark Hanna, but despite his protests to the contrary, it had become common—if incorrect—knowledge that Rove saw himself as Mark Hanna, version 2.0.

Not every report that connected Hanna and Rove missed the mark as badly. A few months after Bush's inauguration, in July 2001, Juan Williams hosted the National Public Radio (NPR) program *Talk of the Nation*. During the program, the guests included NPR correspondent Mara Liasson and David Gergen, and Rove's name emerged during a discussion about the crisis caused by the U.S. Navy's use of the island Vieques, just off Puerto Rico, as a practice bombing range. President Bush had recently announced that the bombing runs would stop, and the move was noted as part of Bush's attempt to reach out to Hispanic voters. Karl Rove was given credit for what was seen as a brilliant strategic plan. Liasson said:

> And there are some people who think that that could be a political master stroke. Karl Rove, who's the president's political adviser, during the campaign, was often fond of talking about the 1896 election, which I think was the election that elected McKinley—and David Gergen will correct me if I'm wrong. . . . He put together—Mark Hanna, who was, I guess, McKinley's Karl Rove, if you could call him that, put together—had this vision of how you would make this grand alliance between the new immigrants that were coming into America and the big business interests, and that was this incredible coalition that became a majority coalition and Karl Rove has a similar vision for Bush.[10]

Gergen concurred with everything Liasson said, and there was a clear feeling in the group that if the Bush administration was playing smart politics in trying to enlarge the Republican coalition, Rove was the figure in the administration making the decisions. The panel deserves some credit. Hanna did, in fact, play an important role in making sure that the campaign of McKinley reached out to a kind of rainbow coalition of potential voters and saw to it that campaign materials were published in many different languages.

However, Gergen, a frequent guest pundit in print and on television, made several inaccurate references to the Hanna-Rove connection in various venues. For instance, in an article published in *Newsweek* in 2002, Gergen wrote, "Rove, a man who loves history, doesn't mind being compared to Mark Hanna, the legendary kingmaker of Republican politics at the turn of the twentieth century who played it any way he had to—as long as he won in the end."[11] Here Gergen both reiterated a standard interpretation of Mark Hanna as a politician who only cared about winning and repeated the inaccurate notion that Rove liked being compared to Hanna.

Another group of commentators once again linked Hanna and Rove on election night 2004. The ABC coverage of the election featured a panel that included news anchor Peter Jennings, politico-turned-commentator George Stephanopoulos, columnist George Will, and commentator Fareed Zakaria. The panel discussed President Bush's apparent reelection to a second term and the fact that the Republicans seemed to have a firm lock on all three branches of the government. The conversation included this exchange:

> Fareed Zakaria: This is a dramatic defeat for the Democratic party. The president and the Republican party have made very significant gains everywhere. The president has, as George Stephanopoulos has mentioned often, new legitimacy because of the popular vote. And I think the legacy that President Bush is looking for is the one that they talked about a couple years ago, which was remaking the politics of the country kind of William McKinley, Mark Hanna, realignment of the country.
>
> Peter Jennings: Not everybody's going to get that one.
>
> Fareed Zakaria: The late nineteenth century, an attempt to create a permanent Republican majority. Which will be done through redistricting, through state legislatures, through control of the House and the Senate, through control of the Supreme Court. So . . .
>
> Peter Jennings: But Fareed, hold it for just a second. Because one of the things that surely are gonna be said about the Republican party for all its success this year with its base, the base hasn't grown very significantly.

Fareed Zakaria: You don't need it to grow that significantly if you can use the instruments of government. And they will have a majority of the state houses, a majority of the governorships and all three branches of government to entrench them permanently in a way that makes the Democratic party the permanent minority party. That I think is more likely the goal of Karl Rove and George W. Bush than to have, you know, a little bit of nice press from the media about bipartisanship.[12]

There is ample justification for labeling the election of 1896 a realigning election, but Zakaria made a mistake that is all too common among media pundits when he made a very premature conclusion, based on fluid events. It is impossible to identify a realignment as it is occurring. It takes time after the fact to analyze the data and reach an accurate conclusion. For all the dire predictions Zakaria made about the Democratic Party in 2004, the situation seemed to be reversed in 2006. Many of the same commentators who pronounced the Democrats dead in 2004 spoke about how Karl Rove was not such a genius after all and proclaimed the Republicans doomed after the 2006 midterm elections. Reporters continually err by treating politics as a series of discrete, disconnected events, rather than the fluid, never-ending cycle it is.

In writing about Rove and his influence in the Bush administration, Texas journalists James Moore and Wayne Slater made the connection between Rove and Hanna in the first of three books they wrote, *Bush's Brain: How Karl Rove Made George W. Bush Presidential* (2003).[13] In so doing, they printed nearly all the exaggerations and mistruths ever written or said about Hanna in one paragraph when they wrote:

Rove's choice of an icon to represent his efforts with Bush is more revealing than has been considered. An industrialist, Hanna was best known for resisting government efforts to break up the giant trusts being developed by corporate and mining interests. These financial behemoths were able to control labor and wages with oppressive power. Hanna turned to the trusts to raise a record $4 million for the McKinley campaign, which made victory impossible for the Democratic opponent, William Jennings Bryan. . . . Hanna treated labor seriously, but not equally. While arguing he was willing to talk to laborers to improve their situations, Hanna's concerns, like Rove and Bush, were for business, assuming big companies did well, everyone else would, too. According to the *New York Times* in 1896, that is not the way things turned out.[14]

In referring to Hanna as "Rove's choice of an icon," Moore and Slater repeated the mistake many other reporters made, a claim that Rove consistently denies.

The curious thing about the many stories that asserted Rove's devotion to Hanna was that none of them ever contained a direct quote from Rove saying he saw himself as, or wanted to be, the twenty-first-century's Mark Hanna, while evidence to contrary was easy attainable from Rove. An e-mail to Rove for this book prompted a curt reply to the question, "Did you ever express a desire to be the new Mark Hanna?" Rove's answer was, "No, never. For reasons you now understand," referring to his interpretation of Hanna's relationship with McKinley.[15]

In an earlier discussion with the author for this book, Rove elaborated on his understanding of Hanna's contributions to McKinley's career. Rove conducted his research on McKinley at the University of Texas under the guidance of the prominent McKinley biographer Lewis Gould. Rove approached Gould to see if he would advise him on an independent-study project, and Gould told Rove he would supervise him on the condition that he read through all of the McKinley Presidential Papers, which are available on microfilm from the Library of Congress at many libraries around the country. Rove agreed to this; and, based on his analysis of the McKinley papers and Gould's books about McKinley, Rove concluded that Hanna was most definitely not the power behind the throne, not a Warwick or a Svengali, who used McKinley to advance his own agenda. To Rove, Hanna's role was overblown by many historians, amateur historians, the press, and the public.[16]

In November 2006, the national editor of *Vanity Fair,* Todd Purdum, appeared on *Hardball with Chris Matthews,* in which Purdum discussed his article about Rove in *Vanity Fair,* titled "Karl Rove's Split Personality." On the program, Matthews asked Purdum about

Rove's response to his reporting. Matthews asked, "Did you feel any claw marks on you this morning when you got up . . . claw marks on you from Rove after getting tough with him . . . when you write about him with objectivity and a bit of—a little bit of contact, does he react?" Purdum responded, "Oh, I say in the piece that in the past, in my comparatively limited experience of dealing with him, he does react. He reacted very strongly, in a friendly sort of way, to a piece I wrote for the *New York Times* . . . when I said that his political hero was Mark Hanna, the Ohio businessman who helped William McKinley become president."[17]

The incident was reported with more detail by Purdum in his 2006 article in *Vanity Fair*. It took place in 2004 when Purdum coauthored a piece in the *New York Times* about Rove's role in Bush's reelection effort. Purdum and his coauthor wrote, "Mr. Rove's role model is Mark Hanna, the Ohio power-broker who helped William McKinley win the White House in 1896—and Republican domination of Washington until the New Deal—by moving beyond the party's natural big-business base to appeal to Northeastern and Midwestern immigrants and city dwellers who were afraid of labor unrest and alienated by that era's fire and brimstone agrarian Democrats."[18] According to Purdum, Rove is highly aware of things that are reported about him and contacted Purdum to refute the assertion that Hanna was his role model. Purdum wrote,

> On the Thursday morning after the 2004 election, Rove called me, full of zip. He was mildly upset over an article I had co-authored about him in that morning's *New York Times,* which stated that his role model was Mark Hanna, the Ohio kingmaker and businessman who backed the career of William McKinley. . . . Rove said he had not idolized Hanna, whom he described as merely "the Don Evans of the McKinley campaign," referring to George W. Bush's old oil-patch friend, leading fund-raiser, and first Secretary of Commerce. Instead, Rove cited a more intriguing idol, one hinting at grander ambition, erudition, and complexity. His real hero, he said, was another McKinley campaign strategist, Charles G. Dawes, who went on to become Calvin Coolidge's vice president and Herbert Hoover's ambassador to Britain.[19]

In this passage, Purdum explained Rove's objection to comparisons to Hanna, which was much like Rove's objection, on the record, to reporter Ron Suskind's suggestion that he wanted to be a latter-day Hanna.

In an article on the Bush administration, reporter Ron Suskind focused on Rove's influence in the Bush administration. The article, titled "Why Are These Men Laughing?," was published shortly after the 2002 midterm elections. In the article, Suskind offered a scathing indictment of the internal operation of the White House, based largely on a characterization offered by the former director of the White House Office of Faith Based Initiatives, John DiIulio, after his resignation. The problems at the White House, according to Suskind and DiIulio, were due largely to the influence of Karl Rove. It was, in essence, the fulfillment of the dire predictions made in an earlier article by Suskind, about the departure of senior adviser Karen Hughes from the administration and how that would leave a power vacuum in the White House to be filled by Rove.[20] Of the comparison to Hanna, Suskind wrote,

> Finally, I asked if one of his role models was Mark Hanna, the visionary political guru to President William McKinley who helped reshape Republicans into the party of inclusion and ushered in decades of electoral victory at the turn of the twentieth century. Rove's a student of McKinley and Hanna. He has talked extensively in the past about lessons he's learned from this duo's response to challenges of their era. "No, this era is nothing like McKinley's. I'm not at all like Hanna. Never wanted to be." Since then, I've talked to old colleagues, dating back twenty-five years, one of whom said, "Some kids want to grow up to be president. Karl wanted to grow up to be Mark Hanna. We'd talk about it all the time. We'd say, 'Jesus, Karl, what kind of kid wants to grow up to be Mark Hanna?'"[21]

Compared to what many modern journalists have reported about Mark Hanna, Suskind's one-sentence statement about him was not terribly inaccurate. It neither claims too big, nor too small, a role for Hanna in McKinley's administration. In this sense, he was far more accurate than many other journalists. However, at the same time, Suskind perpetuated a different untruth—that Rove saw himself as a latter-day Hanna, even after Rove explicitly rejected the idea.

Suskind's article made a big splash in the press during the early years of the Bush administration and was discussed frequently in different forums. For instance, the article was a subject on the Fox News Channel. In addressing DiIulio's complaints about the depth of Karl Rove's involvement in the decision-making process in the Bush White House, Brit Hume, the host of the program *Fox Special Report with Brit Hume,* led a panel discussion that featured political pundits Fred Barnes, Mort Kondracke, and Juan Williams. In introducing the discussion, Hume quoted DiIulio's characterization of the White House as being controlled by what he called the "Mayberry Machiavellis." Hume elaborated, "Mayberry presumably being a reference to Mayberry RFD. The country, rural Andy Griffith-mythical 'Andy Griffith Show' setting. So, what to make of all this? One did not think of him as a particularly disgruntled employee when he left. So, what about this?" Mort Kondracke responded, "Well, he seems to say that— well, see he has it right that Karl Rove is everywhere in the White House. He is there in domestic policy and there in foreign policy and probably has . . . and he does have a sort of historic role there. *It is like Mark Hanna during the McKinley administration, he's got broad gauge authority and he's involved in practically everything"* (emphasis added).

Later, Fred Barnes said,

> In the Bush White House, the most powerful aide by far is Karl Rove. Now, the writer of this article in *Esquire* treats it as saying he is the political adviser, so he shouldn't be in all these other areas. Well, Karl from the beginning has been involved in everything, except foreign policy directly. He is not in the War Cabinet and doesn't go to those meetings, I believe. But you know, you could have said the same thing about Karen Hughes. She was involved in every issue well beyond communications and so on, because she and Karl Rove were the most trusted advisers the president has. So, everything is going to be run through Karl Rove for sure, as it was through Karen Hughes when she was there. I think that was a bit of a shock for John DiIulio. On the other hand, he is right. They are a little thin on domestic policy since September 11.[22]

The commentators were in general agreement with much of what Suskind reported, without necessarily endorsing the dire tone in which it was written. It is worth noting, however, that no one contradicted Kondracke's statement that Hanna had "broad gauge authority" and that he was "involved in practically everything." Hanna simply was not the player in the McKinley administration that Rove was alleged to be in the Bush administration, and not even Suskind made such claims about Hanna. The fact that no one on the panel disagreed with Kondracke's statement is evidence of the enduring power of political myths perpetuated by the media. Once such a myth has been registered on the American psyche, even a panel of well-informed observers like these did not have a better understanding of history nor a desire to relate that history properly to modern-day politics.

Rove's objection to being compared with Hanna was informed by his understanding of Hanna's contributions. In comparing Hanna to Don Evans, as he did for Purdum, Rove portrayed Hanna as an effective fundraiser but little else. Rove saw his role in the Bush campaigns and presidency differently, and he argued there is ample evidence that while Hanna was a very important figure in the political success of William McKinley, other trusted lieutenants like Charles Dawes played equally critical, if different, roles in the campaign and were far more influential than Hanna once McKinley became president.

Purdum included one direct quote from Rove about what Purdum called Rove's "grander ambition" in professing admiration for Dawes. He wrote, "'But,' Rove told me just before hanging up, 'I'll never live up to his reputation!'"[23] When asked to comment for this book, Rove repeated his praise for Dawes. For example, in one e-mail exchange with the author, when Rove was asked if he saw himself as being closer to Dawes than to Hanna, he wrote, "No, I'm not Dawes either. He had more talent, more ability, and greater promise than me."[24]

Purdum was unlike most reporters in sharing with readers the fact that Rove took him to task for making an inaccurate comparison with Hanna. Even Suskind, who got a very direct denial from Rove, felt compelled to follow Rove's statement with an anonymous quote calling Rove's denial into question. Many reporters besides Suskind have asserted that Mark Hanna is Karl Rove's hero or that Karl Rove is a self-styled reincarnation of Mark Hanna or something similar. The reality is that Rove has never told a reporter that he viewed Hanna as a hero or a role model or that he grew up wanting to be Mark Hanna. Nevertheless, this bit of Rove mythology has become an accepted truth, regardless of the media personality's political stripes.

Conservative columnist Robert Novak, for example, responded to Ron Suskind's article about Rove in a column titled, "Esquire Article All about Hurting Bush." Novak's column was partisan and angry in tone, but he also wrote, "Republicans fear magazine cover stories about Rove, and two planned biographies of him will attempt to stigmatize Bush as poet Vachel Lindsay described William McKinley: Hanna's 'echo, his slave, his suit of clothes.'"[25] Rove was undoubtedly at least partly responsible for the comparisons with Hanna because of his regular references to the Republican realignment of 1896. But in this regard, he was not well served in the press even by his friends and allies, such as in this column by Novak.

Novak suggested Rove was responsible for creating this comparison by not only invoking the memory of the McKinley administration but by comparing himself to Hanna. Novak wrote that Rove "cannot escape his early self-identification as another Mark Hanna," but Novak does not cite where or when Rove made this comparison, which Rove denies ever making.[26] Since Hanna was almost never referred to by modern journalists in a positive light, it is easy to understand both Novak's concern over and Rove's bristling at comparisons between him and Hanna. Perhaps most notable in Novak's column was the fact that it took a conservative to remind people of Vachel Lindsay's famous poem that was so negative in its treatment of Hanna, "Bryan, Bryan, Bryan, Bryan." It is hard to imagine what Robert Novak, who claimed to be worried on Rove's behalf, thought he was doing when he reminded people of this long-forgotten poem and, no doubt, sent some of them surfing the Internet looking for it.

In an article by reporter James Harding in the *Financial Times*, published just after the Republicans' successful effort in the 2002 midterm election, Harding wrote of his interview with Rove and of Rove's stated desire to create a lasting Republican legacy, much like what was begun with the election of McKinley. Harding wrote, "To reinforce his point, Mr. Rove faxes over a biography of president he much admires, by a favourite historian: Lewis L. Gould's *The Presidency of William McKinley.*"[27] Harding suggested that references like this, made by Rove himself, lead people to the inevitable next step:

"The similarities between Mr. McKinley and Mr. Bush mean that Mr. Rove is sometimes cast as a modern-day Mark Hanna, the legendary political operator who led the McKinley fundraising effort in 1896. 'There are two important things in politics. The first is money and I can't remember the second,' Hanna once said, perhaps one reason Mr. Rove does not like the comparison."[28]

In a later article, Harding quoted another well-known Republican strategist, Frank Luntz: "Frank Luntz, the Republican Party consultant, pollster, and pundit, says Rove is to Bush what Mark Hanna was to William McKinley in the 1890s: the political organiser building up an underestimated president into the driving force behind an enduring Republican majority. A self-taught historian, Rove himself has been quick to seize on the parallels between Bush and McKinley, but shuns the comparison with Hanna."[29] Luntz is a pioneer of using high-tech market-research techniques to promote the Republican political agenda, and his comparison of Hanna and Rove is apt in terms of what each man did for the president they served. Harding is one of the few journalists to acknowledge Rove's assertion that he was nothing like Hanna.

The conservative commentator Fred Barnes addressed the Rove phenomenon and the Suskind articles during a June 8, 2002, broadcast of the Fox News Channel program *The Beltway Boys;* this time, Barnes's earlier concerns were gone. Barnes and his cohost Mort Kondracke discussed the Ron Suskind story in *Esquire* about Karen Hughes's departure from the White House staff and Andy Card's apparent concern about a lack of balance in the administration with her absence and Karl Rove's being left to pick up her power. Barnes dismissed such concerns when he said,

> Yes. You know, I found these remarks kind of goofy, actually. I, I wasn't sure what he was talking about. I talked to other White House aides. . . . Some of them wondered whether Andy Card had actually said these things. But he hasn't repudiated them. You know, Karl Rove is that kind of indispensable person at the White House. We see, there were a number of them in other administrations, but somebody who is a smart political operative who also has mastered policy. It doesn't happen often, you know, Karl Rove

is not even a college graduate. But I think he's probably among the smarter people there. And while Andy Card could leave, and, and Karen Hughes can leave, and the White House would survive, I think Bush would really be hurting some if he didn't have Karl Rove around there.[30]

Mort Kondracke responded, "His Mark Hanna," and Barnes said, "Right."[31] In this exchange, Barnes was much more positive than Suskind in his assessment of Rove's contribution to the efforts of the Bush Administration, suggesting that, without Rove, the president would be in serious trouble.

However, in a different way, Barnes was making a very similar point to Suskind's—Bush was a product of his advisers. That may or may not be true. History will have to reveal if Bush was his own man in the White House, as Eisenhower was revealed to be the "hidden hand" president, or if he was captive to the neocons in the Defense Department, to Dick Cheney, and to Karl Rove. Just as it took decades to understand the legacies of Truman, Johnson, Nixon, and Reagan, it will take just as long to sort out George W. Bush's legacy.

The problem for Americans who rely on the press for their information about politics is that journalists never want to take the long view. They comment on what happened yesterday as if it will forever change the course of human events. Even while Barnes was taking exception to Suskind's reporting, he was reinforcing it. Both Barnes and Kondracke clearly felt that Rove was an indispensable part of the Bush presidency, and they both made the mistake of characterizing Rove as Bush's Hanna. Hanna was never the White House policy adviser for McKinley that Rove was for Bush. Hanna was in regular contact with the president, but he visited the White House infrequently and was very much occupied with his positions as senator and head of the Republican Party.

An article published in the *Economist* in 2002 compared the Republican realignment of 1896 to the party's fortunes in the twenty-first century. The article's thesis was that Rove's dream of creating an enduring Republican majority was a fleeting fantasy. The article drew a connection between Hanna and Rove and, like so many others, did so with great inaccuracy. According to the article, "The real problem with Mr. Rove is his growing belief that politics is about bribing specific pressure groups, such as steel workers in important Rustbelt states, rather than pursuing the national interest. . . . Nothing could be more Washingtonian, or downright Clintonian, than calculating the electoral advantage to be squeezed from every action. What would Mark Hanna have said?"[32] The implication is that Hanna would disapprove of putting together a large and disparate coalition, but this is clearly untrue because that is exactly what he did in 1896. Compared with the many media stories that invoke the names of Rove and Hanna together, this article's mistake is the opposite of what most such stories do. Rather than overstating Hanna's role, this article understates it. While he did not control McKinley in the White House, he did work hard to craft a new, enduring coalition of Republican voters, and Rove was trying to do the same. Like so many stories that commented on the campaign of 1896, the *Economist* article lacks real understanding of history.

As many scholars have shown, the brilliance of McKinley's campaign in 1896 was that it appealed directly to many different constituencies, representatives of which gladly traveled to Canton, Ohio, to appear on McKinley's front stoop with him. The McKinley campaign saw to it that campaign materials were published in dozens of languages and were distributed to people across the economic spectrum.

The campaign coordinated with the titans of industry to see that their workers understood the Republican view that, if Bryan won, the economy would be greatly harmed and they might lose their jobs. The Bryan campaign and press sympathetic to Bryan's campaign alleged that workers were coerced to support McKinley, but the evidence for this was circumstantial at best. In his autobiography written after the campaign, the best evidence Bryan could offer of this alleged coercion were quotes from newspapers sympathetic to his campaign.

The McKinley campaign also coordinated with the rail barons to ensure that group after group could travel inexpensively to Canton to appear on McKinley's front porch and in his yard. It was suggested by reporters at the time that it was cheaper to visit Canton than it was to stay home.[33]

The story in the *Economist* contained a further mischaracterization of history in an argument that Rove had lost his way with his electoral strategy. It stated,

Yet it also represents a much more significant volte-face: a betrayal of Mr. Rove's plan to transform his party. Two years ago, Mr. Rove, a history buff who brought 148 boxes of books to Washington with him, frequently spoke about his admiration for William McKinley. McKinley's election victory in 1896 ended a long period of deadlocked politics, ushering in an era of Republican dominance. For this, McKinley had to thank . . . a political seer called Mark Hanna who masterminded the reorientation of the party, bringing into its fold the rising industrial elite and the new urban political machines.[34]

This passage directly contradicted the point made in the previous paragraph, in which the author attacked Rove for trying to appeal to too many constituencies. Which was it—too many or too few? Rather than write that Hanna ran McKinley's White House, this author properly credited Hanna with his campaign innovations. Hanna understood that American society was changing, due to industrialization, and he helped the party reach out to new constituencies. However, it does not credit Rove for making similar changes.

Interestingly, the liberal columnist Harold Meyerson, writing in the *American Prospect,* looked at the same evidence as the author of the article in the *Economist* and arrived at a conclusion that was 180 degrees different. Meyerson recognized that Rove's efforts to reach out to voters who did not traditionally vote Republican could be very harmful to the Democrats. He saw Rove's moves as negative for the Democrats but also recognized them as politically prudent, whereas the *Economist* article missed the point entirely by lamenting the fact that Rove chose to focus on specific constituencies, as opposed to campaigning to a broad coalition of voters. Meyerson wrote,

> Much was made during the 2000 campaign of Rove's appreciation of Mark Hanna. . . . Hanna not only persuaded the CEOs of his day to invest mightily in the party, he also dashed the designs of the William Jennings Bryan Democrats to restructure American politics along lines of class. . . . Hanna's strategy was to align voters not by class but by sector. Industrialists and urban workers both benefited from the tariffs that McKinley championed, though Bryan's

farmers most certainly did not. Even though those industrialists paid their workers a miserably low wage, Hanna found common ground between these two conflicting classes—and there built a Republican coalition that lasted for more than 30 years. Follow the Bush White House over the past few months and it's apparent that Rove grows more Hanna-like by the week. At bottom, the administration remains the pluperfect expression of class politics. . . . But Rove knows that an administration devoted solely to the care and feeding of the rich is not politically sustainable. So he's developed a series of discrete policies that appeal to distinct groups in the electorate by sector.[35]

Meyerson completed his column by paying Rove a grudging compliment: "Rove's strategic initiatives stand in sharp contrast to the Democrats' torpor. While Rove has shown himself willing and able to deviate from core GOP policy to cut into the Democratic base, the Democrats have been unable even to formulate a core policy, let alone deviate from it. . . . That's our Democrats. Alas, that's not Karl Rove."[36]

One of Karl Rove's deputies in the White House, Peter Wehner, who served in many posts, including director of the White House Office of Strategic Initiatives, commented on the strategy of expanding the base in 2000, 2002, and 2004 for this book. Wehner said,

In fact, what Karl succeeded in doing in the 2004 election is both deepening and expanding the party base. President Bush would not have won otherwise. In 2004, President Bush was popular among Republicans; there's no question about that. But he also expanded his popularity among (a) seniors, (b) women, (c) Hispanics, (d) Asians, (e) Jewish voters, and (f) African Americans. He was the first candidate in sixteen years to receive a majority of the popular vote; and he received a higher percentage of the vote than any Democratic nominee since 1964. And the president increased his percentage of the vote from 2000 in forty-eight out of fifty states. I could put forth more data, but you get the point. This was hardly "base mobilization" alone. It was Karl Rove when he's given wide latitude to work.[37]

Although it undoubtedly pained Meyerson, as a liberal columnist, to write it, Wehner's insider comment lends weight to Meyerson's comparison of Rove to Hanna as a campaign strategist.

Accurate or not, however, the coverage of Hanna during his lifetime was influential. It sullied his reputation for much of his political career and continued to sully his reputation into the twenty-first century. An exchange on the CNN program *Capital Gang* served as evidence of the enduring negativity of Hanna's legacy in the press. On June 21, 2003, the panel addressed the changing of the guard at the Republican National Committee, when Chairman Marc Racicot was replaced by Ed Gillespie. The change was noteworthy for the panelists because Gillespie was a lobbyist, and government watchdog groups were concerned about a lobbyist having such a close tie to the elected officials in the White House and Congress. The panelists' discussion of this topic concluded with the following exchange:

> Mark Shields: Al Hunt just made the key, the key point. The only time it matters to be party chair is when your party doesn't hold the White House. And I do want to underline, in spite of looking by a lot of people, there have been no serious charges leveled against either Marc Racicot or Terry McAuliffe during their stewardships as national chairmen.
>
> Bob Novak: Let me just say there have been previous chairmen in both parties who used that office to benefit their clients.
>
> Mark Shields: No!
>
> Kate O'Beirne: Oh!
>
> Mark Shields: "Bob, you know, you've been around here longer. . . . I'm tired of—I'm tired of people knocking Mark Hanna. He's been dead too long.
>
> (Laughter)[38]

This exchange goes to the root of the enduring reputation of Mark Hanna. Many Americans do not know who Mark Hanna was, but many of those who know his name have an inaccurate picture of who he was in their minds. This is due, in large measure, to the enduring power of the media myth propagated by the sensational media coverage of him in newspapers owned by his political enemies, first in

Cleveland and then across the United States. Hanna was the chairman of the Republican National Committee for several years and oversaw two successful presidential elections from that vantage point. When the "capital gang" casually painted him as one of the "previous chairmen" who used his office to benefit his clients—corruptly, one infers—they played jokingly into that century-old myth.

A century later, Karl Rove lived in a wide-open media environment with objective journalism on the wane, making it similar to the one in which Hanna lived; and, like Hanna, there were many media outlets that were sympathetic to his political point of view. Many changes in the media universe during the 1990s were driven by conservative forces who felt they had allowed liberal media outlets to control their fates for too long. One wonders, however, which media version of Rove will stand the test of time. Characters, especially caricatures of characters, endure. While historians tried to change people's understanding of Hanna and the presidency of William McKinley, the Hearstian version of Hanna is the character that survives in the public's imagination. An aura of mystery and raw, brutal power surrounded the public image of Hanna, and a similar aura surrounded Karl Rove during his years in the White House. That aura had a powerful attraction for liberal critics and conservative allies alike. It remains to be seen what the popular culture's memory of Karl Rove will be, but just as a sinister version of Hanna stood the test of time, so too might a sinister version haunt Rove's legacy.

Several books tell basically the same story about Rove's childhood and life in politics before George W. Bush's 2000 presidential campaign. These books also make reference to Mark Hanna. One book, by three highly respected political reporters, Lou Dubose, Jan Reid, and Carl Cannon, was called *Boy Genius: Karl Rove: The Brains behind the Remarkable Political Triumph of George W. Bush.* On the subject of Rove and Hanna, they related the story of how Rove came to his understanding of the election of 1896 and what lessons it held for 2000. As previously noted, while at the University of Texas, working to finish his undergraduate degree, Rove studied McKinley and the campaign of 1896. In doing this research, Rove concluded that Mark Hanna was "little more than a fundraiser" and was not the brilliant genius behind the campaign, or the president, he was thought to be. The book also mentions the fact that Rove was much more impressed with both Teddy Roosevelt and Charles Dawes than he was with Mark Hanna.[39]

In the prologue of their book, Dubose, Reid, and Cannon make a compelling case for why Americans ought to know about Karl Rove. For example, they asserted, "Karl Rove is now in a category of major figures in American politics notable because the people in it are often relatively unknown. Rove is to George W. Bush what Kenny O'Donnell was to John F. Kennedy, what Michael Deaver was to Ronald Reagan, what Lee Atwater was to George H. W. Bush, and what James Carville was to Bill Clinton."[40] Everyone loves to make comparisons. Dubose et al. are not the only journalists to try to find other historical figures to compare with Rove. For instance in a piece of Rove's possible involvement in the Valerie Plame affair, Tim Harper, a reporter for the *Toronto Star,* writes,

> All presidents have had their gurus to lean on. Bush's father turned to political strategist Lee Atwater, the "Darth Vader of the Republican party," who passed on much of his dark science to Rove. Clinton used pollster and consultant Dick Morris—until he was caught with a prostitute. For Dwight Eisenhower, the go-to guy was Sherman Adams, who fell from grace after a scandal over the gift of a vicuna fur coat. Some historians here suggest the prototype of the strong political adviser dates back to William McKinley, who relied on Ohio industrialist Mark Hanna after being elected in 1896.[41]

Both Harper's and Dubose et al.'s comparisons are interesting, if not necessarily apt. Atwater, Carville, Morris, and Hanna all make poor comparisons to Rove. None of these men was ever more than a paid political consultant to the presidents he helped elect; none served in a presidential administration the way Rove, Deaver, O'Donnell, or Adams did.

At the end of their book, Dubose, Reid, and Cannon compared Rove to a couple of different presidential advisers:

> As the media started to pay attention to Rove, he demurred when asked for comparisons to lustrous former presidential advisers. The names ranged from Clintonistas James Carville and George Stephanopolous to Reaganite Michael Deaver

and on into the historic stratosphere, to Eisenhower's Sherman Adams and even to McKinley's Mark Hanna. Rove shook his head when asked about these names. But some of those who have worked in the White House, including those who worked for George W. Bush's father, said they aren't far off. [42]

A problem with comparing Adams to Rove is that Adams did not play a major role in Eisenhower's election to the White House. From 1948 to 1952, Adams was the governor of New Hampshire and joined Eisenhower in a full-time capacity only when he was asked to become the chief of staff. He did not serve in a campaign role like Stephanopolous, Deaver, or Rove. Better comparisons might be to Edward "Colonel" House, who helped Woodrow Wilson get the Democratic nomination for president in 1912 and then worked closely with Wilson throughout most of his presidency; or Martin Van Buren, who played a critical role in mass marketing the Democratic Party and ensuring Andrew Jackson's election in 1828.

Dubose et al.'s reference to Mark Hanna also makes a weak comparison to Rove. Hanna was an important campaign strategist and fundraiser who deserves a great deal of the credit for McKinley's successful nomination and campaign in 1896 and 1900, but he played no official role in the administration. McKinley had much less contact with Hanna in Washington than Charles Dawes.

In Tim Harper's article, he concluded, "The relationship between Rove and Bush could turn out to be the strongest of them all."[43] That's right—it *could* turn out to be the strongest of them all. There are many signs pointing to this conclusion. The problem, however, is that we cannot answer any of these questions with certainty now, despite the desire of reporters like Dubose et al. and Harper to do so.

In another book by James Moore and Wayne Slater, who have published three books about Karl Rove, the authors address the Hanna-Rove comparison. In *Bush's Brain,* the authors suggested Rove *chose* Hanna as his icon.[44] They wrote, "An amateur historian, Rove styled the Bush campaign after the work of Mark Hanna, an industrialist at the turn of the twentieth century. Hanna, who was more of an outside expert than a consultant, counseled William McKinley to ignore the post–Civil War influences on the electorate. . . . Similarly visionary thinking by Rove, about the transformation of the Republican party and twenty-first-century demographics, lifted his premier client to the White House and reconfigured the role of political consultant."[45] In one sense, they characterized Hanna correctly. He was not a political consultant per se, but neither was he merely a guy who occasionally chatted with McKinley about politics.

Hanna was so dedicated to McKinley's, and his own, political goals that he ceded control of the family business to his brother Leonard in 1895 to work full time on the presidential campaign. As Croly observed, "He had come to the parting of the ways. Politics had become more absorbing than business. He decided to make his political ambition the salient one in his life."[46] He was not a political consultant in the mode of Lee Atwater, Dick Morris, or James Carville, a gun for hire, but neither was he an "outside expert." He was dedicated entirely to the cause of getting his "client," William McKinley, elected president. Time and again, one journalist after another has failed to get the story of Hanna right.

Why does it matter if the reputation of a figure who died a hundred years ago is besmirched by the reporters of today? In part because of the way this false impression of Hanna is used. As time passes, scholars may agree with today's journalists and find that there were many valid reasons to criticize the actions and power of Karl Rove. There may well be ways he handled winning elections of which both Democrats and fair-minded Republicans would disapprove. Building a case against him with a false interpretation of the historical record, however, does nothing but cause well-informed readers to question the veracity of everything else that was reported about Rove.

Reporters, whose job it is to report facts, often report in a vacuum, ignoring or unknowingly misreporting what has happened in the past. Journalism lives in the moment, and it shapes how people think about events. The problem is that such reporting may cause people to have incorrect impressions about those events—and what they report becomes fodder for the historians of the future. Errors born of ignorance become "fact," and the error is compounded through the ages.

The facts show that Rove and Hanna served their presidents in very different ways, but this reality did little to stop journalists from equating the two men. In June 2008, a book written by journalist Paul Alexander, *Machiavelli's Shadow: The Rise and Fall of Karl*

Rove, was published. It purports to be an account of Rove's role in the Bush administration and an account of his legacy. The inside flap of the book jacket, advertising copy designed to entice people to read the book, contains the following sentence in the first paragraph: "Not since Mark Hanna, special assistant to President William McKinley, has someone not elected to public office played such a vital role in the governance of our nation."[47] There are a number of errors in this one sentence, as we now know. Mark Hanna was never a "special assistant" to William McKinley when he was president. He was a campaign manager, and he remained McKinley's close friend, but he never served in an official capacity in McKinley's White House. Furthermore, Mark Hanna was not unelected to public office but rather was a United States senator from Ohio while McKinley was president, and while McKinley was president, Hanna was much less important as an adviser than men like Charles Dawes and William R. Day.

Later in the book, Alexander repeats common errors about Hanna that should have been easy to correct with research—which he perhaps chose not to do because it would have unveiled information inconvenient to the theme Alexander was developing about Rove.[48] Instead, Alexander repeated the errors of other reports about the McKinley-Bush and Hanna-Rove connections, which necessarily brings many of his conclusions into question.

For his part, Rove claims not to be affected by what is said about him. Like Hanna did, he claims to be immune to negative comments in the media. This is debatable, but just as Hanna tried to act as though nothing got to him, so did Rove. Judy Keen, a reporter for *USA Today,* quoted Rove's denying that negative reporting and rumors bothered him. Rove told Keen, "Look, that comes with the territory. I grew up in small towns. Despite the large number of people in Washington, it's really like a small town. If you try and spend your day correcting what people are saying about you or saying about the White House, you won't get your job done."[49] Of course, in the same article, Keen asserted about Rove what he has consistently denied: that Mark Hanna is his role model or his hero. She wrote, "Rove, a passionate student of history, has said that his role model is Mark Hanna, William McKinley's closest adviser."[50]

In this analysis, how Rove felt about his coverage is not important. What is important is how the stories that were reported about him will influence the history that will be written of the first eight years of American politics in the twenty-first century. There are some descriptions of Karl Rove that everyone can agree upon: he appeared to have a great deal of power, and he was a cagey political strategist who enjoyed winning elections for Republicans. There are also many things said about Rove that are far less certain at this point, like whether he wielded *too* much power in the Bush administration. It is legitimate to make and debate that assertion, but it will remain nothing more than assertion until historians unpack and analyze the Bush presidency. The version of Mark Hanna that is known by most people today is a political myth that was established by the press more than one hundred years ago. Karl Rove is well on the way to having an image that, like Hanna's, is based more on rumor than truth, and it will be up to historians, not journalists, to divine the real Karl Rove and analyze his influence on the administration of George W. Bush.

Notes

Introduction: Mark Hanna in the Twenty-first Century

1. James Harding, "As 2004 Looms, Bush Sets Out to Double His Campaign Funds," *Financial Times,* May 20, 2003, 21.

2. According to searches on Lexis-Nexis of all articles from 1999 to 2007 mentioning both Rove and Svengali; both Rove and Warwick; and both Rove and Hanna.

3. Linda McQuaig, "Davis Scores One for Red Tories," *Toronto Star,* June 15, 2003, A13.

4. Tom Rosenstiel and Amy Mitchell, "The Web: Alarming, Appealing and a Challenge to Journalist Values: Financial Woes Now Overshadow All Other Concerns for Journalists," Pew Research Center for the People and the Press/Project for Excellence in Journalism, 2008, http://www.stateofthemedia.org/2008/Journalist%20report%202008.pdf (accessed November 10, 2009).

5. Mitchell V. Charnley, *Reporting* (New York: Holt, Rinehart and Winston, 1975), 29–30.

6. Robert Ruby, "Special Reports: Public Attitudes," *The State of the News Media 2008: An Annual Report on American Journalism,* http:// www.stateofthemedia .org/ 2008/narrative_special_attitudes.php?cat=1&media=13 (accessed November 10, 2009).

7. Mitchell V. Charnley, "Preliminary Notes on a Study of Newspaper Accuracy," *Journalism Quarterly* 13 (December 1936): 401.

8. Scott Maier, "Getting It Right? Not in 59 percent of Stories," *Newspaper Research Journal* 23 (2002): 15.

9. Ibid., 16–17.

10. Scott Maier, "Accuracy Matters: A Cross-Market Assessment of Newspaper Error and Credibility," *Journalism and Mass Communication Quarterly* 82 (2005): 545.

11. Scott Maier, "Tip of the Iceberg: Published Corrections Represent Two Percent of Factual Errors in Newspapers," paper presented at the national conference for the Association for Education in Journalism and Mass Communication, Newspaper Division, Washington, DC, August 9–12, 2007, 13.

12. Ruby, "Special Reports: Public Attitudes."

13. Gary Hanson, "When Mistakes Happen," Newslab (2001), http:// www.newslab.org/research/mistakes.htm (accessed April 22, 2009).

14. Gary Hanson and Stan Wearden, "The Accuracy of Local TV News: A Study of News Coverage in Cleveland," Newslab (2001), http://www.newslab.org/research/accurate.htm (accessed April 22, 2009).

15. Gary Hanson and Stan Wearden, "Developing a New Measurement for Television News Accuracy," paper presented at the Association for Education in Journalism and Mass Communication annual meeting, Toronto, August 4–7, 2004.

16. Deborah Potter and Amy Mitchell, "Getting It Right," Newslab (2001), http://www.newslab.org/research/gettingright.htm (accessed April 24, 2009).

17. "Making It Right: Corrections Politics in TV Newsrooms," Newslab (2001), http://www.newslab.org/research/makingright.htm (accessed April 24, 2009).

18. Hanson and Wearden, "Accuracy of Local TV News."

19. Maier, "Accuracy Matters," 546.

20. Craig Silverman, Regret the Error: How Media Mistakes Pollute the Press and Imperil Free Speech (New York: Union Square Press, 2007), 8–9. See also Silverman's Web site: http://book.regrettheerror.com/background-material/ (accessed April 24, 2009).

21. For studies that demonstrate enduring nature of this problem, see Phillip E. Converse, "The Nature of Belief Systems in Mass Publics," in Ideology and Discontent, ed. David Apter (New York: Free Press, 1964), 202–61; Michael X. Delli Carpini, and Scott Keeter, What Americans Know about Politics and Why It Matters (New Haven, CT: Yale University Press, 1996); and Robert Luskin, "Measuring Political Sophistication," American Journal of Political Science 31 (1987): 856–99.

22. Marcus Prior, "News vs. Entertainment: How Increasing Media Choice Widens Gaps in Political Knowledge and Turnout," American Journal of Political Science 49 (2005): 577–92.

23. Pew Research Center for the People and the Press, Maturing Internet News Audience—Broader Than Deep: Online Papers Modestly Boost Newspaper Readership (2006), http://people-press.org/reports/pdf/282.pdf (accessed April 24, 2009).

24. Martin Kaplan, Ken Goldstein, and Matthew Hale, Local News Coverage of the 2004 Campaigns: An Analysis of Nightly Broadcasts in 11 Markets (Los Angeles: Lear Center Local News Archive, 2005), 12.

25. David Von Drehle, "The Incredibly Shrinking Court," Time, October 22, 2007, http://www.time.com/time/magazine/article/0,9171,1670489,00.html (accessed November 10, 2009).

26. Bill Bradley, Time Present, Time Past: A Memoir (New York: Knopf, 1996), 166.

27. Ibid.

28. Ibid., 163.

29. Herbert D. Croly, Marcus Alonzo Hanna (New York: Macmillan, 1912), 114–15.

30. Thomas Beer, *Hanna* (New York: Knopf, 1929), 5.

31. Bradley, *Time Present, Time Past,* 193.

32. Ibid., 170.

33. Ibid., 166.

34. Ibid., 406.

35. Al Kamen, "Pay and Polls' Opposite Pulls," *Washington Post,* August 4, 1999, A19.

36. These books are Ron Suskind, *The Price of Loyalty: George Bush, the White House, and the Education of Paul O'Neill* (New York: Simon and Schuster, 2004), and Richard Clarke, *Against All Enemies: Inside America's War on Terror* (New York: Free Press, 2004).

37. Ron Suskind, "Why Are These Men Laughing?" *Esquire,* January 1, 2003, 6. An online version is available at http://www.ronsuskind.com/articles/000032.html (accessed April 24, 2009).

38. Scott McClellan, *What Happened: Inside the Bush White House and Washington's Culture of Deception* (New York: Public Affairs, 2008).

Chapter 1: Hanna—A Man Very Much Misunderstood

1. Arthur M. Schlesinger Jr., "Blazing the Way," introductory essay to *Marcus Alonzo Hanna,* by Herbert D. Croly (New York: Chelsea House, 1983), iv.

2. James Ford Rhodes, *The McKinley and Roosevelt Administrations, 1897–1909* (New York: Macmillan, 1922), 8.

3. Herbert D. Croly, introduction to *Marcus Alonzo Hanna* (New York: Macmillan, 1912), xi.

4. Fred C. Shoemaker, "Mark Hanna and the Transformation of the Republican Party" (PhD diss., Ohio State University, 1992), 5.

5. Croly, *Marcus Alonzo Hanna,* 156.

6. Charles Willis Thompson, *Presidents I've Known and Two Near Presidents* (Indianapolis, IN: Bobbs-Merrill, 1929), 16.

7. Margaret Leech, *In the Days of McKinley* (New York: Harper and Bros., 1959), 64–65.

8. Joe Mitchell Chapple, introduction to *Mark Hanna: His Book* (Boston: Chapple, 1904), 10.

9. Croly, *Marcus Alonzo Hanna,* 65–83.

10. Shoemaker, "Mark Hanna . . . Transformation," 11.

11. Croly, *Marcus Alonzo Hanna,* 114.

12. Ibid., 115.

13. Clarence Stern, *Resurgent Republicanism: The Handiwork of Hanna* (Ann Arbor, MI: Edwards Bros., 1963), 1.

14. Croly, *Marcus Alonzo Hanna,* 110.

15. Ibid., 44.

16. Statement of C. August Rhodes Hanna to J. B. Morrow, box 4, Hanna-McCormick Papers, Library of Congress, 1–2.

17. Croly, *Marcus Alonzo Hanna,* 44.

18. Ibid., 111.

19. Rhodes, *McKinley and Roosevelt*, 2.

20. Croly, *Marcus Alonzo Hanna*, 114–15.

21. See Croly's and Beer's treatments of Hanna's early life: Croly, *Marcus Alonzo Hanna*; Thomas Beer, *Hanna* (New York: Knopf, 1929).

22. Croly, *Marcus Alonzo Hanna*, 119.

23. Beer, *Hanna*, 5.

24. Croly, *Marcus Alonzo Hanna*, 140–41.

Chapter 2: 1880—Hanna Buys Trouble with the Press and Helps Elect Garfield

1. James Wallen, *Cleveland's Golden Story: A Chronicle of Hearts That Hoped, Minds That Planned, and Hands That Toiled to Make a City Great and Glorious* (Cleveland: Taylor and Son, 1920), 78.

2. Ibid., 78; Charles E. Kennedy, *Fifty Years of Cleveland* (Cleveland: Weidenthal, 1925), 6.

3. Kennedy, *Fifty Years*, 9.

4. Ibid., 8.

5. Ibid., 9.

6. Ibid., 10.

7. Wallen, *Cleveland's Golden Story*, 79.

8. Kennedy, *Fifty Years*, 7.

9. Ibid., 10.

10. When William Randolph Hearst bought the *New York Journal,* one of his major tactics was to hire away reporters and editors from his competitors, especially from Joseph Pulitzer.

11. "Sale of a Cleveland Newspaper," *New York Times*, May 8, 1880, 5.

12. Statement of J. B. Morrow to J. B. Morrow, box 4, Hanna-McCormick Papers, Library of Congress, 1.

13. Ibid.

14. Herbert D. Croly, *Marcus Alonzo Hanna* (New York: Macmillan, 1912), 119.

15. Fred C. Shoemaker, "Mark Hanna and the Transformation of the Republican Party" (PhD diss., Ohio State University, 1992), 64.

16. Croly, *Marcus Alonzo Hanna*, 117.

17. Kennedy, *Fifty Years*, 27.

18. Ibid., 26.

19. Ibid.

20. Croly, *Marcus Alonzo Hanna*, 69.

21. Statement of James H. Kennedy to J. B. Morrow, box 4, Hanna-McCormick Papers, 2.

22. Statement of Morrow, Hanna-McCormick Papers, 2.

23. "An Old Newspaper Sold," *New York Times*, March 12, 1885, 5.

24. Kennedy, *Fifty Years*, 58.

25. Croly, *Marcus Alonzo Hanna*, 68.

26. Ibid., 126.

27. Statement of Morrow, Hanna-McCormick Papers, 2.

28. Ibid., 3.

29. Ibid.

30. Croly, *Marcus Alonzo Hanna*, 68.

31. Ibid., 120.

32. James Ford Rhodes, *The McKinley and Roosevelt Administrations, 1897–1909* (New York: Macmillan, 1922), 3.

33. Croly, *Marcus Alonzo Hanna*, 119.

34. Statement of Andrew Squire to J. B. Morrow, box 4, Hanna-McCormick Papers, 3.

35. Rhodes, *McKinley and Roosevelt*, 3.

36. Washington did not seek a third term in office and thereby established a precedent of serving only two terms. However, it did not become a tradition until the next president with the chance to run for a third term, Thomas Jefferson, chose not to run. Jefferson had long expressed the opinion that there should be what he called "rotation in office." In a letter from Jefferson to John Taylor, Jefferson wrote, "My opinion originally was that the President of the United States should have been elected for seven years, and forever ineligible afterwards. I have since become sensible that seven years is too long to be irremovable, and that there should be a peaceable way of withdrawing a man in midway who is doing wrong. The service for eight years, with a power to remove at the end of the first four, comes nearly to my principle as corrected by experience." See Andrew Lipscomb and Albert Bergh, *The Writings of Thomas Jefferson,* memorial edition, vol. 11 (Washington, DC: Thomas Jefferson Memorial Association, 1903), 56–57.

37. Statement of Kennedy, Hanna-McCormick Papers.

38. Kennedy, *Fifty Years*, 33–34.

39. Malcolm Moos, *The Republicans: A History of Their Party* (New York: Random House, 1956), 159.

40. Croly, *Mark Alonzo Hanna*, 118–19.

41. Ibid., 116.

42. Ibid.

43. Statement of Charles Leach to J. B. Morrow, box 4, Hanna-McCormick Papers, 2.

44. Ibid., 2.

45. Statement of Senator Charles Dick to J. B. Morrow, Hanna-McCormick Papers.

46. For a discussion of this, see Shoemaker, "Mark Hanna . . . Transformation," 77.

47. Croly, *Mark Alonzo Hanna*, 117.

48. Moos, *Republicans*, 199.

49. Ibid., 160.

50. "Grand Rally at Warren," *New York Times*, September 29, 1880, 1.

51. Ibid.

52. "Senator Conkling in Ohio," *New York Times,* September 30, 1880, 1.

53. Croly, *Mark Alonzo Hanna,* 117. See also the statement of Kennedy, Hanna-McCormick Papers.

54. Thomas Edward Felt, "The Rise of Mark Hanna" (PhD diss., Michigan State University, 1961), 75–76.

55. Croly, *Mark Alonzo Hanna,* 117.

56. Moos, *Republicans,* 162.

57. "The Day before Burial," *New York Times,* September 26, 1881, 1; "The Last Sad Journey," *New York Times,* September 25, 1881, 1.

58. Shoemaker, "Mark Hanna . . . Transformation," 73.

59. Ibid., 75. See also *Cleveland Leader,* July 27, 1880, 8.

60. Shoemaker, "Mark Hanna . . . Transformation," 78.

61. Croly, *Mark Alonzo Hanna,* 118.

Chapter 3: The Sherman Years

1. "Cleveland Not for Arthur," *New York Times,* April 19, 1884, 2.

2. Ibid.

3. "The Struggle in Politics," *New York Times,* April 20, 1884, 1.

4. Herbert D. Croly, *Marcus Alonzo Hanna* (New York: Macmillan, 1912), 120.

5. Fred C. Shoemaker, "Mark Hanna and the Transformation of the Republic Party" (PhD diss., Ohio State University, 1992), 84.

6. "Republicans in Council," *New York Times,* April 24, 1884, 2.

7. Ibid.

8. "Ohio's Chosen Delegates," *New York Times,* April 25, 1884, 2.

9. Croly, *Marcus Alonzo Hanna,* 126.

10. Hanna to Foraker, June 11, 1884, box 1, Joseph Foraker Papers, Cincinnati Historical Society.

11. Croly, *Marcus Alonzo Hanna,* 125.

12. Foraker's version of events regarding the breakup of his relationship with Hanna and what he views as the reason McKinley, and not he, became president, is presented in his statement given to J. B. Morrow. Statement of Joseph B. Foraker, box 4, Hanna-McCormick Papers, Library of Congress, 2–3.

13. Statement of Theodore Burton to J. B. Morrow, Hanna-McCormick Papers, Library of Congress, 1.

14. "Booming the Candidates," *New York Times,* June 1, 1884, 1.

15. "Ohio Blaine Men Defeated," *New York Times,* June 14, 1884, 1.

16. Croly, *Marcus Alonzo Hanna,* 124.

17. Marvin Rosenberg and Dorothy Rosenberg, "The Dirtiest Election," *American Heritage* 13 (1963): 170.

18. Ibid.

19. For very detailed, state-by-state election data for every presidential election, see David Leip's *Atlas of U.S. Presidential Elections,* http://uselectionatlas.org/RESULTS/ (accessed April 28, 2009).

20. Rosenberg and Rosenberg, "Dirtiest Election," 170.

21. Malcolm Moos, *The Republicans: A History of Their Party* (New York: Random House, 1956), 170.

22. Croly, *Marcus Alonzo Hanna*, 131.

23. Statement of J. B. Morrow to J. B. Morrow, box 4, Hanna-McCormick Papers, 5.

24. Croly, *Marcus Alonzo Hanna*, 130.

25. Shoemaker, "Mark Hanna . . . Transformation," 87–89.

26. Statement of Morrow, Hanna-McCormick Papers, 4.

27. Thomas Beer, *Hanna* (New York: Knopf, 1929), 113.

28. Statement of Morrow, Hanna-McCormick Papers, 5.

29. Ibid.

30. Croly, *Marcus Alonzo Hanna*, 126–27.

31. Ibid., 128.

32. Statement of Foraker, Hanna-McCormick Papers, 2.

33. Ibid.

34. Statement of Burton, Hanna-McCormick Papers, 1.

35. Ibid., 2–3.

36. Everett Walters, *Joseph Benson Foraker: An Uncompromising Republican* (Columbus: Ohio History Press, 1948), 82.

37. Beer, *Hanna*, 112.

38. Croly, *Marcus Alonzo Hanna*, 132–33.

39. Statement of Morrow, Hanna-McCormick Papers, 5.

40. Moos, *Republicans*, 172.

41. Beer, *Hanna*, 110.

42. Thomas Edward Felt, "The Rise of Mark Hanna" (PhD diss., Michigan State University, 1961), 176.

43. H. Wayne Morgan, *William McKinley and His America* (Syracuse, NY: Syracuse University Press, 1963), 111.

44. Herman Henry Kohlsaat, *From McKinley to Harding: Personal Recollections of Our Presidents* (New York: Scribner's Sons, 1923), 2.

45. James Ford Rhodes, *The McKinley and Roosevelt Administrations, 1897–1909* (New York: Macmillan, 1922), 10–11.

46. Moos, *Republicans*, 170.

47. Telegram (first) from Hanna to Sherman, June 23, 1888, box 3, Hanna-McCormick Papers.

48. Telegram (second) from Hanna to Sherman, June 23, 1888, Sherman Papers, Library of Congress.

49. Morgan, *William McKinley*, 111.

50. Felt, "Rise of Mark Hanna," 182.

51. Morgan, *William McKinley*, 119.

52. Statement of Morrow, Hanna-McCormick Papers, 5.

53. Statement of Foraker, Hanna-McCormick Papers, 2.

54. Ibid., 3.

55. Beer, *Hanna,* 111.
56. Croly, *Marcus Alonzo Hanna,* 138.
57. Ibid.
58. Statement of James Dempsey to J. B. Morrow, box 4, Hanna-McCormick Papers, 3.
59. Beer, *Hanna,* 110.
60. Croly, *Marcus Alonzo Hanna,* 149.
61. Statement of Charles Dick to J. B. Morrow, box 4, Hanna-McCormick Papers, 1.

Chapter 4: The Wilderness Years, 1888–92

1. Herman Henry Kohlsaat, *From McKinley to Harding: Personal Recollections of Our Presidents* (New York: Scribner's Sons, 1923), 96.
2. Statement of Andrew Squire to J. B. Morrow, box 4, Hanna-McCormick Papers, Library of Congress, 1.
3. Margaret Leech, *In the Days of McKinley* (New York: Harper and Bros., 1959), 67.
4. Paul W. Glad, *McKinley, Bryan, and the People* (Philadelphia: Lippincott, 1964), 20.
5. Ibid.
6. Herbert D. Croly, *Marcus Alonzo Hanna* (New York: Macmillan, 1912), 150.
7. Statement of Theodore Burton to J. B. Morrow, box 4, Hanna-McCormick Papers, 2.
8. Statement of J. B. Morrow to J. B. Morrow, box 4, Hanna-McCormick Papers, 5.
9. Leech, *In the Days of McKinley,* 48.
10. Ibid., 47.
11. Statement of J. C. Donaldson to J. B. Morrow, box 4, Hanna-McCormick Papers, 2.
12. Leech, *In the Days of McKinley,* 48.
13. Ibid.
14. Croly, *Marcus Alonzo Hanna,* 164.
15. Ibid., 158.
16. Ibid., 159.
17. Everett Walters, *Joseph Benson Foraker: An Uncompromising Republican* (Columbus: Ohio History Press, 1948), 101.
18. Statement of James Dempsey to J. B. Morrow, box 4, Hanna-McCormick Papers, 2.
19. Ibid.
20. Ibid.
21. Ibid.
22. H. Wayne Morgan, *William McKinley and His America* (Syracuse, NY: Syracuse University Press, 1963), 111.

23. Statement of Donaldson, Hanna-McCormick Papers, 3.

24. Ibid., 2.

25. Ibid., 4.

26. Ibid., 3–4.

27. Croly, *Marcus Alonzo Hanna,* 162.

28. Statement of Dempsey, Hanna-McCormick Papers, 1.

29. Ibid.

30. Ibid.

31. Croly, *Marcus Alonzo Hanna,* 162.

32. Ibid., 162–63.

33. Statement of Burton, Hanna-McCormick Papers, 2.

34. Croly, *Marcus Alonzo Hanna,* 153.

35. Statement of Charles Dick to J. B. Morrow, box 4, Hanna-McCormick Papers, 1–2.

36. Ralph G. Martin, *The Bosses* (New York: Putnam's Sons, 1964), 73.

37. Malcolm Moos, *The Republicans: A History of Their Party* (New York: Random House, 1956), 184.

38. Morgan, *William McKinley,* 164.

39. Statement of Dick, Hanna-McCormick Papers, 2.

40. Croly, *Mark Alonzo Hanna,* 165.

41. Morgan, *William McKinley,* 165.

42. Statement of Morrow, Hanna-McCormick Papers, 6.

43. Ibid.

44. Thomas Beer, *Hanna* (New York: Knopf, 1929), 123; see also Morgan, *William McKinley,* 164.

45. Moos, *Republicans,* 188.

46. Ibid.

47. Leech, *In the Days of McKinley,* 56.

48. Statement of Morrow, Hanna-McCormick Papers, 6.

49. Ibid.

50. Ibid.; Moos, *Republicans,* 190–91; Morgan, *William McKinley,* 164.

51. Statement of Morrow, Hanna-McCormick Papers, 6.

52. Richard Welch Jr., *The Presidencies of Grover Cleveland* (Lawrence: University Press of Kansas, 1988), 103.

Chapter 5: The Hearst Effect on the Hanna-McKinley Legacy

1. Lewis L. Gould, *The Presidency of William McKinley* (Lawrence: Regents Press of Kansas, 1980), 8.

2. Louis Koenig, *Bryan: A Political Biography of William Jennings Bryan* (New York: Putnam, 1971), 239.

3. H. Wayne Morgan, *William McKinley and His America* (Syracuse, NY: Syracuse University Press, 1963), 185.

4. Statement of J. B. Morrow to J. B. Morrow, box 4, Hanna-McCormick Papers, Library of Congress, 6.

5. Ibid.

6. Koenig, *Bryan*, 243.

7. David Nasaw, *The Chief: The Life of William Randolph Hearst* (Boston: Houghton Mifflin, 2000), 117.

8. Mrs. Freemont (Cora) Older, *William Randolph Hearst: American* (New York: Appleton-Century, 1936), 159.

9. Ibid., 158.

10. Ibid., 160.

11. Ibid.

12. Ibid.

13. Ibid.

14. Nasaw, *Chief*, 118.

15. See ibid., 118. See also Willis Abbot, *Watching the World Go By* (Boston: Little, Brown, 1933), 181–82.

16. Older, *William Randolph Hearst*, 161.

17. Nasaw, *Chief*, 118.

18. Herbert D. Croly, *Marcus Alonzo Hanna* (New York: Macmillan, 1912), 224.

19. Koenig, *Bryan*, 205.

20. Older, *William Randolph Hearst*, 161.

21. Ibid.

22. Koenig, *Bryan*, 259.

23. Arthur McEwen, "Davenport's Cartoon Book Is Out," *New York Journal*, January 21, 1898, 8.

24. Horace Traubel, "The Problem, the Cartoon and the Artist," foreword to *The Dollar or the Man? The Issue of To Day*, by Homer Davenport (Boston: Small, Maynard, 1900), 8.

25. Koenig, *Bryan*, 239.

26. Croly, *Marcus Alonzo Hanna*, 224.

27. Walt Curtis, "Homer Davenport: Oregon's Great Cartoonist," Oregon Cultural Heritage Commission (2002), http://www.ochcom.org/davenport (accessed April 28, 2009).

28. For a fascinating autobiography of his journey through Arabia hoping to get an Arabian horse, a species that the Bedouins of Arabia guarded in much the same way the People's Republic of China now controls the flow of pandas in and out of China, see Homer Davenport, *My Quest of the Arab Horse* (New York: Dodge, 1909).

29. Curtis, "Homer Davenport."

30. Statement of Morrow, Hanna-McCormick Papers, 3.

31. Statement of Elmer Dover to J. B. Morrow, box 4, Hanna-McCormick Papers, 25.

32. Speech of Nathan B. Scott, April 7, 1904, in *Marcus A. Hanna (Late a Senator from Ohio)* (Washington, DC: Government Printing Office, 1904).

33. Statement of Morrow, Hanna-McCormick Papers, 6.

34. Croly, *Marcus Alonzo Hanna*, 224.

Chapter 6: The Campaign of 1896—The Issues, McKinley, and Hanna

1. Robert S. McIntyre, "President George W. McKinley? Bush Waxes Nostalgic for Robber Baron Era Tax Policies," *American Prospect,* December 16, 2002, 21.

2. See Margaret Leech, *In the Days of McKinley* (New York: Harper and Bros., 1959), 140–42; H. Wayne Morgan, *William McKinley and His America* (Syracuse, NY: Syracuse University Press, 1963), 280–81; and Lewis L. Gould, *The Presidency of William McKinley* (Lawrence: Regents Press of Kansas, 1980), 40–43.

3. Gould, *William McKinley,* 43–44.

4. Herbert D. Croly, *Marcus Alonzo Hanna* (New York: Macmillan, 1912), 276.

5. The years 2004 and 2008 seemed to witness a revival of the kind of very active citizen campaigning that once existed in American politics. It remains to be seen, through careful research, if this anecdotal observation is accurate.

6. Croly, *Marcus Alonzo Hanna,* 173.

7. Gould, *William McKinley,* 8.

8. Mark Harris, *City of Discontent* (Indianapolis, IN: Bobbs-Merrill, Inc., 1952), 180.

9. Ibid., 251.

10. Ann Massa, *Vachel Lindsay: Fieldworker for the American Dream* (Bloomington: Indiana University Press, 1970), 214.

11. Eleanor Ruggles, *The West-Going Heart: A Life of Vachel Lindsay* (New York: Norton, 1959), 264.

12. Vachel Lindsay, "Bryan, Bryan, Bryan, Bryan," in *The Golden Whales of California and Other Rhymes in the American Language* (New York: Macmillan, 1920), 18. Also published in *Collected Poems* (New York: Macmillan, 1923), 102–4.

13. Stanley L. Jones, *The Presidential Election of 1896* (Madison: University of Wisconsin Press, 1964), 276.

14. Joseph B. Foraker, *Notes of a Busy Life,* vol. 1 (Cincinnati, OH: Stewart and Kidd, 1916), 498–99.

15. Jones, *Election of 1896,* 12.

16. Statement of J. B. Foraker to J. B. Morrow, box 4, Hanna-McCormick Papers, Library of Congress, 3.

17. Statement of Charles Dick to J. B. Morrow, box 4, Hanna-McCormick Papers, 3.

18. Croly, *Marcus Alonzo Hanna,* 175.

19. Gould, *William McKinley,* 9.

20. Croly, *Marcus Alonzo Hanna,* 175.

21. Herman Henry Kohlsaat, *From McKinley to Harding: Personal Recollections of Our Presidents* (New York: Scribner's Sons, 1923), 30.

22. Jones, *Election of 1896,* 105.

23. Ibid.

24. Croly, *Marcus Alonzo Hanna*, 215.

25. T. Bentley Mott, *Myron T. Herrick, Friend of France: An Autobiographical Biography* (Garden City, NY: Doubleday, Doran, 1929), 64.

26. Bascom Timmons, *Portrait of an American: Charles G. Dawes* (New York: Holt, 1953), 57.

27. Charles Leach, *That Man Dawes* (Chicago: Reilly and Lee, 1930), 87.

28. James Ford Rhodes, *The McKinley and Roosevelt Administrations, 1897–1909* (New York: Macmillan, 1922), 12.

29. Ibid., 13.

30. Leech, *In the Days of McKinley,* 69.

31. Ibid., 68–69.

32. Gould, *William McKinley,* 52.

33. Statement of George B. Cortelyou to J. B. Morrow, box 4, Hanna-McCormick Papers, 1–2.

Chapter 7: The Campaign of 1896—The Nomination of William McKinley

1. Herbert D. Croly, *Marcus Alonzo Hanna* (New York: Macmillan, 1912), 176.

2. Charles Leach, *That Man Dawes* (Chicago: Reilly and Lee, 1930), 64.

3. McKinley to Hanna, February 25, 1895, William McKinley Papers, Library of Congress, microfilm, ser. 2, reel 17.

4. McKinley to Walter H. Johnson, January 8, 1896, McKinley Papers, ser. 1, reel 1.

5. McKinley to Alfred E. Buck, January 8, 1896, McKinley Papers, ser. 1, reel 1.

6. Leach, *That Man Dawes,* 46–47.

7. Bascom Timmons, *Portrait of an American: Charles G. Dawes* (New York: Holt, 1953), 43.

8. Ibid.

9. Ibid., 42.

10. Charles G. Dawes, *A Journal of the McKinley Years,* ed. Bascom Timmons (Chicago: Lakeside Press, R. R. Donnelley and Sons, 1950), 63.

11. Dawes to Joseph Smith, October 22, 1894, box 278, Charles G. Dawes Papers, Northwestern University, Evanston, Illinois.

12. See Dawes to Hanna, November 28, 1894, and December 20, 1894, box 278, Dawes Papers.

13. Hanna to Dawes, December 11, 1894, box 278, Dawes Papers.

14. Ibid.

15. Dawes, *Journal,* 51.

16. Ibid.

17. Leach, *That Man Dawes,* 57.

18. Timmons, *Portrait of an American,* 45.

19. Hanna to Dawes, December 30, 1895, box 278, Dawes Papers.

20. Timmons, *Portrait of an American,* 44.

21. Dawes, *Journal*, 67.
22. Timmons, *Portrait of an American*, 45.
23. Hanna to Dawes, January 4, 1896, box 279, Dawes Papers.
24. Hanna to Dawes, January 13, 1896, box 279, Dawes Papers.
25. Hanna to Dawes, March 17, 1896, box 279, Dawes Papers.
26. Leach, *That Man Dawes*, 63.
27. Ibid.
28. Hanna to Dawes a, February 24, 1896, box 279, Dawes Papers.
29. Hanna to Dawes b, February 24, 1896, box 279, Dawes Papers.
30. Hanna to Dawes, March 12, 1896, box 279, Dawes Papers.
31. Dawes to McKinley, March 13, 1896, McKinley Papers, ser. 1, reel 1.
32. Hanna to Dawes, April 7, 1896, box 279, Dawes Papers.
33. Joseph Smith to Dawes, April 3, 1896, box 279, Dawes Papers.
34. Smith to Dawes, April 9, 1896, box 279, Dawes Papers.
35. Dawes, *Journal*, 73.
36. Dawes to McKinley, March 14, 1896, McKinley Papers, ser. 1, reel 1.
37. Hanna to Dawes, March 24, 1896, box 278, Dawes Papers.
38. Hanna to Dawes, April 3, 1896, box 278, Dawes Papers.
39. Smith to Dawes, April 16, 1896, box 278, Dawes Papers.
40. Hanna to Dawes, April 18, 1896, box 278, Dawes Papers.
41. McKinley to T. C. Evans, November 30, 1895, McKinley Papers, ser. 1, reel 1.
42. Ibid.
43. McKinley to W. M. Osborne, December 2, 1895, McKinley Papers, ser. 1, reel 1.
44. McKinley to Jacob Meitzler, February 18, 1896, McKinley Papers, ser. 1, reel 1.
45. Moses Handy to Hanna, April 22, 1896, box 278, Dawes Papers.
46. Smith to Dawes, April 22, 1896, box 278, Dawes Papers.
47. Hanna to Dawes, April 14, 1896, box 278, Dawes Papers.
48. Leach, *That Man Dawes*, 61.
49. Hanna to Dawes, April 23, 1896, box 278, Dawes Papers.
50. Leach, *That Man Dawes*, 65.
51. Handy to Hanna, April 22, 1896, Dawes Papers.
52. Leach, *That Man Dawes*, 66.
53. Timmons, *Portrait of an American*, 46.
54. Smith to Dawes, April 30, 1896, box 278, Dawes Papers.
55. Dawes, *Journal*, 81.
56. McKinley to Dawes, April 30, 1896, box 278, Dawes Papers.
57. Smith to Dawes, March 3, 1896, box 278, Dawes Papers.
58. Timmons, *Portrait of an American*, 47.
59. Stanley L. Jones, *The Presidential Election of 1896* (Madison: University of Wisconsin Press, 1964), 169.

60. Herman Henry Kohlsaat, *From McKinley to Harding: Personal Recollections of Our Presidents* (New York: Scribner's Sons, 1923), 37.

61. Timmons, *Portrait of an American,* 50.

62. Hanna to the *Philadelphia Press,* undated 1896, McKinley Papers, ser. 1, reel 1.

63. Jones, *Election of 1896,* 168.

64. Ibid., 171.

65. William Jennings Bryan, *The First Battle: A Story of the Campaign of 1896* (Chicago: Conkey, 1896), 25.

66. Jones, *Election of 1896,* 173.

67. Croly, *Marcus Alonzo Hanna,* 191. See also "Garret Augustus Hobart, 24th Vice President (1897–1899)," http://www.senate.gov/artandhistory/history/common/generic/VP_Garret_Hobart.htm (accessed April 28, 2009).

68. Croly, *Marcus Alonzo Hanna,* 191.

69. Dawes, *Journal,* 86.

70. Croly, *Marcus Alonzo Hanna,* 205.

71. Ibid., 207.

72. Ibid.

73. Timmons, *Portrait of an American,* 49.

74. Croly, *Marcus Alonzo Hanna,* 213.

75. Jill Lawrence, "GOP's Savior in 2000? Republicans Clamoring for Bush to Make the Leap," *USA Today,* March 8, 1999, 1A.

76. David Von Drehle, "A Century-Old Blueprint Inspires GOP; Republicans Look to President McKinley for a Makeover Lesson," *Washington Post,* July 24, 1999, A1.

77. Ibid.

78. "McKinley Mania?" *Cleveland Plain Dealer,* August 8, 1999, H1.

79. Paul Greenberg, "George W.'s First Mistake," *Jewish World Review,* June 17, 1999, http://www.jewishworldreview.com/cols/greenberg061799.asp (accessed November 10, 2009).

80. Ibid.

81. Von Drehle, "Century-Old Blueprint."

82. Jonathan Alter, "Toying with the R Word," *Newsweek,* December 13, 1999, 46.

83. Dawes to McKinley, August 1, 1896, McKinley Papers, ser. 1, reel 1.

84. Alter, "Toying with the R Word," 46.

85. Nicholas Lemann, "The Redemption: Everything Went Wrong for George W. Bush, until He Made It All Go Right," *New Yorker,* January 31, 2000, http://www.newyorker.com/archive/2000_01_31_048_TNY_LIBRY_000020107 (accessed November 10, 2009).

86. See the interview with Lewis Gould by Rick Shenkman on the History News Network, http://hnn.us/articles/17872.html (accessed April 28, 2009). Gould also denies being a Republican in his book about the Republican Party: Lewis L. Gould, *Grand Old Party* (New York: Random House, 2003).

87. Vincent P. DeSantis, "Book Review," *American Historical Review* 86 (1981): 1158–59; Richard Welch "Book Review," *Journal of American History* 68 (1981): 417; and Louis W. Koenig, "Book Review," *Presidential Studies Quarterly* 12 (1982): 448–50.

88. Koenig, "Book Review," 448.

89. DeSantis, "Book Review," 1159.

90. Welch, "Book Review," 417.

91. Lemann, "Redemption."

92. Welch, "Book Review," 417.

Chapter 8: The Campaign of 1896 — Battling Bryan

1. Stanley L. Jones, *The Presidential Election of 1896* (Madison: University of Wisconsin Press, 1964), 294–95.

2. Louis Koenig, *Bryan: A Political Biography of William Jennings Bryan* (New York: Putnam, 1971), 226.

3. Margaret Leech, *In the Days of McKinley* (New York: Harper and Bros., 1959), 81.

4. Joseph E. McLean, *William Rufus Day: Supreme Court Justice from Ohio* (Baltimore, MD: Johns Hopkins Press, 1946), 26.

5. Herman Henry Kohlsaat, *From McKinley to Harding: Personal Recollections of Our Presidents* (New York: Scribner's Sons, 1923), 16.

6. Ibid.

7. Charles S. Olcott, *The Life of William McKinley*, vol. 1 (Boston: Houghton Mifflin, 1916), 321.

8. McLean, *William Rufus Day*, 28.

9. Leech, *In the Days of McKinley*, 50.

10. Jones, *Election of 1896*, 6.

11. William Jennings Bryan, *The First Battle: A Story of the Campaign of 1896* (Chicago: Conkey, 1896), 24.

12. Koenig, *Bryan*, 222.

13. Jones, *Election of 1896*, 13.

14. Ibid., 24.

15. Koenig, *Bryan*, 158.

16. Bryan, *First Battle*, 153–54.

17. Jones, *Election of 1896*, 24.

18. Bryan, *First Battle*, 199–206.

19. Bascom Timmons, *Portrait of an American: Charles G. Dawes* (New York: Holt, 1953), 49.

20. Alfred Henry Lewis, "Mark Hanna, M'Kinley and the Labor Unions," *New York Journal*, August 8, 1896, 8.

21. Herbert D. Croly, *Marcus Alonzo Hanna* (New York: Macmillan, 1912), 224.

22. Jones, *Election of 1896*, 294.

23. Croly, *Marcus Alonzo Hanna*, 184.

24. Ibid., 188.

25. Dawes to Hanna, July 30, 1896, McKinley Papers, Library of Congress, ser. 1, reel 1.

26. Koenig, *Bryan*, 223.

27. Ibid.

28. Ibid., 228.

29. Jones, *Election of 1896*, 270–74.

30. Koenig, *Bryan*, 253.

31. Charles G. Dawes, *A Journal of the McKinley Years*, ed. Bascom N. Timmons (Chicago: Lakeside Press, R. R. Donnelley and Sons, 1950), 90–91.

32. Timmons, *Portrait of an American*, 57.

33. Dawes to McKinley, August 1, 1896, McKinley Papers, ser. 1, reel 1.

34. Dawes, *Journal*, 92.

35. Osborne to McKinley, September 1, 1896, McKinley Papers, ser. 1, reel 1.

36. Croly, *Marcus Alonzo Hanna*, 219.

37. Ibid., 220.

38. Dawes, *Journal*, 97.

39. Koenig, *Bryan*, 247.

40. Allan Nevins, *Grover Cleveland: A Study in Courage* (New York: Dodd, Mead, 1933), 418.

41. Ibid., 420.

42. Jacob Weisberg, "Karl Rove's Dying Dream," *Slate.com*, November 2, 2005.

43. Ibid.

44. Croly, *Marcus Alonzo Hanna*, 220.

45. Matthew Josephson, *The Politicos, 1865–1896* (New York: Harcourt, Brace, 1938), 693.

46. Ibid., 698.

47. Ibid., 699.

48. Croly, *Marcus Alonzo Hanna*, 220.

49. There is no such law in existence today at the federal level. Several states have experimented with such laws but are running into trouble with legal challenges, e.g., Missouri and Vermont.

50. Croly, *Marcus Alonzo Hanna*, 221.

51. Koenig, *Bryan*, 231.

52. Timmons, *Portrait of an American*, 63.

53. Joseph Benson Foraker, *Notes of a Busy Life* (Cincinnati, OH: Stewart and Kidd, 1916), 498.

54. See letters from Whitelaw Reid to McKinley, June 13,1896, McKinley Papers, ser. 1, reel 1; Reid to Hanna, June 13, 1896, McKinley Papers, ser. 1, reel 1.

55. Dawes to McKinley, August 1, 1896, McKinley Papers, ser. 1, reel 1.

56. Dawes, *Journal,* 106.

57. Statement of J. B. Morrow to J. B. Morrow, box 4, Hanna-McCormick Papers, Library of Congress, 6.

58. Croly, *Marcus Alonzo Hanna,* 218.

59. W. M. Osborne to McKinley, August 11, 1896, McKinley Papers, ser. 1, reel 1.

60. Bryan, *First Battle,* 604; Koenig, *Bryan,* 242.

61. Jones, *Election of 1896,* 279.

62. Ibid., 291.

63. Ibid., 292.

64. Koenig, *Bryan,* 225.

65. Untitled, *New York Times,* October 4, 1896, 1.

66. Koenig, *Bryan,* 248.

67. Ibid.

68. For discussion of labor leaders and support of Bryan, see Koenig, *Bryan,* 247.

69. Jones, *Election of 1896,* 316.

70. Leach, *That Man Dawes,* 86.

71. Timmons, *Portrait of an American,* 60.

72. Dawes, *Journal,* 104.

73. Koenig, *Bryan,* 252.

74. Bryan, *First Battle,* 617.

75. Martin Ridge, *Ignatius Donnelly: The Portrait of a Politician* (Chicago: University of Chicago Press, 1962), 365.

76. "How the Fight Was Won," *New York Times,* November 11, 1896, 2.

77. Ibid.

Chapter 9: Mr. Hanna Goes to the Senate

1. McKinley to Hanna, November 12, 1896, McKinley Papers, Library of Congress, ser. 1, reel 1.

2. Whitelaw Reid to McKinley, December 5, 1896, McKinley Papers, ser. 1, reel 1.

3. Russell Alger to Foraker, February 1, 1897, McKinley Papers, ser. 1, reel 1.

4. Herbert D. Croly, *Marcus Alonzo Hanna* (New York: Macmillan, 1912), 230–31.

5. Joint Statement of Elmer Dover and Charles Dick to J. B. Morrow, box 4, Hanna-McCormick Papers, Library of Congress, 19.

6. McKinley to Hanna, February 18, 1897, box 2, Hanna-McCormick Papers.

7. Statement of James Dempsey to J. B. Morrow, box 4, Hanna-McCormick Papers, 1–2.

8. McKinley to Hanna, February 18, 1897.

9. Alger to Foraker, February 1, 1897, McKinley Papers, ser. 1, reel 1.

10. Joseph B. Foraker, *Notes of a Busy Life,* vol. 1 (Cincinnati, OH: Stewart and Kidd, 1916), 498.

11. Ibid., 504.

12. Ibid.

13. Hanna to McKinley, February 1, 1897, McKinley Papers, ser. 1, reel 1.

14. Governor Asa S. Bushnell, contained in the statement of Capt. J. C. Donaldson to J. B. Morrow, box 4, Hanna-McCormick Papers.

15. Statement of Senator Charles Dick to J. B. Morrow, box 4, Hanna-McCormick Papers, 19.

16. Croly, *Marcus Alonzo Hanna,* 233.

17. Statement of Donaldson, Hanna-McCormick Papers, 3.

18. Croly, *Marcus Alonzo Hanna,* 242.

19. Ibid., 243.

20. Ibid., 248.

21. Margaret Leech, *In the Days of McKinley* (New York: Harper and Bros., 1959), 142.

22. McKinley to Carl Schurz, October 16, 1897, McKinley Papers, ser. 1, reel 2.

23. Charles Grosvenor to J. L. Carpenter, December 24, 1897, McKinley Papers, ser. 1, reel 2.

24. Croly, *Marcus Alonzo Hanna,* 248.

25. Statement of Dick, 20.

26. Ibid.

27. Statement of Theodore Burton to J. B. Morrow, box 4, Hanna-McCormick Papers, 3.

28. Croly, *Marcus Alonzo Hanna,* 177.

29. Thomas Beer, *Hanna* (New York: Knopf, 1929), 183–84.

30. Statement of Charles Dewstoe to J. B. Morrow, box 4, Hanna-McCormick Papers, 2.

31. Statement of Burton, 3.

32. Statement of Dick, 21; Statement of James R. Garfield to J. B. Morrow, box 4, Hanna-McCormick Papers, 4.

33. Statement of Garfield, 3.

34. Croly, *Marcus Alonzo Hanna,* 256.

35. Statement of Estes Rathbone to J. B. Morrow, box 4, Hanna-McCormick Papers, 4.

36. Statement of Dick, 21.

37. Statement of Garfield, 5.

38. C. C. Shayne to McKinley, January 7, 1898, box 55, Cortelyou Papers, Library of Congress.

39. Shayne to McKinley, January 10, 1898, box 55, Cortelyou Papers.

40. Statement of Dick, 21–22.

41. Statement of Rathbone, 5.

42. Statement of Burton, 3.

43. Statement of Garfield, 13.

44. Ibid., 14.

45. Ibid., 11.

46. Ibid.

47. Ibid.

48. Statement of Dick, 24.

49. Ibid.

50. Statement of Garfield, 4.

51. McKinley to Hanna, January 10, 1898, box 55, Cortelyou Papers.

52. Charles G. Dawes, *A Journal of the McKinley Years*, ed. B. N. Timmons (Chicago: Lakeside Press, R. R. Donnelley and Sons, 1950), 138.

53. McKinley to John P. Jones, January 10, 1898, box 55, Cortelyou Papers.

54. Alger to Hanna, January 6, 1898, McKinley Papers, ser. 1, reel 3.

55. Dawes, *Journal,* 139.

56. Alfred Henry Lewis, "Hanna Senator for Another Seven Years," *New York Journal,* January 13, 1898, 1.

57. Hanna to McKinley, January 12, 1898, box 55, Cortelyou Papers.

58. Croly, *Marcus Alonzo Hanna,* 265.

59. Garfield to McKinley, January 12, 1898, box 55, Cortelyou Papers.

60. Arthur McEwen, "The Men Who Master the Republic: What Hanna, Quay, and Platt Have Done for Their Country," *New York Journal,* October 16, 1898, 26.

61. Myron Herrick to William McKinley, June 3, 1899, William McKinley Papers, ser. 1.

62. McKinley to Hanna, June 5, 1899, McKinley Papers, ser. 2, reel 7.

63. Dawes to McKinley, June 4, 1899, box 58, Cortelyou Papers.

64. Hanna to McKinley, June 5, 1899, McKinley Papers, ser. 1, reel 7.

65. Hanna to McKinley, July 25, 1899, McKinley Papers, ser. 1, reel 7.

66. Ibid.

Chapter 10: The Country Goes to War

1. "Mr. Hanna to Live with M'Kinley," *New York Journal,* January 25, 1898, 1.

2. Charles Leach, *That Man Dawes* (Chicago: Reilly and Lee, 1930), 94.

3. Bascom Timmons, *Portrait of an American: Charles G. Dawes* (New York: Holt, 1953), 72.

4. Charles G. Dawes, *A Journal of the McKinley Years,* ed. B. N. Timmons (Chicago: Lakeside Press, R. R. Donnelley and Sons, 1950), 52.

5. Timmons, *Portrait of an American,* 65.

6. Dawes to McKinley, January 21, 1897, McKinley Papers, Library of Congress, microfilm, ser. 1, reel 1.

7. Dawes, *Journal,* 112–13.

8. Ibid., 113.

9. Lewis L. Gould, *The Presidency of William McKinley* (Lawrence: Regents Press of Kansas, 1980), 51–53.

10. Dawes, *Journal,* 116.

11. Paul Krugman, "Victors and Spoils," *New York Times,* November 19, 2002, 31.

12. Herbert D. Croly, *Marcus Alonzo Hanna* (New York: Macmillan, 1912), 297–98.

13. Statement of George B. Cortelyou to J. B. Morrow, box 4, Hanna-McCormick Papers, Library of Congress, 1.

14. Dawes, *Journal,* 131–32.

15. Ibid., 133.

16. Dawes to McKinley, November 12, 1897, McKinley Papers, ser. 1, reel 2.

17. Timmons, *Portrait of an American,* 73.

18. Hanna to McKinley, November 15, 1898, McKinley Papers, ser. 1, reel 5.

19. Margaret Leech, *In the Days of McKinley* (New York: Harper and Bros., 1959), 234.

20. Hanna to McKinley, June 30, 1898, McKinley Papers, ser. 1, reel 4.

21. Hanna to McKinley, July 6, 1898, McKinley Papers, ser. 1, reel 4.

22. Hanna to McKinley, July 20, 1898, box 56, Cortelyou Papers.

23. Andrew Squire to McKinley, July 19, 1898, box 56, Cortelyou Papers.

24. Leech, *In the Days of McKinley,* 234.

25. Dawes, *Journal,* 146.

26. Ibid., 137–79.

27. Louis Koenig, *Bryan: A Political Biography of William Jennings Bryan* (New York: Putnam, 1971), 272.

28. Dawes, *Journal,* 150.

29. Ibid., 151.

30. Hanna to McKinley, April 3, 1898, McKinley Papers, ser. 1, reel 3.

31. "McKinley Mania?" *Cleveland Plain Dealer,* August 8, 1999, H1.

32. Harold Meyerson, "Karl Rove's Hedges," *American Prospect,* April 8, 2002, 2.

33. Ibid.

34. Herbert D. Croly, *Marcus Alonzo Hanna* (New York: Macmillan, 1912), 280.

35. Unattributed note to McKinley, December 27, 1897, McKinley Papers, ser. 1, reel 3.

36. The only source of this quote is in the autobiography of one of Hearst's correspondents, James Creelman. See David Nasaw, *The Chief: The Life of William Randolph Hearst* (Boston: Houghton Mifflin, 2000), 127, for a discussion of this. See also James Creelman, *On the Great Highway: The Wanderings and Adventurings of a Special Correspondent* (Boston: Lothrop, 1901), 177–78.

37. Nasaw, *Chief*, 127–28.

38. Hearst to Ida McKinley, August 22, 1897, McKinley Papers, ser. 1, reel 2.

39. For a thorough description of the Evangelina Cisneros story, see Nasaw, *Chief*, 127–28, and Mrs. Freemont (Cora) Older, *William Randolph Hearst: American* (New York: Appleton-Century, 1936), 169–79.

40. "Long's Peace Statement a Part of Hanna's Stock-Jobbing Plot," *New York Journal*, March 4, 1898, 8.

41. Croly, *Marcus Alonzo Hanna*, 276.

42. Dawes to McKinley, May 25, 1897, McKinley Papers, ser. 1, reel 2.

43. Reid to McKinley, March 8, 1898, McKinley Papers, ser. 1, reel 3.

44. The text of the letter is available in many places, e.g., http://www.spanamwar.com/Delome.htm.

45. For a discussion of this, see Nasaw, *Chief*, 129; John Offner, *An Unwanted War: The Diplomacy of the United States and Spain over Cuba, 1895–1898* (Chapel Hill: University of North Carolina Press, 1992), 117; Willis Abbot, *Watching the World Go By* (Boston: Little Brown, 1933), 217–18; and Walter LaFeber, *The New Empire* (Ithaca, NY: Cornell University Press, 1963), 347.

46. For a summary of the explosion and subsequent investigations, see the Navy Historical Center at http://www.history.navy.mil/faqs/faq71-1.htm (accessed May 5, 2009).

47. Croly, *Marcus Alonzo Hanna*, 278.

48. Edward Morris, *The Rise of Theodore Roosevelt* (New York: Ballantine Books, 1980), 602.

49. Dawes to McKinley, August 10, 1898, McKinley Papers, ser. 1, reel 4.

50. Dawes to McKinley, February 10, 1899, McKinley Papers, ser. 1, reel 5.

51. Hanna to McKinley, November 10, 1898, McKinley Papers, ser. 1, reel 5.

52. Hanna to McKinley, November 15, 1898.

Chapter 11: Election 1900

1. Lewis L. Gould, *The Presidency of William McKinley* (Lawrence: Regents Press of Kansas, 1980), 201–4.

2. Ibid., 221–24.

3. Bascom Timmons, *Portrait of an American: Charles G. Dawes* (New York: Holt, 1953), 86–87.

4. Margaret Leech, *In the Days of McKinley* (New York: Harper and Bros., 1959), 533.

5. Timmons, *Portrait of an American*, 87.

6. Charles G. Dawes, *A Journal of the McKinley Years*, ed. Bascom N. Timmons (Chicago: Lakeside Press, R. R. Donnelley and Sons, 1950), 214.

7. Ibid., 235.

8. Dawes to Cortelyou, October 1, 1900, McKinley Papers, Library of Congress, microfilm, ser. 1, reel 13.

9. Herbert D. Croly, *Marcus Alonzo Hanna* (New York: Macmillan, 1912), 320.

10. Ibid.

11. Leech, *In the Days of McKinley,* 533.

12. Croly, *Marcus Alonzo Hanna,* 321.

13. Ibid.

14. Leech, *In the Days of McKinley,* 534.

15. Gould, *William McKinley,* 215.

16. Ibid.

17. Thomas Beer, *Hanna* (New York: Knopf, 1929), 234.

18. Leech, *In the Days of McKinley,* 535.

19. Charles Leach, *That Man Dawes* (Chicago: Reilly and Lee, 1930), 96.

20. Gould, *William McKinley,* 215.

21. Croly, *Marcus Alonzo Hanna,* 318.

22. Ibid., 283–85.

23. Ibid., 285.

24. Ibid.

25. Gould, *William McKinley,* 216.

26. Edmund Morris, *The Rise of Theodore Roosevelt* (Ballantine Books, 1980), 583.

27. Various treatments of this are in Leech, *In the Days of McKinley,* 535–42, Croly, *Marcus Alonzo Hanna,* 309–17, and Morris, *Rise of Theodore Roosevelt,* 717–29.

28. Timmons, *Portrait of an American,* 88.

29. Dawes, *Journal,* 233.

30. Croly, *Marcus Alonzo Hanna,* 314.

31. Leech, *In the Days of McKinley,* 542.

32. Hanna to McKinley, June 24, 1900, McKinley Papers, ser. 1, reel 10.

33. Gould, *William McKinley,* 218.

34. Croly, *Marcus Alonzo Hanna,* 318.

35. Ibid., 327.

36. Ibid., 325.

37. Ibid., 323.

38. Dawes to McKinley, October 30, 1900, box 59, Cortelyou Papers, Library of Congress.

39. Louis Koenig, *Bryan: A Political Biography of William Jennings Bryan* (New York: Putnam, 1971), 300.

40. Ibid., 301.

41. Ibid.

42. Ibid., 321.

43. Ibid., 326.

44. Ibid., 327.

45. Ibid., 302.

46. Ibid., 339.

47. Ibid., 331.

48. Ibid.

49. Gould, *William McKinley*, 226–27.

50. Koenig, *Bryan*, 332.

51. Gould, *William McKinley*, 226.

52. Dawes to McKinley, June 4, 1899, box 58, Cortelyou Papers.

53. Gould, *William McKinley*, 227.

54. Koenig, *Bryan*, 334.

55. Ibid.

56. Ibid.

57. Ibid., 333.

58. Gould, *William McKinley*, 8.

59. "Mr. Hanna's Labor Record . . . ," *New York Times*, September 7, 1896, 1.

60. "Delegate Cohen Excited: Says Cleveland Central Labor Union Members Are Arming," *New York Times*, August 31, 1896.

61. "Mr. Hanna's Labor Record . . . ," *New York Times*, 1.

62. Stanley L. Jones, *The Presidential Election of 1896* (Madison: University of Wisconsin Press, 1964), 290.

63. Croly, *Marcus Alonzo Hanna*, 387.

64. Ibid., 94.

65. Linda McQuaig, "Davis Scores One for Red Tories," *Toronto Star*, June 15, 2003, 13.

66. Croly, *Marcus Alonzo Hanna*, 410.

67. Jones, *Election of 1896*, 290.

68. Gould, *William McKinley*, 17.

69. Croly, *Marcus Alonzo Hanna*, 89–90.

70. Hanna to McKinley, July 24, 1900, McKinley Papers, ser. 1, reel 11.

71. Gould, *William McKinley*, 228; Koenig, *Bryan*, 334.

72. Leech, *In the Days of McKinley*, 557.

73. Gould, *William McKinley*, 228.

74. Morris, *Rise of Theodore Roosevelt*, 730.

75. Statement of Elmer Dover to J. B. Morrow, box 4, Hanna-McCormick Papers, Library of Congress, 3. Hanna's personal secretary, Elmer Dover, reported that Hanna only made four or five speeches outside of Ohio before 1900.

76. Croly, *Marcus Alonzo Hanna*, 332; statement of Dover, 4. Dover said Congressman Charlie Landis, of Indiana, was the first to get Hanna to agree to speak: "Mr. Hanna liked Landis and finally consented to make a speech for him because Landis was having a close fight."

77. Gould, *William McKinley*, 225.

78. Leech, *In the Days of McKinley*, 556.

79. Ibid.

80. Statement of Dover, 4.

81. Richard Pettigrew to McKinley, April 17, 1899, McKinley Papers, ser. 1, reel 6.

82. Statement of Dover, 4. Dover claimed otherwise in his statement: "He had said something disagreeable in the Senate about Mr. Hanna, but that did not influence Mr. Hanna; it was simply because Pettigrew was a traitor to his party."

83. Judy Crichton, *American 1900: The Turning Point* (New York: Holt, 1998), 152.

84. Hanna to McKinley, July 10, 1900, McKinley Papers, ser. 1, reel 11.

85. Statement of Dover, 4.

86. Beer, *Hanna,* 232.

87. Statement of Dover, 4–6.

88. Chase Lichtman to Hanna, July 31, 1900, box 59, Cortelyou Papers.

89. Hanna to McKinley (I), August 3, 1900, box 59, Cortelyou Papers.

90. Hanna to McKinley (II), August 3, 1900, box 59, Cortelyou Papers.

91. McKinley to Hanna, August 7, 1900, box 59, Cortelyou Papers.

92. Ibid.

93. Ibid.

94. Croly, *Marcus Alonzo Hanna,* 331; Leech, *In the Days of McKinley,* 554.

95. Croly, *Marcus Alonzo Hanna,* 331.

96. Leech, *In the Days of McKinley,* 554.

97. Hanna to McKinley, July 23, 1900, box 59, Cortelyou Papers.

98. Cortelyou to Smith, July 7, 1900, box 59, Cortelyou Papers.

99. Hanna to McKinley, August 10, 1900, McKinley Papers, ser. 1, reel 11.

100. Heath to Cortelyou, August 29, 1900, McKinley Papers, ser. 1, reel 12.

101. Ibid.

102. Heath to Cortelyou, September 27, 1900, McKinley Papers, ser. 1, reel 13.

103. Heath to Cortelyou, August 31, 1900, McKinley Papers, ser. 1, reel 13.

104. Heath to Cortelyou, August 29, 1900.

105. Dawes to McKinley, September 23, 1900, box 59, Cortelyou Papers.

106. Gould, *William McKinley,* 229.

107. Hanna to McKinley, November 7, 1900, McKinley Papers, ser. 1, reel 14.

108. Elisabeth Bumiller, "A Democratic Rallying Cry: Vote Bush out of Rove's Office," *New York Times,* January 19, 2004, 16.

109. Ibid.

110. David Tell, "Who's Afraid of George Soros?" *Weekly Standard,* March 8, 2004, http://www.weeklystandard.com/Content/Public/Articles/000/000/003/797eiqkh.asp (accessed November 10, 2009).

111. Howard Fineman, "In the Driver's Seat," *Newsweek,* September 26, 2004, 24.

Epilogue: Mark Hanna's Legacy in the Twenty-first Century

1. See, for example, Walter Dean Burnham, *Critical Elections and the Mainsprings of American Politics* (New York: Norton, 1970).

2. James O'Toole, "Philadelphia Has Rich History of Party Conventions," *Pittsburgh Post-Gazette*, July 30, 2000, A11.

3. Jack Kelly, "What Republicans Forget: McCain Can Beat Gore, but Bush Will Be Clobbered," *Pittsburgh Post-Gazette*, March 5, 2000, E3.

4. Ibid.

5. Jonathan E. Kaplan, "Oliver: The Good Son Comes Home," *The Hill*, June 21, 2005, http://thehill.com/business--lobby/oliver-the-good-son-comes-home-2005-06-21.html (accessed May 6, 2009).

6. Weston Kosova, "Pumping Iron, Digging Gold, Pressing Flesh," *Newsweek*, November 20, 2000, 50.

7. Ibid.

8. Alison Mitchell, "The Election: Trying to Escape the Purgatory of Parity," *New York Times*, November 26, 2000, sec. 4, 3.

9. *The Beltway Boys*, Fox News Channel, December 30, 2000.

10. *Talk of the Nation*, NPR, July 16, 2001.

11. David Gergen, "The Message in the Ballots?" *Newsweek*, November 18, 2002, 16.

12. "ABC News Special Report: Introduction," ABC, November 3, 2004.

13. The other books by the journalists are *Rove Exposed: How Bush's Brain Fooled America* (New York: Wiley and Sons, 2006), and *The Architect: Karl Rove and the Master Plan for Absolute Power* (New York: Random House, 2006).

14. James Moore and Wayne Slater, *Bush's Brain: How Karl Rove Made George W. Bush Presidential* (New York: Wiley and Sons, 2003), 16.

15. Karl Rove, interview by the author via e-mail, December 2006.

16. Karl Rove, interview by the author via e-mail, March 2006.

17. *Hardball with Chris Matthews*, MSNBC, November 1, 2006.

18. Todd Purdum and David Kirkpatrick, "Campaign Strategist Is in Position to Consolidate Republican Majority," *New York Times*, November 4, 2004, 22.

19. Todd Purdum, "Karl Rove's Split Personality," *Vanity Fair*, December 2006, http://www.vanityfair.com/politics/features/2006/12/rove200612?currentPage=6 (accessed November 10, 2009).

20. Ron Suskind, "Mrs. Hughes Takes Her Leave," *Esquire*, July 2002, http://www.ronsuskind.com/articles/000005.html (accessed November 10, 2009).

21. Ron Suskind, "Why Are These Men Laughing?" *Esquire*, January 2003, http://www.ronsuskind.com/newsite/articles/archives/000032.html (accessed November 10, 2009).

22. *Fox Special Report with Brit Hume*, Fox News Channel, December 2, 2002.

23. Purdum, "Karl Rove's Split Personality."

24. Karl Rove, interview by the author via e-mail, December 2006.

25. Robert Novak, "Esquire Article All about Hurting Bush," *Chicago Sun-Times*, December 5, 2002, 35.

26. Ibid.

27. James Harding, "As 2004 Looms, Bush Sets Out to Double His Campaign Funds," *Financial Times*, May 20, 2003, 21.

28. Ibid.

29. James Harding, "Power behind the Throne," *Financial Times*, October 25, 2003, 12.

30. *The Beltway Boys*, Fox News Channel, June 8, 2002.

31. Ibid.

32. "Karl Rove's Fading Ambition," *Economist*, June 22, 2002, 54.

33. Louis Koenig, "The First Hurrah," *American Heritage* 31 (April/May 1980), http://www.americanheritage.com/articles/magazine/ah/1980/3/1980_3_4.shtml (accessed November 10, 2009).

34. "Karl's Rove's Fading Ambition," 55.

35. Harold Meyerson, "Karl Rove's Wedges," *American Prospect*, April 7, 2002, 2.

36. Ibid.

37. Peter Wehner, interview by the author, November 20, 2006.

38. *Capital Gang*, CNN, June 21, 2003.

39. Lou Dubose, Jan Reid, and Carl M. Cannon, *Boy Genius: Karl Rove: The Brains behind the Remarkable Political Triumph of George W. Bush* (New York: Public Affairs, 2003), 130.

40. Ibid., 131.

41. Tim Harper, "'Bush's Brain' Examination," *Toronto Star*, July 17, 2005, A14.

42. Dubose, Reid, and Cannon, *Boy Genius*, 234.

43. Harper, "'Bush's Brain' Examination," A14.

44. Moore and Slater, *Bush's Brain*, 16.

45. Ibid.

46. Herbert D. Croly, *Marcus Alonzo Hanna* (New York: Macmillan, 1912), 174.

47. Paul Alexander, *Machiavelli's Shadow: The Rise and Fall of Karl Rove* (New York: Modern Times, 2008), inside flap of book jacket.

48. For example, see ibid., 11, 13, 70, 117, 172.

49. Judy Keen, "Finger-Pointing Finds a Familiar Target in Rove," *USA Today*, September 30, 2003, 6A.

50. Ibid.

Bibliography

Archives

Charles G. Dawes Papers, Northwestern University, Evanston/Chicago, IL.
George B. Cortelyou Papers, Library of Congress.
Hanna-McCormick Family Papers, Library of Congress.
Joseph B. Foraker Papers, Cincinnati Historical Society.
William McKinley Papers, Library of Congress.

Newspapers

Cleveland Plain Dealer. "McKinley Mania?" August 8, 1999.
New York Journal. "Half a Billion Back of McKinley." August 3, 1896.
———. "Long's Peace Statement a Part of Hanna's Stock-Jobbing Plot." March 4, 1898.
———. "Mr. Hanna to Live with M'Kinley." January 25, 1898.
———. "Subscription Blank." September 12, 1896.
New York Times. "Booming the Candidates." June 1, 1884.
———. "Cleveland Not for Arthur." April 19, 1884.
———. "The Day before the Burial." September 26, 1881.
———. "Delegate Cohen Excited: Says Cleveland Central Labor Union Members Are Arming." August 31, 1896.
———. "The Last Sad Journey." September 25, 1881.
———. "Mr. Hanna's Labor Record: Central Labor Union Gets a Report and Puts It on File." September 7, 1896.
———. "Ohio Blaine Men Defeated." June 14, 1884.
———. "Ohio's Chosen Delegates." April 25, 1884.
———. "An Old Newspaper Sold." March 12, 1885.
———. "Republicans in Council." April 24, 1884.
———. "Sale of Cleveland Newspaper." May 8, 1880.
———. "Senator Conkling in Ohio." September 30, 1880.
———. "The Struggle in Politics." April 20, 1884.

Published Articles and Books

Abbot, Willis. *Watching the World Go By.* Boston: Little, Brown, 1933.
Alexander, Paul. *Machiavelli's Shadow: The Rise and Fall of Karl Rove.* New York: Modern Times, 2008.

Alter, Jonathan. "Toying with the R Word." *Newsweek,* December 13, 1999, 46.

Ansolabehere, Stephen, Roy Behr, and Shanto Iyengar. *The Media Game: American Politics in the Television Age.* New York: Macmillan, 1994.

Bai, Matthew. "The Framing Wars." *New York Times Magazine,* July 17, 2005, 38.

Balutis, Alan P. "The Presidency and the Press: The Expanding Presidential Image." *Presidential Studies Quarterly* 7, no. 4 (1977): 244–51.

Bartels, Larry. "Uninformed Votes: Information Effects in Presidential Elections." *American Journal of Political Science* 40, no. 1 (1996): 194–241.

Baum, Matthew A. *Soft News Goes to War: Public Opinion and American Foreign Policy in the New Media Age.* Princeton, NJ: Princeton University Press, 2003.

Beer, Thomas. *Hanna.* New York: Knopf, 1929.

Berelson, Bernard, Paul F. Lazarsfeld, and William N. McPhee. *Voting.* Chicago: University of Chicago Press, 1954.

Blum, John Morton. *Liberty, Justice, Order: Essays on Past Politics.* New York: Norton, 1993.

Bradley, Bill. *Time Present, Time Past: A Memoir.* New York: Knopf, 1996.

Brands, H. W. *T. R.: The Last Romantic.* New York: Basic Books, 1997.

Brian, Dennis. *Pulitzer: A Life.* New York: Wiley and Sons, 2001.

Brody, Richard A. *Assessing the President: The Media, Elite Opinion, and Public Support.* Stanford, CA: Stanford University Press, 1991.

Bryan, William Jennings. *The First Battle: A Story of the Campaign of 1896.* Chicago: Conkey, 1896.

Bumiller, Elisabeth. "A Democratic Rallying Cry: Vote Bush Out of Rove's Office." *New York Times,* January 19, 2004.

Burnham, Walter Dean. *Critical Elections and the Mainsprings of American Politics.* New York: Norton, 1970.

Burton, Theodore E. *John Sherman.* Boston: Houghton Mifflin, 1906.

Calhoun, Charles W. *Benjamin Harrison.* New York: Times Books, 2005.

Callow, Simon. *Orson Welles: The Road to Xanadu.* London: Vintage, 1995.

Campbell-Copeland, Thomas. *Harrison and Reid—Their Lives and Record: The Republican Campaign Book for 1892.* New York: Webster, 1892.

Canes-Wrone, Brandice, and Scott de Marchi. "Presidential Approval and Legislative Success." *Journal of Politics* 64, no. 2 (2002): 491–509.

Chapple, Joe Mitchell. *Mark Hanna: His Book.* Boston: Chapple, 1904.

———. "Senator Hanna as Man and Statesman." *National Magazine* 19, no. 1 (1903): 751–80.

Charnley, Mitchell V. "Preliminary Notes on a Study of Newspaper Accuracy." *Journalism Quarterly* 13 (December 1936): 394–401.

———. *Reporting.* New York: Holt, Rinehart and Winston, 1975.

Clarke, Richard. *Against All Enemies: Inside America's War on Terror.* New York: Free Press, 2004.

Contosta, David R., and Jessica R. Hawthorne, eds. *Rise to World Power: Selected Letters of Whitelaw Reid, 1895–1912*. Philadelphia: American Philosophical Society, 1986.

Converse, Philip E. "The Nature of Belief Systems in Mass Publics." In *Ideology and Discontent*, edited by David Apter, 202–61. New York: Free Press, 1964.

Cook, Timothy, and Lyn Ragsdale. "The President and the Press: Negotiating Newsworthiness at the White House." In *The Presidency and the Political System*, edited by Michael Nelson, 29–63. 6th ed. Washington, DC: CQ Press, 2000.

Cornwell, Elmer E. "Presidential News: The Expanding Public Image." *Journalism Quarterly* 36 (Summer 1959): 275–83.

Cortissoz, Royal. *The Life of Whitelaw Reid*. New York: Scribner's Sons, 1921.

Creelman, James. *On the Great Highway: The Wanderings and Adventurings of a Special Correspondent*. Boston: Lothrop, 1901.

Crichton, Judy. *America 1900*. New York: Holt, 1998.

Croly, Herbert D. *Marcus Alonzo Hanna*. New York: Macmillan, 1912.

Curtis, Walt. "Homer Davenport: Oregon's Great Cartoonist." Oregon Cultural Heritage Commission, 2002. http://www.ochcom.org/davenport.

Davenport, Homer. "All the Comforts of Home." *New York Journal*, January 26, 1898.

———. "And They Called Him Napoleon." *New York Journal*, April 7, 1898.

———. "Final Charge of the Buncombe Brigade." *New York Journal*, October 31, 1896.

———. "Honest Money." *New York Journal*, September 12, 1896.

———. "How Can He Lose Me?" *New York Journal*, October 18, 1896.

———. "Idol of Yellow Patriotism." *New York Journal*, March 16, 1898.

———. *My Quest of the Arab Horse*. New York: Dodge, 1909.

———. "The Personal Narrative of Homer Davenport." Pts. 1 and 2. *Pacific Monthly* 14, no. 4 (1905): 409–22; no. 5 (1905): 517–25.

———. "A Tight Squeeze." *New York Journal*, November 4, 1897.

———. "What a Difference Being Appointed and Being Elected to the Senate." *New York Journal*, October 28, 1897.

———. "What Further Use Can Hanna Have for a Charter of Rights?" In *The Dollar or the Man? The Issue of To Day*, edited by Homer Davenport and Horace L. Traubel. Boston: Small, Maynard, 1900.

———. "Where Mr. Hanna Stands on the Labor Record." *New York Journal*, September 8, 1896.

Dawes, Charles G. *A Journal of the McKinley Years*. Edited by Bascom N. Timmons. Chicago: Lakeside Press, R. R. Donnelley and Sons, 1950.

Dearing, James W., and Everett M. Rogers. *Agenda-Setting*. Thousand Oaks, CA: Sage, 1996.

Delli Carpini, Michael X., and Scott Keeter. *What Americans Know about Politics and Why It Matters*. New Haven, CT: Yale University Press, 1996.

DeSantis, Vincent P. "Book Review." *American Historical Review* 86, no. 5 (1981): 1158–59.

Dobson, John. *Reticent Expansionism: The Foreign Policy of William McKinley*. Pittsburgh: Duquesne University Press, 1998.

Druckman, James. "Does Political Information Matter?" *Political Communication* 22, no. 4 (2005): 515–19.

———. "Media Matter: How Newspapers and Television News Cover Campaigns and Influence Voters." *Political Communication* 22, no. 4 (2005): 463–81.

———. "The Power of Television Images: The First Kennedy-Nixon Debate Revisited." *Journal of Politics* 65, no. 2 (2003): 559–71.

———. "On the Limits of Framing Effects: Who Can Frame?" *Journal of Politics* 63, no. 4 (2001): 1041–66.

Druckman, James, and Michael Parkin. "The Impact of Media Bias: How Editorial Slant Affects Voters. *Journal of Politics* 67, no. 4 (2005): 1030–1049.

Dubofsky, Melvyn. *Industrialism and the American Worker, 1865–1920*. Arlington Heights, IL: Harlan Davidson, 1975.

Dubose, Lou, Jan Reid, and Carl M. Cannon. *Boy Genius: Karl Rove, the Brains behind the Remarkable Political Triumph of George W. Bush*. New York: Public Affairs, 2003.

Duncan, Bingham. *Whitelaw Reid: Journalist, Politician, Diplomat*. Athens: University of Georgia Press, 1975.

Economist. "Karl Rove's Fading Ambition." June 22, 2002, 54–56.

Entman, Robert. "Framing: Toward Clarification of a Fractured Paradigm." *Journal of Communication* 43, no. 1 (1993): 51–58.

Felt, Thomas Edward. "The Rise of Mark Hanna." PhD diss., Michigan State University, 1961.

Fineman, Howard. "In the Driver's Seat." *Newsweek*, September 26, 2004, 24.

Fischer, Roger A. *Them Damned Pictures: Explorations in American Political Cartoon Art*. New Haven, CT: Archon Books, 1996.

Foraker, Joseph Benson. *Notes of a Busy Life*. 2 vols. Cincinnati, OH: Stewart and Kidd, 1916.

Gergen, David. "The Message in the Ballots?" *Newsweek*, November 18, 2002, 16.

Glad, Paul W. *McKinley, Bryan, and the People*. Philadelphia: Lippincott, 1964.

Goodwyn, Lawrence. *Democratic Promise: The Populist Moment in America*. New York: Oxford University Press, 1976.

Gould, Lewis L. *Grand Old Party*. New York: Random House, 2003.

———. *The Modern American Presidency*. Lawrence: University Press of Kansas, 2003.

———. *The Presidency of William McKinley.* Lawrence: Regents Press of Kansas, 1980.

Gould, Lewis L., and Craig H. Roell. *William McKinley: A Bibliography.* Westport, CT: Meckler, 1988.

Graber, Doris. *The President and the Public.* Philadelphia: ISHI, 1982.

Green, James R. *The World of the Worker: Labor in Twentieth-Century America.* New York: Hill and Wang, 1980.

Greenberg, Paul. "George W.'s First Mistake." *Jewish World Review,* June 17, 1999.

Grossman, Michael Baruch, and Martha Joynt Kumar. *Portraying the President: The White House and the News Media.* Baltimore: Johns Hopkins University Press, 1981.

Hanson, Gary. "When Mistakes Happen." Newslab. http://www.newslab.org/research/mistakes.htm.

Hanson, Gary, and Stan Wearden. "The Accuracy of Local TV News: A Study of News Coverage in Cleveland." Newslab. http://www.newslab.org/research/accurate.htm.

———. "Developing a New Measurement for Television News Accuracy." Paper presented at the Association for Education in Journalism and Mass Communication Annual Meeting, Toronto, August 4–7, 2004.

Harding, James. "As 2004 Looms, Bush Sets Out to Double His Campaign Funds." *Financial Times,* May 20, 2003, 21.

———. "Power behind the Throne." *Financial Times,* October 25, 2003, 12.

Harper, Tim. "'Bush's Brain' Examination." *Toronto Star,* July 17, 2005.

Harpine, William D. *From the Front Porch to the Front Page: McKinley and Bryan in the 1896 Presidential Campaign.* College Station: Texas A&M University Press, 2005.

Harris, Mark. *City of Discontent.* Indianapolis, IN: Bobbs-Merrill, 1952.

Hart, Roderick P., Deborah Smith Howell, and John Llewellyn. "The Mindscape of the Presidency: *Time Magazine,* 1945–1985." *Journal of Communication* 41, no. 3 (1992): 6–23.

Heald, Edward Thornton. *The William McKinley Story.* Stark County, OH: Stark County Historical Society, 1964.

Heldman, Caroline, Susan J. Carroll, and Stephanie Olson. "She Brought Only a Skirt: Print Media Coverage of Elizabeth Dole's Bid for the Republican Presidential Nomination." *Political Communication* 22, no. 3 (2005): 315–35.

Hess, Stephen, and Milton Kaplan. *The Ungentlemanly Art: A History of American Political Cartoons.* New York: Macmillan, 1975.

Iyengar, Shanto. *Is Anyone Responsible?* Chicago: University of Chicago Press, 1991.

Iyengar, Shanto, and Donald R. Kinder. *News That Matters.* Chicago: University of Chicago Press, 1987.

Iyengar, Shanto, Helmut Norpoth, and Kyu Hahn. "Consumer Demand for Election News: The Horserace Sells." *Journal of Politics* 66, no. 1 (2004): 157–75.

Johns, A. Wesley. *The Man Who Shot McKinley.* New York: Barnes, 1970.

Jones, Stanley L. *The Presidential Election of 1896.* Madison: University of Wisconsin Press, 1964.

Josephson, Matthew. *The Politicos: 1865–1896.* New York: Harcourt, Brace, 1938.

Juergens, George. *Joseph Pulitzer and the* New York World. Princeton, NJ: Princeton University Press, 1966.

Kamen, Al. "Pay and Polls' Opposite Pulls." *Washington Post,* August 4, 1999.

Kaplan, Jonathan E. "Oliver: The Good Son Comes Home." *The Hill,* June 21, 2005. http://thehill.com/business--lobby/oliver-the-good-son-comes-home-2005-06-21.html.

Kaplan, Martin, Ken Goldstein, and Matthew Hale. *Local News Coverage of the 2004 Campaigns: An Analysis of Nightly Broadcasts in 11 Markets.* Los Angeles: Lear Center Local News Archive, 2005.

Kazin, Michael. *The Populist Persuasion.* New York: Basic Books, 1995.

Keen, Judy. "Finger-Pointing Finds a Familiar Target in Rove." *USA Today,* September 30, 2003.

Keene, John Henry. *The Power-Holding Class versus the Public: Imaginary Dialogue of McKinley and Hanna.* Newport, RI: Brotherhood of Liberty, 1900.

Kelly, Jack. "What Republicans Forget: McCain Can Beat Gore, but Bush Will Be Clobbered." *Pittsburgh Post-Gazette,* March 5, 2000.

Kennedy, Charles E. *Fifty Years of Cleveland.* Cleveland: Weidenthal, 1925.

Kent, Noel Jacob. *America in 1900.* Armonk, NY: Sharpe, 2000.

Kernell, Samuel. *Going Public: New Strategies of Presidential Leadership.* Washington, DC: CQ Press, 2006.

———. "Presidential Popularity and Negative Voting." *American Political Science Review* 71, no. 1 (1977): 44–66.

Kernell, Samuel, and Gary C. Jacobson. "Congress and the Presidency as News in the Nineteenth Century." *Journal of Politics* 49, no. 4 (1987): 1016–35.

Klein, M. W., and N. Maccoby. "Newspaper Objectivity in the 1952 Campaign." *Journalism Quarterly* 31 (Summer 1954): 285–96.

Koenig, Louis. "Book Review." *Presidential Studies Quarterly* 12, no. 2 (1982): 448–50.

———. *Bryan: A Political Biography of William Jennings Bryan.* New York: Putnam, 1971.

———. "The First Hurrah." *American Heritage* 31 (April/May 1980). http://www.americanheritage.com/articles/magazine/ah/1980/3/1980_3_4.shtml.

Kohlsaat, Herman Henry. *From McKinley to Harding: Personal Recollections of Our Presidents.* New York: Scribner's Sons, 1923.

Kosova, Weston. "Pumping Iron, Digging Gold, Pressing Flesh." *Newsweek,* November 18, 2002, 50.

Krugman, Paul. "Victors and Spoils." *New York Times,* November 19, 2002.

LaFeber, Walter. *The New Empire.* Ithaca, NY: Cornell University Press, 1963.

Lakoff, George. *Don't Think of an Elephant: Know Your Values and Frame the Debate—the Essential Guide for Progressives.* White River Junction, VT: Chelsea Green, 2004.

Lauer, Solon. *Mark Hanna: A Sketch from Life and Other Essays.* Cleveland: Nike, 1901.

Lawrence, Jill. "GOP's Savior in 2000? Republicans Clamoring for Bush to Make the Leap." *USA Today,* March 8, 1999.

Lazarsfeld, Paul F., Bernard R. Berelson, and Hazel Gaudet. *The People's Choice.* New York: Duell, Sloan and Pearce, 1944.

Leach, Charles. *That Man Dawes.* Chicago: Reilly and Lee, 1930.

Leech, Margaret. *In the Days of McKinley.* New York: Harper and Bros., 1959.

Leip, David. "Election 2008." David Leip's Atlas of U.S. Presidential Elections. http://www.uselectionatlas.org.

Lemann, Nicolas. "The Redemption: Everything Went Wrong for George W. Bush, until He Made It All Go Right." *New Yorker,* January 31, 2000. http://www.newyorker.com/archive/2000_01_31_048_TNY_LIBRY_000020107.

Lewis, Alfred Henry. "Hanna Senator for Another Seven Years." *New York Journal,* January 13, 1898.

———. "Mark Hanna, M'Kinley and the Labor Unions." *New York Journal,* August 8, 1896.

———. *The President.* New York: Barnes, 1904.

Lichter, S. Robert, and Richard E. Noyes. *Good Intentions Make Bad News: Why Americans Hate Campaign Journalism.* New York: Rowman and Littlefield, 1996.

Liebovich, Louis W. *The Press and the Modern Presidency.* Westport, CT: Praeger, 1998.

Lindsay, Vachel. *Collected Poems.* New York: Macmillan, 1923.

———. *The Golden Whales of California and Other Rhymes in the American Language.* New York: Macmillan, 1920.

Lipscomb, Andrew, and Albert Bergh. *The Writings of Thomas Jefferson.* Memorial edition. 20 vols. Washington, DC: Thomas Jefferson Memorial Association, 1903.

Lipsitz, Keena, Christine Trost, Matthew Grossman, and John Sides. "What Voters Want from Political Campaign Communication." *Political Communication* 22, no. 3 (2005): 337–54.

Littlefield, Roy Everett, III. *William Randolph Hearst: His Role in American Progressivism.* New York: University Press of America, 1980.

Lorant, Stefan. *The Glorious Burden: The American Presidency.* New York: Harper and Row, 1951.

———. *The Presidency: A Pictorial History of Presidential Elections from Washington to Truman.* New York: Macmillan, 1952.

Luskin, Robert C. "Measuring Political Sophistication." *American Journal of Political Science* 31, no. 4 (1987): 856–99.

Maier, Scott. "Accuracy Matters: A Cross-Market Assessment of Newspaper Error and Credibility." *Journalism and Mass Communication Quarterly* 82, no. 3 (2005): 545–46.

———. "Getting It Right? Not in 59 Percent of Stories." *Newspaper Research Journal* 23, no. 1 (2002): 10–24.

———. "Tip of the Iceberg: Published Corrections Represent Two Percent of Factual Errors in Newspapers." Paper presented at the national conference of the Association for Education in Journalism and Mass Communication, Newspaper Division, Chicago, August 9–12, 2007.

Marcus, Robert D. *Grand Old Party: Political Structure in the Gilded Age: 1880–1896.* New York: Oxford University Press, 1971.

Marcus A. Hanna (Late a Senator from Ohio). Washington, DC: Government Printing Office, 1909.

Martin, Ralph G. *The Bosses.* New York: Putnam's Sons, 1964.

Massa, Ann. *Vachel Lindsay: Fieldworker for the American Dream.* Bloomington: Indiana University Press, 1970.

McClellan, Scott. *What Happened: Inside the Bush White House and Washington's Culture of Deception.* New York: Public Affairs, 2008.

McCombs, Maxwell E., and Donald L. Shaw. "The Agenda-Setting Function of the Mass Media." *Public Opinion Quarterly* 26 (Summer 1972): 176–87.

McCook, Henry Christopher. *The Senator: A Threnody.* Philadelphia: Jacobs, 1905.

McEwen, Arthur. "Davenport's Cartoon Book Is Out." *New York Journal,* January 21, 1898.

———. "The Men Who Master the Republic: What Hanna, Quay, and Platt Have Done for Their Country." *New York Journal,* October 16, 1898.

McGraw, Kathleen, and Kristina Ling. "Media Priming of Presidential and Group Evaluations." *Political Communication* 20, no. 1 (2002): 23–40.

McIntyre, Robert S. "President George W. McKinley? Bush Waxes Nostalgic for Robber Baron Era Tax Policies." *American Prospect,* December 16, 2002, 21.

McLean, Mrs. C. F. "Mark Hanna and His Family: Personal Sketch of 'The Great Organizer.'" *Midland Monthly* 7 (1897): 19–29.

McLean, Joseph E. *William Rufus Day: Supreme Court Justice from Ohio.* The Johns Hopkins University Studies in Historical and Political Science 64. Baltimore, MD: Johns Hopkins Press, 1946.

McQuaig, Linda. "Davis Scores One for Red Tories." *Toronto Star,* June 15, 2003.

Merrill, J. C. "How *Time* Stereotyped Three U.S. Presidents." *Journalism Quarterly* 42 (Autumn 1965): 563–70.

Meyerson, Harold. "Karl Rove's Wedges." *American Prospect,* April 7, 2002, 2.

Milburn, Michael A., and A. B. McGrail. "The Dramatic Presentation of News and Its Effects on Cognitive Complexity." *Political Psychology* 13, no. 4 (1992): 613–32.

Mitchell, Alison. "The Election: Trying to Escape the Purgatory of Parity." *New York Times,* November 26, 2000.

Moore, James, and Wayne Slater. *The Architect: Karl Rove and the Master Plan for Absolute Power.* New York: Random House, 2006.

———. *Bush's Brain: How Karl Rove Made George W. Bush Presidential.* New York: Wiley and Sons, 2003.

———. *Rove Exposed: How Bush's Brain Fooled America.* New York: Wiley and Sons, 2006.

Moos, Malcolm. *The Republicans: A History of Their Party.* New York: Random House, 1956.

Morgan, H. Wayne, ed. *The Gilded Age: A Reappraisal.* Syracuse, NY: Syracuse University Press, 1963.

———. *William McKinley and His America.* Syracuse, NY: Syracuse University Press, 1963.

Morris, Edmund. *The Rise of Theodore Roosevelt.* New York: Ballantine Books, 1980.

———. *Theodore Rex.* New York: Random House, 2001.

Mott, T. Bentley. *Myron T. Herrick: Friend of France.* Garden City, NY: Doubleday, Doran, 1929.

Mowry, George E. *The Era of Theodore Roosevelt: 1900–1912.* New York: Harper and Bros., 1958.

Nasaw, David. *The Chief: The Life of William Randolph Hearst.* Boston: Houghton Mifflin, 2000.

Neuman, W. Russell, Marion R. Just, and Ann N. Crigler. *Common Knowledge: News and the Construction of Political Meaning.* Chicago: University of Chicago Press 1992.

Nevins, Allan. *Grover Cleveland: A Study in Courage.* New York: Dodd, Mead, 1933.

Newslab. "Making It Right: Corrections Politics in TV Newsrooms." 2001. http://www.newslab.org/research/makingright.htm.

Novak, Robert. "Esquire Article All about Hurting Bush." *Chicago Sun-Times,* December 5, 2002.

Nunberg, Geoffrey. *Talking Right: How Conservatives Turned Liberalism into a Tax-Raising, Latte-Drinking, Sushi-Eating, Volvo-Driving,* New York Times *Reading, Body-Piercing, Hollywood-Loving, Left-Wing Freak Show.* New York: Public Affairs, 2006.

Offner, John. *An Unwanted War: The Diplomacy of the United States and Spain over Cuba, 1895–1898.* Chapel Hill: University of North Carolina Press, 1992.

Olcott, Charles S. *The Life of William McKinley.* Vol. 1. Boston: Houghton Mifflin, 1916.

Older, Mrs. Freemont (Cora). *William Randolph Hearst: American.* New York: Appleton-Century, 1936.

Opper, Frederick. "If Willie Is a Good Boy." *New York Journal,* n.d., 1900.

O'Toole, James. "Philadelphia Has Rich History of Party Conventions." *Pittsburgh Post-Gazette,* July 30, 2000.

Page, Benjamin I., and Robert Y. Shapiro. "Presidential Leadership through Public Opinion." In *The Presidency and Public Policy Making,* edited by George C. Edwards III, Steven A. Shull, and Norman C. Thomas, 22–36. Pittsburgh, PA: University of Pittsburgh Press, 1985.

Parker, Elliot. "New York City Press and the McKinley Assassination." Paper presented at the Association for Education in Journalism and Mass Communication Conference, Washington, DC, August 2001.

Penrose, Charles. *George B. Cortelyou: Briefest Biography of a Great American.* New York: Newcomen Society in North America, 1955.

Perry, Franklin D. "Marcus A. Hanna: A Progressive Republican in a Conservative Era." Master's thesis, Xavier University, 1968.

Pew Research Center for the People and the Press. "Maturing Internet News Audience—Broader Than Deep: Online Papers Modestly Boost Newspaper Readership." July 30, 2006. http://people-press.org/reports/pdf/282.pdf.

Phillips, Kevin. *William McKinley.* New York: Times Books, 2003.

Potter, Deborah, and Amy Mitchell. "Getting It Right." Newslab. http://www.newslab.org/research/gettingright.htm.

Press, Charles. *The Political Cartoon.* Rutherford, NJ: Fairleigh Dickinson University Press, 1981.

Price, Vincent, and John Zaller. "Who Gets the News? Alternative Measures of News Reception and Their Implications for Research." *Public Opinion Quarterly* 57, no. 2 (1994): 133–64.

Pringle, Henry F. *The Life and Times of William Howard Taft: A Biography.* Vol. 1. New York: Holt, Rinehart and Winston, 1964.

Prior, Marcus. "News vs. Entertainment: How Increasing Media Choice Widens Gaps in Political Knowledge and Turnout." *American Journal of Political Science* 49, no. 3 (2005): 577–92.

Purdum, Todd. "Karl Rove's Split Personality." *Vanity Fair,* December 2006. http://www.vanityfair.com/politics/features/2006/12/rove200612.

Purdum, Todd, and David Kirkpatrick. "Campaign Strategist Is in Position to Consolidate Republican Majority." *New York Times,* November 4, 2004.

Rauchway, Eric. *Murdering McKinley: The Making of Theodore Roosevelt's America.* New York: Hill and Wang, 2003.

Reid, Whitelaw. *Some Newspaper Tendencies: An Address.* New York: Holt, 1879.

Republican Party. *Handbook of the St. Louis Convention.* Cleveland, OH: Press of J. B. Savage, 1896.

———. *Proceedings of the Tenth Republican National Convention.* Minneapolis, MN: Harrison and Smith Co., Printers, 1892.

———. *Proceedings of the Twelfth Republican National Convention.* Philadelphia, PA: Press of Dunlap Printing Co., 1900.

———. *Republican Campaign Textbook.* Washington, DC: Hartman and Cadick, 1896.

Rhodes, James Ford. *The McKinley and Roosevelt Administrations, 1897–1909.* New York: Macmillan, 1922.

Ridge, Martin. *Ignatius Donnelly: The Portrait of a Politician.* Chicago: University of Chicago Press, 1962.

Rosenberg, Marvin, and Dorothy Rosenberg. "The Dirtiest Election." *American Heritage* 13 (August 1962). http://www.americanheritage.com/articles/magazine/ah/1962/5/1962_5_4.shtml.

Rosenstiel, Tom, and Amy Mitchell. "The Web: Alarming, Appealing, and a Challenge to Journalist Values: Financial Woes Now Overshadow All Other Concerns for Journalists." The Pew Research Center for the People and the Press / Project for Excellence in Journalism. http://www.stateofthemedia.org/2008/Journalist%20report%202008.pdf.

Ruby, Robert. "Special Reports: Public Attitudes." *The State of the News Media 2008: An Annual Report on American Journalism.* http://www.stateofthemedia.org/2008/narrative_special_attitudes.php?cat=1&media=13.

Ruggles, Eleanor. *The West-Going Heart: A Life of Vachel Lindsay.* New York: Norton, 1959.

Russell, Francis. *The President Makers: From Mark Hanna to Joseph P. Kennedy.* Boston: Little, Brown, 1976.

Rutkow, Ira. *James A. Garfield.* New York: Times Books, 2006.

Ryfe, David. "Betwixt and Between: Woodrow Wilson's Press Conferences and the Transition toward the Modern Rhetorical Presidency." *Political Communication* 16, no. 1 (1999): 77–93.

Sabato, Larry. *Feeding Frenzy.* New York: Free Press, 1991.

———. "Open Season: How the News Media Cover Presidential Campaigns in the Age of Attack Journalism." In *Under the Watchful Eye: Managing Presidential Campaigns in the Television Era,* edited by Mathew D. McCubbins, 127–51. Washington, DC: CQ Press, 1992.

Saltzman, Joe. "Sob Sisters: The Image of the Female Journalist in Popular Culture." *Image of the Journalist in Popular Culture: Resources.* Los Angeles: Norman Lear Center, University of Southern California, 2003. http://ijpc.org/sobsessay.pdf.

Schiffer, Adam J. "Assessing Partisan Bias in Political News: The Case(s) of Local Senate Election Coverage. *Political Communication* 23, no. 1 (2006): 23–29.

Schlesinger, Arthur M., Jr. "Blazing the Way." Introductory essay to *Marcus Alonzo Hanna* by Herbert D. Croly, edited by A. M. Schlesinger. New York: Chelsea House, 1983.

Searight, Frank T. "Early Ideals of Great Men: What Rockefeller and Hanna Wrote Fifty Years Ago." *National,* July 1904, 394–405.

Shanno, Jasper B. *Money and Politics.* New York: Random House, 1959.

Shenkman, Rick. "Lewis Gould Interview." History News Network. http://www.docstoc.com/docs/1018675/Lewis-Gould-Interview/.

Shepp, J. W. *Lives of Gen. Benjamin Harrison and Whitelaw Reid.* New York: Political Publishing, 1892.

Sherman, Henry T. *Myron T. Herrick: Cleveland Banker, Governor of Ohio, Ambassador to France—and the Society for Savings, 1849–1949.* New York: Newcomen Society in North America, 1949.

Shoemaker, Fred C. "Mark Hanna and the Transformation of the Republican Party." PhD diss., Ohio State University, 1992.

Silverman, Craig. *Regret the Error: How Media Mistakes Pollute the Press and Imperil Free Speech.* New York: Union Square Press, 2007.

Sitkoff, Robert H. "Corporate Political Speech, Political Extortion and the Competition for Corporate Charters." *University of Chicago Law Review* 69 (Summer 2002): 1103–66.

———. "Politics and the Business Corporation." *Regulation* 26 (Winter 2003): 30–36.

Skowronek, Stephen. *The Politics Presidents Make: Leadership from John Adams to George Bush.* Cambridge, MA: Belknap Press, 1993.

Smoller, Frederic T. *The Six O'Clock Presidency: A Theory of Presidential Press Relations in the Age of Television.* New York: Praeger, 1990.

Socolofsky, Homer E., and Alan B. Spetter. *The Presidency of Benjamin Harrison.* Lawrence: University Press of Kansas, 1987.

Spear, Joseph C. *Presidents and the Press: The Nixon Legacy.* Cambridge, MA: MIT Press, 1984.

Stern, Clarence A. *Resurgent Republicanism: The Handiwork of Hanna.* Ann Arbor, MI: Edwards Bros., 1963.

Suskind, Ron. *The Price of Loyalty: George Bush, the White House, and the Education of Paul O'Neill.* New York: Free Press, 2004.

———. "Why Are These Men Laughing?" *Esquire,* January 1, 2003. http://www.ronsuskind.com/newsite/articles/archives/000032.html.

Swanberg, W. A. *Citizen Hearst.* New York: Scribner's Sons, 1961.

Tarbell, Ida M. *The History of the Standard Oil Company.* New York: Peter Smith, 1950.

Tell, David. "Who's Afraid of George Soros?" *Weekly Standard,* March 8, 2004. http://www.weeklystandard.com/Content/Public/Articles/000/000/0031797eiqkh.asp.

Thayer, William Roscoe, ed. *The Letters of John Hay.* 2 vols. New York: Kraus Reprint, 1969.

Thompson, Charles Willis. *Presidents I've Known and Two Near Presidents.* Indianapolis, IN: Bobbs-Merrill, 1929.

Timmons, Bascom. *Portrait of an American: Charles G. Dawes.* New York: Holt, 1953.

Trachtenberg, Alan. *The Incorporation of America: Culture and Society in the Gilded Age.* New York: Hill and Wang, 1982.

Traxel, David. *1898.* New York: Knopf, 1998.

Tulis, Jeffrey. *The Rhetorical Presidency.* Princeton, NJ: Princeton University Press, 1987.

U.S. Senate Historical Office. "Garret Augustus Hobart, Vice President (1897–1899)." http://www.senate.gov/artandhistory/history/common/generic/VP_Garret_Hobart.htm.

Von Drehle, David. "A Century-Old Blueprint Inspires GOP: Republicans Look to President McKinley for a Makeover Lesson." *Washington Post,* July 24, 1999.

———. "The Incredible Shrinking Court." *Time,* October 22, 2007. http://www.time.com/time/magazine/article/0,9171,1670489,00.html.

Wallen, James. *Cleveland's Golden Story: A Chronicle of Hearts That Hoped, Minds That Planned, and Hands That Toiled to Make a City Great and Glorious.* Cleveland, OH: Taylor and Son, 1920.

Walters, Everett. *Joseph Benson Foraker: An Uncompromising Republican.* Columbus: Ohio History Press, 1948.

Wanta, Wayne. "The President, Press, and Public Agenda Building." PhD diss., University of Texas at Austin, 1989.

———. *The Public and the National Agenda: How People Learn about Important Issues.* Mahwah, NJ: Erlbaum, 1987.

Wanta, Wayne, Mary Ann Stephenson, Judy Van Slyke Turk, and Maxwell McCombs. "How President's State of Union Talk Influenced News Media Agendas." *Journalism Quarterly* 66, no. 3 (1989): 537–41.

Warken, Philip. *The First Election of Marcus A. Hanna to the United States Senate.* Master's thesis, Ohio State University, 1960.

Weaver, David. "Media Agenda Setting and Elections: Voter Involvement Alienation?" *Political Communication* 11, no. 4 (1994): 347–57.

Weisberg, Jacob. "Karl Rove's Dying Dream." Slate.com, November 2, 2005. http://www.slate.com/id/2129292/.

Welch, Richard E. "Book Review." *Journal of American History* 68, no. 2 (1981): 417.

———. *The Presidencies of Grover Cleveland.* Lawrence: University Press of Kansas, 1988.

White, William Allen. "In the World's Arena." *The Idler: An Illustrated Monthly Magazine,* 1900, 172.

———. *Masks in a Pageant.* New York: Macmillan, 1928.

Wolff, Gerald W. *Mark Hanna and the Labor-Capital Question.* Master's thesis, Bowling Green State University, 1962.

Wood, B. Dan, Chris T. Owens, and Brandy M. Durham. "Presidential Rhetoric and the Economy." *Journal of Politics* 67, no. 3 (2005): 627–45.

Yearley, C. K. *The Money Machines.* Albany: State University of New York Press, 1970.

Young, Garry, and William B. Perkins. "Presidential Rhetoric, the Public Agenda, and the End of Presidential Television's 'Golden Age.'" *Journal of Politics* 67, no. 4 (2005): 1190–1205.

Zaller, John R. *The Nature and Origin of Mass Opinions.* New York: Cambridge University Press, 1992.

Index